Paul ...

Craig Eddy

Jon Price

SAMS

Teach Yourself

MS Access
2002

in 21 Days

SAMS

201 West 103rd St., Indianapolis, Indiana, 46290 USA

Sams Teach Yourself Microsoft Access 2002 in 21 Days

Copyright © 2002 by Sams Publishing

International Standard Book Number: 0-672-32103-3

Library of Congress Catalog Card Number: 00-109717

Printed in the United States of America

First Printing: December 2001

04   03   02   01   4   3   2   1

Trademarks

Warning and Disclaimer

ASSOCIATE PUBLISHER
Linda Engelman

ACQUISITIONS EDITORS
Neil Rowe
Rosemarie Graham

DEVELOPMENT EDITOR
Robyn Thomas

MANAGING EDITOR
Charlotte Clapp

PROJECT EDITORS
Heather McNeill
Leah Kirkpatrick

COPY EDITOR
Michael Dietsch

INDEXER
Becky Hornyak

PROOFREADER
Plan-It Publishing

TECHNICAL EDITOR
Robyn Thomas

TEAM COORDINATOR
Lynne Williams

MEDIA DEVELOPER
Dan Scherf

INTERIOR DESIGNER
Gary Adair

COVER DESIGNER
Aren Howell

PAGE LAYOUT
Joe Millay

Contents at a Glance

Contents

DAY 21 Access on the Web   523

WEEK 3 In Review   543

Appendixes   545

APPENDIX A Answers to Quizzes   545

About the Authors

PAUL CASSEL started using computers by converting accounting systems to automated ones back in the mainframe days of yore. When minis such as the DEC PDP series made computing more accessible, he moved to that platform. His first PC database experience came in the early days of personal computing with dBASE II and the BASIC language on the first IBM PCs. His experience with Access goes back to the first version. He has been recognized by Microsoft with several MVPs for Access, Windows, and Visual Basic and by Borland (Inprise) as a TeamB member.

He has taught computers and computing concepts to students at the University of New Mexico. He has written over a dozen books and published hundreds of articles. His database consulting business is based in New Mexico and includes such clients as the Department of the Navy, University Hospital, University of New Mexico, New Mexico Tech, AMREP, Lovelace Health Systems, the New Mexico State Bar Association, the State of New Mexico Finance Division, the Zuni Nation, and the Jicarilla Apache Nation, plus many others. He is also the chief information officer for a series of community health centers in northern New Mexico.

CRAIG EDDY resides in San Jose, California with his wife, two children, a dog, and a cat. A devout fan of Virginia Tech football, Craig graduated from Virginia Tech with a Bachelor of Science in Electrical Engineering. He is currently a Senior Software Engineer for Peregrine Systems. He came to Peregrine via its acquisition of Remedy Corporation and Remedy's acquisition of Pipestream Technologies, which he helped to found. Craig's expertise lies in the areas of C++, Web development, and database design. Craig's hobbies include reading, cycling, leading a Cub Scout den, and helping his kids in their current sport-du-jour.

JON PRICE is a Senior Developer/Project Lead at Reynolds and Reynolds. His Access experience dates back to Access 2.0 and includes many successful database applications. He has successfully put Access to good use in a variety of industries including automotive retailing, banking, insurance, engineering, and government. He also has contributed as coauthor or editor to several fine Access books. Jon can be reached at jonprice@donet.com.

Dedication

Craig Eddy   I dedicate my work in this book to my family: my wife Susan, my children, and especially to my parents who continue to inspire me in all areas of my life.

Jon Price   I dedicate my portion to the most stalwart Christian I know—my father. He is a branch stirred, but not shaken either by the winds of change or the clouds of uncertainty. He is a tree firmly planted by the rivers of water as can be seen in Psalms 1:1–3.

Acknowledgments

Craig Eddy   I wish to thank all of the editors at Sams for their patience and tireless work. In particular, Robyn Thomas did a fantastic job on technical and development editing, catching my many references to sections whose names had changed and helping to clarify my thoughts. Things that seem so obvious to the author probably aren't to the reader, and Robyn was fantastic at pointing these out.

Jon Price   Many hours of long and sometimes tedious work goes into putting a book together and the staff at Sams has again done a wonderful job. The development editor, Robyn Thomas has had the unenviable task of trying to meld three different authors into one seamless book. Many thanks go to her and Michael Dietsch for their insight and helping to catch many mistakes.

A special thanks goes to you, the reader, for purchasing this book. It is my hope that from this book you will be able to take a basic understanding of Access and learn to apply it to developing applications that can be used at a professional level.

A final thanks goes to my wife. Because of the short time frames allowed for writing a book, most of my free time has been spent at the computer. Her support in my writing has always been a critical factor in the success of this and my other books.

Tell Us What You Think!

As the reader of this book, *you* are our most important critic and commentator. We value your opinion and want to know what we're doing right, what we could do better, what areas you'd like to see us publish in, and any other words of wisdom you're willing to pass our way.

As an Associate Publisher for Sams, I welcome your comments. You can fax, e-mail, or write me directly to let me know what you did or didn't like about this book—as well as what we can do to make our books stronger.

Please note that I cannot help you with technical problems related to the topic of this book, and that due to the high volume of mail I receive, I might not be able to reply to every message.

When you write, please be sure to include this book's title and authors, as well as your name and phone or fax number. I will carefully review your comments and share them with the authors and editors who worked on the book.

Fax: 317-581-4770

E-mail: feedback@samspublishing.com

Mail: Linda Engelman
          Sams Publishing
          201 West 103rd Street
          Indianapolis, IN 46290 USA

Introduction

Just as the title suggests, this book is designed to help you teach yourself Microsoft Access 2002 in 21 days. This is the seventh edition of the book originally written for Access 1.0 in the early-1990s. As the Access product has matured, so has this series. This edition introduces concepts used by Access 2002 and steps you through tasks to let you experience firsthand how to implement these concepts. This book was written following the format of "tell me," "show me," and "let me try." Each of the 21 days takes a topic and steps you through it so that by the time you have completed all 21 days, you will be ready to apply what you have learned to your real-world situations.

This seventh edition adds Jon Price and Craig Eddy as co-authors with Paul Cassel, the author of the original book. Together, these authors have created sample databases on which you can experiment without the drudgery of creating your own data.

Following the format of the *Teach Yourself* series, each lesson ends with a set of frequently asked questions and answers, a quiz, and exercises. These sections provide thought provoking questions and exercises that let you use the skills you have learned to reinforce your mastery of Access 2002.

Who Should Read This Book

You do not need any previous experience in programming to learn how to program in Microsoft Access 2002. This book is intended for the beginner and intermediate-level programmer. It will teach you every principle you need to succeed in using Access as an individual, a corporate guru, or an independent developer.

This book concentrates on the product and database concepts. It is meant for the person who is comfortable using a computer and has some familiarity with Microsoft Windows products. You do not need Access experience to use this book successfully as a self-teaching tool. All but the most advanced Access 2002 developers will benefit. Even accomplished developers will benefit from lessons on SQL and VBA.

Conventions

 Note

These boxes highlight information that can make your Access programming more efficient and effective.

| Tip | These focus your attention on helpful hints that will benefit you in specific situations. |

This book uses various typefaces to help you distinguish VBA code from regular English. Actual VBA code is typeset in a special monospace font. Placeholders—words or characters temporarily used to represent the real words or characters you would type in code—are typeset in *italic monospace*. New or important terms are typeset in *italic*.

Task: Reinforcing the Concepts You Learn

1. Tasks are included in the lessons to provide you the opportunity to put into action the skills introduced in each section.

2. The tasks contain numbered steps to lead you through their execution.

WEEK 1

At a Glance

This first week, you will learn some of the theory on which Access is based and then you will begin actually using Access to create your own applications.

Day 1, "Database Concepts," you will learn the difference between data and information. In addition, you will be introduced to the basic concepts on which Access is based. You will also learn how relationships between data determine how you design your database.

Day 2, "Learning the Basics to Develop an Access Database Application," you will learn about the Access user interface and the different objects in Access. Once you are familiar with the "parts" of Access, you will learn how to plan your database.

Day 3, "Automatic Access," will introduce you to the power of Access wizards. Access has automated many tasks you must perform to create and maintain your databases.

Day 4, "The Data Foundation—The Table," will show you the important role that tables have in the Access database. When you have stepped through this lesson, you will be able to create your own tables from scratch.

Day 5, "Simple Forms," will show you how to create forms to present users with a friendly interface for entering and modifying information. You will learn to use controls, such as buttons, to simplify manipulation of information for your users.

Day 6, "Introducing Queries," you will learn all about how to use queries to find, sort, and update information.

1

2

3

4

5

6

7

Day 7, "Basic Reports," you will learn how to create reports for display or printing information. You will see how creating reports is much like creating forms.

Does all of this sound confusing? Don't worry, many of the skills you learn are transferable to other tasks, such as the building of forms being much like building a report. Don't forget to try the exercises at the end of each day to reinforce what you have read.

DAY 1

Database Concepts

Most people who try to use Access either use it poorly or fail to use it at all. In the first few sections of this book, you will learn about the use of Access as a relational database and other database concepts. These database concepts are important in learning to use Access properly.

Today You Will Learn

In today's lesson you will learn these fundamental concepts:

- The difference between data and information
- How to change data into information
- The relational model that Access uses
- Relationship types
- An introduction to normalization
- Informally stated rules for data structures

- The mission of Access in this world
- Examples of converting data to information
- Hardware requirements and maintenance notes

In this lesson, you will notice "theory" mentioned many times. Do you need to know this theory enough to be able to explain it to someone else? I don't think so, but you do need to know the practical application of the underlying theory if you hope to be able to use Access to its fullest.

Access in Theory and Practice

Note

Read This Even If You Read Nothing Else
Read this, the first section of this book, to gain valuable insight as to the use of Access. It's only a few paragraphs and it can make an enormous difference in your success with Microsoft Access.

Writing about using Access is fun and entertaining, but it's not all fun and games when it comes to using Access successfully. Access is unique among Microsoft Office applications in that using the components of the program doesn't mean you can apply the program to your needs. In theory, a person might be an expert in Access tables, forms, queries, reports, and programming, but still not be able to use the program as intended. This is because Access relies on an organizational theory common to all relational databases. You need to understand the nature of this theory and be good enough at it to apply it to your data if you're to obtain good results from Access.

I'm asking you to read and read again (if necessary) the theoretical material in the following sections. If you feel ambitious, read another book on the theory of the relational database. The topic itself is rich enough for several volumes, but you don't need that much knowledge to use Access well.

What you don't need to do is to read and understand the following material now. You can put it off until you've played around a little with Access. My suggestion is to skim the theoretical material now, move on to learn the mechanics of using Access, and then come back to this after you have a feel for the parts of the program. This way you'll have some idea of the theory behind the practice. When you've learned Access well, come back here to see how to use your newly gained skills to the greatest advantage.

That said, let's move on to the theory of data and relational database organization.

Data Isn't Information

The purpose of a database system such as Microsoft Access, is to change data into information. Many people use those two terms interchangeably, but there is a world of difference between the two if you consider information as being the same as knowledge. Data is a collection of facts. Information is that data organized or presented in such a way as to be useful for decision making.

Take a look at Figure 1.1. This shows actual voter registration data for a particular county. The table you see is shown in Access 2002. It includes voters' names, addresses, registration information such as political party, and also the voting records for each person registered. It doesn't, of course, include for whom voters voted (that's unavailable as data). It does include, but not show, whether and how the voters voted for each election cycle. Voters can cast votes by mail-in ballot, by early voting, or at the polls.

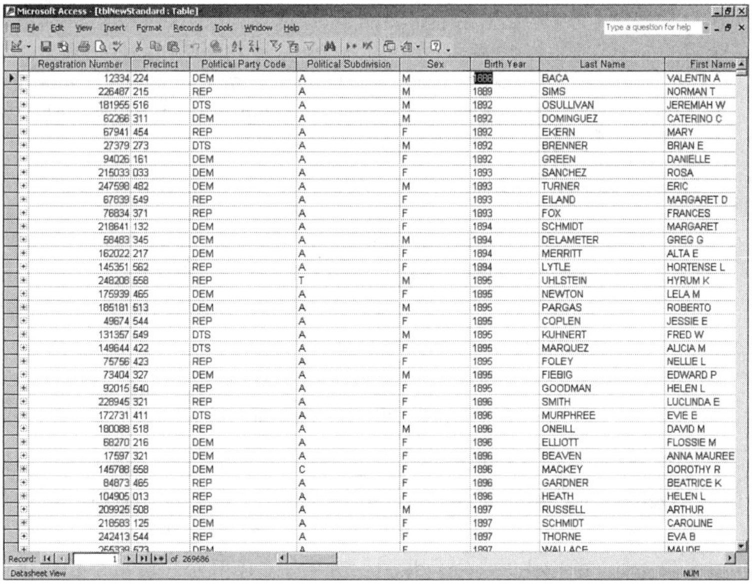

Regstration Number	Precinct	Political Party Code	Political Subdivision	Sex	Birth Year	Last Name	First Name
12334	224	DEM	A	M	1886	BACA	VALENTIN A
226487	215	REP	A	M	1889	SIMS	NORMAN T
181955	516	DTS	A	M	1892	OSULLIVAN	JEREMIAH W
62266	311	DEM	A	M	1892	DOMINGUEZ	CATERINO C
67941	454	REP	A	F	1892	EKERN	MARY
27379	273	DTS	A	M	1892	BRENNER	BRIAN E
94026	161	DEM	A	F	1892	GREEN	DANIELLE
215033	033	DEM	A	F	1893	SANCHEZ	ROSA
247598	482	DEM	A	M	1893	TURNER	ERIC
67639	549	REP	A	F	1893	EILAND	MARGARET D
76834	371	REP	A	F	1893	FOX	FRANCES
218641	132	DEM	A	F	1894	SCHMIDT	MARGARET
58483	345	DEM	A	M	1894	DELAMETER	GREG G
162022	217	DEM	A	F	1894	MERRITT	ALTA E
145351	562	REP	A	F	1894	LYTLE	HORTENSE L
248208	558	REP	T	M	1895	UHLSTEIN	HYRUM K
175939	465	DEM	A	F	1895	NEWTON	LELA M
185181	513	DEM	A	M	1895	PARGAS	ROBERTO
49674	544	REP	A	F	1895	COPLEN	JESSIE E
131357	549	DTS	A	M	1895	KUHNERT	FRED W
149644	422	DTS	A	F	1895	MARQUEZ	ALICIA M
75756	423	REP	A	F	1895	FOLEY	NELLIE L
73404	327	DEM	A	M	1895	FIEBIG	EDWARD P
92015	540	REP	A	F	1895	GOODMAN	HELEN L
228945	321	REP	A	F	1896	SMITH	LUCLINDA E
172731	411	DTS	A	F	1896	MURPHREE	EVIE E
180088	518	REP	A	M	1896	ONEILL	DAVID M
68270	216	DEM	A	F	1896	ELLIOTT	FLOSSIE M
17597	321	DEM	A	F	1896	BEAVEN	ANNA MAUREE
145788	558	DEM	C	F	1896	MACKEY	DOROTHY R
84873	465	REP	A	F	1896	GARDNER	BEATRICE K
104905	013	REP	A	F	1896	HEATH	HELEN L
209925	508	REP	A	M	1897	RUSSELL	ARTHUR
218583	125	DEM	A	F	1897	SCHMIDT	CAROLINE
242413	544	REP	A	F	1897	THORNE	EVA B
255339	573	DEM	A	F	1897	WALLACE	MAUDE

FIGURE 1.1

County clerk records showing voter information and voting behavior is data.

Figure 1.1 is a table with a mass of data—hundreds of thousands of people each with over 60 data points. In other words, there are millions of items to look at and correlate. In the real world of databases, this isn't a terribly large dataset, but it's still too large for the human mind to gain insight from.

Note

> Don't worry if you don't understand the Microsoft Access screens shown here. The use of tables, as well as the parts of Access, are both easy to learn and you'll pick them up in subsequent lessons. For now, just concentrate on the concepts discussed.

Changing Data into Information

Now let's take that data and organize it into information. Let's say that in the 2000 congressional race the Democrat candidate lost by 3,216 votes. Using the Count() function built into Access, the database user notes that Republican voters mailed in 5,423 more ballots than the Democrat voters. This is information. Using it, the Democrats can see that if their candidate had emphasized mail-in balloting more (perhaps by mailing out applications for such ballots) he might have won.

Note

> This lesson skips over the technicalities of how to perform most operations such as using the Count() function. You'll see how to do this and perform other exercises in subsequent days. However, it's not too early to tell you that getting such a count of mail-in votes for a particular party from a dataset of this size takes only a few seconds once you know how to use Access. You'll consider such feats child's play once you've finished this book.

Of course, you must approach such information using your own common sense or specific knowledge of the task at hand. Knowing that Republicans mailed in more ballots than Democrats did imply more mail-in votes for the Republican candidate, but that's imputed information. In reality, nobody can know if this is the case, because all you really know is that those mail-in ballots came from registered Republicans. The votes themselves might have been for the Democrat, Libertarian, Green, or other candidate.

There is a world of information possible from any proper dataset. Let's say that the Democrat candidate won by those 3,216 votes, but you see that Republicans outvoted (in all modes) Democrats by 7,987 votes. This is rather irrefutable information that the Democrats fielded a candidate attractive to Republicans, that the Republican candidate wasn't what Republicans wanted in a representative, or both.

Discovering Information

I've used the voter registration and voting record example because it's simple but large in scope. Manually counting the Democrat and Republican mail-in ballots is possible even with a dataset of 270,000 voters as in this example. Using Access for such tasks speeds things up quite a bit, but only barely scratches the surface of this program's power.

Let's say instead of voter records, you have a database of shopper behavior. This shows each shopper's visit cataloged by day, date, time, weather conditions, and purchases. The behavior is tracked using those shopper "discount" cards issued by most large grocery stores today. Using date data, you summarize the following dataset for purchases of a particular laundry detergent. Table 1.1 shows the summarized data.

TABLE 1.1   Purchases by Date

Date	Packages of Detergent Purchased
2/3/01	23
2/4/01	90
2/5/10	20
2/6/01	25
2/7/01	15
2/8/01	87
2/9/01	12
2/10/01	10
2/11/01	97
2/12/01	101
2/13/01	9

Looking at this so-called information gives you no hint as to why some days this detergent sells like crazy, but on most days it sells roughly the same number of boxes per day.

Recasting the data to correlate boxes sold to a different criterion creates useful information. Table 1.2 illustrates this scenario.

TABLE 1.2   Purchases by Weather Conditions

Date	Packages of Detergent Purchased
Sunny	23
Rainy	90
Partly Cloudy	20

TABLE 1.2   continued

Date	Packages of Detergent Purchased
Partly Cloudy	25
Sunny	15
Snowy	87
Sunny	12
Sunny	10
Rainy, foggy	97
Rainy	101
Sunny	9

A quick glance at this table will give you all the knowledge you need to understand the buying patterns of your customers when it comes to this detergent. The key is to try different correlations until you find one that clicked.

The Key to the Transformation

The means to transform data into information is organizing that data so you can view it in a useful form. The earlier examples—the number of voters voting in a particular way and the correlation between weather and sales—show you this transformation.

Access itself won't do the entire job for you even though help in that area has been a major design goal of Microsoft for many years. You need to structure your database in such a way as to make the transformation possible.

The key here is to keep foremost in your mind what form the information you hope to derive will take. In other words, when creating a database structure, think about how you'll extract information from the dataset. This is clearly the most difficult task for a person new to databases.

Note   Failure to properly structure your database will always lead to suboptimal database performance. It often leads to useless collections of data.

Tip   Master carpenters have a saying: "Measure twice, cut once." Master database developers have a similar saying, "Plan long, work short." The mechanics of making most database projects should be undertaken only after a

> thorough planning stage. If, project after project, you find yourself having to revise your structure from that which you planned, you need to plan more.

The Relational Model and Access

Access is a relational database. Some purists claim that few, if any, databases today are truly relational because they fail one or another theoretical test. The best thing to do if you run into one of these zealots is to agree that Access (as well as most other products) aren't fully and truly relational, and then continue to use it (or those products) to get your work done.

The father of the relational model is Edgar F. Codd. I'll be the first to agree that Access doesn't fully meet all the rules that Codd said make up the relational model, but it does meet the spirit of that model. Here is a list, not of all the relational rules, but of the idea behind the relational model.

- All data is stored in tables or two-dimensional grids. See Figure 1.1 for an example of such a grid. The columns of that grid are called fields and the rows are called records. Referring to Figure 1.1, note that the columns `Precinct`, `Political Party Code`, and so forth are all fields. The rows contain the data corresponding to the fields.

- Each record in a table has a primary key to positively identify it. The *primary key* value for a record is unique to that table. In Figure 1.1 the `Registration Number` field is the primary key. No two records in this table have the same value for their `Registration Number` field. In addition, Access, by default, orders (sorts) the table according to the primary field. This particular table is ordered on the `Birth Year` field. You can see this sorting in the ascending order of primary field values within this table. Since the primary sort order is `Birth Year`, you'll find that `Registration Number` is sorted (ordered) within `Birth Year`. For example, there are many folks born in 1892 in this table. You'll find the registration numbers sorted in order within the scope of the `Birth Year`.

- Data within a database is broken into small, but logically consistent, parts. Each of these parts has its own table. The breaking up of data into these parts is called *normalization*. For example, a database of student registrations (for a college, let's say) will contain a table with the students' personal information. Another table will contain data relating to the students' classes, while another table will contain class data such as class time and place. Each table will have logically consistent contents. For example, no table will contain class instructor data and student scholarship data because those two datasets aren't logically connected.

- Data can be assembled from the various tables by linking those tables by fields containing identical data. For example, the student personal table will contain the student ID as the primary key because it's a unique value for each student. The table containing student classes taken will contain this student ID for each record. This will enable the database engine to link the students with their classes without error.

You can see these concepts in action by following along in the next section and looking at the figures as you read the text.

Note

Don't be concerned if you don't understand the mechanics of how to view and manipulate the database objects shown in the following figures. The purpose of this section is to illustrate how data can follow the relational model. In a few days, you'll be able to do the operations shown here with ease.

Figure 1.2 shows the Relationships window. This window currently contains the table structure for the sample database Northwind, which is included in Access. Let's focus on the tables Suppliers and Products. The Suppliers table contains data such as the suppliers' ID number, company name, contact, and address. The Products table contains data about product details. The two tables are linked on the SupplierID which contains the same data in each table. Note the link on the SupplierID field. This will allow the database manager to associate the suppliers with their products.

FIGURE 1.2

You can view the Relationships window by choosing Tools, Relationships from the main Access menu.

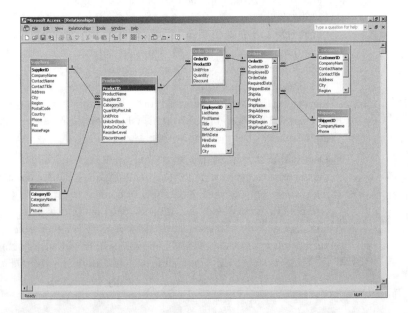

> **Note**
>
> Feel free to either open the Northwind sample database and follow along with this lesson, or just leave it alone. The material here is fully illustrated in the figures. Unlike some parts of Access, you don't need a hands-on approach to learn the subject matter.

Figure 1.3 shows the two tables, Suppliers and Products open at the same time. Note how the SupplierID field exists in both tables. Also note also the same entries in both fields in the two tables. Access "knows" from the SupplierID field in Products which products are from the Supplier with the identical SupplierID. For example, the product Chai is from the Supplier Exotic Liquids, which has a SupplierID of 1.

> **Note**
>
> I've modified the tables in Northwind to display like those in Figure 1.3. If you open the database, you'll see the Supplier Name in the Supplier field. Microsoft's sample data includes a statement that essentially says to Access, "Instead of showing the SupplierID value, look up this value and display the Supplier Name instead." I've edited the sample data for display and theory simplicity.
>
> I also have highlighted the two records (or rows) to illustrate the linked data.

FIGURE 1.3

When Access sees the same data in two tables, it knows that the records in both tables have some relationship to each other.

Figure 1.4 shows the Suppliers table with one supplier's record expanded to show the products it has. While most relational databases rely exclusively on queries to assemble linked data, Access allows you to view linked data in the table view by clicking on the plus sign.

FIGURE 1.4

You can view linked data in Access by expanding the table view.

Figure 1.5 shows the Products table with a record (row) expanded to show some details about a product. The Products table has linked data to the Suppliers table. Look at Figure 1.2 for correlation between the two tables.

The display in Figure 1.5 isn't very clear, nor is it easy to use. It shows the order details for each product from the Order Details table. However, by creating a query with these tables, you can put together a piece of information from the data contained in the tables. Figure 1.6 shows this query being designed, and Figure 1.7 shows it running.

In this case, I think you can see what I did here even though you might have little, if any, idea what a query is. I've asked Access to create a simple report containing a list of products, their supplier's names, the quantity on hand of each, and the level at which each product will be restocked (or reordered) from the supplier.

Note

At this point, you might think that the trick shown in Figures 1.6 and 1.7 is pretty neat. Actually, it's rather lame compared to what you can do with Access, and what you will be able to do when you're done reading this book.

FIGURE 1.5

The Products table has linked data.

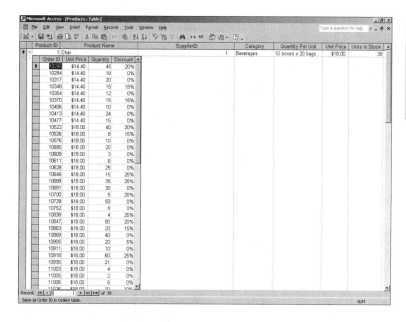

FIGURE 1.6

First you design a query using the tables in this dataset.

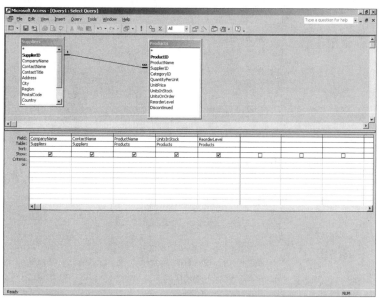

Usually you only care about restocking level if it is lower than stock on hand. Figure 1.8 shows that I've added a field to the query which will return a number 1 if the restocking level is greater than stock on hand, and 0 if not. That is, this field will show 1 if the product needs to be restocked. I used the following statement in the design phase:

```
Reorder: IIf([Products.ReorderLevel]>[Products.UnitsInStock],1,0)
```

FIGURE 1.7

*Then you can see the
data from two tables
put together in a
cogent and easy-to-use
manner.*

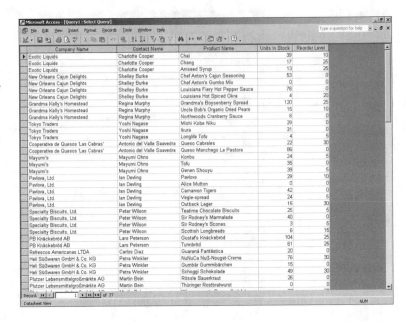

> **Note**
>
> At the risk of repeating myself, keep in mind that unless you are quite famil-
> iar with relational databases, the operations I'm doing here to illustrate
> some principles will confuse you to say the least. Remember, I'm doing this
> to give you some idea of how Access takes data and assembles it into useful
> information. In this case, the data is product inventory and restocking level.
> The information will be what products need ordering today.

Finally, I've instructed Access to return only those products that need reordering now
because their inventory count is less than their reorder points. Figure 1.9 shows the
results of the updated query.

> **Note**
>
> The method I used to convert the data into information is clumsy at best,
> but it also was the simplest. By the time you are halfway done with this
> book, you'll laugh at this example, having found much more elegant solu-
> tions on your own.

FIGURE 1.8

This query shows a flag indicating when a product should be reordered.

Microsoft Access - [Query1 : Select Query]

Company Name	Contact Name	Product Name	Units In Stock	Reorder Level	Reorder
Exotic Liquids	Charlotte Cooper	Chai	39	10	0
Exotic Liquids	Charlotte Cooper	Chang	17	25	1
Exotic Liquids	Charlotte Cooper	Aniseed Syrup	13	25	1
New Orleans Cajun Delights	Shelley Burke	Chef Anton's Cajun Seasoning	53	0	0
New Orleans Cajun Delights	Shelley Burke	Chef Anton's Gumbo Mix	0	0	0
New Orleans Cajun Delights	Shelley Burke	Louisiana Fiery Hot Pepper Sauce	76	0	0
New Orleans Cajun Delights	Shelley Burke	Louisiana Hot Spiced Okra	4	20	1
Grandma Kelly's Homestead	Regina Murphy	Grandma's Boysenberry Spread	120	25	0
Grandma Kelly's Homestead	Regina Murphy	Uncle Bob's Organic Dried Pears	15	10	0
Grandma Kelly's Homestead	Regina Murphy	Northwoods Cranberry Sauce	6	0	0
Tokyo Traders	Yoshi Nagase	Mishi Kobe Niku	29	0	0
Tokyo Traders	Yoshi Nagase	Ikura	31	0	0
Tokyo Traders	Yoshi Nagase	Longlife Tofu	4	5	1
Cooperativa de Quesos 'Las Cabras'	Antonio del Valle Saavedra	Queso Cabrales	22	30	1
Cooperativa de Quesos 'Las Cabras'	Antonio del Valle Saavedra	Queso Manchego La Pastora	86	0	0
Mayumi's	Mayumi Ohno	Konbu	24	5	0
Mayumi's	Mayumi Ohno	Tofu	35	0	0
Mayumi's	Mayumi Ohno	Genen Shouyu	39	5	0
Pavlova, Ltd.	Ian Devling	Pavlova	29	10	0
Pavlova, Ltd.	Ian Devling	Alice Mutton	0	0	0
Pavlova, Ltd.	Ian Devling	Carnarvon Tigers	42	0	0
Pavlova, Ltd.	Ian Devling	Vegie-spread	24	5	0
Pavlova, Ltd.	Ian Devling	Outback Lager	15	30	1
Specialty Biscuits, Ltd.	Peter Wilson	Teatime Chocolate Biscuits	25	5	0
Specialty Biscuits, Ltd.	Peter Wilson	Sir Rodney's Marmalade	40	0	0
Specialty Biscuits, Ltd.	Peter Wilson	Sir Rodney's Scones	3	5	1
Specialty Biscuits, Ltd.	Peter Wilson	Scottish Longbreads	6	15	1
PB Knäckebröd AB	Lars Peterson	Gustaf's Knäckebröd	104	25	0
PB Knäckebröd AB	Lars Peterson	Tunnbröd	61	25	0
Refrescos Americanas LTDA	Carlos Diaz	Guaraná Fantástica	20	0	0
Heli Süßwaren GmbH & Co. KG	Petra Winkler	NuNuCa Nuß-Nougat-Creme	76	30	0
Heli Süßwaren GmbH & Co. KG	Petra Winkler	Gumbär Gummibärchen	15	0	0
Heli Süßwaren GmbH & Co. KG	Petra Winkler	Schoggi Schokolade	49	30	0
Plutzer Lebensmittelgroßmärkte AG	Martin Bein	Rössle Sauerkraut	26	0	0
Plutzer Lebensmittelgroßmärkte AG	Martin Bein	Thüringer Rostbratwurst	0	0	0

Record: 1 of 77

Datasheet View NUM

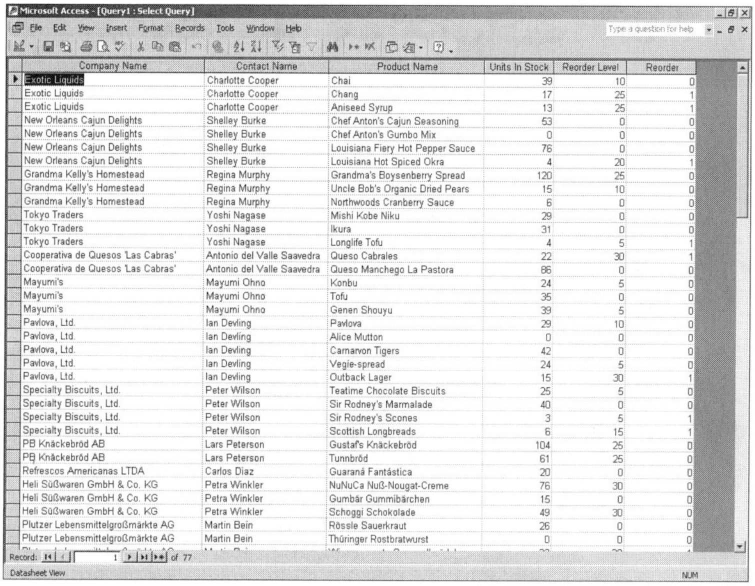

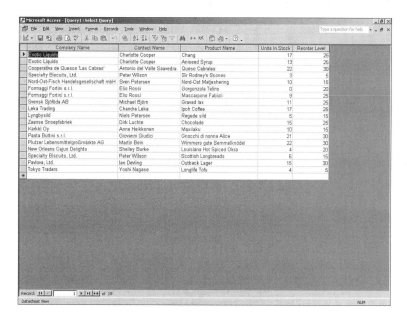

FIGURE 1.9

Here the query is stripped of superfluous data, giving us the information we wanted from the gathered data.

Microsoft Access - [Query1 : Select Query]

Company Name	Contact Name	Product Name	Units In Stock	Reorder Level
Exotic Liquids	Charlotte Cooper	Chang	17	25
Exotic Liquids	Charlotte Cooper	Aniseed Syrup	13	25
Cooperativa de Quesos 'Las Cabras'	Antonio del Valle Saavedra	Queso Cabrales	22	30
Specialty Biscuits, Ltd.	Peter Wilson	Sir Rodney's Scones	3	5
Nord-Ost-Fisch Handelsgesellschaft mbH	Sven Petersen	Nord-Ost Matjeshering	10	15
Formaggi Fortini s.r.l.	Elio Rossi	Gorgonzola Telino	0	20
Formaggi Fortini s.r.l.	Elio Rossi	Mascarpone Fabioli	9	25
Svensk Sjöföda AB	Michael Björn	Gravad lax	11	25
Leka Trading	Chandra Leka	Ipoh Coffee	17	25
Lyngbysild	Niels Petersen	Røgede sild	5	15
Zaanse Snoepfabriek	Dirk Luchte	Chocolade	15	25
Karkki Oy	Anne Heikkonen	Maxilaku	10	15
Pasta Buttini s.r.l.	Giovanni Giudici	Gnocchi di nonna Alice	21	30
Plutzer Lebensmittelgroßmärkte AG	Martin Bein	Wimmers gute Semmelknödel	22	30
New Orleans Cajun Delights	Shelley Burke	Louisiana Hot Spiced Okra	4	20
Specialty Biscuits, Ltd.	Peter Wilson	Scottish Longbreads	6	15
Pavlova, Ltd.	Ian Devling	Outback Lager	15	30
Tokyo Traders	Yoshi Nagase	Longlife Tofu	4	5

Record: 1 of 18

Datasheet View NUM

Database Structure in Theory

Many people believe that structuring real-world data for a relational database is more art than science. Perhaps a better way to state this is that database design is an art based on a science. For example, keep in mind that there might be practical considerations that will make you create a database structure that's less than optimal. Knowing when that is the right way to go is the art form. Knowing what the optimal structure is remains the science.

Here, in summary form, are your goals for structuring your data:

- You should create a dataset optimized for selection and retrieval of data as information.
- You should make data entry easy and economical. This tends to mean making sure any datum only appears once in your database. For example, if you have a student's address in a table, you shouldn't have that address anywhere else, but you should instead link to that data (through common fields) whenever you need it.
- You should have the data structured in a logical form so the database documents (explains itself) by its very structure. This also means that alterations to the database or the data are simple to carry out.

The tables in your database represent groups of real-world objects either tangible or abstract. For example, a table might hold inventory data (tangible) or addresses (abstractions). The fields in tables (columns in the grid) determine what type of data the table holds while the rows (records) give values to the fields. Figure 1.10 shows a table from the Microsoft supplied database Northwind.

The field Last Name in Figure 1.10 tells the user that this field contains last names for the employees of this company. The name Davolio, the first value in Figure 1.10, tells the user that this is the specific value for one record.

 Note

If you have Northwind open to the Employees table as shown in Figure 1.10, you can expand Davolio's linked table by clicking on the plus sign immediately to the left of the Employee ID field.

The primary key for this table is EmployeeID (shown as Employee ID in this figure). This field also will appear in other tables as a link value. The inclusion of this field in the Orders table allows this database to track the orders with the employees who took the order. Figure 1.11 shows the Orders table in design view with the row showing the EmployeeID field highlighted.

FIGURE 1.10

Fields or columns define the type of data, while rows or records give specific values to fields.

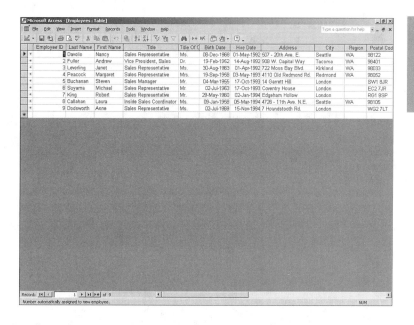

> **Note**
>
> Old hands at database work refuse to use white spaces (blanks) for field names. This is because some operating systems and other databases cannot handle white space (they use them for delimiters). This isn't necessary if you use only Access, but it's worthwhile if you are a belt-and-suspenders type of person. Access can use different labels for the field names and the display of those field names. Here, the actual field name is the safe EmployeeID, while the display name is the friendly Employee ID.

Foreign key is the name of a primary key field of one table when included as a linking field in another table. Here EmployeeID from Employees (a table) appears in Orders (another table) as a foreign key. Figure 1.12 shows that with a little bit of magic, Access can display the employee name instead of the ID number. In a real application, you'd want your data-entry people to select employees by name, not numbers, but Access will link on number.

Again, this can't possibly seem clear to you in total at this point unless you're a database prodigy. However, as you get to working with Access later in the book, these concepts will fall into logical places.

> **Note**
>
> As I did before, I altered the Northwind database to show the EmployeeID label and number in Figure 1.11. I did this to make clear the contents of the

foreign key field `EmployeeID` in the `Orders` table. The table, as supplied by Microsoft, displays the name of the employee and not the ID number in the `Employee` field as shown in Figure 1.12.

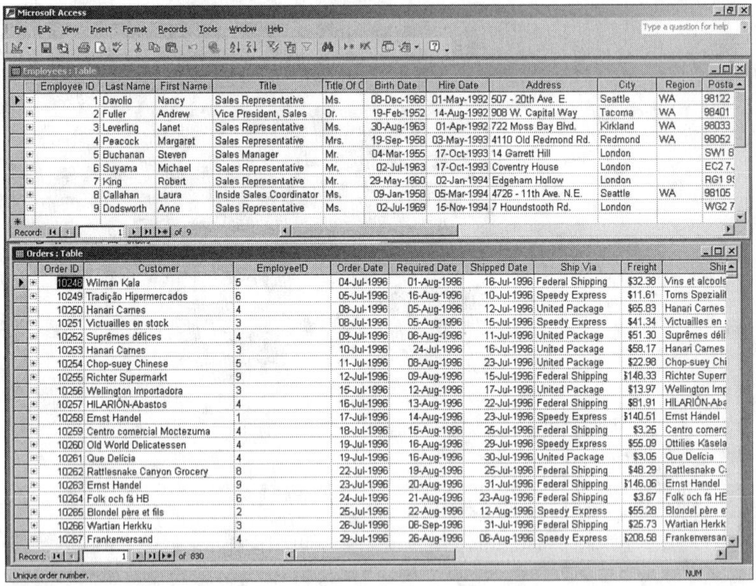

FIGURE 1.11

*The foreign key
EmployeeID appears in
Orders to link this
table to Employees.*

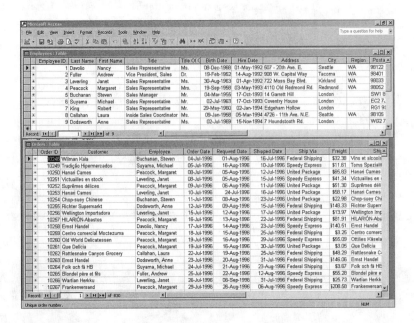

FIGURE 1.12

*Access can display the
field in a factual man-
ner or a friendly one.*

1

For those of you who just have to know how it's done, Access displays the employee name in the `EmployeeID` field by the following SQL statement:

`SELECT DISTINCTROW Employees.EmployeeID, [LastName] & ", " & [FirstName] AS Name FROM Employees ORDER BY Employees.LastName, Employees.FirstName;`

The statement also contains a sorting statement to sort the table by `LastName` and `FirstName` within `LastName`.

The reason the field name is `Employee` instead of `EmployeeID` is a simple entry in the design part of the table instructing Access to label the field differently from its name.

Figure 1.13 shows the form used by data-entry people to enter order information. The links in this database mean that once entered, data never needs to be entered again. The combo box shown here links to the `Employees` table through the inclusion of the foreign key field `EmployeeID` in the `Orders` table shown in Figure 1.11.

FIGURE 1.13

Once the tables are linked, forms based on those tables can benefit from those links.

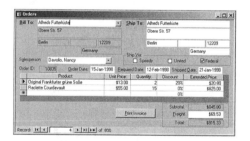

Database Structure in Practice

Deciding what to use for a primary key and how to 'break up' or normalize your real-world data is the primary skill for a database designer. Don't expect to get it right at first—nobody does. Instead, do the best you can using the guidelines given in this section. When things go wrong (as they will) downstream in your database projects, reflect how the structure could be made better to avoid the problems you have encountered. Over time, you'll find yourself making fewer and fewer mistakes and those will be easily correctable.

Choosing the Primary Key

Access has a built-in primary key generator called the `AutoNumber` type field. This will generate either unique sequential or random numbers for use as a primary key. While this works, and Microsoft seems to encourage this practice, database purists sneer at including any non-data values in a table.

Don't be afraid of using the generator even if it means a slight increase in your table sizes. However, don't automatically figure that this is the only way to choose a primary key or even the optimal one. Your first approach should be to examine your table data to see if you can find a natural primary key. A natural primary key is a field or fields that exist as data, but are also unique so can serve as such keys.

The use of Social Security Number (SSN) in a student personal table is an example of natural data that's useful for a primary key. Access will also allow the use of several fields used in aggregate to form a composite primary key. For example, the composite of a date of birth field with a home phone number field can serve as a primary key as there is little likelihood that two people will have the same date of birth and home phone numbers. While that's unlikely, it's not impossible.

Neither field by itself is suitable for a primary key if it is possible for two students to have the same date of birth (likely) or the same home phone number (sisters). This scheme will fail, however, in the case of twin sisters attending your school at the same time. If you wish to avoid such cases, you'll need to add more fields to your composite key (first name) until you've achieved uniqueness again. Here you can see the advantage of using the AutoNumber facility in Access as there is no chance you will end up having to restructure your data in the event of an unanticipated event ruining the uniqueness of your primary key.

While you shouldn't be afraid of creating an artificial field in tables for use as a primary key, use real data whenever possible. Keep in mind that a natural field or fields for a primary key is suitable if it is unique and simple.

Choosing Relationship Types

When structuring your data, keep in mind the different type of relationships that can occur between tables. The following list uses a hospital database for the examples. The tables are

- Patients
- Procedures
- Providers (doctors)
- Beds

Of course in a real-world hospital database there would be more tables than these. The relationships are

- One to many   Patients to Procedures. One patient can have many procedures performed during his stay at the hospital.
- Many to many   Patients to Providers. One doctor can have many patients while one patient can have many doctors as well.
- One to one   Patients to Beds. One patient can have only one bed while one bed can have only one patient.

You will need to keep these relationship types in mind when designing your tables. For now, just remember there are these three relationship types.

Note

Relational theory is replete with its own often confusing jargon using terms such as domain, tuple, entity integrity, and constructor. Whenever possible, I'll avoid using such jargon in this lesson and instead either use common terms (such as *row* instead of the technically correct *tuple*) or discuss concepts descriptively, rather than by relying on jargon.

Understanding Normalization

The terms *normal* and *normalization*, when used in a database context, don't refer to behavioral, chemical, or biological normalcy, but stem from the mathematical concept of being perpendicular to a plane.

From the Mathematical Concept of Being Perpendicular to a Plane

Isn't very clear, is it? I've given you the technical definition of what normalization is just so you could have it. The important thing to keep in mind is that it doesn't refer to normal as in common usage—that of adhering to a standard.

Relational theory has its roots in set theory, but has been extended well beyond the types of unions postulated in that theory. This basis in mathematics is the reason for some of the unusual jargon including the often confusing terms *normal* and *normalization* which refer to proper table structure rather than an alteration from an abnormal state to one more common (normal). Because there is no alternative word that conveys the same concept as *normal*, and the use of this word is widespread even among novices, I haven't tried to avoid its use.

The structure data in tables, or the contents of tables, can be described as being in various normal forms. Ideally, you'll construct your tables and by extension your relationships will be in the first, second, or third normal forms, which are described below. In practice, you might violate normalization rules for some of your tables, although purists will sneer at such practice.

Well, we can't live our lives or base our database practices on the often impractical ideas of theorists, so let's move on to learn about four normal forms. Keep in mind that all higher normal forms are supersets of lower forms.

The first normal form is the so-called atomic form, as there is no possibility of splitting it further. Consider a table of department personnel, shown in Figure 1.14, in which the Employees field contains the composite of the first and last name.

FIGURE 1.14

The first normal form prevents multiple entries such as these entries in the Employees column.

Department	Employees
1	Bob, Ted
2	Alice, Phil
3	John, Tirilee

The table shown in Figure 1.14 presents problems in data selection and manipulation, especially as the numbers of employees grow. It is not in the first or any normal form. While Access can handle such violations fairly gracefully when departments hold three or four people, it will fall apart fast when the numbers get into the hundreds, thousands, or even higher.

The correct way to structure the data you see in Figure 1.14 is to have a row for each distinct value in the Employees field. That is, you'd not have two employees in the Employees field, but a single entry for each field.

In most systems, there also will be another table with an employee's personal data, such as home address and phone. There also will be another table with other linked data, such as employee review dates and outcomes.

You'd link the first table to the other tables by using a foreign key field in the other tables, linked to a primary key field in this first table. Each table you wished to link (or relate) employees to, would have a foreign key in it. Generally speaking, even if you use a foreign key in a table you'll want to display a more user-friendly value than that key as you've seen Microsoft do with the Northwind database (and as you've seen me undo several times).

As a preview of things to come, the following SQL statement retrieves and then displays sorted data from a source table called tblEmployees:

```
SELECT DISTINCTROW tblEmployees.EmployeeID, [LastName] & ", "
    ¦ & [FirstName] AS Name FROM tblEmployees
¦ ORDER BY Employees.LastName, Employees.FirstName;
```

Figure 1.15 shows the results of restructuring the data from this table into the first normal form.

FIGURE 1.15

This is a simple and small table that works well. Usually, you'd want more information in a table to manage table quantities within the database, but this is all right.

EmployeeID	FName	LastName
1	Tirilee	Cassel
2	Jose	Jones
3	Sammy	Schultz
4	Carol	Young
*		

The second normal form is the first normal form plus the criterion that all non-primary key fields must be dependent on the entire value in the primary key field. The word *entire* is important to include due to cases where a primary key is made up of more than one field.

Figure 1.16 shows a table meeting the requirements of the second normal form. The two fields `PurchaseOrder` and `LineNumber` form a composite primary key for this table. The two non-key fields derive all their identity from this composite key, but are useless as information without the entire key.

FIGURE 1.16

The non-key fields in this table depend on the entire primary key. Thus this table meets the requirements of the second normal form.

PurchaseOrder	LineNumber	Quantity	ItemID
1	1	3	5
1	2	9	6
3	2	3	4
4	3	4	3
*			

The third normal form calls for all non-key fields to be mutually independent of each other. Remember they still must be dependent on the entire primary key as this is a superset of the second normal form. Mutual independence means simply that the values of the non-key fields can't vary depending upon the contents of another field.

For example, if you had a table with the price and quantity information. If you add a third field that calculates the total cost by multiplying the price times the quantity, you'd violate the rules for the third normal form as this field would be dependent upon the values in two other non-key fields. You can use a query, a form, or a report to do this calculation if such a calculation is needed for your project.

Note   While Access can handle errors in structure such as including total cost in a table by multiplying cost and quantity and storing the product in a field, it does waste resources to do so.

In some instances you might wish to violate this or other normalization rules. Asking a query to do this calculation will take some time, which your users might find irksome. In a case like this, you can calculate the total cost and place that value in a table in violation of the math rules, but to the benefit of your users.

The fourth normal form specifies that the relation be in the third normal form and that there be no more than one set of facts in that relationship. For example, consider the facts that would be found in the `Patients-to-Providers` relationship (found in the previous section). Including these facts in a single table would violate the fourth normal form. To properly model this many-to-many relationship, you would create a third table, `PatientsProviders`, that would store the patient and provider relationship separately.

Note   Most database developers stop the normalization process at the third normal form, but by following the fourth normal form, you will produce well-designed databases.

Keep in mind that normalization is just common sense applied to the database problem. If your application works well and meets the needs of your users, its structure is right even if it violates some theoretical mathematical model.

Note   **DO** include a primary key for every table.
DON'T worry overly that your tables meet the criteria set for a particular normal form.

Informal Rules to Live By

Here are some of my made-up rules to live by when structuring your database. These are based on the examples so far. There are more to come, but you don't need to memorize them. I list them here in way of taking a break, and for review.

- Always include a primary field in every table. No exceptions are allowed ever for any reason (there are no good reasons to avoid this one).

- Choose a primary key from the data if possible. Don't immediately rely on adding a field just for a primary field.

- Determine the units from which you want to extract or order on (sort) data later. Because you might want to order on last name, don't include both first and last names as one field. You probably won't ever want to extract just house numbers, so you don't need to break apart street names and numbers in an address field. If you will need to extract these fields separately, then do break them apart. Access does have the ability to select on partial fields, but this isn't fully realized.

- Create a picture of what your data looks like in the abstract. For example, a company has many products, but each product has only one company that creates it (per the Northwind database). A logical way to represent this is to have a table with CompanyID as a primary field, and another table for products with the CompanyID as a foreign key in it. This allows you to have many products for each company, and also retrieve product information along with the associated company.

The Mission of Access

Access was originally conceived by Microsoft as a defensive product. At that time, the common knowledge said that Microsoft led in every office software category other than databases, so the Redmond giant decided it needed to address that type of software. When Access was introduced, both leading database products were written for MS-DOS. The dominant but waning dBase line was being supplanted by the MS-DOS version of Borland's Paradox, with a version of Paradox for Windows close over the horizon. At the time, both dBase and Paradox owned the personal computer database territory.

Access differed from both these products in several ways, but perhaps the most important was that it adhered more closely to the relational model than Paradox or dBase did (or do now), and that it used BASIC (Access BASIC then, VBA now) rather than the PAL language of Paradox. When Paradox for Windows arrived, it relied on the technically excellent OPAL (Object PAL) language. However OPAL's C-like syntax and obscure keywords condemned it to seasoned developers only. BASIC was accessible to all users from advanced novice on up. BASIC was, and remains, Bill Gates' favorite language for this reason—accessibility to the non-advanced market.

Microsoft extended Access for version 2.0 by making it much easier to use and capable of serious data handling. Access 95, the next version, saw the concurrent creation of the Upsizing Wizard allowing Access applications to be migrated to SQL Server applications with very little work or fuss. Subsequent versions of Access (including Access 2002) address the needs most demanded by private and corporate users: power and ease of use. While Access 2002 is a paragon of ease of use, the need to know how to structure your data remains as difficult for many folks as it did in earlier versions.

The Upsizing Wizard is vital even though few Access users know of its existence, and fewer will ever use it. Prior to the Upsizing Wizard, users had to size their applications before they chose a program to host it. The choice came down to a modestly capable, but relatively easy to use, database program such as Paradox or dBase. The alternative was to use a highly capable, but expensive and difficult to use, package such as Oracle or SQL Server.

If your Paradox data outgrew the program's capacity, you had to redo the entire package using a more capable program. However, the wizard lets you use Access with a clear mind. If your data outgrew Access, you could migrate easily up to SQL Server, which for the vast majority of applications can't be outgrown.

For several reasons—including its ease of use, fast database development, and the popularity of Microsoft Office—by the time Access 95 hit the streets, it had eclipsed both dBase and Paradox to become the leading database product for personal computers. Subsequent versions of Access, up to the current 2002, only extend its lead above its almost non-existent competitors.

Today you don't even need the Upsizing Wizard, because, beginning with Access 2000, the program supports SQL Server development natively through a new type of file called an Access project (as opposed to *.mdb files).

Hardware Requirements

Unlike Word or Excel, which for the most part reach diminishing performance returns shy of even the aging Pentium II, Access will continue to improve in performance as you feed it better equipment. It will run on the minimum specified by Microsoft, but it won't sparkle.

While a faster processor will boost the program's speed, more RAM and a faster disk will better serve most systems. Access uses temporary files to a great extent when it runs short of RAM, so the further you can extend that point and the faster you can read and write those temporary files, the better Access will perform.

As of this writing, SCSI disks are the fastest, but they also run hotter and cost more than ATA IDE disks, which are catching SCSI in performance. If you have a fast ATA disk, you won't see much performance increase by moving to a SCSI setup. If you're building a system from scratch or have an older and slower IDE disk, installing a SCSI drive will reward your extra expense.

The minimum RAM for decent Access performance depends on your operating system. Figure on 32MB for Windows 98 or Me, and 64MB for Windows NT/2000 (and its successors). These are the minimums. Windows 98 and Me run much better at 64MB, while Windows 2000 really starts to shine at 256MB. Increasing beyond these numbers will yield some benefit, but unless you run many tasks at the same time as you run Access, you won't see drastic performance improvements.

Don't refuse a faster processor because that's not the area of greatest sensitivity. Rather, if you currently have a 400MHz Pentium with 64MB RAM and Windows 2000, you'd be better off moving to 128MB RAM, rather than moving to a 850MHz Pentium III with the same 64MB RAM. Better still, get that III, but also get the 128MB RAM. And even better yet, get a computer with two processors for even faster performance. Keep in mind that a dual-processor Windows 2000 machine won't be improved with Access as much as with other applications (such as rendering programs) that are heavily processor dependent.

Access Databases Maintenance

You've probably heard it before—it's not if you'll lose data, but when. Computers aren't infallible, power fails, and parts, especially disk drives, go bad. The only defense is to back up your data.

A full discussion of backup devices is beyond the intended scope of this book. The two fundamental methods are some sort of network backup—either through your LAN or by subscription over the Internet—and backup to removable media such as tape, removable hard disk, or writable CD's. Pick a method and use it.

Access files are somewhat more susceptible to corruption due to power failure than other non-database programs such as Microsoft Word. While you always should be able to restore your files from a backup, sometimes that isn't possible or desirable. For example, you might have done quite a bit of data entry after your last backup in which case you'd prefer not to restore from backup, which would require repeated data entry.

Access 2002 does have a facility that will repair many instances of damage to a database. You can find this in the main Access menu under Tools, Database Utilities. Compact and repair are now one operation.

If you have a database open and choose Tools, Database Utilities, Compact and Repair Access will operate on the open database. If you have no database open, it will prompt you for a file to work on. This latter method is how you'd attempt a fix on a file you can't open.

Access has a quirk that forces the occasional compaction of a database. While Access will dynamically expand to accommodate additional database objects and data, it won't dynamically compress itself as objects or data are removed. You need to do this either programmatically or manually, or you can turn on the Compact On Close feature by going to Tools, Options, General and selecting the Compact on Close option.

While the repair and compact operation are as foolproof as Microsoft can make them, nothing is truly 100% reliable. Unless you like playing with fire, back up your old databases before doing the repair and compaction routine. If you do a compaction or repair on a non-open database, Access will prompt you for a name for the output. This is a form of backup, but since it's not to an external source such as a CDR disk, it's not as foolproof as a real backup.

Tip

In some cases, the repair facility will fail to fix a corrupted database. Occasionally, you can work around this failure by creating a new database container and then importing the objects from the old corrupted database container into the new one. If they import alright, they'll almost always run properly. You can find the import facility in the main Access menu under File, Get External Data, Import.

Summary

Few people care about data. The point of a data manager such as Access is to allow you to turn data into information. Data are entries in a table. Information is what that data means. For example, a list of voters' behavior in a particular election is data. That Republicans outvoted Democrats in mail-in balloting is information. You manipulate and extract (select) data to turn it into information.

Deriving poorly structured data into information is difficult or even impossible. The relational model was created to simplify this conversion, but it only works if you understand and use it. This model specifies that all data reside in tables or two-dimensional grids. You decompose data masses into logically related groups that can be relinked using fields of common data. While the entire relational theory is large and complex, using a relational database, such as Access, is more a matter of common sense than mathematical precision.

Access was originally conceived to fill a missing piece in Microsoft's Office suite. Due to its ease of use and scalability, it has grown to be the dominant data manager for personal computers.

While you need to keep your data, including your databases, backed up, Access has the ability to repair some types of damage.

Q&A

Q. **I'm still unclear about relational theory and its application. Do you have any suggestions?**

A. There are many books out on relational theory, but most of them are either dense or superficial. I won't discourage you from trying this route, but eventually you'll have to get down to actually using the Access product. Practical use will teach you what works and what doesn't—and that's the acid test of whether your database structure is right or wrong.

Q. **What's wrong with including data twice in a database?**

A. There is nothing wrong about doing this, but you lose some efficiency and your database increases somewhat in size. In many cases, your users will demand that you do this. Don't adhere to arbitrary rules to the detriment of your users' reasonable demands.

Q. **How important is it to include a primary key in every table?**

A. This is one rule you can't violate. You can't be sure Access is doing a proper and complete selection of data in a table lacking a primary key. Don't leave the table without one.

Q. **How often should I compact?**

A. There is no rule about this. It depends upon your usage frequency. Some heavily used databases are backed up then compacted daily. Moderately used ones can get away with a compaction every week, or even a lesser frequency. Just make sure to back up when it will take you longer to replace data than it takes to do the backup.

Workshop

The Workshop helps you solidify the skills you learned in this lesson. Answers to the quiz appear in Appendix A, "Answers to Quizzes."

Quiz

1. What's it called when a primary key field is the linked field in another table?
2. Would you classify the following statement as data or information? "In the last election, Republicans outvoted Democrats 5 to 3."

3. Would you agree with the statement "Because Access is a relational database, there is no need to backup its files"?

4. Can Access dynamically shrink the database to reflect deleted data?

DAY **2**

Learning the Basics to Develop an Access Database Application

People have different levels of comfort with computers. This lesson contains mostly basic information about Access and its objects (tables, forms, queries, and so forth). You need to know this information to use Access and to develop database applications for your use.

Today You Will Learn

In today's lesson, you learn the basics of Access that you can put to good use while planning a database application. Specifically in this lesson, you will learn about:

- The Access user interface
- The Objects bar
- Groups

- The types of Access objects
- Opening and closing objects
- Access object views
- Global options
- How to plan your database application

Even if you've never seen Access before, you might be familiar with the items presented in this lesson. If you're comfortable with computers or have a good idea what a table, form, and other Access objects are, feel free to either skim or skip this lesson. If, later on, in the book, you get stuck, come back to it.

The Access User Interface

Access 2002 has a slightly revamped user interface designed to be cosmetically more appealing than its immediate predecessor, Access 2000. The previous version had a significantly revised interface that made things not only easier for the beginner to navigate through, but also made the life of the Access expert simpler.

The main user interface is made up of the Task Pane and the Database View. Office Task Panes, new in Office 2002, are unobtrusive windows that contain frequently used tasks. The Database View is a window that shows all the permanent objects within the database. Each object is grouped on its own page with similar types of objects. For example, all the permanent table objects are shown when you select the Tables tab.

You will use both the Task Pane and the Database View extensively, so let's dig into more detail about each.

Task Pane

Perhaps the largest change in the Access user interface is the Task Pane addition. The Task Pane generally shows up docked on the right side of the display window. If you don't see the Task Pane, you can open it by choosing the menu option View, Toolbars, Task Pane. The Task Pane is aptly named, for it provides quick access to frequently used tasks.

Particularly within Access, the New File Task Pane allows you to open existing databases and create new databases, including new databases from the sample templates. The New File Task Pane also offers a link to Help. Not shown normally is the Clipboard Task Pane, the Basic Search Task Pane, and the Advanced Search Task Pane. The Clipboard Task Pane allows you to collect up to 24 items to be pasted. The Basic Search Task Pane allows you to search for words within files on your computer. The Advanced Search Task

Pane allows you to be more specific with your search. You can specify a particular property (such as "number of pages"), a condition (such as "more than"), and the value. Within Advanced Search, you can specify multiple conditions. An example of multiple conditions would be "Search for files where the number of characters is greater than 10,000 AND the number of paragraphs is fewer than 250." You also can specify where to search and in which type of files to search.

Like so many concepts in small computers, gaining familiarity with the Access interface is best done by a hands-on approach, so let's get started. Launch Access by choosing it from the Start menu. In some administrative (network) installs, Access will be part of a group under Programs, in which case you'll need to locate where Access is to launch it. For most people, Access will be an entry directly under Start, Programs.

Upon launching, Access, via the New File Task pane, offers you several choices: open a file, create a new database, create a new file from an existing file, or create a new file from a template. See Figure 2.1 for a typical screen upon an Access launch.

FIGURE 2.1

The New File Task Pane.

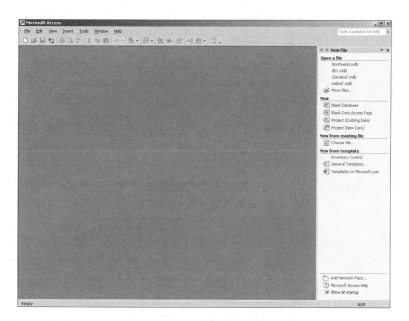

If this is the first time you've launched Access, you won't have any entries in the list box at the top of the New File Task Pane. Here are explanations of the New File Task Pane entries:

- Open a File—Opens existing Access databases and Access Projects. You also can Browse for Access databases and projects on your computer.

- New-Blank Database—Creates a new blank database, ready for you to populate with your database objects.
- New-Blank Data Access Page—Starts the process of creating an HTML form useful for presenting data in an intranet application.
- New-Project(existing data)—Creates an Access Project that connects to an existing Microsoft SQL Server database. Such applications are called client/server applications.
- New-Project(new data)—Creates an Access Project and creates a new Microsoft SQL Server database.
- New from existing file—Creates a new copy of an Access database or project.
- New from template-General Templates—Brings up the Templates dialog to allow you to select installed templates. A template is a Microsoft supplied sample database application replete with sample data. More templates are available at Microsoft's Web site; the last entry in the Task Pane links you to those templates.

In addition, you can drop down the File menu to see the usual Open and New options, which will open the New File Task Pane if it's not visible.

For this, a first tour of Access, choose More files... from the Open a File section. That action will open up a standard File Open browsing dialog box. Navigate to the Northwind database. This is usually located wherever your Microsoft Office is installed in a folder called Samples. The Northwind database has the standard extension MDB. You might or might not see extensions based on the way your Windows is customized.

 Note

If you have difficulty locating Northwind.mdb, use Office's search utility. To get to that from the New File Task Pane, click the down arrow and choose Search. Fill in the Search text box and then click the Search button. Alternatively, you can use Windows Explorer (not Internet Explorer) and use Search (or Find for Windows 9.x) to locate the file.

Objects and Actions

Northwind is part of most installs, but it might not be present in your machine. If not, you can still get a good idea of the Access user interface by the screens within this section, or you can run Office Setup again to install it. After you've opened Northwind, click OK to close the introduction splash screen. When the splash screen is closed, the

Main Switchboard display appears. A switchboard is a navigational aid, rather than a data entry form. Your screen should resemble Figure 2.2.

FIGURE 2.2

The Database View holds a collection of all database objects within your project.

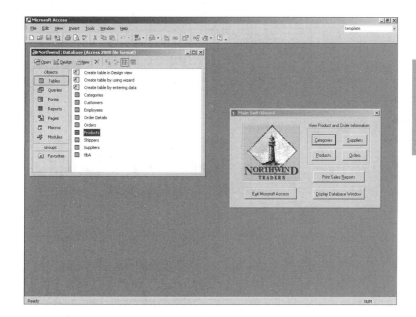

The Main Switchboard is a way for users to use this application in various ways. If you want, you can close the switchboard by clicking on the Close Window icon (it's an X) in the upper-right corner.

The remaining object, the one that says Northwind: Database in its title bar, is the Database View. It displays all the items or objects within your database. The `Object Bar` down the left side of the Database View gives you a classification choice of different types of objects. Click the Forms button (or any button other than the one currently selected) and the Database View will filter all the database objects to only let the one type selected appear within the Database View. Figure 2.3 shows the Form objects within the database. Choosing different object types changes the display within the Database View. Compare Figure 2.3, which shows the Form objects, to Figure 2.2, which shows the Table objects.

Note

The first few objects on display within the Database View aren't truly objects, but actions. You can differentiate these actions from true objects by their icons located to the immediate left of the object name.

FIGURE 2.3

The Database View is showing the forms in the database.

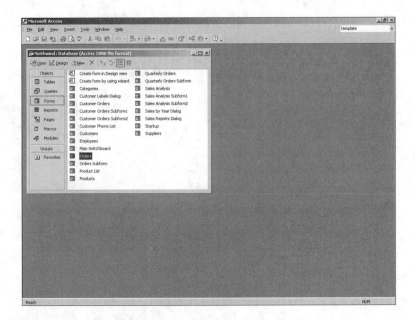

At the top in the toolbar of the Database View, you can see a set of icons telling you what actions you can perform on the objects listed within the Database View. The first four entries left to right provide important actions:

- Open: Launches an object in its native mode such as for data entry. Access uses the term *view* for different object modes.
- Design: Launches an object so you can edit its structure rather than its data.
- New: Creates a new object of the type highlighted within the Object list.
- Delete: Deletes the highlighted object.

The four buttons to the right of the three action entries allow you to view the database objects in large icons, small icons, list view, and details view. These views correspond with the identically named Explorer views of your files and folders.

Right-clicking is alive and well in Microsoft Access 2002. Right-click any true object (as opposed to an action within the Database View) and you'll see a context (or shortcut) menu containing all the actions within the Database View, as well as a few more. True to its name, the context menu for each type of objects will vary. Figure 2.4 shows the context menu for form type objects. The specific actions within a context menu will vary based on the type of object.

You also can right-click the Objects group button to see shortcuts to Access facilities such as the VBA editor or the database startup dialog box.

FIGURE 2.4

The context menu for Form objects.

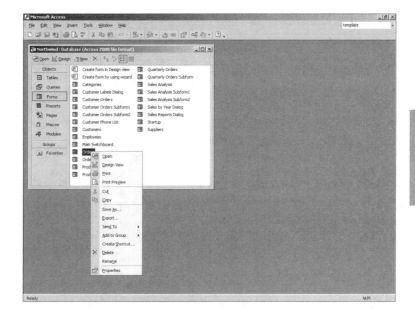

2

Groups

Note the Groups Add to Group button within the context menu for Figure 2.4. This facility, new in Microsoft Access 2000, allows different types of objects within user-defined groups. Prior to Access 2000, there was no simple way to collect and display different categories of objects (such as Forms and Reports both) within one "button" of the Database View. Now you can by creating user-defined groups. To create a new group, right-click any type of object (such as Forms or Reports) listed down the left side of the Database View, and choose New Group from the context menu. Enter Tirilee Traders in the New Group dialog and press Enter.

Now that you have a multiple category capable group, you can add objects to it by right-clicking the object you want to add, choosing Add to Group from the context menu, and then specifying the group from the submenu. Figure 2.5 shows a form being added to the Tirilee Traders group.

Figure 2.6 shows the new group, Tirilee Traders, with different types of objects within it. You can tell that the objects are heterogeneous by their differing icons. I've changed the view from List to Large icons to make the point clearer.

Tip

You also can use drag-and-drop to create a shortcut to an object from its object classification (such as Queries) to a user-defined group.

FIGURE 2.5

You can use the context menu for an object to add it to a group.

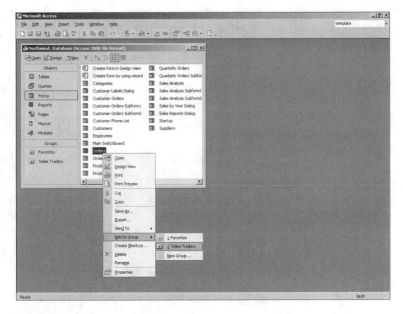

FIGURE 2.6

The Microsoft Access 2002 user-defined groups can hold diverse objects.

Object Views

Access uses the term "*view*" to refer to different object modes. The two main views used throughout Access are normal view (just called view) and design view. Normal view is the mode you use to interact with the object and its data (if relevant). Design view is the mode you use to change the characteristics, or design, of an object.

Opening and Closing Object Views

If you double-click an object within the Database View, it will open in normal view. If you have Northwind, try opening the Employees form by selecting (clicking on) the

Forms group and then double-clicking the Employees form in the database view. Figure 2.7 shows the resulting form opened for data entry.

FIGURE 2.7

The normal view, or the default mode, for an Access object is the view ready for data entry, viewing, or editing.

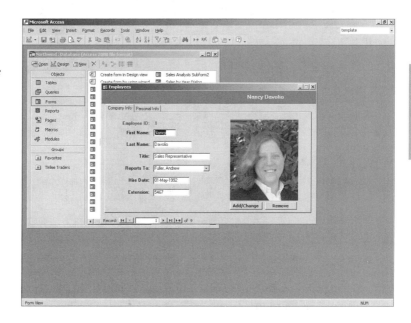

> **Note**
>
> The Database View is a resizable window. I've resized it quite a bit for these screen shots for clarity and to show all the objects contained in it.

You also could highlight the Employees form and then click the Open button along the top of the Database View to open Employees in this view. To close an object, click the close button in the upper-right corner of the window or choose File, Close from the main menu when the object is selected (active). Remember your "right" to right-click if you prefer manipulating objects that way.

To see an object in design view, highlight it in the Database View, and choose design from the toolbar of the Database View. Figure 2.8 shows the Employees form opened in design view.

You also can dynamically switch views by clicking on the View button in the main Access toolbar, or from the View menu. The View button is on the extreme left on the bottom toolbar shown in Figure 2.8. Try switching back and forth from design to normal view using the View toolbar button until you get a feel for it. This is an important switch that you'll use quite a bit when designing certain Access objects—especially forms.

FIGURE 2.8

*Design view is the
mode you use to
manipulate the object's
design rather than the
underlying data.*

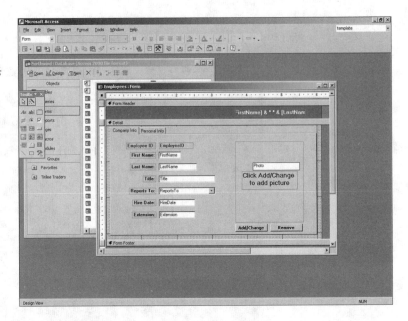

When you're ready to, close the Employees form. If Access prompts you to save or discard changes, that means you made some modification to the form. Don't save any
changes now.

Managing Access Object Views and Windows

The windows containing Access objects, such as the Employees form, act just like any
other Windows window. Once you have one open, you can maximize it, minimize it,
move it around, stretch it, and shrink it just like any usual window. The only restriction
is that, except for Page objects, all Access objects must remain within the main Access
window.

Try opening Employees again in normal view. Maximize it and then minimize it. When
it's in windowed mode, move it around. Grab a corner or other border with your mouse
cursor and try shrinking and then stretching it in all directions until you have a good feel
for how things work within Access. You can likewise shrink, maximize, minimize, and
manipulate the Database View window. Closing Database View window will, however,
close the database.

Note

If you minimize and then lose track of an object, pull down the Windows
menu from the main Access menu bar and then select the missing or lost
object. This will restore it to its former size and location.

Options—Customizing Access Globally

Microsoft Access 2002 has several options allowing you to customize the way it looks and acts. This customization means that, to the extent Microsoft has foreseen, you can make Access behave in a way most comfortable and convenient to you.

To see the Options dialog box, choose Tools, Options from the main Access menu. Figure 2.9 shows the resulting dialog box.

FIGURE 2.9

The Options dialog box for Microsoft Access 2002 sports the familiar tabbed look.

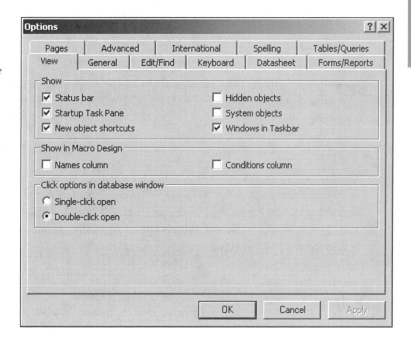

Many of the options on these tabs refer to advanced topics best left to later sections of the book after you're more familiar with this product. However, there are several options of interest to users of any level. Table 2.1 is a short list of these options, the tabs they appear on, and a short explanation of what they can do for you.

TABLE 2.1   Global Options

Entry	Tab	Description
Click options in database window	View	Specifies that to open objects, you double-click or single-click.
Default database folder	General	Specifies where Access stores database files by default.

TABLE 2.1   continued

Entry	Tab	Description
Confirm	Edit/Find	Specifies whether to confirm major record changes.
Windows in Taskbar	View	Specifies that each object shows up in the taskbar, or only Access shows.
Fonts and Formatting	Datasheet	Specifies various entries for the default appearance of Access grids, otherwise known as datasheets.

> **Note**   The default state for the size and font of a datasheet (table or query) display is 10 point Arial. Some people find this hard to see. Feel free to change this to a larger size or more easily discerned font, but keep in mind that if you do so, your screens will vary cosmetically from those in the book.

The option that causes the most confusion for users, especially those used to versions of Access prior to 2000, is the Windows in Taskbar option. Prior to Access 2000, a single window would be represented in the taskbar, no matter how many database objects you had opened. However, Access, unlike some other Office applications, gives you the option to turn this feature on or off.

> **Note**   The Windows in Taskbar requires the Active Desktop (part of Internet Explorer 4.x and greater) in order to work as advertised.

With Windows in Taskbar checked, every open object within your database has its own entry on the taskbar. With Windows in Taskbar unchecked, only the Access program and the currently active object have an entry on the taskbar. It might seem that turning Windows in Taskbar on is the way to go as it places all objects in easy reach; this is true. The downside of this, however, is that many open objects mean a cluttered taskbar.

Add a few other applications, such as Word or Notepad, to a Windows session and you can end up with a miserably cluttered taskbar. The Windows in Taskbar option isn't terribly useful if your application or work habits require many Office documents open simultaneously. Figure 2.10 shows the results of many windows open at the same time.

Figure 2.11 shows the same computer with the same documents, objects and applications open, but with the Windows in Taskbar option turned off. Note how much less cluttered the taskbar looks.

FIGURE 2.10

A number of applications with the Windows in Taskbar option turned on.

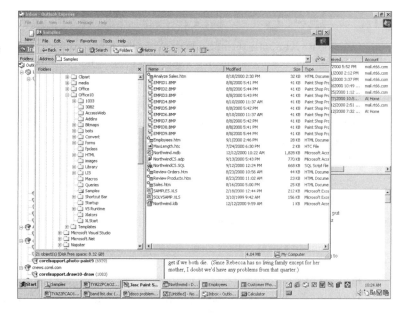

FIGURE 2.11

The same number of applications with Windows in Taskbar option turned off.

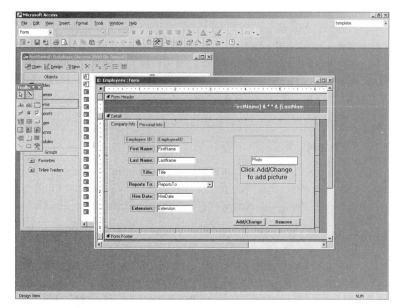

Tip

Access 2002 can dynamically change its display from a single window represented in the taskbar to all open objects represented unlike Access 2000, which needed a shutdown and restart to accomplish the same thing.

The Objects of Access

It's time to get a little technical here. A database is an orderly collection of data for presentation and manipulation. The data itself is all stored in tables, which are two-dimensional grids (matrices). Other database objects, such as forms and reports, present, select, filter, or otherwise modify the presentation of the data within tables.

While you have no choice in where you store data, you have a wide variety of tools when choosing its presentation and manipulation. The two elements defining an Access expert are

- A working or descriptive knowledge of all the tools within Access and perhaps its big brother, SQL Server.
- The ability to apply those tools ideally for each given task.

Becoming an expert sounds easy, doesn't it? Well, in theory it is, but as in many things, the fundamentals are simple, but the details don't quite fall in place so easily. If they did, there would be nothing but Access experts and clearly that situation doesn't exist. However, there's nothing about learning Access that's overly difficult if taken in small bites.

The first part of learning Access is to gain a working familiarity with the nature of the objects within the Database View. To proceed, launch Access, if necessary, and then open the Day 2 database located on your CD in the Day 2 folder. You can do this by choosing More Files… from the Open a File section in the Task Pane. Alternatively you can choose Open from the File menu or double-click the file after locating it using Windows Explorer.

Tables

A table is the fundamental element of a relational database and is where Access stores all data. Learning your way around in tables is important for understanding Access. Let's get some hands-on experience with tables. Open the Start (found in the Day 2 folder).

Once Start is open, if necessary, click the Tables button on the Object Bar of the Database View to make the table objects visible. Open the table object tblFriends by double-clicking it or clicking the Open button on the toolbar, with it highlighted. Your screen should resemble Figure 2.12. The prefix tbl is a shorthand flag indicating that this object is a table. Although this is obvious when looking at the collection of tables, it's not so obvious at other places within Access. For example, if you're in a group, would you rather try to figure out if that icon is a table or a query, or just see a three-letter prefix for each object positively identifying it? Also in some areas of Access, you won't have an icon to help you.

Note

This book uses the most common naming convention, derived from an early convention by Greg Reddick and Stan Lyszynski and modified by Lyszynski and the Kwery Corporation.

FIGURE 2.12

Fields go up and down, whereas records go across in rows. Keep that in mind and you'll never get your fields crossed with your records.

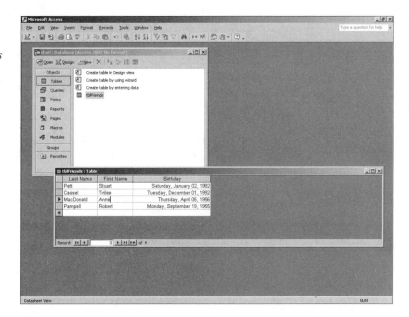

This table has only a few entries. It holds the first name, last name, and birthday for a few people now, but of course can be expanded to hold millions of names, if necessary or desired. The headings across the top of the grid are field names. The rows are records. The concept of which are the fields and which are the records is vital to understanding and using Access or any other database product.

- Fields hold similar data such as text, numbers or dates. Fields classify data according to its data type. Each field in Figure 2.12 holds text classified by last name, first name, or birthday.

- Records classify data in the sense of a data picture of the table's purpose. In Figure 2.12, each record holds all the pertinent data for a particular person.

Click the View button at the far left of the toolbar to move into design view. Figure 2.13 shows this view for this table. Remember, design view is the view where you modify the actual design of an object. It excludes all data information.

FIGURE 2.13

The design view of an object allows you to examine or edit its properties.

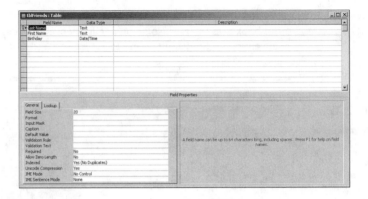

Note   Remember that I'm resizing windows as I go to make the display clear. Your specific screens will surely vary cosmetically from those in the book unless you bother to resize them as you go as the book does.

You can get a pretty good idea of how to design a table based on examination of Figure 2.13. The design view is again a grid, but one with columns having fixed labels and uses. The first column is the field name which also, by default, appears as a table heading. The second column is the data type where you tell Access what kind of data its going to store in that field, whereas the third column holds comments.

The design view is context-sensitive. Click the Birthday field and watch how the bottom portion of the grid (the Field Properties) change to reflect the properties associated with a date/time field, as opposed to a text field (Last Name).

Very soon, all these table properties will become second nature to you, but before proceeding there, let's move on to finish our tour of objects. The next stop is queries.

Queries

While tables hold all data, clearly the heart of Access is its query system. Using queries, you can select, order, present, filter, modify, and otherwise party it up with your data. Access has two basic ways to create queries, by directly entering SQL statements (difficult for beginners) or using the query by example grid. By the time you're done with the 21 days, you'll have gained expertise in both systems.

To see a query in action, close the table object tblFriends if it's still open. Click the Queries button and open the query qryFilteredFriends. Your screen should resemble Figure 2.14.

FIGURE 2.14

A query allows you to select, order, and otherwise present or modify your data.

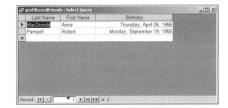

This query filters the table tblFriends to only present people who have birthdays before January 1, 1980. Keep in mind that doing this doesn't, by itself, affect the data in the underlying table. This is called a select query because it selects data according to your criteria. Also keep in mind that unless you take measure to prevent it, all select queries in Access are live. Modifications to the data shown in Figure 2.14 will affect the data in the underlying table. The query itself doesn't do the modifications, but any editing will.

To see the magic behind the query, click the View button to move to design view. Again you'll see a grid, this time the query by example grid.

FIGURE 2.15

The query by example grid uses a visual metaphor to construct queries.

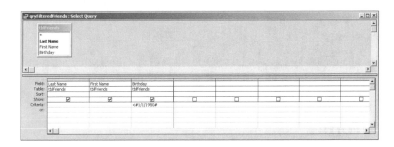

Again, you probably can determine how the query works by simple examination. The box just below the title bar represents the fields in the linked (bound) table, tblFriends. This is the source for the query's data. In this case, all the fields from tblFriends are included in qryFilteredFriends, but they don't all need to be. You also can use more than one table in a query to combine data from more than one table, as you'll see later in Day 4, "The Data Foundation—The Table." Feel free to peek ahead to see how this looks.

The key to filtering or selecting within this query is the statement

```
<#1/1/80#
```

in the criteria line under the Birthday field. This restricts the display of records to those that have a value less than (or, in other words that are before) January 1, 1980.

Note

> The pound symbol (#) is special syntax that tells the query parser in Access to treat the portion between the pound signs as a date value. If you didn't have to specify this syntax, Access might treat the date 1/1/80 as a string or even a number (1 divided by 1 divided by 80.)

The other important view of a query is the SQL (Structured Query Language) behind it. Pull down the combo box view button at the far left of the toolbar and choose SQL View from the drop-down list. Your screen should resemble Figure 2.16.

FIGURE 2.16

The particulars of SQL are complex, but the language itself is plain English.

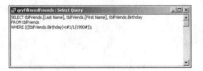

Again, even if you've never seen SQL before, you should be able to have an idea of how it works by examining the statement in Figure 2.16 and seeing the results in the query view.

See how easy this can be? SQL is one of the most complex topics in Access and you already have an idea of how it works. However, next on the tour of Access is forms—the fun part of database design.

Forms

Forms display data for viewing, editing, or entering. In addition, you can use form tools to help in data entry, data validation, or other related duties. Most people find that entering or editing data within forms is a lot easier than using the grid format of a query or table.

In short, like queries, there is a lot of depth in forms, but also like queries, getting started with forms is fairly easy. The Day 2 folder on the accompanying CD has a form based on the object tblFriends called frmFriends. This is a simple form created by a wizard. It took about a minute to make, because the special formatting is part of the designs supplied by Microsoft with Access 2002.

To see this form in action, close any open objects, click the Forms button in the Database View, and double-click the object frmFriends. The form will open in normal (or data) view. Your screen should resemble Figure 2.17.

FIGURE 2.17

The simple but attractive form bound to the `tblFriends` *table.*

This form shows the first entry in the table, the one for Tirilee Cassel. The table has as its key field `Last Name` (a design mistake we'll get to later), so it orders its records by that field. As Tirilee's last name is first alphabetically, it appears as the first record.

Take a look at the bottom of your screen, the status bar. You'll see the word *Record* and a box with the number 1 in it. That tells you that the record shown is first, and farther to the right you can see that there are four records in total. Click the VCR-like control—the one with the wedge pointed to the right. That moves you one record at a time through the records until you're at the last record. You can jump forward and backward using the buttons with lines on them. The button with a star on it jumps you to a new record—the expressway to data entry.

Pull down the View button on the toolbar and choose Datasheet view from the pull-down list. That changes your screen to look similar to the underlying table. Figure 2.18 shows this view.

FIGURE 2.18

The datasheet view is a form, too.

Finally, click the View button to go to design view. The result will be the form design grid shown in Figure 2.19. Although this grid is a bit more complex than the grids you've seen before, you should be able to have a general idea of how the form is constructed.

Again, as in the query design grid, there's a box (a window really) showing the available fields for this form based on the table it's bound to (`tblFriends`). The toolbox (a toolbar that, by default, floats) toward the center of the screen holds the tools (or controls) you can use to construct your forms.

The `Detail` section of the form holds three fields (or controls) for data, and three labels to tell users what the fields represent. Try switching back and forth between design and form view to see how the controls and their labels make the transition. When you're done, close the form, discarding any changes you've made, because it's time reports took the center stage.

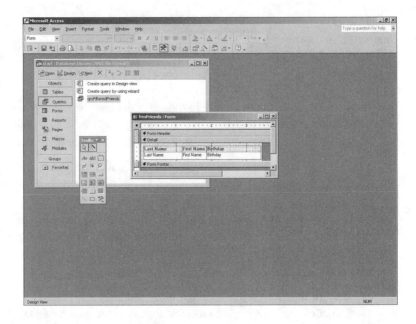

FIGURE 2.19

The form design view is more complex than some of the grids in Access, but the actual use of the grid is, paradoxically, easier.

Reports

Novices to Access tend to be a bit confused as to why there are both forms and reports within the product, because you can print forms and show reports on your screen. The simple answer is that reports are forms optimized for printing while forms are, well, forms optimized for screen use. The more complex answer is that forms have facilities for data manipulation, whereas reports don't. This brings to bear issues such as database security. That tends to beg the question a bit as you can make forms that won't tolerate any data manipulation, so let's just leave it that forms are optimized for screens, while reports are designed for the printer.

Open the report rptFriends by choosing the Reports button in the Database View, and double-clicking that object. Your screen should resemble Figure 2.20.

When you open a form by double-clicking or choosing Open from the action buttons in the Database View, Access puts you in Print Preview view. This shows the report as it should print out from your printer. Like the form, the report can scroll through records using the VCR-like buttons at the bottom of the screen. As all the records from tblFriends easily fit on one screen, this facility isn't relevant to this report.

Click the now-familiar View button on the toolbar to switch to design view for this report. Your screen should resemble Figure 2.21.

FIGURE 2.20

To put it simply, a report is a form optimized for the printer, but as you can see, it works all right on the screen, too.

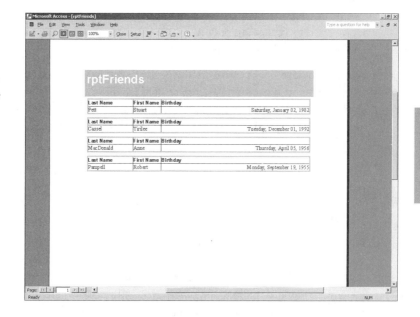

FIGURE 2.21

The report design grid is very similar to the form design grid. That's by design (ahem), not accident.

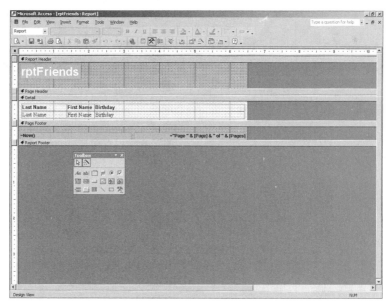

This should look familiar to you by now. The report design grid is very similar to the form design grid. There is a toolbox, a list of available fields, a Detail section, and two header sections that are available in the report where they weren't in the form. However, they're there in both forms and reports, although the entire business of headers and footers is a bit more complex in reports than forms.

Again, you have field controls in the Detail section where the actual data will appear when the report runs/prints. There are field labels, and some more labels in the header and footer sections. By switching between design and Print Preview views, you can gain a good idea of how all the design features work in the actual report.

One of the greatest things about Access is that you can transfer skills from one part of Access to another. Just about anything you learn about designing forms is applicable to reports. The characteristic is commutative.

Pages

Figure 2.22 shows a simple data access page (the First Data Access Page) included with your sample data. Figure 2.23 shows the same page in design view. You should notice some similarities between forms, reports, and pages. Skills learned in one area generally are transferable to the others. The only place where this isn't true is in the instance of a specific task that one object does what no other object does. My guess is that at least 80% of the skills in any of these objects are transferable to the others.

FIGURE 2.22

The data access page is a form useful for display in Internet and intranet sites.

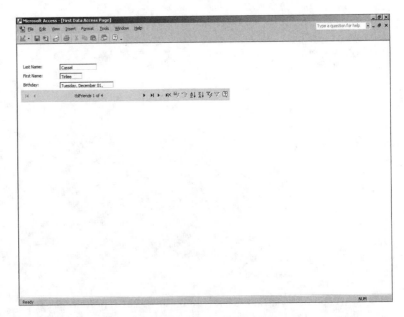

FIGURE 2.23

The design view of the data access page is similar to the form design view, but not identical.

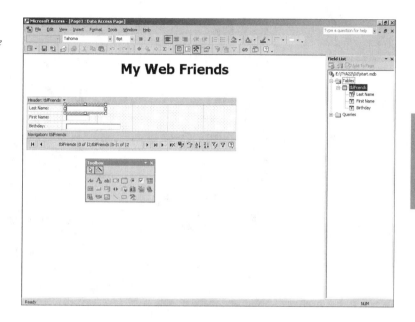

Macros

The macro language within Access is a simple way to program Access for foreseen events or to automate tasks. Close any open objects in the Day 2 database, click the Macros button in the Database View, and open the macro mcrMessage by either the Open button or double-clicking. Your screen should resemble Figure 2.24.

Click OK to clear the message box. If necessary, highlight the macro named mcrMessage in the Database View and click the design button to see the macro's design. Your screen should resemble Figure 2.25.

Once again, you should be able to examine the macro design grid and get a good idea of how this macro operates. The Action column should be self-explanatory—this macro's action is to display a message box (msgbox). Pay special attention to the Action Arguments Pane where you'll see entries for both the title bar and the message itself.

If you want to see the macro in action so you can observe the transition from the design elements to the running elements, click the Run button on the toolbar. This has an exclamation point for an icon. When you're satisfied that you have this macro figured out, close it discarding changes.

"Well," you might wonder, "that was interesting, but useless." So let's continue with the macro demonstration by showing an admittedly trivial, but good for demonstration purposes, macro activation upon an event.

FIGURE 2.24

The macro design grid is yet another grid resembling the table design grid, but vastly different in use.

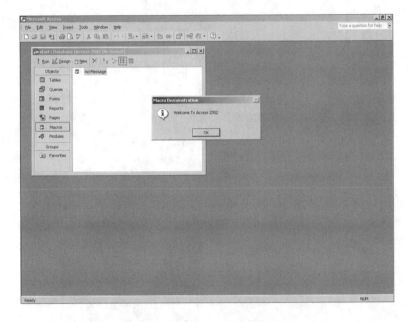

FIGURE 2.25

The chief characteristic of this simple macro is the macro action specified in the left column.

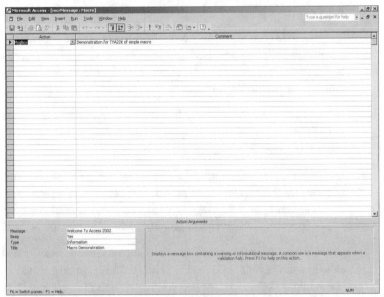

Return to the Forms button of the Database View, and open in form view the form frmMacroDemo. Move your mouse all around the form making sure to avoid the red rectangle labeled Mouse Corral. When you're satisfied that nothing's strange, pass your mouse cursor over the Mouse Corral. Your screen should resemble Figure 2.26.

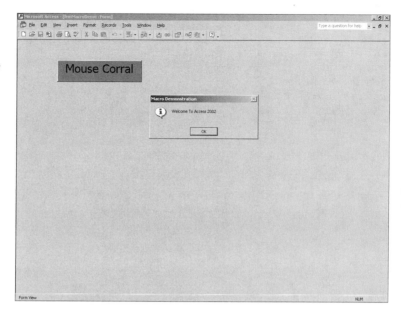

Obviously, this is a rather silly example of what you can use macros for, but I think you understand the principle, so let's move onward to modules.

Modules

Modules are Visual Basic for Applications (VBA) code—real computer programming. The extent of VBA programming is enormous, and often needed for externally distributed Access projects. The enormousness (but not enormity) of VBA tends to discourage some otherwise adept Access users, but it needn't be that way. While the potential for VBA is huge, just like anything else, taking it in small bites will surely be in the reach of anybody who cares to take the time.

This example of a VBA module is overly simple to demonstrate that VBA as a topic doesn't have to overwhelm even the most novice user. Close all database objects discarding changes. Click the Modules button of the Database View. Double-click the module, modDemo. Your screen should resemble Figure 2.27.

Click the Run button on the toolbar. That's the one close to the middle with the right-pointing wedge. Or, if you prefer, press F5 (run). Access will prompt you for which procedure to run; because you have only one choice, just click run. Your screen should resemble Figure 2.28.

FIGURE 2.27

The module design area is considerably different in look, behavior, and use from any other Access design facility.

Tip

Don't confuse the Macro dialog with Access Macros mentioned in the previous section. These macros mentioned here are really VBA procedures.

FIGURE 2.28

A VBA module can contain complex code or as simple as the message box shown.

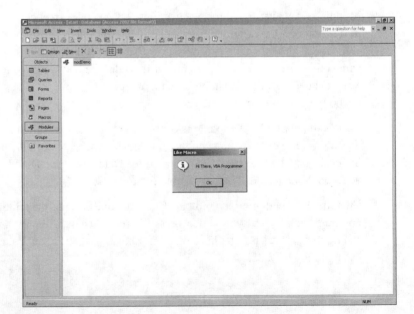

Again, by examining the code in Figure 2.27, you should have a pretty good idea of how this routine works. To return from the screen in Figure 2.27 to the standard Access screen, click the View Microsoft Access button on the toolbar. That's the one at the far left in Figure 2.27. It has a key for an icon.

Well, that's it for your fast tour of the various Access objects. Close all objects and Access itself as the next sections don't make use of the Day 2 database.

Planning Your Database Application

Bluntly put, the success of any database application depends on the quality of its planning. Access is much more forgiving of poor data design than other database systems, but even Access can't make a good database application from no planning.

You, as the developer, need to find a planning method that suits you best, but most people do at least roughly similar tasks. Since the point of a database system is data organization (or information), you need to pay attention to the output. In fact, it's a fairly common practice to design the database system around what it needs to output. Here is one way a certain developer goes about planning a database application. You can use this list, modifying it to suit your tastes and needs.

1. **Determine the purpose of the database application.** What will come out of it? What level of users will have to manipulate the data? How much flexibility do they need?

2. **Determine the workflow and see how it will integrate into the organization.** Most of the time your database applications need to conform to the system and personnel already in place, but this is not always the case. What is the level of the expertise available to you within the company? What is the time available for this project?

3. **What data is available to you?** Is what you need already structured in another computer system or will you need to have your people enter the data from scratch? Can this system save time or steps in another area of the organization?

4 **Conceptualize the data for use within the system.** Think of your data not in human terms, but computer ones. For a relational database like Access, this boils down to normalizing your data or breaking it into a table system with data linked by key fields and no (or as little as possible) duplication between tables (normalization). That is, if you have a person's address anywhere in a database table, you should not have that address repeated anywhere. Instead, think of a structure where you can link the address onto any other data (such as name) you want to display.

5. **Prototype the system.** This is an optional part useful for large database applications where a do-over will cost you dearly. Create a model of your proposed system. Test it with live data. If you're working externally in any aspect, show it to users and approvers to get their input. This latter step can be a disaster if you lose control of the input sessions, but it is very useful if there is any doubt that the people you will be depending upon to make use of this system are at all reluctant to use it. Reluctant users can destroy any database system.

Don't Be a Slave to Convention

When reviewing currently used systems, don't try to duplicate them utterly. A well-designed paper system (or a mainframe one) isn't necessarily a good template for a modern database system. Always keep in mind the parts of Access, its particular abilities, and its strengths.

For example, a paper system can't have a pull-down text box (combo box) whereas Access can. A paper system can't validate entry, but Access can. Access can automatically call up information based on partly-entered data; paper can't.

While you can automate and improve a paper or mainframe system by simply duplicating it using Access, you won't be using the program to its fullest. You've got the most able and up-to-date database program in existence, so use it like it should be used.

Don't Worry Yet

If you've considered actually putting these steps into action using a database problem you currently face and despaired, don't worry. Putting these fundamentals into action requires a good working knowledge of Access. That's something you'll gain in the next 19 days or so.

The point is to keep this information on hand:

- Knowledge of your data source
- Knowledge of your informational output
- Knowledge of user characteristics
- Knowledge of current workflow
- Knowledge of your workers' task mutability—will they adjust to the system or must the system come to them?
- Knowledge of the objects of Access

Trying to visualize putting all these elements into action at this point is asking too much of yourself. After you've finished this book, come back to this section and it'll be much clearer.

Getting Help—The Office Assistant

Microsoft has a goal for Office applications such as Access—this goal is called "accessibility." This differs from the Accessibility Options in Windows—special aids for users with unusual needs. However, it's thematically similar.

It's fairly easy for Microsoft or another company to pack a program with features, but two things prevent users from availing themselves of those features:

- They can't find them
- They can't figure out how to use them once they've found them

Microsoft has decided the best way to aid users is to pump up the online help facility. This has several advantages for users and Microsoft itself.

- Users will call for Microsoft support less often.
- Users will get better use from the product and presumably talk up the wonders of the program to their friends, family, and coworkers.
- Microsoft can have a less guilty conscious about eliminating almost all written documentation thus forcing users to buy third-party instruction manuals such as this one.

The first iteration of the Office Assistant (OA) showed up in Office 97—the infamous or famous paper clip. Some users loved this iteration and thought it cute, but too many considered it patronizing or even an interference with their work. Microsoft has improved the OA for Office 2002.

Right-click assistant you have active. Choose Options from the context menu. If you have no assistant available, choose the menu selections Help, Show the Office Assistant. If this isn't available, you'll need to install the OA using Office setup.

Figure 2.29 shows the Office Assistant dialog box with the Options tab active.

The Gallery tab allows you to choose from a selection of Office Assistants. The dog shown in Figure 2.30 is Rocky. Microsoft promises to issue new Office Assistants from time to time, and distribute them free through its Web site.

Real Experts Shun Help—Ha!

If you ever get a chance to visit an Access convention where the heavyweight Access programmers hang out, ask a few if they use the help facility in Access. They will universally tell you that they do. There is no shame in not wanting to memorize thousands of properties, keywords, functions, and other folderol you need to develop an Access application. Why should you bother?

FIGURE 2.29

The Options for the Office Assistant allows you to choose the OA you wish to talk to, and also its behavior.

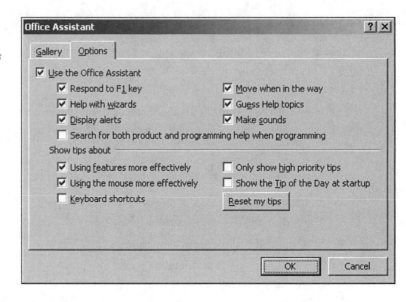

FIGURE 2.30

Rocky, the Office Assistant ready to answer your questions.

Microsoft also has included many examples you can copy and paste directly into your application from the help facility. These are guaranteed to run flawlessly (bug free) so why not paste them in, and then modify them to your specific needs? There is no reason not to!

The Ways of Accessing Help

To see the help facilities in action, you can press F1. Alternatively, you can click Help, Microsoft Access Help on the menu.

Figure 2.31 shows a real help page about programming. The underlined entries in the text screen at the right are links to other topics. These work identically, and are really identical in all important aspects, to the links on a Web page. If you want to drill down deeper in any area summarized in the page shown, just click it.

FIGURE 2.31

The format of the Office help system is identical to Web pages. You can drill down (hypertext) by clicking on any link.

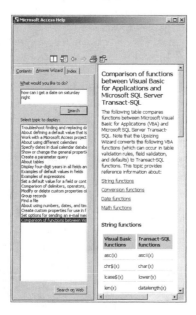

If you have some time, browse through the help system now, looking at the organization of the Contents. Locate a word within help that you think might be a keyword, and enter it in the Index Pane to see what the Help system brings up. Try asking the Answer Wizard a few questions such as "How can I get a date on Saturday night?" (a famous question asked of the wizard by all too many Access programmers).

What's This?

Help also includes a contex-sensitive system called "What's this?". To use this facility, locate a dialog box with a question mark for an icon in its title bar, click it, and then click objects in the dialog box. If a context subject exists, Access brings up a short cheat sheet type balloon help with a hint as to what goes in the dialog box, or what an object is.

Here's an example. From the main menu, choose Tools, Security, Set Database Password. Click the question mark icon next to the close icon in the title bar of the resulting dialog box. The cursor changes to a pointer with a question mark attached. Click the Password field. Your screen should resemble Figure 2.32.

Note

If you get a message box explaining that you need to open the database exclusively when you try to Set Database Password, close the database, then select File, Open, and highlight the database in the dialog box. Pull down the combo box (which is integrated into the OK button in the File Open dialog box), choose Exclusive and then you'll be able to do so. You can set the password on the database when Access can be assured that you are the only one in the database. The only way that can happen is if you open it as described.

FIGURE 2.32

Context-sensitive help also can call up the main help facility.

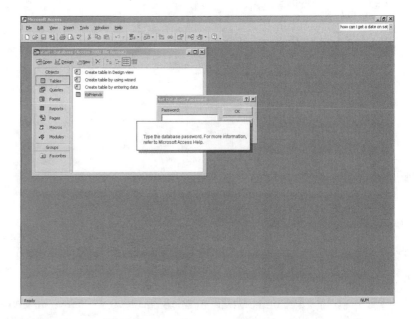

This tool tip–like help has a button in it that will bring up a lot more information about this topic. Don't, at this point, actually add a password to your database or you'll risk locking yourself out.

You also can call up context help by pressing Shift+F1. Try this: Return to the Database View (Database View) itself. Press Shift+F1 and click the title bar of the database window. In this way, you can call upon context help for objects that don't have the question mark icon.

Toolbars

If you're familiar with using toolbars in any Office application, you have a good working knowledge of how to use them in Access. Access does allow you to link certain toolbars to objects, but that's an advanced topic to be covered later. That day will also cover how to place custom macros and other user defined objects on a standard or custom toolbar. This section only covers use of toolbars in the standard Office way.

To modify or create toolbars, click on View, Toolbars, Customize menu. This brings up the Customize dialog box. To add any command to a toolbar, locate it using the left and right panes of the dialog box and then drag it to the toolbar, dropping it where you want it to reside. To remove a button from a toolbar with the Customize dialog box showing, just drag it off the toolbar, dropping it anywhere on the desktop. To remove a button without the Customize dialog box, press the ALT key while dragging it off the toolbar.

Try this: With the Start database open, open the Customize dialog box. Click the Commands tab and scroll down the left pane (Categories) of the dialog box until you can highlight the All Macros entry. This will bring up the macMessage macro in the Commands (right) pane. Your screen should resemble Figure 2.33. Drag this macro to any toolbar dropping it in a convenient place. Close the dialog box by clicking on OK. Now click the new button you just added.

FIGURE 2.33

Adding user-defined buttons to a toolbar isn't too difficult. This topic is quite complex in its entirety, however.

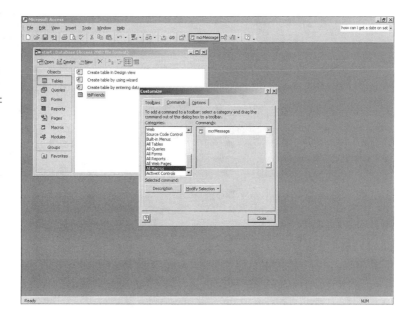

After you're done, you can remove this button by pressing ALT and dragging it off the toolbar.

You can dock your toolbars at any edge of the screen, or let them float around your display. Most people find floating toolbars to be annoying and leave them docked, but this is your call. To move or resize a toolbar, grab it by its handle (the raised portion at the left of a toolbar) and drag. If the cursor is in the shape of a cross, you can move the toolbar. A double arrow cursor is the icon for sliding/resizing. A little experimentation with these toolbars is all you need to get a feel for them.

The menu bar is a type of toolbar too, and like the usual toolbars, you can float it around. Figure 2.34 shows Access with all the standard bars and one optional bar afloat. You also can dock them in any order you wish. Feel free to experiment around with changing how Access looks. You can always return to the standard Access setup by choosing the Reset button in the Customize dialog box on the Toolbars tab.

FIGURE 2.34

You can float all or some toolbars. It's a matter of taste.

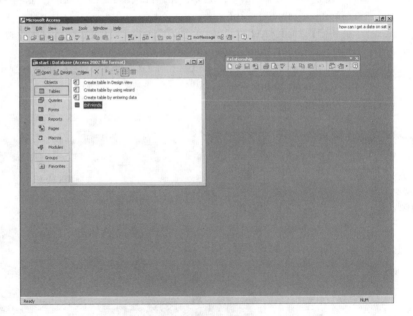

Summary

To use Access or to even plan an Access database, you need a good working familiarity with the Access user interface and the objects that make up a database application. This lesson gave you a good foundation in these areas.

The primary display in Access is the Database View. This is where you can see all the objects within your database either classified by type or clustered within a heterogeneous group. The Database View has an `Object Bar` allowing views of other types of objects and a toolbar (below the title bar) allowing you to take actions upon the selected objects.

There are seven types of Access objects grouped within the Database View: tables, queries, forms, reports, pages, reports, macros, and modules. Tables hold data. The other objects either display or manipulate that data.

You analyze and plan a database application by examining your Access skills, the program's capacities, and your users' needs and facilities. The successful developer finds the ideal synthesis for these often-competing aspects of a database application.

Real Access developers use help almost constantly. You can use the table of content, the answer wizard, or wade through the index. Help can be context-sensitive, and will contain a wealth of examples for you to adapt to your needs.

Q&A

Q. Why can't I store data in a query?

A. Queries query either another query or a table. They can't be the original store for data.

Q. Why not just enter data directly in a table and skip all the form bother?

A. You can if you wish, but most users find forms easier for data entry. Also, forms have extended facilities for data entry not directly available in tables. Few if any good Access developers ask users to add data directly into tables.

Q. Can I print a form?

A. Yes, but the results aren't generally satisfactory, since form controls aren't optimized for printing.

Q. Can I use color in reports? The examples today were all grayscale.

A. Yes, but keep in mind that if your users don't have color printers, doing this can have unpredictable results.

Q. Why does the query date criteria have number (#) signs around it?

A. That's how Access signals that the enclosed string is a date. In most cases, Access will autoformat that for you when you just enter a date as a query criteria.

Workshop

The Workshop helps you solidify the skills you learned in this lesson. Answers to the quiz appear in Appendix A, "Answers to Quizzes."

Quiz

1. What Access object is optimized for display of data on a screen? A printer?
2. Will double-clicking a form in Database View open it in design view?
3. Can you run a macro from the macro design view?
4. What language does a module use?
5. Where does Access store data?
6. Are the columns in a table the fields or the records?
7. Is the type of data in a record always uniform (of the same data type)?

DAY 3

Automatic Access

In the previous two lessons you learned theory and mostly introductory material. Many developers ignore the wizards, because they don't know about the benefits that can be gained by using them. The important concept behind today's lesson is to understand that the wizards can save you a lot of time and that you can study the generated database applications for ideas that you can use in your own database.

Today You Will Learn

In today's lesson, you will see Access wizards in action. Specifically, this lesson covers the following topics:

- Why Automatic Access?
- The Database Templates
- Table Wizard
- Query Wizard
- Form Wizard
- Report Wizard
- Page Wizard

After you finish today's lesson, you will be able to pick and choose what wizard will help you most. Let's put the wizards to work!

Why Automatic Access?

Microsoft has put a lot of time and thought into making Access more accessible to non-professional database users. The result is a somewhat mixed bag of success. Most users get into trouble by not understanding how to structure their data, but creating some sort of wizard process to help users in this area hasn't been easy or even done to any extent.

Most users haven't had much trouble creating Access objects such as tables, forms, or reports, but Microsoft has had a great deal of success in automating the process of making these objects. It also has created wizard processes for making whole database applications.

So you might wonder why Microsoft has applied itself to automating processes that users weren't having much trouble with while not addressing the major block people have with Access. The reason is simple: It did what it could.

There is good reason to learn and use the automatic wizards to create Access objects even when you learn how to do the work manually. The reason is that these wizards save a lot of effort and time. At least some wizards do. It is, for example, a lot easier to create a report using a wizard and modify it to suit your specific needs than to create the same report from scratch. In some cases, the wizard's output is so far from where you want it to be that it won't help, but in many cases, wizards save you a lot of time and effort.

In some cases, like the Mailing Label Wizard in Reports, the wizard will save you vast amounts of effort and misery. In other areas, like the Table Wizard, unless you need a table that the wizard provides, the time savings just isn't there.

I recommend you follow through the next section step by step in any area that interests you. Failing to use wizards at all when you get to know Access well, is similar to not using power tools when building a house. Sure, you can do terrific work using hand tools only, but it will take you a lot longer. Still, there are some workers out there still using hand saws and, for all I know, sharp rocks to do carpentry. Likewise there are some Access programmers who will never use a wizard. It's your life and your time. Spend it like you wish.

Database Wizard or Template

Microsoft calls the wizards that make an entire database application *templates*. Open or launch Access and look at the New File Task Pane. You'll find a section called New from template. There are at least two hyperlinks in this section. The top one, General Templates, is for launching templates stored locally on your personal computer or network. The other, Templates on Microsoft.com, is for using more templates Microsoft created and stored on its Web server. Obviously, you must be connected to the Internet to use the latter templates.

I've seen very few users who have created and used template (or wizard-generated) databases successfully. The wizards run just fine, but user needs tend to vary sufficiently from what the template provides; because of this, the generated applications lack necessary features and have added unneeded features that get in the way.

In theory, you should be able to create an application using a template and modify it to your needs. In practice, this remains one of those good ideas that might not work out. However, these templates do generate database structures that adhere fairly well to relationship structural rules, so at the very least, they're worthwhile to generate a few databases for study.

With those provisos out of the way, let's examine a template by walking through one.

The Template

If you don't want to follow along with the wizard, but want the resulting database, you can find ResourceScheduling1 on the CD, in the Day 3 folder. To create the database based on a template, follow these steps:

1. Launch Access if it's not already open. Locate the New from Template section from the New File Task Pane

2. Click the General Template hyperlink. This brings up the Templates dialog box. Click the Databases tab. Your screen should resemble Figure 3.1

FIGURE 3.1

Access provides several bundled database templates with many more available through the Microsoft Web site.

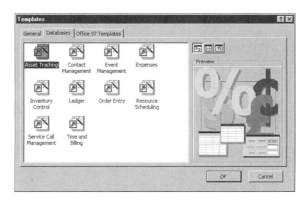

3. Locate the Resource Scheduling template and highlight it by clicking it. Once the template is highlighted, click the OK button.

4. The default name for your new database will be ResourceScheduling1. You can name it whatever you choose, but for this example, just accept the default name. Click the Create button to make a new database from the template.

5. Click Next to move past the introduction screen. In the next step, you can choose to include optional fields. Optional fields are italicized. See Figure 3.2 for the tables and fields that the database wizard will create for you in your database.

FIGURE 3.2

Select the fields that you want in your database.

6. Click Next to move to the style options. Choose the International style.

7. Click Next to move to printed style options. Choose the Formal option.

8. Click Next to get to the last step of the database wizard. In the last step, you can title your database. This is the title that you will see in the Title bar at the top of the main Access window and in message boxes. Leave the default title of Resource Scheduling and click the Next button.

9. In the last step of the wizard, check the option to start the database once it is created and click Finish.

The database wizard creates your database application and should appear as shown in Figure 3.3

If you tried deselecting any fields in step 5, you hit the message box saying you can't deselect this because the field or table is required. Not all is lost. If you choose the last table, Customer Information, then scroll the field list to the bottom, you'll find a few italicized fields that are optional. Even such strange fields like phone extension are mandatory due to the inherent inflexibility of the template.

Tip

If you choose to leave things at default, you can click Finish much earlier in the process to speed the wizard up.

FIGURE 3.3

Access uses a switch-board, or selection form, for its template-generated applications.

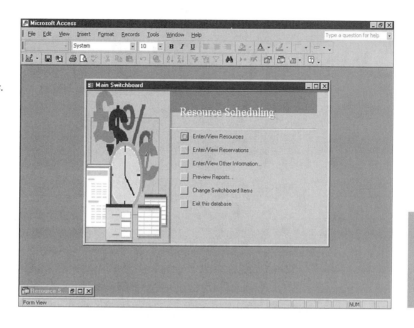

Play around with the switchboard to see all the objects you and the wizard created. Yes, this is a real Access application and in some ways, quite sophisticated too. You can see the database view down in the lower-left corner of your screen and in Figure 3.3, as well. Restore this window to see all the database objects in your new application. Figure 3.4 is the relationships window (choose Tools, Relationships from the menu) for this application. As noted above, this wizard generated application conforms to decent, if not ideal, database practices as far as structure is concerned. You can do a lot worse.

Tip

Press F11 for a quick way to show the database view.

Comments on Templates

At the chance of repeating myself, I've found few people who have used template-generated applications in practice. There always seems to be something missing, or too many things thrown in for this to work. Similarly, there seems to be a negative aspect to an entirely template-generated application compared to one generated one object at a time using the individual wizards that follow. What the template applications will show you is how to structure data well. I encourage you to create template applications and then view their objects in design view. Also try to get a feel for how Microsoft's engineers normalized the data for proper structure.

FIGURE 3.4

Templates adhere to good database programming practices.

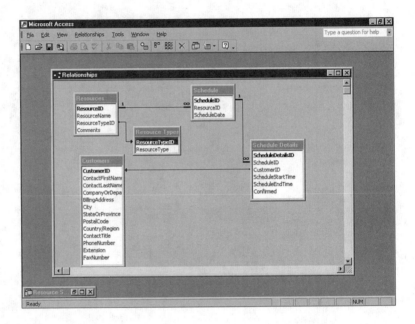

FIGURE 3.4

Templates adhere to good database programming practices.

Table Wizard

Unless you need a table that is exactly what the wizard can generate, I think the Table Wizard is a waste of time and space. It's really another side of the template-created, full-on applications you saw in the last section. Most wizards act on underlying objects, but there is nothing that underlies a table. It is the basic building block of an Access application. I think Microsoft included this just for consistency so it didn't have to answer the question, "Where are the table wizards?"

Again, there are some good lessons to be learned from running a few table-making wizards to see what Microsoft's engineers produce with you as a proxy. Here are the slightly simplified thought steps necessary to create a field in a table.

1. Name a field for a table (such as Last Name).
2. Decide what Data Type of information will go in the field (such as date, number, or text).
3. Set the correct data type.
4. Add any supplemental properties, such as format of the field, in the Properties section of table design view.

To start the table wizard, open the Day 3, then double-click the Create table using wizard hyperlink. Figure 3.5 shows the start of the Table Wizard.

FIGURE 3.5

Unlike other wizards,
the Table Wizard acts
upon no existing
object, but creates the
fundamental building
block of Access, the
table.

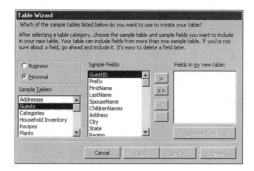

3

Start the table-making process by selecting either Business or Personal type tables from
the option buttons at the middle left of the dialog box shown in Figure 3.5. Then choose
a table and choose the fields to include by using the > or >> buttons. (The > button
chooses the highlighted field, whereas the >> button chooses all fields.) Remove fields
by using the < or << buttons. You can change field names here by choosing a field from
the Fields in my new table list, and then clicking the Rename button. The Rename button
will bring up the Rename dialog box, allowing you to change the name of the field. You
also could wait to rename the field until after you've gotten the table finished if you
want. I've chosen `GuestID`, `Prefix`, `FirstName`, `LastName`, and `ChildrenNames` from the
Personal table `Guests` and clicked Next.

In this step, you can name the table whatever you want. The default name is the name of
the table you selected. You also specify whether you want to select a primary key field or
let Access do it for you. Remember, no matter who does it, you should have such a field
(unique to every record) in each table. In this step I've chosen to let Access set the key
field, then I clicked the Next button.

If you already have tables in your database, the wizard tries to determine the relationships your new table has to these other tables. You will learn more about establishing
relationships to other tables in Day 4, "The Data Foundation—The Table." Because we
don't want to relate our table to any other at this time, just click the Next button.

In the last screen in the wizard, you can specify to modify the table design, enter data
directly into the table or launch a form wizard that creates a form based on your new
table. Look at Figure 3.6. I chose to enter data directly into the table, which is the default
option.

Try entering data directly into the table. Figure 3.7 shows the start of entering some data
into a table.

FIGURE 3.6

The Table Wizard is bone simple. We're almost done.

FIGURE 3.7

Your finished Guest table, ready for data entry.

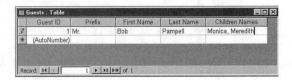

In almost every instance, you will not want to enter data directly into a table, but instead you'll use a form. Also, for a preview of things to come in Day 4, click the design view button.

Tip

> The most important part of table design, aside from the constant of always having a primary key, is making sure the data type is right for each field.

The Query Wizard

Queries choose specifically defined data from another query or a table. For example, if you have a table of all the surnames in the United States, you can create a query to restrict the return to be only those surnames starting with *S*, or those that are *Smith*. Queries in Access also can modify and analyze data in other queries or tables.

Access has made enormous strides in ease of querying by building on the query-by-example method pioneered by other database systems. Older methods required users to write difficult queries using stilted syntax and special keywords. Today you still can (and in some cases must) use this method, but for most daily chores, querying Access is simple and easy. Even so, Microsoft has included a Query Wizard. I've included a table with some data for you to practice querying on. This is a much reduced and simplified table from some real medical data with the personal information (and most fields) stripped out. It's part of your sample data called `tblMiscData`. This example uses that table.

Here's how I made a query using the sample data table. Follow along by doing or just reading about it.

Click the Queries button in the database view to bring up the Queries area. Your sample database, Day 3 should have the query already finished as part of the sample database. To see how I created this query, follow the steps. Click the Create query by using wizard hyperlink. This launches the Query Wizard.

Figure 3.8 shows the first dialog box of the Query Wizard. If you are following along, you need to select a table or query to use for your query. This example uses the tblMiscData from the sample data. It also includes all three fields from the table into the query. You can see the result of this operation in Figure 3.9.

FIGURE 3.8

The first step of the Query Wizard.

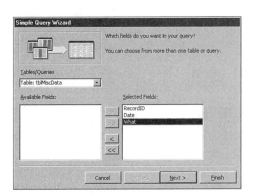

The next dialog box asks whether you want a summary or a detail query. Summary queries return information such as the number of records or the totals of fields. For this example, use the detail option and then click Next.

Finished already! Here you get to name the query and then open or launch it or view it in design view. Note the query only returns exactly the same records and in the same format as the table.

At this point, you might wonder what is the point of a query. If you have the query open, click the design view button (far left); or, if it's not open, open the sample data database to the Queries section and click the object qryMiscData Query. To see this query in more useful action, highlight the sample data query qryDate and then click the Design button in the toolbar right above where the database objects reside. Your screen should resemble Figure 3.9, but at this point without the entry in the Criteria line.

I've added the criterion <#1/1/95# to the criteria area of the query the wizard made in the Date field and saved it using the name qryDate. Other than that, it's the same query as the wizard made.

FIGURE 3.9

Here is the modified wizard made query in design view.

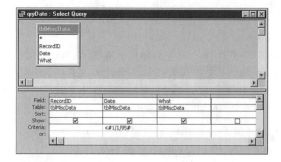

This new query tells Access to pull or select only those records where the date field is less than January 1, 1995. If you have it open, try running this query by clicking the Query View button at the far left on the main toolbar. Scroll around to assure yourself that this simple change vastly changes the query from one the same as the table, to one bearing information.

Automatic Forms

Form wizards (along with Report wizards; see the next section) are the most useful wizards in Access. They also are the most complex. You'll find that in many instances, your life will be much easier if you create a basic form or report using the wizard and then customize it in design view.

There two types of automatic forms. The AutoForm generates a simple data entry form based on the selected table or query. The other type is the multi-step Form wizard, which allows you more control over the creation process.

Creating a Form Using AutoForm

There are two types of AutoForm—the New Object: AutoForm and the builder-based AutoForm. The New Object: AutoForm generates a very simple and uninspiring data entry form. The builder-based AutoForm creates five different types of forms: Columnar,

Tabular, Datasheet, PivotTable, and PivotChart. The AutoForm wizard creates each type of form using the currently selected AutoFormat which is a predefined format. For more information about AutoFormat, while in design view of a form, select the Format, AutoFormat menu.

Tip

> It's important for you to establish standard colors and fonts that you will use in your forms and reports. This is commonly referred to as the "look-and-feel" of an application. After you've settled on a pleasing and useful format, you can create your own AutoFormat that you can then quickly apply to all forms in your database application.

Here is how to use the New Object: AutoForm button:

1. From the database view, click the Tables button.
2. Click the `tblMiscData` to highlight it.
3. Locate the New Object pull-down button on the toolbar (it's the second one from the right with the lightning bolt on it.)
4. Click the button, which selects the New Object: AutoForm option, or pull the button down and choose AutoForm from the list.

The results are seen in Figure 3.10.

FIGURE 3.10

The New Object: AutoForm is simple and fast.

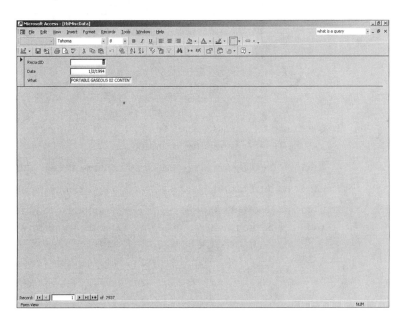

Tip

> If you choose a query for the form to be based on, the form will only show the fields and the records that are in that query. For example, if you chose the query qryDate in the Queries section and clicked AutoForm, you'll have a form that would show only those records having the date before 1/1/1995.

Well, that was easy. I've saved this form using the name frmAuto.

Creating a Form Using the Form Wizard

Now for something a bit more interesting. The Form Wizard gives you more control over how you want your form to appear. Let's create a form using the wizard, following these steps:

1. From the database view, click the Forms button.
2. Click the Create Form by using wizard shortcut to launch the wizard. Figure 3.11 shows the first dialog box of the Form Wizard.

FIGURE 3.11

The first step of the Form Wizard.

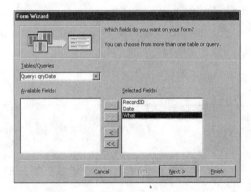

3. Choose all the qryData query from the Tables/Queries list. Then choose all available fields by selecting the >> button.
4. Click the Next button to see the layout options. Choose the Columnar option.
5. Click the Next button to see the style options. Choose the International option.
6. Click the Next button to see the final step in the Form Wizard. This step allows you to name the newly created form. Name the form frmWizard, or something similar, and click the Ok button.

The results of the Form Wizard are seen in Figure 3.12.

FIGURE 3.12

The frmWizard opened
in Form View.

Note that it's a little more complex than the AutoForm by inclusion of the formatting. The real value of using the full wizard instead of the AutoForm is choosing different types of forms in the second dialog box. By including fields from different, but related, tables or queries, you can vastly extend the value of the Form Wizard, but that topic is a bit heavy for this early lesson. I'll come back to it later in Day 10, "Improving Your Forms."

Automatic Reports

The Report Wizard is very similar to the Form Wizard. There is also an AutoReport that works the same as the AutoForm. Figure 3.13 shows the result of the AutoReport option run against the query, qryDate.

FIGURE 3.13

The AutoReport is
similar in all aspects
to the AutoForm.

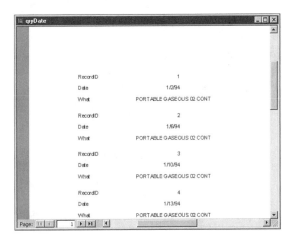

You have this report as part of your sample data saved as rptAuto in the Reports section of the database view. Double-click it to run it from Reports or run the AutoReport yourself against the query qryDate or any other table or report.

The Report Wizard is similar to the Form Wizard, allowing many more options, some of which you'll see here. Again like the Form Wizard, this function is capable of some rather advanced work which I'll cover later in the book. This lesson is supposed to be a light survey of some automatic features of Access, not an exhaustive discussion of all its possibilities.

If you choose to follow along, this section uses the query qryDate to run the Report Wizard against. It likewise includes all fields. The interesting difference in the Report Wizard is in the second dialog box shown in Figure 3.14 where you get to group records. I've chosen to group on the Date field as you can see in the figure.

FIGURE 3.14

Here is the Report Wizard's grouping dialog box. The Grouping Options button will allow grouping by month, day, year, and so on.

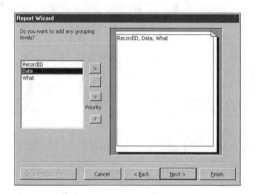

I've also chosen to sort by date as you can see in the next dialog box shown in Figure 3.15. Grouping and sorting are the report's forte.

FIGURE 3.15

Grouping, sorting, and printing are the missions of reports.

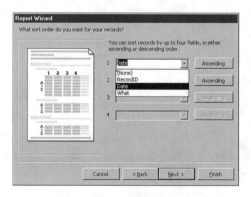

I've left the rest of the options at default, named the report, rptWizard (part of your sample data) and launched it upon the end of the wizard. Figure 3.16 shows the final report.

FIGURE **3.16**

Although quite simple in creation, this report has quite a bit of functionality.

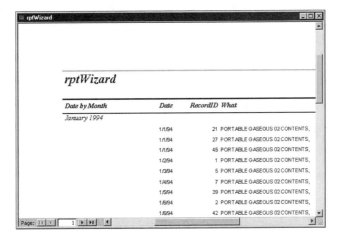

> **Tip**
>
> Now is a good time to spend 15 minutes or so running the Simple Report Wizard using different options. This gives you an idea of the scope of this facility.

If you feel adventurous, open this report in design view. This should give you some idea of the magic behind it. By the time you're done with the Day 12, "Getting Reports Right" lesson, you'll find all the elements in this view to be obvious. Don't expect them to be today, however.

Pages

The Data Access Page Wizard is a duplicate of the Report Wizard (valid for today's discussion anyway) but results in a report suitable for display over the Web. I've run the wizard and saved the page as pgeWizard. You can open the page in the Day 3 database, by choosing the Pages button from the database view. Choose Open from the toolbar. Figure 3.17 shows this open and in action within Access.

Figure 3.18 shows the same page open in Internet Explorer just as it might be in the Web.

I've included this page as the file pgeWizard.html. If you try to open it and find you cannot link to the data source, it's because you've installed the Day 3 database in a different folder from the page, or it's in use by another application (like Access itself).

FIGURE 3.17

You can think of a Page as an interactive report useful for Web work.

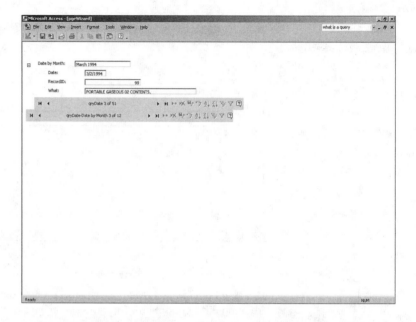

FIGURE 3.18

The pgeWizard.html displayed in Internet Explorer

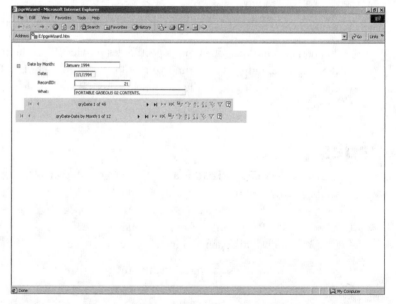

Note

For those of you wondering how to post a database on the Web, you've just done it. That page is connected to the Day 3 database and the display of records is being controlled by the JET engine in Access. Congratulations— you're now a Web database specialist. Well, almost.

Summary

There are five object wizards in Access for tables, queries, forms, reports, and pages. In addition, there is a wizard for creating whole databases. The value of these wizards varies quite a bit from highly useful pages, reports, and forms to less useful queries, to mysterious tables that really just create other tables from predefined data supplied by Microsoft.

All the wizards, especially the Database Template Wizard, are useful for the Access student because you can get to see how Microsoft did it. Creating objects or whole databases using wizards, and then examining those objects in design view, gives you valuable insight into the minds of the Access engineers.

Later on when you move to using Access as a developer, you'd be well-advised to keep these wizards in mind. Rarely, if ever, will you find any wizard that creates an object just as you'd like it, but wizards can come close. Adding a bit of effort to customize a wizard's output results in an object that's just as good as a fully hand-built one and that saves you a substantial amount of time.

Q&A

Q. Why not use the database wizard or template to create an application and then modify it?

A. This is, in theory, what the templates are supposed to do. My personal experience watching many users try this indicates that this entails more work than just making an application from scratch, using object wizards when called for.

Q. How can I arrange the look of a form made with a wizard?

A. You'll need to switch to design view for that form and move the fields around. It's a simple task once you've seen how it's done (as are all tasks). The upcoming lesson, Day 10, "Improving Your Forms," on forms will get you up to speed in a few hours.

Q. Why doesn't the Query Wizard enable you to enter query criteria as part of the wizard's process?

A. This sure seems like a mystery to me. I've never asked Microsoft people about this simply because switching to design view in the query and then adding criteria is so simple it's never seemed very important enough to me. People seem to have problems with the summary queries more than the selection ones and the wizard does handle them all right.

Q. What were the #'s signs you put around the date criterion in the query example you used?

A. Enclosing dates with those signs tells Access that the enclosed expression is a date, not a text string. Access supplies the # signs by default.

Workshop

The Workshop helps you solidify the skills you learned in this lesson. Answers to the quiz appear in Appendix A, "Answers to Quizzes."

Quiz

1. How can you get more templates for your Database Wizard?
2. Which button on the toolbar toggles view and design view?
3. What is a reason to run the full Report Wizard instead of the AutoReport?
4. Is the type of data you intend on using in a field important to specify when designing a table?
5. If you add a criterion to a query, do you end up with a subset or superset of the queried object?

Exercises

1. Open the Day 3 sample data.
2. Open the table, Guests, in design view.
3. Do you think the field, ChildrenNames, meant to hold several names, is good database design?
4. Your answer for question 3 should be no. How do you think the database could have a better design in this area? Keep in mind Day 1's discussion and the one-to-many relationship.
5. Create a query using the wizard based on the table tblMiscData. Switch to design view. Alter the query to display only records where the date is greater than 1995. Run the query.
6. Close the query you just created giving it a name of your choosing.

   Run the AutoReport against this new query from step 6.

DAY 4

The Data Foundation—
The Table

In Day 3, "Automatic Access," you saw the way a table looks in data and design view. Today, you'll learn how to create a table. You'll also gain an understanding of the theory behind various table elements and how to apply that theory to your database applications.

Today You Will Learn

In today's lesson, you will see the importance of tables. Specifically in this lesson you will learn:

- Examining tables
- Creating tables
- Analyzing tables
- Relationships
- Table and field properties
- Sorting and finding

By the time you have finished this lesson, you will understand the place that tables have in the database. You will do well by taking your time to work through the tasks and to follow along.

Understanding the Importance of Table Design

It's worth repeating that a table is the fundamental element in a relational database. It is the place where the system stores all data. The other objects of a database system manipulate or present the data all of which is stored in these tables.

The irony of a table's position in a database system is that while it's the simplest object to create or modify, it's also the most important in the sense that if the table structure is wrong, the database system can't be right.

The most important element in table design is making sure that the table's fields are suitable for all planned data entry. This means making sure the fields are of the type (text, number, date, and so forth), plus they have the correct properties for the data. For example, if you define an address field as being able to hold only 20 characters, you will be in deep trouble when people start entering real addresses in that field.

You can change much of a table's design after the fact, but some changes will cause ripple problems (downstream trouble) if the table is linked to other tables, or if you have other database objects expecting a certain data structure.

The moral of the story is to plan three times and do once.

Examining Tables

Locate and open the database Day 4 on your CD. Click the Tables button in the object bar, and then open the tblAllTypes object in data view, by double-clicking it. Your screen should resemble Figure 4.1.

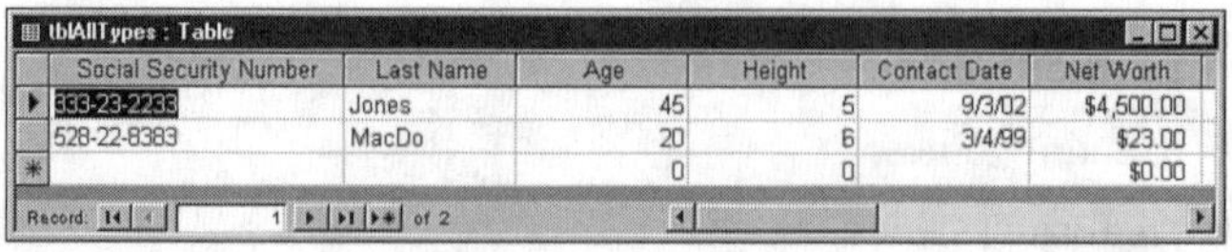

FIGURE 4.1

A table is a simple structure, but holds the key to the success of your database.

Social Security Number	Last Name	Age	Height	Contact Date	Net Worth
333-23-2233	Jones	45	5	9/3/02	$4,500.00
528-22-8383	MacDo	20	6	3/4/99	$23.00
		0	0		$0.00

This table has various field types (data types) and is a trivial example, but should give you a feel for the nature of a table and the types of data they hold.

Click a new record in the Social Security field. The new record can be found at the bottom of the table. Note that when you click on the Social Security field, Access creates a template for a social security number. That template is called an input mask. Enter a social security number. Now click the Last Name field and try entering the last name **Gonzalez**. You can't, because the field size for this field has been defined too small to be useful for a last name field. This is a rather obvious error, but one of the type you, as a developer, needs to watch out for.

Continue to enter data observing from entries that have come before what type of data you suppose the field should hold. The final field, Sound, contains a sound file (.wav) in the first record that you can play if you have a sound enabled computer, but don't worry about entering new sounds in this field. Try entering apparently wrong data like **3/4** in the Contact Date field. The table won't accept data that's inappropriate. You won't need to (or can) enter a number in the Friend Registration Number, as that will auto increment when you're done with the record.

Note

If you want to hear the sound file, try right-clicking the sound entry in the table and then look at the entries under the Wave Sound Object entry in the context menu. Click Play from the context menu to hear the .wav file.

4

When you're done experimenting, switch to design view by clicking the View button at the far left of the toolbar. Your screen should resemble Figure 4.2.

FIGURE 4.2

Here is the design view of a table containing a sample of various data types.

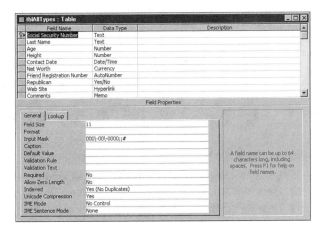

When designing your tables, you need to focus on these main issues:

- What will be the key field for the table?

- What data type shall you use for each field?
- What properties for each field do you need to set?
- How does this table fit into your entire data structure scheme?

Use the `tblAllFields` object in design view to explore the various elements of this elementary table's design. Click in the `Data Type` column of the `Last Name` field and change the field type to something other than `Text`. Examine how the Properties section changes as you change to different data types. Click the `Last Name` field entry and examine the `Field Size` property (in the area at the bottom left of the screen) noting that it's too small to accommodate most of the world's last names (remember the problem you had when you tried to enter "Gonzalez"?).

Return to data view for this table discarding any changes you might have made in design view.

Place your cursor in between any two columns until the cursor changes to a bar with opposite facing arrows. Click and drag, noting how you can change the visible size of a field.

 Note   Changing the visible size of a field will not alter its `Field Size` property.

Click the column head. This highlights the column. Pressing Delete at this point allows you to delete this field from your database. Click to the left of the `Social Security Number` field at the record level to highlight an entire record. Your screen should resemble Figure 4.3.

FIGURE 4.3

Using a record selector, you can highlight a record or a series of records.

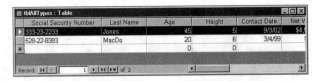

 Tip   Using the keys Ctrl and Shift, you can make multiple selections of fields or records. Ctrl+click selects a series of records. Click one record, move the cursor, and then Shift+click a second record to select all the intervening fields.

Again, pressing Delete removes any highlighted records. Keep in mind that although this works for a few records, an action query discussed in Day 15, "Introduction to VBA Concepts," is a better way to delete records from a live database.

Click any column head, to select it. Click again and keep the mouse button pressed, and then drag the column to the right or left. This changes the column order display, but it won't affect the order of fields in design view.

Finally, click between two rows over on the far left of the table—in the record selector area. Your cursor changes to a double arrow with bar. Drag up or down to change the height of all records.

Note

All rows (records) in a table must be the same height. You can't resize rows individually as you can in Excel.

Finally, click the Format button in the main menu bar. Note the entries there available to you for this table. Microsoft has made some changes to Access to make it work somewhat similarly to Excel for tables and queries (when feasible), so you get the Excel-like options for hiding and freezing columns (fields).

Keep in mind that it should be a very rare, or even nonexistent, event that users even see a table, much less make data entries to it or edit its layout (change column or row order or widths). Microsoft added these table facilities apparently to make Excel experts feel more at home. An adept Access developer will have his or her data entry done all through forms or automated by macros or VBA.

4

Tip

Using the same technique as record selection, you can alter (drag) the field order in design view. This alters the order of fields in table (data) view. Conversely altering the order of fields in table view does not alter their order in the design grid.

Creating Tables

By now, you probably have enough experience in tables and their views to have a good idea how to create the critters, but follow along with this section as you'll likely pick up a few interesting details.

To reiterate, there are three ways to make a table:

- Use the design view grid.
- Use the datasheet view.
- Use the Table Wizard.

Understanding Table Design Basics

The design grid is the way almost all (maybe all) experienced Access developers create their tables. This grid is the only way to have the fine control of your fields' properties you utterly must have in any but the most elementary Access applications.

Here's the basic format you will follow when creating a table using the design grid:

- From the database view, click New, choose Design View from the resulting dialog box, and click OK.

- Enter a field name in the first row of the `Field Name` column.

- Press return or tab to move to the `Data Type` field.

- Enter a data type for this field. Access scrolls using the first letter of the data type. You also can pull down the combo box choosing the data type from a list.

- Alter the Field Properties section of the table design grid appropriately as needed.

- Add a comment in the `Description` column, if desired.

Here are the various data types and their uses.

- `Text`—Alphanumeric data up to 255 characters. Access uses dynamic storage, so specifying a field less than 255 characters does not affect disk storage needs, but it can have an effect on wizard generated forms. The wizard tries to size the field according to the field size that you set it to.

- `Memo`—Text for entries longer than the maximum 255 characters permitted by the `Text` data type. Used for notes or comments. You can't search or index on `Memo` data type fields.• `Number`—Various kinds of numbers from byte (0–255) to decimal. Use the `Number` type only for fields that need to have computational operations on them, otherwise use `Text`. You specify what kind of `Number` data types your field will hold by altering the `Field Size` property. Figure 4.4 shows the combo box for the `Number` data type with its selections exposed.

> **Tip**
>
> Use the least precise `Number` data type you can to preserve database size and to optimize Access' performance.

- `Date/Time`—Really a `Number` data type too as Access stores dates as sequential numbers. Use this data type to store dates or times.

- `Currency`—Another variant on the `Number` data type. This is optimized (it's very precise) for currency calculations and it formats using a currency sign.

FIGURE 4.4

The Number data type uses the Field Size property to specify the type of numbers your field will receive.

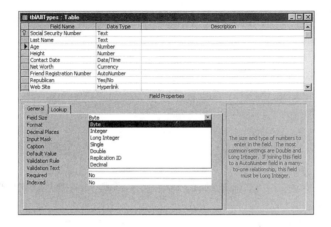

> **Tip**
>
> A Number data type entry can't start with a zero, so use Text for any fields (such as social security number) where there exists the possibility of a leading zero or zeros. Also remember to only use Number data types where you need to do computations. You will never wish to add up the social security numbers in a database for example, so there is no need to use the Number data type. Counterintuitively, Access sorts and searches on Text data type faster anyway.

4

- AutoNumber—A field that either sequentially or randomly assigns a number to each record without any user input.

- Yes/No—A very compact data type that is either on or off (yes or no). Good for checkbox type fields such as "Application Received?".

- OLE Object—A linked or embedded OLE object of any type. Usually used for adding items such as music, sound, or pictures to a table.

- Hyperlink—A URL, such as a Web site address or an e-mail address.

- Lookup wizard—Not really a data type, but a way to link a source to a field within a table.

Using The Table Design Grid

Now that you have a load of the preliminaries, it's time to create your first table using the design grid (Design view). Open the Day 4 database found on the CD, if necessary, and open the tblEmployees table in design view. Click the table to highlight it and then click the Design button on the database view toolbar. That's the table you'll be creating in this and the other task lists. If you get lost, consult this table to see where you went wrong.

Task: Using Design View to Create a New Table.

1. Launch Access and either load the Day 4 database or start a new blank database.

2. Click the Tables button in the Object bar (the vertical bar at the left of the database view). Click New to start a new table. Choose Design View from the dialog box and click OK. That launches the design grid. You also can choose Create Table in Design View from the database view.

3. Enter the field name **Employee ID** in the first row of the Field Name column. Press Enter to enter the Data Type field. Your screen should resemble Figure 4.5.

FIGURE 4.5

The data type of your first table field is entered automatically by default.

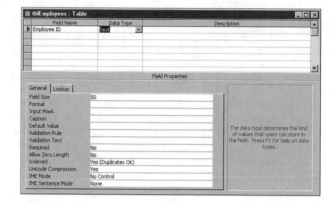

4. Click the Key Field icon in the toolbar (the one with the key on it). This sets the primary key for this table. The Employee ID field will be the field used to link the tables within this database. Click in the Field Size field in the Field Properties section of the grid. Edit the value to read **6**, the size of an employee number in this company.

5. Click in the second row of the Field Name column and enter **Last Name**. Keep the Data Type as Text, but edit the Field Size property to **20**.

6. Enter Field Names for first name and middle name changing the field sizes to **15** for both, but keeping the data type to Text.

7. Enter a Field Name **Vested** and change the data type to **Yes/No**.

8. Enter a field name for vestment date and change the data type to **Date/Time**. Also change the Format property to **Medium Date**.

9. Choose File, Save or click the Save icon on the toolbar. If you're in a new database, use the name **tblEmployees** for a table name. If you're using the Day 4 database, choose another name to prevent overwriting the existing table.

10. Click the View button to switch into table view. Your screen should resemble Figure 4.6.

FIGURE 4.6

*Your new table in data
view is ready to
receive data about
your company's
employees.*

Note

Note that Access automatically knew to use a checkbox for the field you
designated as Yes/No.

While there are more details, such as many other Field Properties you need to gain familiarity with, that's how to create a table using the design view.

Using the Datasheet View to Make a Table

Creating a table by the datasheet view method is commonly referred to as "creating by
example." Microsoft added this facility against some objections from the database community. It's not that using this method necessarily ends up in a bad way, but it really
saves nothing over using the design view method, and can lead to sloppy designs in all
but the most elementary databases.

It's your call if you like using this method. To see this table finished, open the table
tblByDatasheet from the Day 4 database. Here is the method in all its glory.

Task: Using the Datasheet View to Create a New Table

1. Launch Access and either load the Day 4 database, or start a new blank database.
   Click the Tables button in the database view, if you aren't already there.

2. Click the New button or choose Create table by entering data shortcut from the
   database view. If you clicked the New button, choose Datasheet view from the dialog box and click OK.

3. Enter **000234** for the first field in the first row as shown in Figure 4.7.

FIGURE 4.7

*You also can enter
data directly into a
blank datasheet to
design a table.*

4. Right-click the first column header (now labeled `Field1`) and choose Rename from the context menu. That will place the column header in edit mode. Enter a field name **Employee ID** for this field. Note that you also can rename a field this way on an existing table.

5. Enter some name data of your own choosing (why not use your name?) for each of the next three fields editing the field names to **Last Name**, **First Name**, **Middle Name**, respectively.

6. Move to the next column and enter **Yes** and edit the column header to **Vested**.

7. Move to the next column and enter a date such as **2/2/2002** and edit the field name to **Vestment Date**. Your screen should resemble Figure 4.8.

> **Note**
>
> In order for you to see more of the display in Figure 4.8, you can stretch the display sizes of the fields. You can do this by moving your mouse between two columns in the column header, until the mouse pointer turns to a bar with arrows pointing opposite ways. Click and then drag to make the column smaller or larger.

FIGURE 4.8

You can add data that defines the data types for new fields in Access.

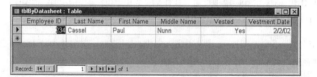

8. Click the Save icon in the toolbar (the one with the disk icon) and name the table `tblByDatasheet` if you're in a new database. If you're in Day 4, choose a unique name to prevent overwriting the existing table.

9. Click the View button to switch to design view refusing the offer to create a primary key. Your screen should resemble Figure 4.9.

FIGURE 4.9

The `tblByDatasheet` table that Access generated based on input in the datasheet.

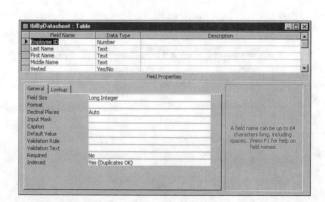

You'll note that Access did a good job of guessing the right data types for the fields based on the data you entered in the first record. However, we want the Text type for Employee ID and there's no control over the field size property except in design view.

To see a limit on the datasheet view method, switch back to table (or data) view and note that the leading zeros have disappeared from the Employee ID field. This is because a Number data type field can't have leading zeros.

From here, you can fine-tune this table to meet the exact criteria you did when you created the same table in design view. It's your call if you think that this method saved time or was simpler than the all design view method.

Using the Table Wizard to Create a Table

The Table Wizard is somewhat misnamed. Other wizards enable you to create objects more or less of your own choosing. The Table Wizard only allows you to pick and choose from predefined tables and fields, yet it still can be a time saver. Remember, you can use design view to edit any fields or field properties created in any table, including those done by a wizard.'

The last lesson gave you an overview of the wizard which you might have followed along with. This lesson gives you a more detailed step-by-step, essentially covering the same material. Feel free to skip past this section if you feel you have a handle on it.

That said, take a look at the table from the database Day4 called tblService Records. This is the table you'll be creating using the wizard. When you're done reviewing the outcome of this experiment, it's time to actually do the work. If you follow along, you will need to delete the tblService Records table that is already in the Day 4 database. You can delete the table by selecting it and then press the Delete key. Press Yes to the next dialog asking you to delete the relationships also.

Task: Using the Table Wizard to Create a New Table

1. Launch Access and either load the Day 4 database or create a new blank database. Click the Tables button on the Object bar in the database view.

2. Double-click the Create table by using wizard shortcut in the database view. Your screen should resemble Figure 4.10.

3. Click the Personal option in the left-center section of the dialog box.

4. Scroll down the Sample Tables list box until you find the table Service Records. Click to highlight it.

5. Click the single right facing caret to move the current field from the sample table to the table you're creating. Use the double caret button to move all fields.

FIGURE 4.10

The first step of the Table Wizard.

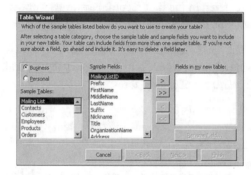

Similarly, you can remove a field, or all fields, from your table by clicking the single or double left-facing carets, respectively. For this table, include all the fields from the sample table into your table. Click the Next button to move on.

6. To maintain our naming conventions, rename the table **tblService Records**. Allow the wizard to set the primary key for you. Click Next.

7. The next screen is rather interesting as Access tries to establish a relationship with existing tables by examination of all the primary keys. Your screen should resemble Figure 4.11. You don't want to establish any relationships now, so just click the next button.

FIGURE 4.11

The Table Wizard is a trooper in that it looks to establish relationships with existing tables.

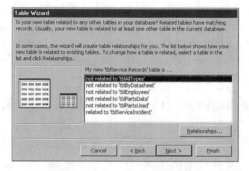

8. Click Next, then Finish to see the table in datasheet view. There is no need to manually save the table. The wizard does that for you.

Analyzing the Wizard's Table

The wizard didn't do a very good job of making a table. While the general table is alright, you should be able to do better and you will be able to before you've finished this book. Let's look at some of the design flaws in this table.

Violation of First Normal Form

With the table in data (or table) view, scroll over to the `Parts Replaced` field. That's a normal text field. As you likely know, most repair jobs require more than one part to be replaced, so how would a data entry person handle this field? Let's say a person wanted to cost this job by linking the parts to their cost?

You might be tempted to solve this problem one of two ways:

- Put a bunch of parts in that one field like shown in Figure 4.12. That the field is of a data type `Memo` implies that this is the designer's intent.

FIGURE 4.12

All the parts used for this job lumped into one field.

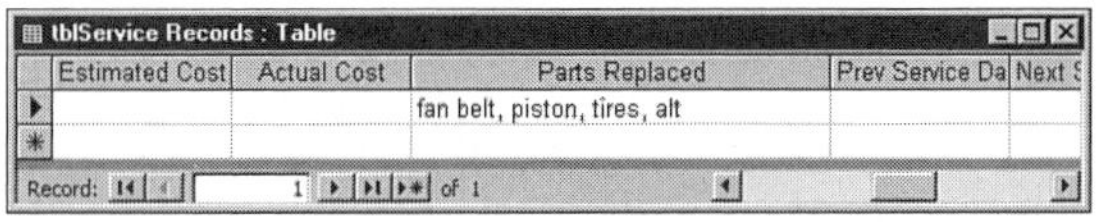

- Put each part in a duplicate record shown in Figure 4.13.

FIGURE 4.13

The solution of a whole new record for each part is worse than the multiple entry solution above.

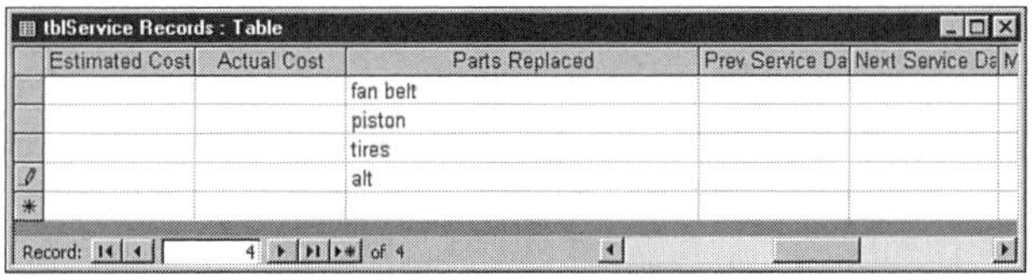

The first method, putting the parts into one field, violates one of the primary rules of relational database design. The second method, duplicating new records for each part is even worse than the first method. It ends up being a waste of time and effort, not to mention the confusion as to whether these are a single service or more than one incident. We'll correct this table in just a moment to show the correct way to structure this type of data.

Possible Wrong Field Types

Switch to design view for the `tblService Records` table. The `Description` field is `Text` data type of 255 characters long. There is also a `Problem Description` field of `Memo` data type. There are no comments to tell you, the programmer, or the user what the difference in these fields is, or if the 255 characters in `Description` is sufficient.

Equally worrisome is the `AutoNumber` data type for the `ServiceRecordID` field. This is alright if you want to allow Access to uniquely generate an ID for each job, but what if the service orders are preprinted or your user wants to use a custom code for each service record?

The `AutoNumber` data type is useful for generating index numbers when you're utterly sure that you won't need to edit or specify the values for this field aside from the starting number, but `AutoNumber` isn't ideal for all uses.

Linking Fields—the Heart of the Relationship

The really serious problem with the `tblService Records` as it stands is the bunching of parts within a single field. Open the `Day 4` database in the `Day 4` folder; close any open objects, if necessary, to clear the deck and get ready to work.

Click the Tables button in the Object bar and locate the two tables, `tblServiceIncident` and `tblPartsUsed`. Those are the two tables you'll be linking.

Here is the purpose of this task. We want to have one record for the service incident and a way to not only record all the parts for this job, but to cost it as well.

The solution is to put the service incident details in one record and the parts in many records. The reasoning will become clearer as you work through this task. We can then further link up the parts used information to cost information for those parts.

Some of the presentation in the rest of this section will be a bit beyond where you've gone, but try not to worry about it. Concentrate on the idea of the link and how it makes the one-to-many relationship of having many parts to a single service job much clearer and more useful than lumping all the parts into one memo field. If you want to perform the next task, you need to delete the existing relationships. You can do this by selecting the links between the tables and then pressing the Delete key.

Task: Creating Relationships between Tables

1. Open the two tables `tblServiceIncident` and `tblPartsUsed` in design view either at the same time, or singly. Note that there is a field called `ServiceRecordID` in both tables. This will be the link field.

> **Note**   Linked fields must be of the same data type. The linked field, `ServiceRecordID` in `tblServiceIncident`, is the data type AutoNumber by increment, which uses Long Integers for incrementing, so the link field in `tblPartsUsed` is the data type number with a field size of Long Integer.

2. Choose Tools, Relationships from the main Access menu.

3. Locate the two tables `tblServiceIncident` and `tblPartsUsed`. Click each and click the Add button to move them from the Show Table dialog box to the

▼   Relationship window. If you want, adjust the size of the field list boxes to show
more fields or to show all the fields. Your screen should resemble Figure 4.14.

> If you want to remove a table from the relationship view, right-click its title
> bar area and then choose Hide table from the context menu. To show the
> table again, click the Show Tables icon on the toolbar or choose
> Relationships, Show Table from the menu.

FIGURE **4.14**

The Relationships window is where you link tables using their common fields.

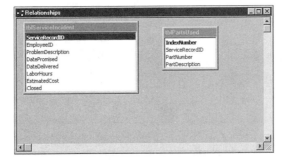

4. This link is one-to-many, meaning that there might be many parts for any single
   service incident. We'll also want to enforce relational integrity. That means that we
   can't assign a part to a job that doesn't exist. In other words, a matching record
   must exist in tblServiceIncident before we can attribute a part to it in
   tblPartsUsed.

5. Click the ServiceRecordID field in tblServiceIncident and drag your cursor to
   the ServiceRecordID in tblPartsUsed. Release the mouse button. After you're
   done, your screen should resemble Figure 4.15.

FIGURE **4.15**

The simple drag method establishes the link.

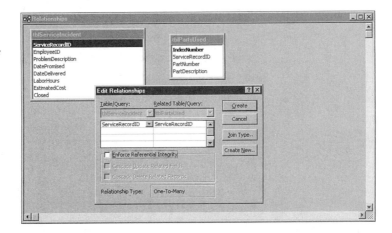

▼

▼   6. You might have noticed that Access guessed that this is a one-to-many relationship. Check the Enforce Referential Integrity box and the two other checkboxes in the dialog box that become enabled.

7. Click Create to close the dialog box and notice that Access graphically shows you the new link (and that it's one-to-many) in the Relationships window. Close the Relationships window by choosing File, Close from the main menu. Your screen should resemble Figure 4.16.

FIGURE 4.16

The link is established with integrity enforced.

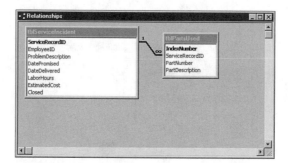

▲

The idea of the link field is to make sure that the items in the tblPartsUsed will match up correctly to the right job listed in tblServiceIncident.

Currently there are two records in the tblServiceIncident table. There are several parts in tblPartsUsed for each of these jobs. Open both tables to examine the entries. Figure 4.17 shows these two tables with their entries, as of this point.

FIGURE 4.17

Each part used is linked to the job it's been used for by the common link field ServiceRecordID.

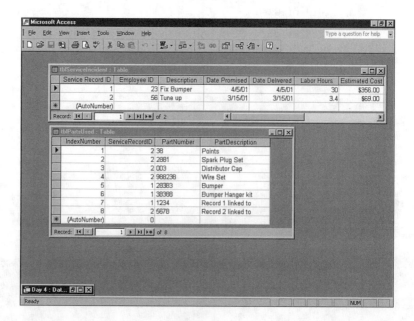

Adding Data to Linked Tables Within the Datasheet View

Access does include a way to add linked records to the many table quite easily, but remember it's not really a good idea to do so. Still, because it's there, it's worth knowing about.

Open the `tblServiceIncident` table. Note the feature—a plus sign at the extreme left of each record. Click the plus sign. That will open up a new table-like window where you can add parts to any job. Figure 4.18 shows the parts window opened for the first record.

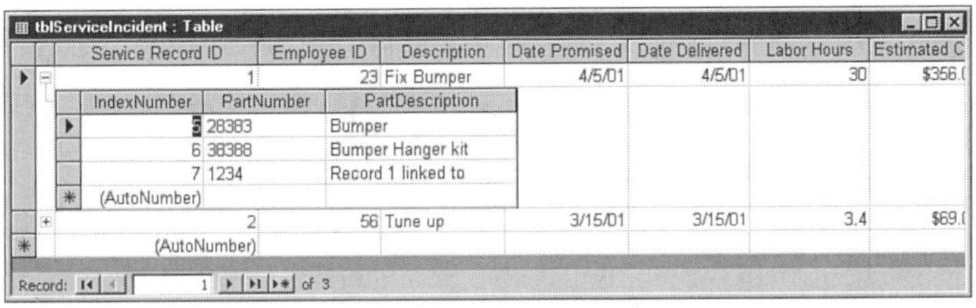

FIGURE 4.18

Access has a table level entry facility to enter items to the many side of a one-to-many relationship.

This is one of those things that appears somewhat confusing in a screen shot. By all means, open `tblServicetIncident` and click the plus sign yourself to see how this facility works.

Most experts believe that the best way to do data entry in a one-to-many relationship is through a form with a subform. You can get a preview of that topic by looking ahead to Day 10, "Improving Your Forms."

Understanding the Benefits of a Relationship

At this point, you might think that this is a lot of work compared to just including all the parts in one memo field like the original table did. Here's where we must jump ahead a bit so you can see the reason for all this foundation work.

There is another table in the database Day 4 called `tblPartsData`. This contains cost and supplier information about each part this auto repair facility stocks or orders. If you examine that table's data or structure and `tblPartsUsed` you'll note a slight violation of proper normalization as the part description is repeated in each table. I've left things that way to make some earlier steps clearer for you, but in an actual application, I wouldn't have had this data duplicated.

Figure 4.19 shows a query where the information in the two tables, `tblServiceIncident` and `tblPartsUsed`, is linked up again. You can see that due to the link between the fields, the query is able to match up the parts used with the job where the parts were used.

FIGURE 4.19

The link field is what lets Access match the parts used with the jobs they were used in. Note this query includes data from both tables.

Service Record ID	Employee ID	Description	Labor Hours	PartNumber	PartDescription
1	23	Fix Bumper	30	26363	Bumper
1	23	Fix Bumper	30	38388	Bumper Hanger kit
1	23	Fix Bumper	30	1234	Record 1 linked to
2	56	Tune up	3.4	38	Points
2	56	Tune up	3.4	2881	Spark Plug Set
2	56	Tune up	3.4	003	Distributor Cap
2	56	Tune up	3.4	988238	Wire Set
2	56	Tune up	3.4	5678	Record 2 linked to
(AutoNumber)					

Record: 1 of 8

The query shown in Figure 4.19 is part of the Day 4 database and has the name qryBasicMatchUp. If you wish to run this query, click the Queries button in the Object bar and double-click the query. Open this query in design view to see how it's been constructed.

The Best Is Yet To Come

That's fine, but you might still be wondering why bother as if you listed all the parts in one huge memo field they'd also be matched up with the right job.

So now it's time for the relationship trump—the match up you can't do using the memo field method of including many items in a single field in a table. Figure 4.20 shows the results of another query this time including costing information from the table tblPartsData. This query is called qryCosting and is also part of your sample data. Open it in design view to see how it works if you want a peek ahead on query construction.

FIGURE 4.20

At last all the extra work pays off. The costing information is yours without any additional work.

Service Record ID	Description	Date Promised	Estimated Cost	PartDescription	PartNumber	Cc
2	Tune up	3/15/01	$69.00	Points	38	
2	Tune up	3/15/01	$69.00	Spark Plug Set	2881	
2	Tune up	3/15/01	$69.00	Distributor Cap	003	
2	Tune up	3/15/01	$69.00	Wire Set	988238	
1	Fix Bumper	4/5/01	$356.00	Bumper	26363	$
1	Fix Bumper	4/5/01	$356.00	Bumper Hanger kit	38388	
(AutoNumber)						

Record: 1 of 6

Yes, you could have manually entered all the cost information in the original table, but why bother? This way, once you've created the relational structure, Access will automatically look up linked information for you.

 Note

The main purpose of a relational database is to have the database look up related data rather than requiring data entry personnel enter it redundantly. Using the relationship model will mean that once you've entered any data (such as part cost) you can use it in as many queries as you need to without ever entering it again.

Not Convinced?

If you're not convinced yet, open up the query qryTotalCost in query view by double-clicking it. Your screen should resemble Figure 4.21.

FIGURE 4.21

Computer programs love to add things up. Here, Access gathers up all cost data for each job and sums that data matching the sum to the job.

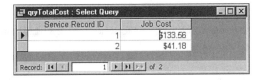

By all means look at the magic behind this query by switching to design view for it. While the workings of this query might not be superficially obvious, you should have a good idea of how it's operating.

There is no reasonable way to duplicate the costing and summation data you've seen in these past two queries by piling data into memo fields. More importantly, having data normalized like this allows for easy lookups, faster data entry, and assured data integrity. The latter simply means that you can't enter a part for a job that doesn't yet exist. You have to create a job first, and then you can add parts to it. Otherwise, you can end up with "data orphans" in your system.

More importantly, referential integrity means that due to having to assign a part to a job, you will be assured that you bill all the parts by having them positively attached to some job. That doesn't necessarily mean the right part is attached to the right job, but that's another topic.

Some of what you saw in this section is a bit too complex to go into right now (such as how the qryTotalCost query did its totaling magic) as the information so far is likely quite a bit of a load for you at this point.

If you remain skeptical that the referential model isn't the best for the vast majority of data tasks, how about just suspending your disbelief for a few days? Give it a while and you'll see why it's worth the bother to create a correct relational structure for your database projects. After a short while, you'll see that using a flat model would be less than satisfactory for most of what you will need to do using Access.

Seeing It Yourself

Grasping the concept of linking relationships between tables is vital to the successful use of Access or other similar products. The following task uses the objects you're now familiar with to see how this concept works in daily use.

Task: Adding Data to a Linked Table and Then Seeing the Result

1. Open the Day 4 database if necessary. Open the tblServiceIncident table in datasheet view (double-click it in the database view).

2. Click the plus sign to the far left of the first record in the table for record number 1. This opens a window containing the linked table tblPartsUsed. Your screen should resemble Figure 4.22.

FIGURE 4.22

Clicking the plus (expand view) sign opens a window to the linked table.

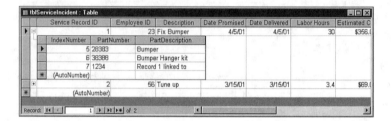

3. Enter a few part numbers and descriptions of your own choosing to simulate entering actual parts for this service order. Keep in mind what you've entered.

4. Click in the same area to the left of the first record on the sign that's now a minus. The window will close.

5. Click the plus sign to the left of the second record to open a window for that record. Again, enter some data in the window distinctive from the data you entered in step 4. Close the table.

6. Click the Queries button in the database view.

7. Run the query qryBasicMatchUp by double-clicking it. Note that the parts you entered for record 1 are now linked to that record and those you entered for record 2 are now linked to that one. That's the essentials of a relational database.

Using Table and Field Properties

You've only seen demonstrated a few table properties as of now. This section starts your tour of a few additional ones plus some overall table settings.

Task: A Beginner's Guide to Field Properties

1. If necessary, open the Day 4 database and the tblEmployees table in design view. Your screen should resemble Figure 4.23.

2. Click the Last Name field to bring up the context sensitive Field Properties list box for this field.

FIGURE 4.23

The tblEmployees table object acts as a test bed to learn about some additional properties available to the developer in Access tables.

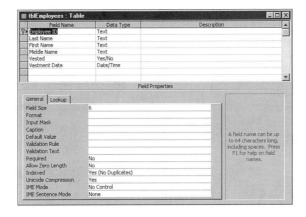

> **Note**
>
> This task uses the tblEmployees, but any table should suffice for these demonstrations.

4

> **Note**
>
> The properties area of the table design view is context-sensitive. Change the field with the focus (where the cursor is) in the upper section of the design view and you'll change the associated properties in the lower half.

3. Edit (or enter) **Surname** for a Caption property. The Caption property controls the label a field has, not only for the table, but any objects (such as forms) derived or bound to the table. If the Caption property is blank, the field uses the field name for a Caption property. Switch to datasheet view saving changes when prompted. Your screen should resemble Figure 4.24.

FIGURE 4.24

The Caption or header for this field now over-rides the default field name for a caption.

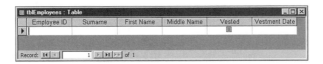

4. Note that the field name is now Surname, reflecting your entry in the Caption property.

5. Use of the Format property is a huge topic in detail, but the concept is bone simple. The idea is to alter the format, or appearance of data. For example, you might

wish to have a data field display in all capital letters. To do this, enter a ">" for a Format property. Try that with the Last Name field. Change to datasheet view, enter some lowercase letters in the field captioned Surname, and then leave the field. The entry appears in all caps. Figure 4.25 shows the Format property to display a field in all caps.

Note

You must leave the field you're entering data into before the formatting will take effect.

FIGURE 4.25

A simple change to the Format property will make a large difference in the display of a table's data.

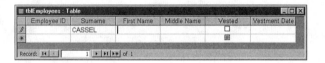

Note

The data stored in the table with a format property of > is in its original form—uppercase or lowercase. The format property only changed the way the data is displayed in the table.

The help system is a good reference for other format properties. Table 4.1 includes several examples to help you get started.

TABLE 4.1 Purchases by Date

Format	Enter	Displayed in table
>	tirilee	TIRILEE
<	Tirilee	tirilee
@@@-@@@@	5558976	555-8976
@;"Empty"		Empty (displays the word Empty until you enter data)

Understanding Key Fields and Indexes

The key field (primary key) is the unique identifier for a record. All tables, without exception, should have a key field identified. For example, you can't generally use a

Last Name field as a key field as most any database will, or at least can, have more than one entry for any last name. I have a fairly common name, Cassel. If you used last names as a key field, you could only have one Cassel in the entire table—surely not a good design concept for general purposes, but a good concept to keep in mind for some special applications where you wish that to be the case. So Last Name won't usually work for a primary key, but social security numbers are unique so that would work as a primary key.

If possible, use natural keys—keys that are part of the data anyway. A good example of this is the previously mentioned social security number. Everybody's is unique and you might have that as part of the data anyway. If you're doing an auto service application, license plate (tag) numbers should work as a primary field. If in doubt, then couple the license plate number with the state for a two field primary key.

Tip

> Make a multi-field primary key by highlighting more than one field (Ctrl+click) and then clicking the primary key button in the toolbar.

4

If nothing works naturally, you can resort to using Access' AutoNumber facility to generate artificial (not part of the data) primary keys. A primary key not only uniquely identifies a record (you can only have one example in any table), but also speeds many Access operations. Don't leave the table without one.

Indexes order data within a database. An index with entries that can't be duplicated in that field within a table is a primary key, but you also can have secondary indexes.

Open the tblEmployees table in design view if you don't already have it open. Click on the Employee ID field to select it. Examine the Field Properties for the Indexed property. The entry reads Yes (No Duplicates) which is the definition of a primary key.

Click the pull-down tab for the Index property, and you'll also note you can set this property to No, for no index, or Yes (Duplicates OK). When you specify the Yes (Duplicates OK) option, Access creates an index for this field.

Index any field you expect you'll be searching on, but don't specify the Yes (No Duplicates) option, unless you know that you will never need to store the same value in different row. Your best bet, is to only specify the Yes (No Duplicates) option only for primary keys. For example, if you will know that you'll be searching employees under last name, index the field, but don't exclude duplicates or you'll only be able to include one unique last name per table.

You can sort (reorder) and filter data in tables, although most developers prefer doing so within queries. The next section shows how you can do these feats while staying within tables.

Sorting and Filtering in Tables

Database design purists cringe that people like to manipulate the views of a table. They complain that other database objects, especially forms and queries, are for that duty. Well, cringe causing or not, people seem to like playing around in table or datasheet view rather than creating additional objects for that purpose. There's really no reason not to use tables for viewing your data other than the data in tables should be normalized (fragmented) into less-than-useful chunks. A query reassembles data into a usually more useful form, but if your needs can be met by viewing, ordering, or filtering data directly in tables, there's no reason not to do so.

 Note

> Edits made in a query are reflected in the underlying tables. For example, edits made in the query shown in this lesson are reflected in the respective tables underlying these multi-table queries.

Sorting

To sort a table or other datasheet is database talk to order it in a determined fashion. Ordering records alphabetically is an "alpha sort" in database lingo.

Sorting a table in datasheet view doesn't really alter its indexes, but just the display of the table. Here's how it's done.

 TASK

Task: Ordering the View of Table Data

1. Close the `Day 4` database if open. Open the `Northwind` database. `Northwind` is part of the sample data supplied by Microsoft. You might need to run Office setup again to install `Northwind` if it's not on your disk. Close the splash screen and the switchboard.

2. Click the Tables button in the Object bar. Locate the `Customers` table and open it in datasheet view by double-clicking it. Your screen should resemble Figure 4.26.

3. Click anywhere in the column (field) named `Contact Name`. This causes your next action to act on that field.

4. Click the toolbar button Sort Descending. Figure 4.27 shows this button (the cursor is on it). Note the change in the table's order.

FIGURE 4.26

When opened, a table orders itself according to its primary key, which is the Customer ID *for this table.*

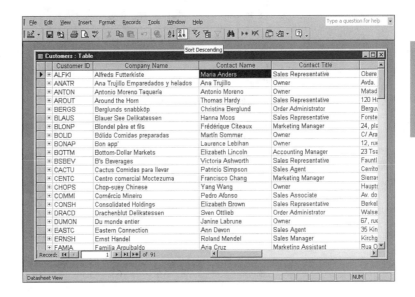

FIGURE 4.27

Changing the sort order changes the display of data, but not the order of the data within the table.

5. Click in the Contact Title field. Click the Sort Ascending button to re-sort the table. This will bring all the accounting managers to the fore.

Note The skills you gained today in filtering and sorting in tables are fully transferable to other objects, such as queries and forms.

That's all there is to changing the sort order. To make sure you return the table or tables to their presort condition, close them discarding layout changes and then reopen.

Filtering

Filtering means to filter out all but the data you let pass your criteria or criterion. Access makes this one as simple as sorting.

Task: Filtering Table Data

1. Open the Northwind table Customers again if you closed it after the last task. Locate a record within the Contact Title column having the entry "owner."

2. Click the Filter by Selection button on the toolbar. Figure 4.28 shows this button and how your screen should look after the clicking is over.

FIGURE 4.28

Filter by selection takes a look at the current selection and filters according to it.

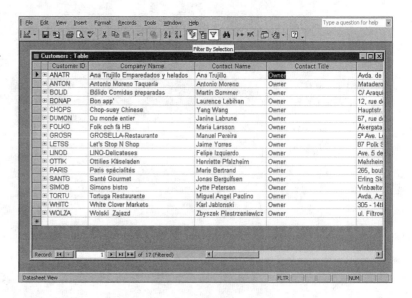

3. Click the Remove Filter (two to the right of the Filter by Selection button) button to remove the filter. Click the same button again to reapply the filter.

4. Click the Remove Filter button to remove any filter by selection. Click the Filter by Form button. This button is in between the Filter by Selection and Apply/Remove Filter. Note the pull-down buttons. Pull down the combo box for Contact Title. Your screen should resemble Figure 4.29.

5. If you haven't already done so, pull down the combo box for Contact Title and choose Accounting Manager. Click the Apply Filter button (the one with the funnel as an icon). This applies the filter as before. You can filter on more than one field using this method. After you apply the filter, your screen should resemble Figure 4.30.

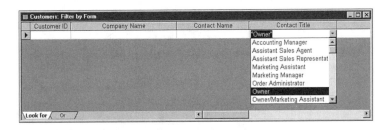

FIGURE 4.29

Ready to select a Contact Title to filter by.

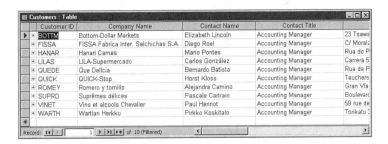

FIGURE 4.30

The Customers table filtered on Accounting Manager.

You can use the Filter by Form to save and recall filters. Here's the trick in a task.

Task: Saving and Recalling Filters

1. Open the Customers table in datasheet view.

2. Click the Filter by Form button. Choose the `Contact Title` field by clicking in it and choosing "Owner" from the drop-down list. Click the Save as Query button in the toolbar. Enter `qryFilterDemo` as a save name. Your screen should resemble Figure 4.31.

3. Click OK to exit this dialog box.

4. Click the Close button on the toolbar to close the Filter by Form screen. Close the table by choosing File, Close. You should discard layout changes, if so offered.

5. Open the table again. Click the Filter by Form button. Click the Load from Query button (far left). Your screen should resemble Figure 4.32.

6. Click OK to load the filter. Click the Apply Filter button and you'll have your table filtered as before.

FIGURE 4.31

You can save a Filter by Form as a query.

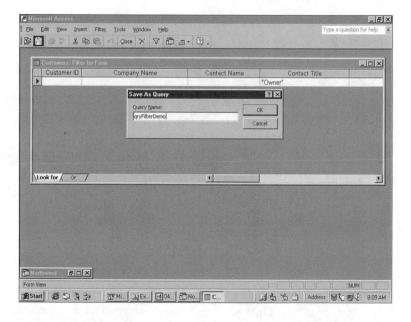

FIGURE 4.32

You can recall saved filters using this dialog box.

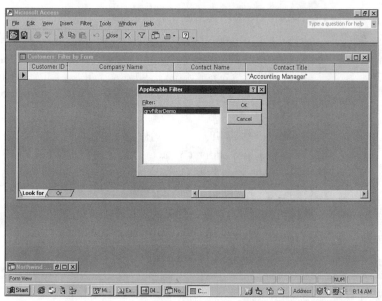

Finding Data

There's one more trick with tables to cover today, but it's an easy one to grasp—finding data within tables. Like the other skills, filtering and sorting, this skill is transferable to other database objects, such as forms and queries.

Task: Finding Data with the Datasheet View

1. Open the Northwind database, if necessary. Open the Customers table in datasheet view.

2. Click in the Company Name field. Click the Find button on the toolbar. The Find button is the one with the binoculars icon. Your screen should resemble Figure 4.33.

FIGURE 4.33

The Find dialog box is a quick route to locate data.

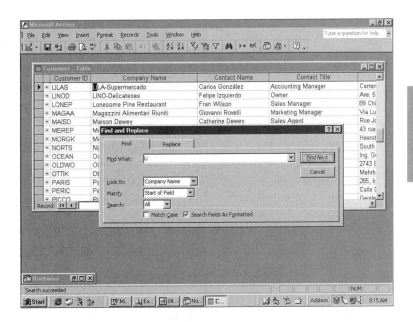

3. Enter **Li** in the Find What text box. Pull down the Match combo box and choose Start of Field. Click Find Next. Access goes out and finds the first entry in the Company Name field that starts with the two letters "Li".

4. Pull down the other combo boxes in this dialog box to gain familiarity with other capabilities of the Find facility. When you're done, close everything up.

Tip

> You also can use Find and Replace instead of just find. This works almost identically to the same facility in Word.

Find Cautions

Many users love the Find dialog box and use it regularly, but a few cautions are worth mentioning. Here they are:

- Applying a find to an entire table (as opposed to a single field) can take a long time.

- Applying a find to an unindexed field will take longer than an indexed field. If you plan on searching regularly within a field, index it in table design view.

- Search and replace can be very dangerous. For example, if you learn that LINO-Delicateses is now LONO Delicateses and decide to search on LI and replace with LO, allowing a Replace All will change LINO-Delicateses to LONO-Delocateses unless you tighten the search criteria. Use with care!

 Note   You can use an action query to change table data. You'll encounter these specialized advanced queries on Day 16, "VBA Language Elements—Part 1."

Summary

Tables store all data within a relational database such as Access. Access offers three ways to make a table: by design view, by entry example, and by a wizard. Each field within a table must have a specific data type conforming to the type of data it's to hold. Each field also has an array of developer set options called Field Properties. The properties for each field depend upon the data type.

Primary fields act as unique identifiers for a record within a table. Although you should try to use actual data as a key, using artificial data such as an incrementing AutoNumber field is a lot better than no key (which should never occur).

By linking fields between tables, the essence of a relational database, you can later construct various views of data from more than one table.

While other database objects, such as forms or queries, might do the job better (to some people's view), you can filter, sort, and find data within tables.

Q&A

Q. If I set a primary key field in my one table, should I also use that field as a primary key in my many table?

A. No. This will make your link useless, as you will need potentially many entries using the data from the one side in the many side. For example, say you have a list of employees with the social security number (SSN) as a primary key in a table called `tblEmployees`. You also have a table called `tblFixedAssets` where each asset is assigned to an employee. The link is the SSN. Because any employee can have many assets, you can't have SSN as the primary key in `tblFixedAssets`. Instead, include SSN as a field in `tblFixedAssets` to link on, but use another unique field (such as asset number) for the primary key in `tblFixedAssets`.

Q. Why do I need a primary key for every table?

A. Access enforces uniqueness for primary fields. Telling Access that a field is the primary key is the only way to be 100% sure you have a unique identifier for every record in that table.

Q. I want to have more than one sort for a table, but every time I change a table's field order, I lose my old sort. How can I have more than one sort for a table?

A. You can order or sort tables using a simple query. Each query can have its own sort order so the answer is to use series of queries, not sorts within tables. You can copy tables and sort them all, but that's a real waste of disk space.

Q. Will the * wildcard work in Access' Find dialog box?

A. Yes. For example *c* will find any field with the letter "c" in it. But you really don't need this as you also can search by the `Any Part of Field` option, which covers the same territory.

4

Workshop

The Workshop helps you solidify the skills you learned in this lesson. Answers to the quiz appear in Appendix A, "Answers to Quizzes."

Quiz

1. Can a primary key field have two records with identical values for the primary key field?

2. Can the value of a primary key appear elsewhere (another field) in a record?

3. How often should identical data appear in a properly designed database?

4. If you create two tables you intend to have a one-to-many relationship, how do you create that relationship?

5. Will the letter Z appear first or last after applying a Sort (Descending) on a field containing all the letters of the alphabet?

Exercises

1. Open the Customers table in the Northwind database.

2. Click the Filter by Form button on the toolbar. Click in the Contact Title field. Enter a filter criterion to show only those records that begin with the letter "A". Hint, use the criterion "A*".

3. Apply the filter. Remove the filter.

4. If you saved the filter in the Task "Filtering Table Data", click Queries in the Object bar.

5. Locate the query qryFilterDemo. Note that the object you saved as a filter is now a query (your first query!).

6. Double-click this object to launch the query.

    Did the result meet your expectations?

Day 5

Simple Forms

Forms are for data entry, editing, and viewing data that's in tables. There are two reasons for using forms in your database application:

- Most people prefer and are used to seeing data in a form. Thus a form can increase people's comfort level with a computer application.
- Forms have facilities for data filtering, automation, and validation beyond that which is possible using tables or queries alone.

Forms consist of a blank work area, the form itself, and various controls existing on the form. Form controls can display fields for editing or consist of tools for various kinds of automation.

Today You Will Learn

Although you can do most, if not all, of your data entry directly into tables, by using forms you gain more control over how the data gets into those tables. In this lesson, you will learn all about forms and some of the properties that control the look of the form. Specifically you will learn:

- How to use the AutoForm Wizard
- How to create a form with the General Form Wizard
- How to use the form design view
- How to control and record sources
- How to customize a form's tab order
- Form control naming conventions
- How to use bound and unbound forms and controls
- How to use option frames
- How to filter, sort, and find in forms
- How to program a command button using a wizard
- Form design properties

Forms, along with tables, are all you need to create a functional database application. So let's get to work!

Why This Chapter Now

The Object bar in the database view has queries as the object following tables, but in the book I've skipped to forms. You've actually had some exposure to queries in the last lesson with sorting and filtering in tables. These two facilities are really query functions.

Forms make sense now because they, added to tables, are all you need for a very rudimentary knowledge of Access. I'm not saying you should never learn queries—they are vital to using Access well—but if you know forms, tables, filtering, and sorting, you can use Access. This lesson also gives you a look at programming Access, which is a lot of fun. The other reason to learn forms is because they are interesting, which will make up a bit for the rather dry table lesson that you just waded through.

 Note

> This lesson jumps around seemingly from topic to topic to cover a lot of territory. It'll all come together for you when you actually go to design forms having some complexity.

Bound and Unbound Forms and Fields

A form can either be bound or unbound. A bound form is linked to an underlying table or query, and derives its data from and writes to that object. An unbound form neither gets data from, nor writes to any object. The Record Source property of a form controls what, if any, object is bound to a form.

Within a form, controls can be either bound or unbound, too. In a manner similar to a bound form, a bound control reads from or writes to a field within a bound object. Many forms mix bound and unbound controls. The property of a control that determines its bound or unbound condition is the Control Source property.

This discussion, so far, has been rather abstract, and because of this it might, at this point, seem a bit more abstruse than it really is. To get an idea of how all these concepts work together, open the database Day 5 located in its folder of your CD.

Control and Record Source Properties

Examine the table tblSales by opening it in both design view and datasheet view. This is a very simple table having only two fields—one for a sale number (primary key field) and one for a sale amount.

Note

> Many of the objects in the sample databases are trivialized. That is, you won't use identical objects for real applications. I've done this to keep the focus on the topic being covered.

Click the Forms button in the Object bar and locate the form called frmFirstDemo. Double-click this object to open it in form view. Figure 5.1 shows this form.

FIGURE 5.1

This form has two bound controls along with one unbound control.

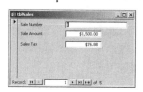

5

This form is bound to the table tblSales you saw earlier. From the top, the first field or control shows the primary key field, or Sale Number. The second control displays the Sale Amount field from the table. The third control is unbound to any underlying object. It calculates the sales tax (5.125% of the Sale Amount) for any sale.

To see how all these items work together, click the View button to move to design view for this form. If the Properties list box isn't open, click the Properties button on the toolbar or choose View, Properties from the main menu. Make sure the current object is the form itself. If it is, the word *Form* will appear both in the formatting toolbar and the title bar for the Properties list box itself. Figure 5.2 shows the form opened in design view with the form itself as the current object. You can tell that the form is the current object by three indicators. The first is the black square within the gray square at the upper-left of the form design grid, the second is the word *Form* in the formatting toolbar, and lastly, the word *Form* in the title bar of the Properties list box.

Tip

> Pressing Alt+Enter in form design view will reveal the Properties dialog box if it's hidden.

FIGURE 5.2

The form is the currently selected object.

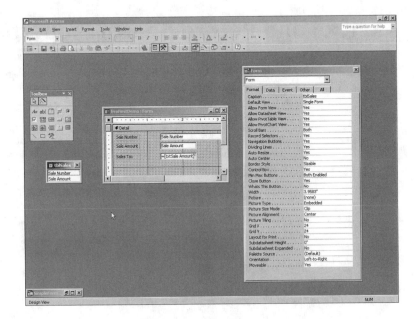

Note

> I've closed down the database view (window) to simplify the screen in Figure 5.2. These screens can get awfully cluttered and confusing until you're used to their various dialog boxes, menus, and toolbars.

Also make sure the Field List list box is open. In Figure 5.2, it's the box with the title bar saying tblSales. Click the Data tab in the Properties list box. Note the Record Source property is tblSales indicating that this form is bound to that table.

Click in the data display part of the first field, Sale Number. The properties in the Properties list box will change from properties for a form to properties for a text box control—the type of control this form uses for the Sale Number field. If necessary, click the Data tab and note that the Control Source is set to Sale Number—the field in the table that's bound to this control.

> **Note**
> The Record Source is the whole object, such as table or query, to which the form control is bound. The Control Source is the specific part of the object, such as field, that's bound. These aren't the names I would have given them, but I have to use them because Microsoft does.

Click in the data area of the next field, Sale Amount. Again, click the Data tab of the Properties list box and note that the Control Source for this control is the Sale Amount field in the bound table.

> **Note**
> Form controls are objects that display data in a graphical format. Examples are text fields, check boxes, and combo boxes.

So far things are likely unfolding about as you'd expect. Now things get interesting. Click in the Sales Tax field—where the sales tax itself appears when you're in form view. Again note the Control Source property in the Data (and All) tab:

```
=[txtSale Amount]*0.05125
```

This time, the Control Source doesn't point to a field within the bound table, but refers to another control and a math formula.

> **Note**
> The brackets ([ ]) around the field txtSale Amount indicate to Access that the enclosed name is a control.

5

Name Property—Standard Naming Conventions

The other important property you should know is the Name property. Click in the All tab. Note the Name property for the bottom field is txtTax. Click in the middle field and note the Name property for that control is txtSale Amount.

> **Note**
> All controls in an Access form must have a name. Access will assign a name to a new control using its own algorithm. It's up to you as an Access developer to use a cogent naming convention for your forms' controls.

All controls on a form, bound or unbound, must have a Name property. Using a logical naming convention for form objects is vitally important for efficient use of Access. The program doesn't care what, if any, naming convention you use, but you should care. Take a look at the Name property for each of the controls in the object frmFirstDemo. Note that each name starts out with the three letters txt followed by a name indicating the type of the control is a text box.

This is a rather standard naming convention. The txt part of the names refers to the nature of the controls—text boxes. If, for example, the controls were combo boxes, the three letter prefix would be cbo. The following part of the name is a mnemonic of some sort to indicate the function of the control to the programmer.

Back in the early days of personal computers programmers had to (or preferred to) use short names for program objects. So, you'd get statements such as these:

```
A = 1
B = .05125
C = 2990
```

This works, but remembering exactly what the objects A, B, and C stand for isn't easy when a programmer is working deep down in the program. Instead, look at a descriptive naming convention:

```
Periods = 1
InterestRate = .05125
PresentValue = 2990
```

This leaves no doubt as to what these values stand for.

Similarly using a naming convention for all Access objects leaves little doubt now, or in the future, about what an object does. Say you show the object named

TxtTaxesDue

Any programmer familiar with Access or modern naming conventions would be able to make a good guess that this object is a text box that holds values stating the tax due. Try it yourself. Table 5.1 shows the naming convention for some of the objects found on a typical form.

TABLE 5.1   Form Object Naming Conventions

Convention	Object
txt	Text box
cbo	Combo box
lbl	Label

TABLE 5.1 continued

Convention	Object
ocx	Custom control
cmd	Command button
chk	Check box
img	Image
opt	Option button
fra	Option button frame (group)
tgl	Toggle button
lst	List box

Now take a look at Table 5.2. This shows named objects and their functions. Does this system make sense to you?

TABLE 5.2 Typical Uses of Naming Conventions

Convention	Object
txtTotalSales	Text box displaying total sales
cboSelectCustomer	Combo box to choose customers from a list
lblKafeeTraders	Label for the form called Kafee Traders
cmdClose	Command button to close form
chkSalesTaxExempt	Check box for tax-exempt customers
optUPS	Option button to select UPS as shipper
tglShowProduct	Toggle button to show a graphic of the selected product
lstProductsAvailable	List box to show available products

Feel free to use a system such as this for your database objects or another of your own choosing. The advantage of using the now standard convention is that others will understand what you've done.

Tip

> Unlike earlier systems, object names in Access can contain spaces, but most database developers prefer to use mixed case to delimit words within a name. So instead of State Tax Owed, they'll use StateTaxOwed as control names.

5

Creating a First Form

There are two fundamental ways to create a form using Access. The first is using form
design view; the second, a bevy of wizards including the super simple AutoForm. Unless
your form needs are quite simple, you'll want to enhance through design view the output
of a form wizard.

Note

> The following sections somewhat duplicate the material you saw in Day 3,
> "Automatic Access." The reasons for inclusion here are that it makes sense
> within this context and the matter is presented as a survey earlier and a
> how-to here. Feel free to skip ahead if you know you have a good handle
> on the form wizards.

This first task creates a two-field form using the wizard, and then modifies the form controls.

Task: Running the AutoForm Wizard to Create a Form

1. Launch Access and open the Day 5 database.

2. Click the Tables button in the Object bar.

3. Locate the table tblSales. Click that object, but don't open it.

4. Locate the New Object button on the toolbar. That's the button that has something
   that looks like an icon with a lightning strike.

5. Click the New Object button to pull it down (it's a combo box).

6. Locate the AutoForm button and click it. Access creates a form using this table as a
   record source. Your screen should resemble Figure 5.3.

7. Save this form by choosing File, Save As from the main menu giving it the name
   frmFirstForm.

8. Close the form. Click the Forms button in the Object bar (if necessary) and note
   that your new form is now part of the form objects in Access.

FIGURE 5.3

The AutoForm isn't terribly artistic, but it is quite functional.

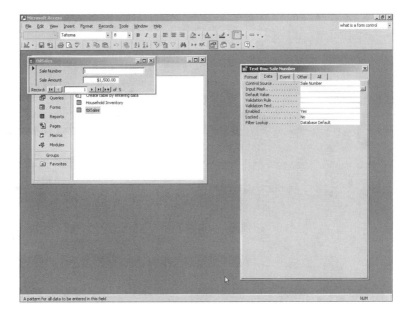

You can also use the form design wizard to create a form. This is a bit more flexible than AutoForm. Here's how it works.

Task: Running the Form Wizard to Create a Form

1. Launch Access and open the Day 5 database.

2. Click the Forms button in the Object bar.

3. Click the New button on the database view toolbar to start a new form. The New Form dialog box displays.

4. Choose the Form Wizard entry from the list box in the New Form dialog box. Note that you also could choose some useful AutoForm wizards from this list box.

5. Pull down the combo box at the bottom of this dialog box and choose tblSales from the list. Your screen should resemble Figure 5.4.

6. Click OK to start the wizard in earnest. The first screen you'll see should be familiar if you've been through a table or query wizard—the field selector list boxes.

7. Because there are only two fields here, include them both for the new form by clicking the >> button. Click Next to move to the layout step.

5

FIGURE 5.4

The New Form dialog box asks whether you want to use a wizard and what the record source for the form should be.

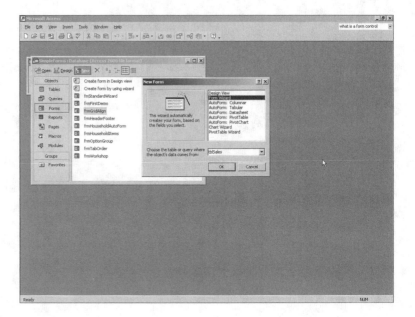

8. Keep the form layout as columnar. You might want to return to this wizard later on to see the output of the other types of form. The wizard does show a graphic representing what the other forms will look like. To see this graphic, click other option buttons. Return the option buttons to default (columnar) and click Next. Your screen should resemble Figure 5.5.

FIGURE 5.5

The form wizard lets you create a sharp look for your new form.

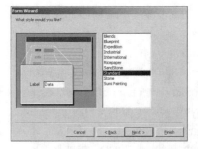

9. Choose a form style. I chose Sumi Painting. Click Next.

10. Use the next screen to name the form **frmStandardWizard**. Click Finish.

11. Access will create the new form and open it in form view. Your screen should resemble Figure 5.6.

FIGURE 5.6

The finished form is, in this case, identical to the AutoForm, but its style is Sumi Painting.

Form Design View

There's nothing wrong with these kinds of forms for the simple two-field bound table. Look at Figure 5.7. This is an AutoForm wizard output based on the table Household Inventory from the Inventory database—part of the sample data that comes with Access. You can find this form supplied with the Day 5 database as frmHouseholdAutoForm.

FIGURE 5.7

The form wizards lack imagination when applied to even a moderately complex object.

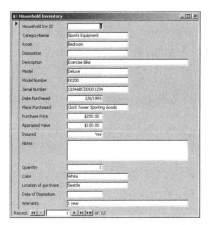

The next task will modify the wizard-generated form from Figure 5.7.

Task: The Form Design View

1. Launch Access and open the Day 5 database. Click the Forms button in the Object bar. Locate the frmHouseholdAutoForm form. Right-click this button. Choose Copy from the context menu. Right-click in the Forms area away from any entry and choose Paste from the context menu. Access will bring up a Paste As dialog box allowing you to enter a new name for this object. Enter **frmHouseholdItems** for a new name. Your screen should resemble Figure 5.8. Click OK to exit the dialog box.

FIGURE 5.8

The Paste command at the database view is really a Paste As command.

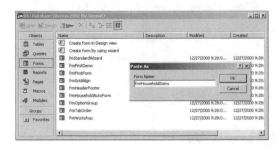

> **Tip**
>
> Step 1 uses the Copy/Paste technique to show you how it works. You also could have opened the form and used the Save As command from the File menu to create a copy of the object sporting a different name.

2. Click the new form, if necessary, to highlight it. Click the Design button in the database view toolbar. This opens the new form in design view. Your screen should resemble Figure 5.9.

> **Note**
>
> I've maximized the form design window and opened the `Properties` dialog box and also the toolbox. I've docked the toolbox (really a toolbar) at the left side of the screen. I find this arrangement most efficient when working on forms. Experiment with other window layouts to find one that suits you best.

3. Depending on the state of your form design view, you might not see all the objects shown in Figure 5.9—or you might have more. To view or hide any object in the form design grid, either click its button in the main toolbar (the buttons are toggles) or select/deselect their entries in the main menu View submenu.

4. The form design grid uses a drag-and-drop approach for most of its layout chores. To move a field, click it. This surrounds the field with some boxes and lines indicating the field has focus (or is highlighted). Figure 5.10 shows the `Description` field with the focus.

5. Click away from the `Description` field, and then back in it but don't release the mouse button. Your cursor will change to look like a hand. Move the mouse and you'll drag the field. Release the mouse button to drop the field into its new location. Note the field and its label moved in synchronization.

FIGURE 5.9

The form design view is quite a bit different from the previous design views for queries and tables.

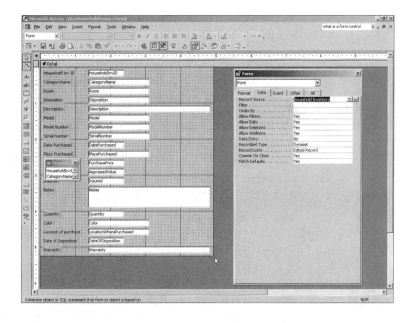

FIGURE 5.10

Access gives a strong visual clue to which field or fields are high-lighted.

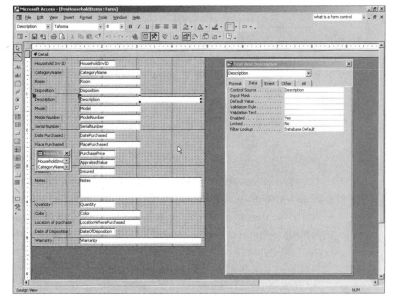

5

> **Tip**
>
> The hand cursor in form design view indicates you can move a form control.

6. Press Ctrl+Z (Undo) to snap the field back to its former position.

7. Again click in the field, if necessary, to highlight it. Locate the larger squares at the upper-left corners of the field data part and the label. Move your cursor to hover over either square. The cursor changes to a hand with an upraised finger. Drag the mouse and you'll move the field or label independently of each other. Drop the object you're moving and click undo again to replace the objects.

8. Move your cursor over any of the little squares at the sides of either the data area or the label of the control that is highlighted. The cursor changes to a double-ended arrow. Click-and-drag to increase or decrease the size of the field. Drop the resized field and then click the Undo button to restore the field to its original size.

> **Tip**
>
> The standard Access toolbar has Undo and Redo buttons that work identically to other Office applications. After doing some actions on a form, pull down the menu in the Undo button to see how much you can rollback.

9. If necessary, click the Description field to highlight it if it's currently not highlighted. Press the Delete key to delete the field from this form. Make sure the field list box for the Household Inventory table is visible. If it's not, choose the Field List button from the View menu in the main menu bar. Locate the Description field in the list box. Click this field and drag it to the form design grid, dropping it where the old Description field existed. Figure 5.11 shows this operation in process.

10. The type of control Access uses for a field depends on the current tool selected from the toolbox. If nothing is selected, Access uses the text box control. Again, delete the Description field from the form design grid. Locate the combo box control within the toolbox and click it to select it as the control you want to use for the next field placement. If the magic wand (wizard) button in the toolbox appears pressed, click it to give it a raised look. The control box wizard is handy as can be, but if you triggered it now, it'd cause some confusion. Click, then again drag the Description field from the field list box to the design grid. Access will add the field, but this time it uses a combo box control to display it. Figure 5.12 shows this procedure finished other than final location of the control.

▼

FIGURE 5.11

Adding fields to a form is a simple matter of dragging and dropping.

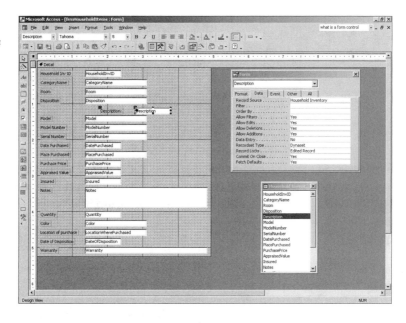

FIGURE 5.12

Access can use various toolbox controls to display a field.

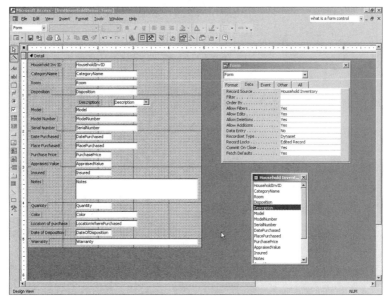

▼

> **Tip**
>
> The More Controls button in the toolbox opens up a list of many more controls, some of which are useful for form design. The exact number and type of controls opened depend on your computer's setup.

11. Close the form discarding changes.

Some form controls make sense for displaying field data, some don't. For example, the standard toolbox contains both command and toggle buttons, neither of which can display data, but instead find use as objects to control the flow of a program. Table 5.3 contains the most often used form controls and their prevalent uses.

TABLE 5.3   Often Used Form Controls

Control Name	Common Use
Text box	Contains text or numbers. Can be bound or unbound or contain a calculation (expression).
Label	Name of form, name of field, or instructions for data entry.
List box	List of values or entries. Usually bound, but can be filled using VBA, too.
Combo box	Familiar pull-down box. Actually a combination of a text box and a list box.
Check box	The square box useful for yes/no data type fields or form choices.
Option button	Another yes/no control often used in option groups. Used to be called radio buttons.
Option group	A group of option buttons or check boxes where only one in a group can be selected.
Unbound object	Displays an object (such as an image) that remains the same as records change.
Bound object	Displays objects that should change for each record. For example, pictures of employees will change as the record changes.
Tab control	Creates tabbed forms that have the look of Office 2000's option dialog boxes.
Subform	Creates forms that are bound to other related objects of the parent's form bound. Most often used to create detail listings, such as order details for customers where the customers table is linked to the order details.
Line	Create lines to visually delineate form elements.
Rectangle	Create squares and rectangles to delineate form elements.

Most of these controls are self-explanatory, but some people have trouble with the idea of option buttons or check boxes within a group until they use the control. If you have any doubt about the use of an option group, glance through the next section. If you're sure about its use, skip ahead.

Option Group

An option group permits only one control at a time to be set. Open the form frmOptionGroup in form view. This form is part of the sample data located in the Forms section of the Day 5 database. Figure 5.13 shows this form open.

FIGURE 5.13

This form has a set of option buttons in an option group and a set not in an option group.

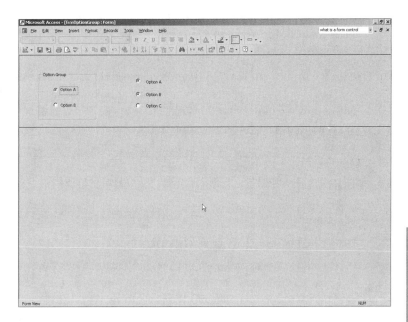

Try to get both option buttons within the group to be "on" at the same time. You can't. Now try to do the same with the three buttons on the right—the ones outside a group.

While this example uses option buttons for the demonstration, it could also use check boxes with the same result.

Use an option group or frame when a record must have one choice selected, but can't have more than one.

Tip

Most users expect to see option buttons, not check boxes in a group. This has become a Windows convention. As a developer, you will have better results following this and other conventions.

To enclose option buttons within a group, create the group using the corresponding control in the toolbox. Place it on the form, size it if necessary, and then place the option buttons within the group. The option group tool in the toolbox is a rectangle with the letters (tiny ones) *xyz* above it.

Form Control Alignment

You might have noticed that the background of the form design grid does in fact look like graph paper or a grid. This isn't just for decoration, but is an enormously helpful aid in form design.

You can set Access to snap controls (auto align) to this grid, to automatically align or space controls, and you also can adjust this grid to whatever fineness you need for your design work.

Open the form frmGridAlign (part of your sample data that's on the CD) in either view. This is a simple, unbound form with three text box controls scattered around it. These are the controls you'll need for this task. The purpose of this task is to give you the skills you'll need to create orderly looking forms and reports.

Note
Most of the skills learned in form design are directly transferable to report design.

Task: Form Grid and Alignment

1. Launch Access and open the Day 5 database. Click the Forms button in the Object bar. Launch the form frmGridAlign in form view (double-click it). Note the three text box controls scattered about the form.

2. Click the View button to move to design view for this form. Make sure the Properties list box is visible. If not, choose it from the toolbar or from the View menu. Also make sure the form itself is the currently selected object. If it is, the word *Form* will appear in the title bar of the Properties list box.

3. Note the look of the grid (graph paper) in the background of the form design area. Click the All or Format tab in the Properties list box. Scroll down until you locate the Grid X and Grid Y properties. Note that they are set at 24 each. This is the number of lines per inch the grid exhibits. Your screen should resemble Figure 5.14.

FIGURE 5.14

The two grid properties control the granularity of the design grid.

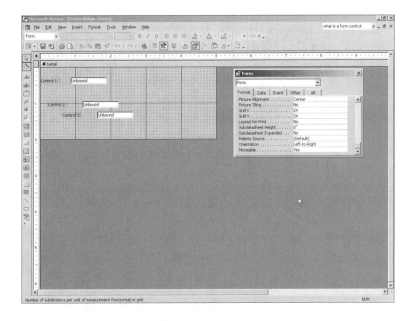

4. Move any control around. Note you can only drop it where the grid is. With the grid set to such a coarse granularity, you're severely limited to where you can place controls.

Note

If you have trouble seeing that you can only drop the controls on the grid, temporarily change the Grid X and Grid Y properties to 5 and then try again.

5. Open the Format menu. Locate the Snap to Grid option and click it to deselect it. Again, try moving a control around the form. You can drop it anywhere. Reactivate Snap to Grid.

Tip

Activating Snap to Grid won't snap to grid objects currently off the grid until you move them.

5

▼ 6. Click anywhere on the form away from the three text box controls. Drag a box around the three controls. Release the mouse. This is called a marquee selection— the marquee being the rubber band–like rectangle you saw during the drag opera- tion. Figure 5.15 shows the marquee selection in process.

FIGURE 5.15

The marquee selection is one way to select several form objects at the same time.

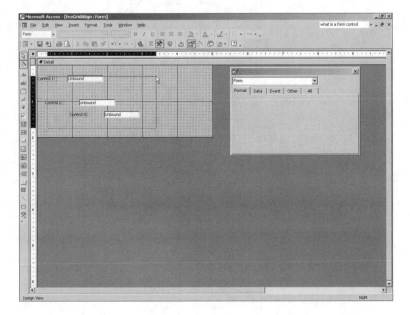

7. Open the Format menu. Locate the Align button and move your mouse cursor down to that button. Note the flyout menu has several alignment options. Try aligning these controls—left and right, top and bottom—to get a feel for what the effect of these choices will be.

Tip

Shift+click will allow multiple selections of form objects as well.

8. Open the Format menu and locate the entries for Horizontal spacing and Vertical spacing. Experiment with the submenu entries for both these entries to see what effect they can have.

9. Separate (if necessary) any overlapping controls to give them some spread again. Highlight all three using either the Shift or the marquee method. Choose the ▼ Format menu's Group button. This places a rectangle around all three controls.

A grouped set of controls can act in design view as a linked set of controls. Click away from the group, and then click again in the group area on any of the grouped controls. Try moving one control of the group. Now click the black square at the upper-left of the group rectangle. Drag the square to drag the group. Figure 5.16 shows a group.

FIGURE 5.16

Grouped controls can act in concert.

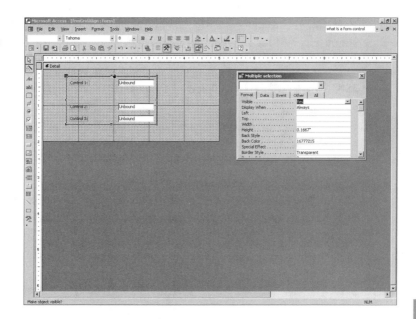

Note

You still can select and individually move controls within a group. They aren't locked to the group.

10. You also can change the entire size of the form. Move your cursor to the extreme bottom-right corner of the form. When at the corner, your cursor changes to look like an oval with four arrows pointing out of it. Drag to increase or decrease the size of the form in both directions. You also can change the vertical or horizontal size of the form by clicking and dragging on the right or bottom edge of the form design screen.

11. Close the form, saving or discarding changes as you see fit. If you want to preserve the original form and the modified one, choose File, Save As from the menu to save your modified form under a new name.

Form Headers and Footers

A form header is an area at the top of the form that remains the same no matter what record the form's Detail area displays. The form's footer is the same but is at the form's lower edge.

Form headers and footers are useful for displaying form titles or other data you want to persist from record to record. There are two classes of headers and footers. Form headers/footers persist for all records while page headers/footers persist for a particular form page.

Task: Experimenting with Form Headers and Footers

1. Launch Access and open the Day 5 database. Click the Forms button in the Object bar. Locate the form frmHeaderFooter. Open it in form view. Click the forward and back buttons at the bottom of the form to move through the records. This form is a simple form based on some of the field in the Household Inventory table also in this database.

2. Note how the label in the header section remains no matter what record is displayed in the Detail section of the form. Also note the same thing for the forward and back buttons in the footer section.

3. Switch to design view. Note the construction of this form shown in Figure 5.17.

FIGURE 5.17

The Form Header section of this form holds a label control that remains static no matter what is displayed in the Detail section.

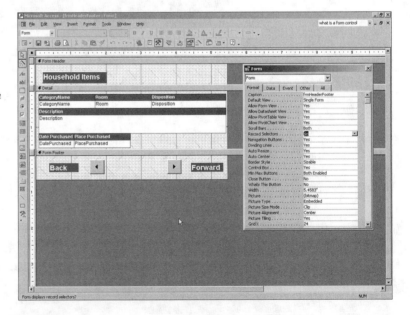

4. You can use headers and footers not only for labels, but also for navigation controls (such as the forward and back buttons), totals or subtotals. Close the form discarding or saving changes as you prefer.

Other Form Format Properties

Forms default to having certain properties that almost always aren't all needed at the same time on the same form. These are shown in Table 5.4.

TABLE 5.4 Default Form Controls

Property Name	Usage
Default View	Specifies the default view the Form or datasheet displays (forms can display in the datasheet format too).
Scroll bars	Specifies which scroll bars, horizontal or vertical or both, appear on the form.
Record Selectors	Specifies that a record selector appears in the form.
Navigation buttons	Specifies that the navigation buttons appear on the form. Navigation buttons are on the bottom of the form and moves one record forward or backward or to end or beginning of records.
Control box	Specifies that the control box appears in the title bar of the form. The control box appears to the extreme left of the title bar in standard Windows applications. Opens the Control menu.
Min Max buttons	Specifies that the minimize and maximize buttons appear in the title bar of the form.
Close button	Specifies that the close button appears in the title bar of the form. Use this button to close the form.
What's this button	Specifies that the question mark button appears in the title bar of the form. This button is for context-sensitive help.

To see some of these properties in action, open the form frmHeaderFooter in design view. If it's not visible, click the Properties button in the toolbar or choose it from the View menu.

Click in the Record Selectors property and enter **No** or pull down the combo box choosing **No** from the list. Switch to form view to see the results of your action.

> **Tip**
>
> You can toggle many properties, such as those that are Yes or No by double-clicking them.

5

Access removes the gray bar to the left of the form Detail section. As you can see, removal of this element doesn't detract at all from the usefulness of the form.

> **Tip**
>
> You can change some properties of some form objects (controls) while in form view. The objects must be able to accept focus which puts the form itself off limits. To do this, open the form in form view, make the Properties dialog box visible by either pressing F4 or choosing the menu View, Properties. Then experiment away.

Similarly, change or toggle some of the other properties listed in Table 5.4. Watch the form, noting what element each property controls. Some properties, such as the close, minimize and maximize buttons will require you to switch from form to design and back to form view for the changes to take effect. If in doubt, toggle your view.

Tab Order

When you're in any Windows-standard dialog box or form, you'll notice that there is a standard order for cursor movement. In other words, when you leave a field or object in Windows, your cursor doesn't randomly move to another object, but rather the programmer or program (by default) determines the cursor progression order for the available objects.

Like so many things, this is easier seen than explained. Open the database Day 5, if necessary. Locate the form frmTabOrder by clicking the Forms button in the Object bar and finding it in the list of available forms for this database.

Double-click this form to open it in Form view. This is a simple form bound to the Household Inventory table from the sample data Inventory database supplied with Office 2002.

> **Note**
>
> An object is said to have the focus when an object can accept input, or in other words has the "attention" of the cursor.

Note that the cursor starts out in the primary key field for this table, the Household Inv ID field. Press the Tab key to move to the next field in the tab order. The cursor jumps to the Category Name field. This makes sense logically for data entry, but it's distracting to see the cursor moving in a disorderly fashion around the form.

Note | Access assigns the tab order for a form based on the order that you placed objects into the form's sections or areas. In this case, the Category Name field was placed on the form Detail area right after the Household Inv ID field causing the tab order to be 2 and 1, respectively.

To get a feel for how annoying a disoriented tab order can be, click the New record button on the toolbar (to the right of the Find button). This brings up a blank record for your data entry. Tab out of the Household Inv ID field as that auto-increments. Enter a Category Name and then press Enter. Enter a room name or number and then press Enter (or Tab) again. Note the Stop (close form) command button now has the focus. This surely isn't a sensible way to design a form! If you press Enter to move on to the next field, you'll end up closing the form.

Tip | Ctrl++ (Ctrl plus the plus sign) also jumps you to a new record.

Even leaving the Stop button out of it, having the cursor jump all over the form is distracting. The next task assigns a planned tab order to these fields and prevents an accidental closing of the form.

Task: Setting Tab Order and Tab Stops

1. Launch Access and open the Day 5 database. Click the Forms button in the Object bar. Locate the form frmTabOrder. Open it in design view. If you have the form open in form view by following along in the introduction of this section, switch to design view now.

2. Choose Tab Order from the View menu. This opens the Tab Order dialog box. Your screen should resemble Figure 5.18.

3. The Tab Order dialog box has two ways to change the tab order of a form's controls. You can click the Auto Order button to order the controls from left to right and top to bottom, or you can click the gray square to the left of each control's name then drag-and-drop the control to a new place in the order.

4. Using either method, alter the tab order so the fields are ordered from left to right and top to bottom. The order of the fields in the Tab Order list box should end up as follows:

   1. Model
   2. CategoryName

▼   3. Room

        4. HouseholdInvID

        5. ModelNumber

        6. cmdClose

FIGURE 5.18

The Tab Order dialog box shows the current tab order for the object in each section of a form.

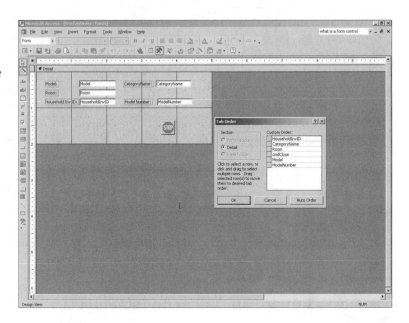

> **Note**
>
> The field names for the controls differ from the labels associated with those fields because the field names and the Caption property for those fields vary. Open the Household Inventory table in design view to see the two labels.

5. Return to form view. Again click the New record button in the toolbar and enter a new record. While the current field order is less logical (to some ways of thinking), the data-entry person will find the order of the field progression to be predictable, and therefore not as worrisome as it was before.

6. There is still a problem. There is no need to give the focus to the Stop (close form) button for each record entered in this form. In fact, it's a bad idea because the data entry person might erroneously close the form and therefore lose time relocating
▼   and opening it. To fix this, return to design view for this form.

7. Click the Stop (close form) button to highlight it. Open the `Properties` list box, if necessary, by clicking its button in the toolbar. Click the Other or All tab and locate the Tab Stop property. Edit that to No (or double-click it that will toggle it to No). Your screen should resemble Figure 5.19.

FIGURE 5.19

The Tab Stop property enables or disables the object's ability to accept focus from the tab order.

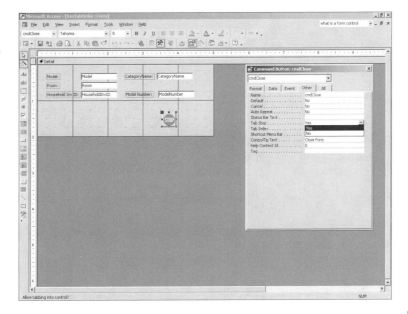

8. Save the changes you made to the form by clicking the Save button in the toolbar. Return to form view and tab through the fields. Note that the cursor doesn't ever land on the Stop button. However if you need to, you can click the Stop (close form) button using a mouse click. This avoids the possibility of an accidental form closure and removes the extra tab keystroke for every record entry, but preserves the use of the Stop button for when it's needed.

9. There's a further improvement you can make to this form. The `HouseholdInvID` field is an `Auto Increment` field so it requires no user entry at any time. In fact, there's no reason for this field to ever have focus as users can't edit values within this field or make entries here.

10. Return to design view. Click in the `Household Inv ID` field. Locate the property `Enabled` in the Data (or All) tab. Toggle this value from Yes to No.

11. Return to form view. Again click the New record button to enter a new record for your household possessions. Note that this time the cursor skips over not only the Stop button, but the auto increment field (`HouseholdInvID`) as well. Compare how

easy data entry is in the form now that you've set a proper tab order and tab stops compared to when you started with this form. The Enabled property is the property that controls "graying out" in Access applications, as you can see in Figure 5.20.

Tip

Setting the Enabled property to No prevents the control from getting the focus and therefore prevents the user from editing data values. Setting the Locked property to Yes allows focus, but prevents data editing.

FIGURE 5.20

To set the Enabled property to No grays out a control in Access or in Windows.

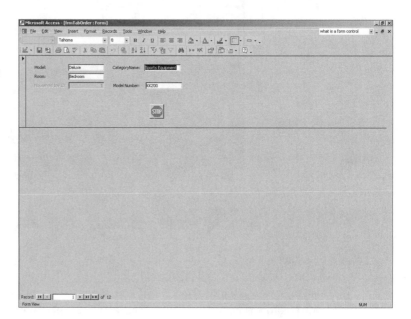

Finding, Filtering, and Sorting in Forms

This is the easiest and simplest section you can imagine. Filtering by form, filtering by example, and sorting data within forms are all identical in every way to doing these procedures in a datasheet whether that datasheet is a query or a table.

Remember, a bound form doesn't represent different data than a table or query but only a different presentation of that data. All the skills you learned in Day 4, "The Data Foundation—The Table," are directly transferable without any changes to use in forms.

If you have any doubts about your abilities, review the material in Day 4 about filtering, finding, and sorting data in datasheets. Then try the same procedures from the form view. You'll note no differences whatsoever.

Similarly, much of the skill set you picked up today will be transferable to reports, coming tomorrow.

Summary

Forms present data in a way most people find easier to edit or view than simple datasheets. You can create forms using the AutoForm Wizard, the regular form wizard, or design view. You can always modify the wizard-generated forms using design view. Many developers let the wizard make a simple form and then modify the layout using design view.

Forms have up to five sections. These are Form Header, Page Header, Detail, Page Footer, and Form Footer. You can add controls, either bound or unbound, to any of these sections. To add a bound control to a section, click the field name in the field name list box and drag it to the section on the form where you wish it to appear. To add a non-default (non-text box) control to a form, click in the toolbox on the control type, click the field in the list box, and click the form where you wish the control to reside.

Forms are heavily equipped with properties to control their function and appearance. This lesson covered some of the appearance and tab order properties, but there are many more to come. For example, you can alter the entire tab order of a form using the Tab Order dialog box, remove a control from the tab order by setting the Tab Stop property to No, and remove a control's ability to get the focus by setting the Enabled property to No.

5

Q&A

Q. I've seen datasheets using only horizontal lines. How was that done?

A. Here's one way. Open the form frmTabOrder in datasheet view by highlighting double-clicking it in the database view. Then choose datasheet view from the View button on the toolbar (it's a pull down control). Locate the Gridlines button in the Formatting (datasheet) toolbar. If necessary, right-click any toolbar and open the Formatting (datasheet) toolbar. Locate the Gridlines (horizontal only) button and choose it. Your screen should resemble Figure 5.21.

FIGURE 5.21

*You have control over
the gridlines in a
datasheet.*

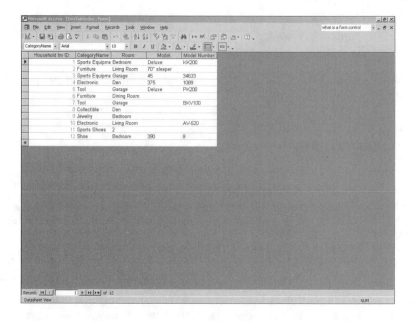

Q. Are there global properties I can set for all controls on a form?

A. Yes. Select the form itself and then open the `Properties` list box to the Data tab.
Note that you can set the form to either edit or not edit all records, as well as several other related properties.

Q. Can I set several properties at the same time for related controls?

A. Yes, you can select several controls using Shift+click or marquee. The `Properties`
list box displays Multiple Selection in its title bar. Any common properties appear
in the various tabs. Setting any property sets that property for all selected controls.

**Q. I am trying to set the color of a form, but can't find any property that sounds
right for the form. Is there a way to do this?**

A. You set color for each section, not the form. For example, click in the Detail section away from any object, and then choose the Format tab from the Properties list
box. Locate the Background color property. Click the ellipsis button that appears
when that property has focus. Choose your color from the displayed palette.

Q. Can I copy a control and paste it elsewhere on the form?

A. The clipboard works the same in form design view as elsewhere in Windows. You
can copy, cut, and paste any object.

Workshop

The Workshop helps you solidify the skills you learned in this lesson. Answers to the quiz and exercises appear in Appendix A, "Answers to Quizzes."

Quiz

1. What allows the dragging of a control separate from its label?
2. How do you remove a control from a form?
3. How can you alter a control's size on a form?
4. Will a form header appear for all records on a form?
5. Can two option buttons in an option frame both be set to Yes?
6. How does filtering by form differ in a datasheet and a form?

Exercises

1. In the Forms section of the database view, choose New. Choose the Form Wizard to create a form bound to the table tblSales. Include both fields in this new form. Save the form using a name of your choosing or use this example's choice: frmWorkshop. That form is part of your sample data. If you have trouble following along with this exercise, consult that form. Accept all the wizard's defaults for this form.

2. Switch to design view. If the form footer isn't visible, choose (or toggle it) from the View menu. Enlarge the form footer to be the length of the form, but about one inch (2.5 cm) deep. You might have to move your cursor around directly under the lower gray bar to see it switch to the look, which means you are in resizing mode.

   Your screen should resemble Figure 5.22.

3. Make sure the toolbox is visible. If not, make it visible using the View menu or the toolbar. Make sure the Control Wizards button is selected in the toolbox's toolbar. That's the button with the magic wand on it.

4. Locate the command button control in the toolbox. Click it. Click in the form footer area of the form toward the right of the footer area. This will place a button on the form and launch a wizard. Your screen should resemble Figure 5.23.

5. Choose Form Operations and Form Close from the two list boxes shown in Figure 5.23. Click Next.

5

Tip

This is a good place to pause and study the other operations a command button wizard can do.

FIGURE 5.22

You are about to add a new control to a wizard form.

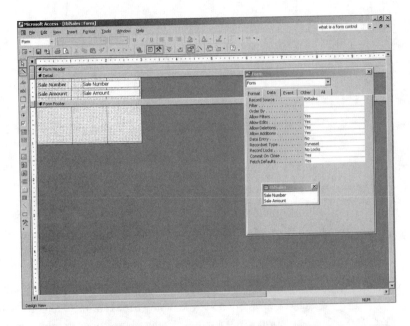

FIGURE 5.23

Some controls can trigger wizards. A command button is one of these.

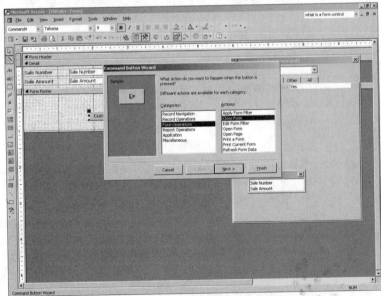

6. Choose the Stop Sign from the next screen. Click Next.

7. Name the command button `cmdExit`. Click Finish. Your screen should resemble Figure 5.24.

FIGURE 5.24

You've just created and programmed a command button to close this form.

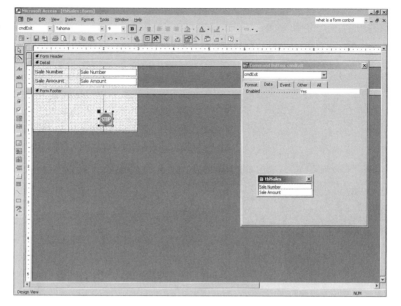

8. Save the form. Change to form view. Try your new button to see if it works as you expected it to. It should.

9. Return to design view. Remove the new command button from the tab order, but allow it to have focus. Return to form view.

10. Test the tab order to see if it includes your command button. It shouldn't. Return to design view. Open the Tab Order dialog box from the View menu. Does the footer section include the cmdExit object in its list?

11. Close the form, saving changes if you choose.

5

DAY 6

Introducing Queries

As promised, today you'll get a look at queries. In the early days of databases—really, before they existed on small computers—queries were the heart of what it meant to be a database administrator. You had to write the query in an often-complex, syntactically abstruse language. It took a lot of study and practice to get it right.

Clearly small-computer users weren't interested in making such a large educational investment. Most had day jobs they needed database programs to assist them with. They did not want to become professional database administrators. The solution for most was the query by example. Instead of entering your query using a language, you'd give the database an example of what you wish to select on. The query by example is the model that Access uses.

Today You Will Learn

Queries are the part of database work some folks find most intimidating. This likely is due to older database programs that were quite difficult to use. I think you'll find that learning queries in Access is a simple process. In today's lesson, you will learn

- How to use the design view to create a query
- How to use the Query Wizard
- How to filter records by using simple query criteria
- How to use AND and OR in queries
- How to query on multiple tables
- How to create relationships within queries
- What you can do with expressions

This lesson restricts itself to select queries—by far the most common type in all database work. Select queries pull selected data from one or more tables or queries. For the purpose of this lesson, think of a query as a subset of data in a table or tables selected according to criteria entered by you. Later in this book, you'll learn other neat query tricks Access can do.

The Query in Access

Many developers call queries the heart of Access. While tables store all data, it's the queries that most objects derive their data from. Queries allow much more flexibility when selecting or manipulating data than do tables.

 Note

> Structured Query Language (SQL) is the standard language for querying a relational database, such as Access. While Access accepts query by example (QBE), it is really a full SQL engine. The Access user interface translates your QBE into SQL which, in turn, does the actual query duties.

The most important thing to remember at this point is that all Access queries are live. Changes made to data in a query datasheet view are reflected in the underlying table just as they'd be if you made those changes (or edits) directly in the table. This includes multi-table queries where changes made to any part of the query reflect in the underlying tables. You can even add new data to tables through queries.

 Tip

> Although you can edit or add data to tables directly through queries, most applications work better if the developer uses forms for those changes.

A First Query

If you've been working your way through this book sequentially, you already should have a good idea of what the query design grid looks like. You also should have a fair idea of how to construct a query. This next task covers some familiar ground, but within the task are details that previous Days glossed over, so take some time to review this task even if you think you've got a grasp on simple query construction.

There are three ways to create a query:

- Using the design view
- Using a wizard
- Directly entering SQL commands using the SQL view

This lesson covers only the first two, as the third method requires some understanding of SQL commands. SQL, in and of itself, is an intermediate-level topic covered later in the book. As you'd need an understanding of that language before doing much in SQL view, this book will largely skip over that topic for now.

Task: Creating a Query Using the Design View

1. Launch Access and open the database called Day 6. This database contains several tables from the Northwind database.

> **Note**
>
> This lesson uses some Northwind data, but doesn't work in that database itself for two reasons. Using a separate database allows the book to focus on the subject matter, and working outside Northwind prevents that database from being clogged up with practice database objects.

2. Click the Queries button in the Object bar. Click the New button on the toolbar in the database view. Your screen should resemble Figure 6.1.
3. Click OK to accept the default of starting a query in design view. The Show Table dialog box opens.
4. Click the Customers table and then click the Add button to add this table to the query.

> **Note**
>
> You also can drag-and-drop objects from the Show Table dialog box to the design grid.

FIGURE 6.1

Starting a new query from the database view.

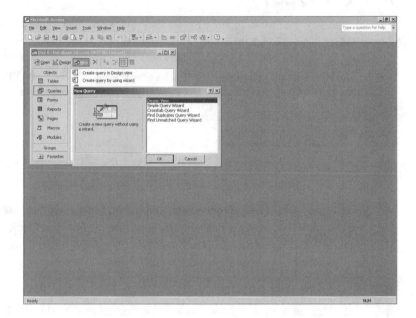

5. Click Close to close the Show Table dialog box. Each table or query you add is represented as a field list box in the upper portion of the query design view.

> **Tip**
>
> As the tabs in the Show Table dialog box indicate, you can include tables, queries, or both, in any particular query. That is, you can query a query—an important technique as you'll later learn.

6. Adjust the size of the field list box to suit your taste.

7. Click and drag the first four fields (one at a time) from the field list box and drop them in the first four columns, respectively. Figure 6.2 shows this operation in progress for the last column.

8. Click the next field down—the Address. Then Ctrl-click the next field, City. This highlights both fields. Drag them to the grid, dropping them to the right of the Contact Title field. You can drag and drop as many fields as you wish by using the Shift or Ctrl selection method which works identically here, as in the Explorer.

9. Click in the next column to the right of the City field. This brings up a pull-down caret (combo box). Pull down that combo box and choose Region from the drop-down list. Figure 6.3 shows this technique of adding a field to a query.

FIGURE 6.2

Dragging a field from the field list box to the grid includes that field in the query.

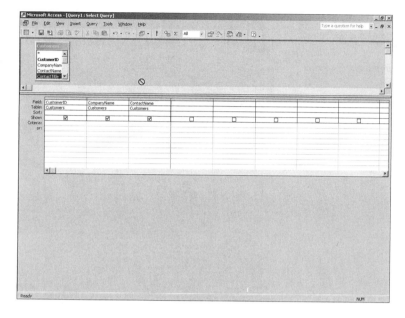

FIGURE 6.3

You can drag and drop to include fields in a query or choose from a pull-down list.

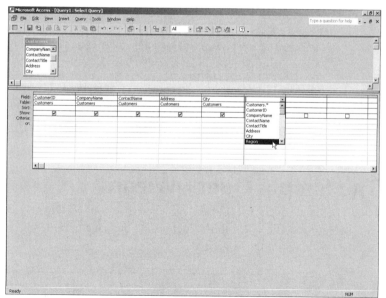

6

10. Click the Run button on the toolbar to see how the query is coming along. The Run button has an exclamation point on it. Your screen should resemble Figure 6.4.

FIGURE 6.4

At this point, the query selects all records from the included fields.

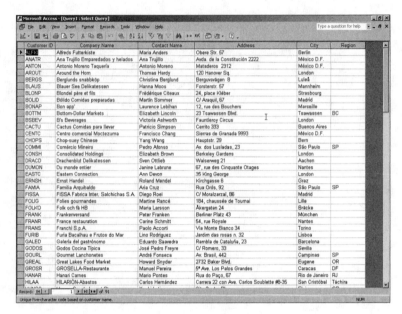

11. Click the disk icon on the toolbar to save this query as qrySelectCustomers1, or just qrySelectCustomers if you don't mind overwriting the sample query. Close the query (File, Close) and take a break if you want. If you prefer, leave it open, as you'll be using it again later in this lesson.

That's it. You've just constructed a query by dragging fields from the list box labeled Customers (the name of the table) to the query design grid. At this point, the query is a subset of the Customers table in the sense that it contains all records, but only some of the fields.

The Simple Query Wizard

The simple query wizard can save some time constructing queries like the one done in the previous Task. It's almost identical to the table wizard you saw in the last lesson. Here's a tour of this wizard:

Note

This section duplicates, to some extent, the material covered in Day 3, "Automatic Access." Here it's covered in somewhat more detail and in a how-to format, rather than a survey format. Feel free to skip over this section if you feel you have a decent handle on this subject.

Task: Creating a Query Using the Simple Query Wizard

1. If necessary, launch Access and open the database called Day 6 located on your CD.

2. Click the Queries button in the Object bar. Double-click the Create query by using wizard shortcut in the Queries section of the database view. You also could click the New button on the toolbar and choose Simple Query Wizard from the dialog box. In either case, Access responds with the dialog box shown in Figure 6.5.

FIGURE 6.5

The simple query opening dialog box is familiar territory to anyone familiar with the Table Design Wizard.

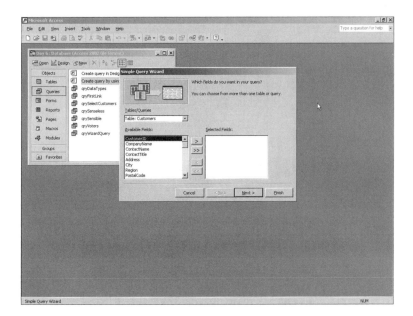

3. The wizard defaults to the Customers table because that is the first table in your database. You can pull down the combo box labeled Tables/Queries to see other objects you can query.

4. Add the fields Customer ID through Region to the query by clicking several times on the right-pointing caret button.

Tip

> The double caret buttons add or remove all fields from the query at one time.

5. Click Next to move on.

6. Name the query **qryWizardQuery1** and click Finish. This runs the query. Your screen should resemble Figure 6.6.

▼ 7. As you can see, the results are the same as you saw when making a query using the design view.

FIGURE 6.6

There's no difference between the wizard-generated query and the one you did manu-ally using the design view.

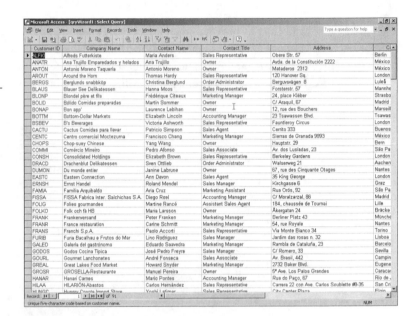

▲

Filtering and Sorting in Queries

You can use the same techniques you used with tables to filter and sort data within queries when you're in a datasheet view. However, queries have the ability to store such settings by using the query design grid (or SQL view) to create variations on a query.

Task: Quick Filtering and Sorting in Queries

TASK

▼ 1. Launch Access and open the database called Day 6 located on your CD.

2. Locate the query qrySelectCustomers. Double-click it to open it in datasheet view. Your screen should resemble Figure 6.4.

3. Click in the Contact Name field. Click the Sort Ascending button in the toolbar. The Sort Ascending button is the one with the A over the Z and an arrow pointing downward. As you saw in the table datasheet view, Access sorts the current field in alphabetical order.

4. Click in the Customer ID field and click Sort Ascending again to return the
▼   datasheet to its original view.

Warning You can't undo a sort in datasheet view, but the changes aren't saved by default when you close the query. A short-cut to returning a datasheet to its former sort order is to close the table, discard layout changes, and then reopen it.

5. Try clicking in various fields and then clicking the Sort Ascending or Sort Descending buttons.

6. Locate the first entry of Order Administrator in the Contact Title field and click in it.

7. Click the Filter by Selection button on the toolbar. Your screen should resemble Figure 6.7.

FIGURE 6.7

You can filter by example in a query as you can in a table.

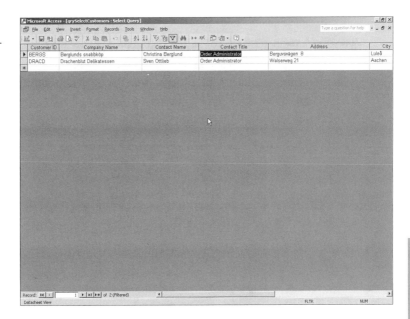

Tip You can filter by form from a query-generated datasheet, but you'll find it more flexible to do so using the design view of the query.

8. Remove the filter by clicking the Remove Filter button on the toolbar. Close the query discarding layout changes (if any).

Query Criteria

Using criteria in queries to select only certain records is perhaps the most frequent use for queries. This facility is very similar to filtering in datasheet view. In fact, there's only a small difference for most queries.

▲ TASK

Task: Specifying an "OR" Criteria in the Query

1. Launch Access and open the database called Day 6 located on your CD. This database contains several tables from the Northwind database.

2. Locate and open in design view either the query qrySelectCustomers, or the qrySelectCustomers1, depending on whether you wish to use the sample query or one of your own making.

3. Note the checkboxes in the Show row of the query design grid. This controls whether an included field displays in the query. As all the fields are currently checked, all will display. Very soon, you'll see the importance of an included non-displayed query field.

4. Enter **Du monde entier** in the Criteria row under the Company Name column.

5. Tab out of the Company Name column. Access adds quotes to your entry. This indicates that the limit of this criteria is the string between the quote marks. Your screen should resemble Figure 6.8.

FIGURE 6.8

Access almost always guesses correctly about adding delimiters to query criteria.

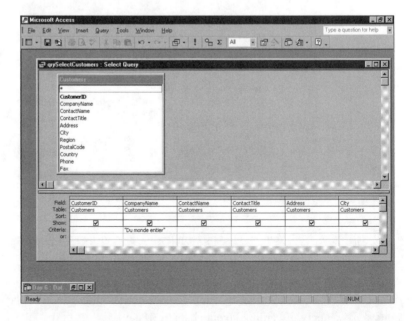

▼   6. Click the Run button to view the query's output.

       7. You'll note that the query is now limited to those companies bearing the name "Du monde entier"—or one single company. Return to design view for this query.

       8. Locate the column `Contact Title` and enter **Sales Agent** in the second row of the criteria area. By placing a criterion on two rows, you create an "OR" criteria that returns records matching either criterion. Your screen should resemble Figure 6.9.

       9. Run the query. Your screen should resemble Figure 6.10.

FIGURE 6.9

This query returns records that have "Sales Agent" in the `Title` *or "Du monde entier" as the* `Company Name`.

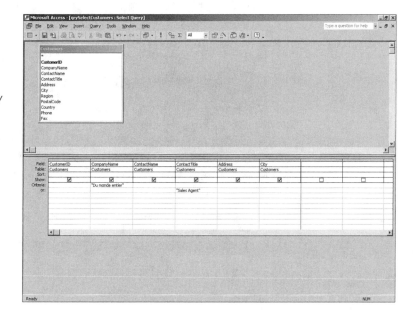

    10. The next query type worth examining is the AND criteria query. This query demands validity in both columns (fields) for any returned record. Return the query to design view.

Tip

> OR queries are inclusive. AND queries are exclusive. This is somewhat different from natural speech where we might say "I want the records for those customers living in Chicago and Denver." The human will return customers who live in either place. The computer will only return those who live in both places.

    11. Cut or delete the entry for Sales Agent and then move it to the first row. Your screen should resemble Figure 6.11.

6

FIGURE 6.10

*An OR query returns
records meeting either
of the entries on the
Criteria row.*

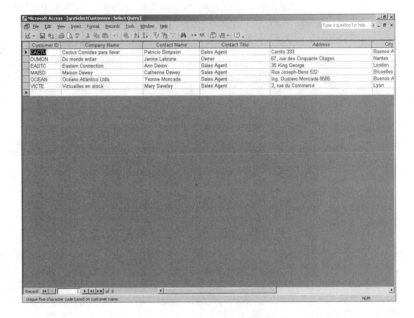

FIGURE 6.11

*You construct an AND
criteria by including
the example on the
same row.*

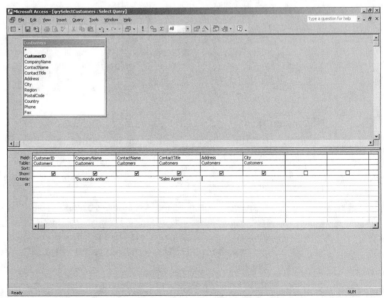

12. Run the query. You should get a null return as there are no records where the
    Company Name is "Du monde entier" and the Contact Title is "Sales Agent."

▼   13. Return to design view. Remove the "Du monde entier" criteria.

    14. Click to the right of the quote marks in the column Contact Title and enter a space followed by the word **or** and the string **"Owner"**. Your screen should resemble Figure 6.12. Be sure to include the quote marks around the second string, but not the OR keyword.

FIGURE 6.12

Using OR in a column selects either criterion from a field.

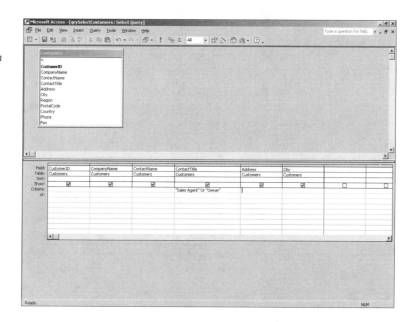

> **Note**
>
> You can alter column widths in the query design view just like you can any other columns, such as table view. I've widened the column in Contact Title for these figures to show the entire criterion.

> **Tip**
>
> Some folks have trouble seeing what they're doing when in the Criteria row. Click in that row, and then click Shift+F2 (Zoom), which opens a large text box where you can edit your criteria easily and clearly.

    15. Run the query. Note that you'll get returns for any record where the Contact Title meets either of your criteria. Note at the bottom of the screen that there are a total
▼   of 22 records returned.

6

16. Return to design view. Uncheck the Show checkbox for the Contact Title field so it won't display when you run the query. Run the query again. Your screen should resemble Figure 6.13.

FIGURE 6.13

Access returns the same 22 records even without the display of the criteria field.

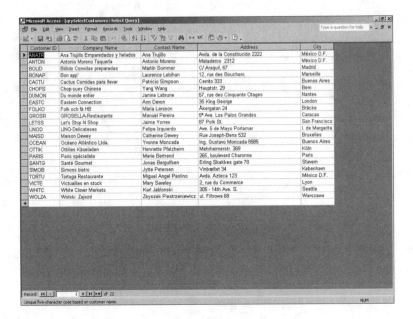

Tip

A field needs to be included in the query design view to have criteria entered for it, but it doesn't have to show in the query's output.

Quick Query Facts

There are a bevy of query tricks and short cuts that experienced Access users learn over time. Here are a few of the more common to give you a boost up to becoming proficient with Access 2002:

- To include all fields in a query, drag the asterisk from the field list box to any column in the query design grid.
- To include all fields of a table or query in a query, and also specify fields for criteria, drag the asterisk to the first column, and the fields to which you wish to add

criteria into the right columns. Add your criteria, but then uncheck the Show checkbox for the added fields.

- To remove a field from the query, highlight its column by clicking the header and then click the Delete key to remove it.

- To remove a field from the query, switch to SQL view and delete the field from the query in that view. SQL view is reflected in design view and vice-versa.

- To add another table or field to a query, click the Show Table button in the toolbar. Doing this opens up the Show Table list box.

- You can move or resize columns in the query's datasheet view just like you can in the table's datasheet view.

- You can widen or narrow rows in a query's datasheet view just like you can in a table's datasheet view.

- Altering column widths in design view does not affect the columns in query view and vice-versa.

- You can widen or narrow columns in the query design grid if you need more room to display long criteria or expressions (expressions come up soon).

- You can shrink the width of a field in design grid to zero to allow for other columns' display without affecting the display of the query in datasheet view.

- You can move a column in the query design grid just like you can move a column in datasheet view. Moving a column in design view changes the column's place in datasheet view. Moving a column in datasheet view does not change that column's location in the design view.

- Pull down the Sort row in any column to change the default order of a query (the default order is the sort created by the primary key).

- You can sort on multiple fields in the design view. Sort priority is from left to right. To give a sort a higher priority, move the column to the left of other sorted columns or drop the fields in a different order. You always can move the column back to the right in datasheet view without affecting the sort priority.

- You do not need to insert fields from the field list box into the query design grid in the same order as they appear in the list box. Access doesn't care.

- You can filter and sort, in datasheet view, queries that have sorts and criteria entered for them.

That's a good list to get you going in simple queries. The next section discusses including more than one table or query in a query.

6

Multi-table Queries

The normalization process splits data into logical, but smaller, "chunks." The point of this split is to increase efficiency, especially in optimizing data-entry chores and storage space requirements. However, there must be a way to reconstruct this split data or the efficiently stored data won't be terribly useful. The prime tool for data reconstruction in an Access database is the query.

The following task shows how to use data from two different linked tables to construct a datasheet containing elements from both tables. You can use this technique for queries using more than two tables. The only important element to remember is that for the rows to make logical sense, there must exist a logical link. In the case of this task, the link is the SupplierID field.

Before starting, take a look at Figure 6.14. This is the Day 6 database with the Tools, Relationships window opened. Note the two tables used for this task and their pre-existing link.

FIGURE 6.14

A multi-table query doesn't require an existing link between tables, but it saves a step.

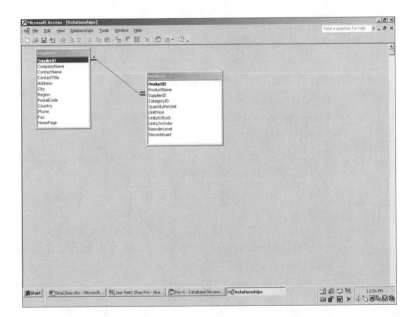

To preview the result of this Task, open up in datasheet view (or run) the query named qryFirstLink.

Task: Creating a Query with Multiple Tables Using the Design View

1. Launch Access and open the database called Day 6 located on your CD. This database contains several tables from the Northwind database.

2. Click the Queries button in the Object bar.

3. Click New to start a new query. Choose the design view.

4. Add the tables Products and Suppliers table to the query design grid. Your screen should resemble Figure 6.15.

FIGURE 6.15

Add in the objects to query to start a multi-table query, like a single table query.

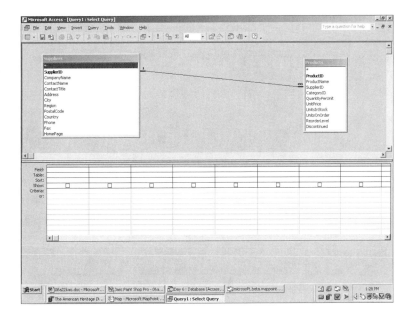

5. Note that the Suppliers table has information about parts suppliers, whereas the Products table includes information about the products of the suppliers. Because any supplier can vend many products, but each product can have only one supplier, the relationship is one-to-many.

6. Drag and drop the CompanyName field from Suppliers to the first column in the grid, and the ProductName field from Products to the second column. Your screen should resemble Figure 6.16.

7. Save the query using a name of your choice other than the name the sample data uses, qryFirstLink. If you wish to use that name, you'll overwrite the sample data.

6

▼

FIGURE 6.16

*Access links field data
from more than one
table even if the link
field doesn't exist in
the query grid or out-
put.*

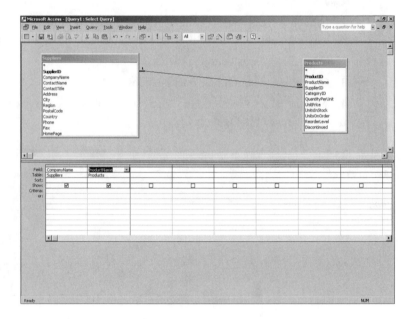

8. Click the Run button or choose datasheet view to see the results of this query. Your
   screen should resemble Figure 6.17.

FIGURE 6.17

*You've matched up all
the products with their
suppliers. In this sim-
ple step, you've con-
structed a new data
view from related
tables.*

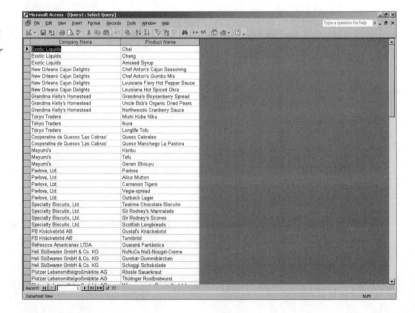

▼

▼

> **Tip**
>
> You don't need to have a link established in Tools, Relationships. You can include two or more tables into the query design grid and drag and drop the link there. Creating a link in Tool, Relationships creates a link in the query design grid, but creating a link in the query design grid does not create a link in Tools, Relationships.

▲

If you want, you can enter additional fields and the data will remain in synchronization due to the link field of SupplierID. To see how this worked, return to design view for this query and choose the SQL view. Figure 6.18 shows this view for the first two fields only.

FIGURE 6.18

The SQL view reveals all. In this case, you can see that Access included the SupplierID link behind the scenes to keep the data records in proper synchronization.

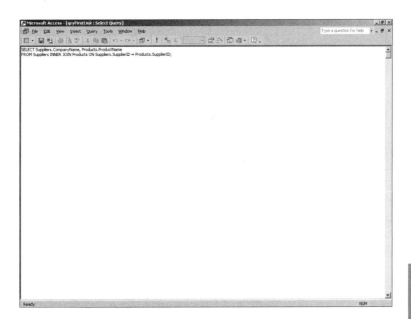

Here is the code from the SQL view. I've included it here because it's easier to read than in a screen shot.

```
SELECT Suppliers.CompanyName, Products.ProductName
FROM Suppliers INNER JOIN Products ON Suppliers.SupplierID =
Products.SupplierID;
```

> **Note**
>
> The SQL keyword ON specifies the link field for two or more tables.

6

Multi-table Queries Without Existing Links

You always can throw extra data into a query and Access won't really mind, but there's no reason to do that.

Your sample data includes a query called `qrySenseless`. Open that query in design view to see that it's the same query as the useful `qryFirstLink`, but with the `Customers` table added. There is no logical link between the `Customers` table and either the `Products` or `Suppliers` tables, so the resulting output doesn't make any sense—thus the name of this query.

Switch to datasheet view or run the query and you'll see that Access, a bit at sea as to how it should proceed given its illogical query, just repeats the same Customer for each record. Figure 6.19 documents Access' distress.

FIGURE 6.19

Adding unrelated data to a query just confuses the issue. Access carries on like a trooper, but there's nothing it can do to make a meaningful return from this query's design.

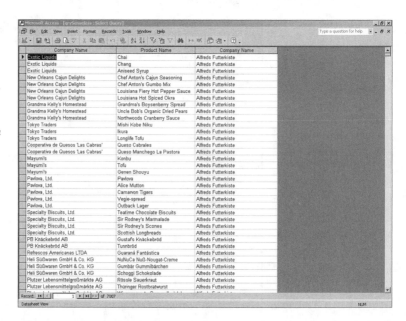

Actually, there is a link between these three tables, but it exists only as a path through two other tables, `Orders` and `Order Details`.

The following task uses those two tables to create a five-table query linking up the currently uncoordinated data shown in Figure 6.19.

Task: Creating a Multiple Table Query by Specifying the Links Between the Tables

1. This task only makes sense in context. If you aren't familiar with the material in this lesson, starting with the heading "Multi-table Queries," take a minute to look it over now.

2. Launch the query qrySensible in the queries group in design view. Your screen should resemble Figure 6.20. Note the two fields CustomerID in Customers and Orders tables.

FIGURE 6.20

You will need to create a link between Orders and Customers table.

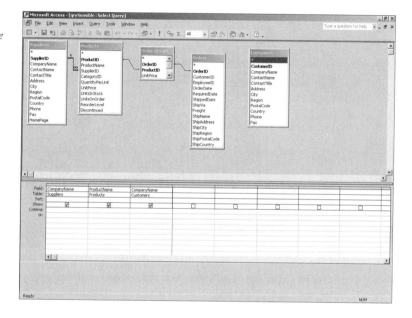

3. To create a link between the two tables, click in either table at the CustomerID field and drag to the CustomerID field in the other table dropping the link when you get to the second table. This establishes a link using the common field CustomerID.

4. Change your view to datasheet view or choose Run from the toolbar buttons.

5. Now the query returns a list of Products sold, the Company vending the product, and the Company who has bought the product.

Note

The Orders and Order Details tables contain information about customer orders.

▼

▼ 6. Return to design view for this query. Open the Sort combo box for the
CompanyName field in the Customers table. Choose Ascending. Switch again to
datasheet view. You now have a list of all Products purchased sorted by Customer
instead of Product. Your screen should resemble Figure 6.21.

7. Close the query, saving or discarding changes as you prefer.

FIGURE 6.21

*The query can be sort-
ed on any field just like
a single table query.*

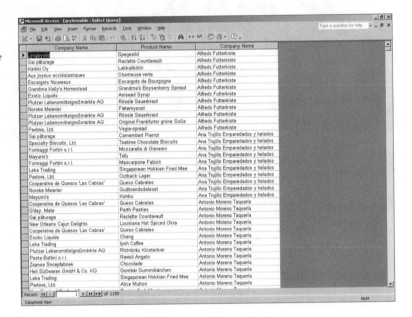

▲ This task has little business value, but it does demonstrate how you can get to anywhere
in a database as long as you can find a series of links to network into a logical construction.

Intermediate Criteria

The criteria examples so far today have been simple query by examples with the addition
of the OR and AND inclusive or exclusive. Criteria by example means using something like
"Cassel" or "Tirilee" on the Criteria row to return specific records.

A simple criteria example is only the very beginning of how you can select records using
a query. Here are a few often used criteria examples.

Wildcards in Like and Between

The following examples use the table, tblVoters, included as one of the objects in the database Day 6. This table is a real list of registered voters minus the voting record section. The key field is the Registration number.

The Like keyword combined with the wildcard asterisk character returns closely matching records. The Like keyword alone returns records the Access engine believes comes close to your example.

The sample database contains a query, qryVoters, that's simply the table tblVoters included with all fields and, at this point, no criteria or sorts. To see how the wildcard and Like keyword behave, proceed to the following task.

Task: Using Wildcards in the Criteria of a Query

1. Open the qryVoters query in design view. Your screen should resemble Figure 6.22.

2. Add the criteria **Like A*** in the Criteria row in the Surname column. Access adds quote marks around the A*. Tab or click out of the column. Switch to datasheet view or run the query.

FIGURE 6.22

Without any criteria, this query returns all the tblVoters records. That's about to change.

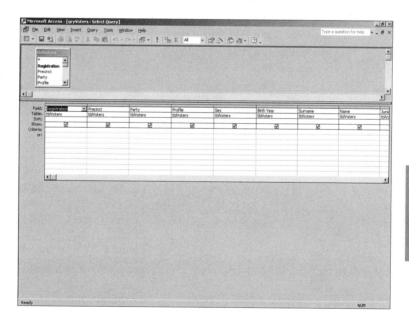

3. Access filters out all records except those having surnames starting with the letter A. Return to design view.

▼   4. Edit the criteria to read **Like "[A-D]*"**. Be sure to include the quote marks as shown. Run the query again. This time Access returns all records where the surname starts with an A, B, C, or D. Access understands the expression [A-D] as inclusive of the letters in between the Roman alphabet (in the English version of Access, anyway).

5. Return to design view. Edit the criteria to read **Like "*av*"**. Again switch to datasheet view. This time Access returns any records where the surname has the letters *a* and *v* sequentially within it.

6. Return to design view for this query. Edit the criteria to read **Like "ave?"**. Run the query. As you can see, the ? wildcard works by replacing a single character. In this case, the query returns all records where the surname starts with *ave* and has one more letter (or number, for that matter).

7. Return to design view. Remove any criterion from the Surname field. Edit the Criteria row of the Birth Year column to read **Between 1950 and 1960**. Run the query. Access selects records for voters born in 1950 through 1960 inclusive.

8. Return to design view. Edit the Birth Year criteria to read **>1960**. Run the query. Access selects records for voters born in 1960 or later.

9. One more example, and then it's on to other things. Return to design view and remove all criteria from the Birth Year field. Edit the Criteria row of Surname to read **Not Like "A*"**. Run the query. Access selects for any record where the surname does not start with the letter A. Close the query, saving or discarding changes
▲   as you see fit.

Table 6.1 shows some of the most often used query criteria expressions and their returns.

TABLE 6.1 Query Criteria Expressions

Expression	Returns
Between #12/1/98# and #2/3/99#	Dates from 12/1/98 and 2/3/98 inclusive
In ("Mary", "Louise", "Annie")	Records with Mary, Louise or Anne
" " (quotes with a space in between)	Records with a blank
IsNull	Records with no entry (null field)
Like "Cas?le"	Cas then any character followed by le
Like "*s"	Ends in s (not case-sensitive)
Like "v*"	Starts with v (not case-sensitive)

TABLE 6.1 continued

Expression	Returns
<1000	Less than 1000
1000	Equal to 1000
Like "[A-C]??"	Starts with A through C and has three characters
????	Any four characters
Len([Surname]) = Val(4)	Any surname of four characters
Right([Surname],2) = "is"	Any surname ending in the letters is.
Left([Surname],4) = "Cass"	Surnames starting with Cass

Summary

You can create a query using either the design view or a wizard. In many cases, the add fields facility of the wizard can save you a lot of time compared to using the design grid exclusively. While you also can create queries using SQL natively, that's an advanced topic, which is covered later.

This lesson covered select queries that are subsets of fields, records, or both, of other queries or tables. Once you've included the fields you wish in your query, you can add criteria to the design grid (or the SQL view) to narrow down the selection of your query. You can add criteria for any field included in a query even if that field doesn't show (or return) when the query's run.

You can do all the datasheet layout manipulation in a query that you can in a table's datasheet. Changes in field order in the datasheet view won't change the design view, but changes in field order in the design view alter the datasheet's layout.

You can sort on fields in the design grid. The sorting priority is left to right. You also can filter and sort in datasheet view just as you can with a table's datasheet view.

Adding criteria to different rows in different columns creates an OR query selecting records based on either criterion. Entering criteria on the same row for two or more columns creates an AND query requiring both criteria to be satisfied for a record return.

Using built-in Access functions and expressions, you can construct sophisticated query selections spanning dates, times, or alphanumeric strings.

6

Q&A

Q. Can I use the OR and AND selections in a filter?

A. Yes. Entering two field criteria in a filter by form creates an AND query. Using the OR keyword in a field creates an OR criterion.

Q. Does sorting in datasheet view take precedence over the design designated sort?

A. Yes it does. The last sort order holds reign.

Q. Can I use the greater than or lesser than signs for dates?

A. Yes. >#12/31/99# returns records where the date is at least the year 2000.

Q. Can I limit the number of records a query returns based on values relative to the dataset?

A. You can edit the Top Values box on the toolbar to a specific number of records or a percentage. Altering the Sort changes the order to the top or bottom values returned.

Workshop

The Workshop helps you solidify the skills you learned in this lesson. Answers to the quiz and exercises appear in Appendix A, "Answers to Quizzes."

Quiz

1. How can you filter for data by example in a datasheet?
2. What does the criterion >100 return?
3. What do the criteria "Cassel" AND "Orchant" yield in the Surname field of qryVoters?
4. You've set two sorts in the design view of a query. Which field is the primary sort?
5. What does the SQL keyword ON mean?
6. Can you select by one table's fields, but show another tables fields in a query?

Exercises

1. Locate the qryDataTypes in the database Day 6. This is a small query based on the table tblDateTypes. It has only a few records consisting of differing data type fields.

2. Open the query in design view to familiarize yourself with its structure. Switch to datasheet view to see that at this point it returns all the records in tblDataTypes. While in datasheet view, examine the field Memo (Data Type Memo and named Memo). Figure 6.23 shows this table in datasheet view.

FIGURE 6.23

The qryDataTypes is a good place to practice criteria.

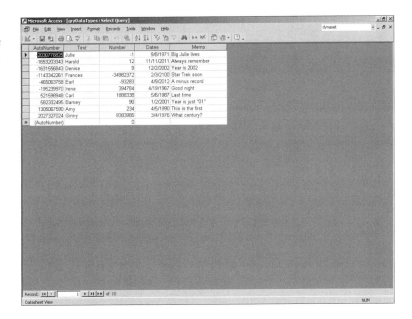

3. Return to design view. Enter a criterion for the Memo field you think should return at least one record. Run the query. Did you get your expected return?

4. Return to design view. Enter a sort order for the Memo field. Run the query. Did Access run as you expected?

5. Say you want to find only records after the year 2000 in this query. Enter >#1/1/2000# in the Dates column. Run the query. Did you get your expected return?

6. Close the query qryDataTypes and open in datasheet view the qryVoters. Click the Filter by Form button. Enter Like "A*" or Like "b*" in the Surname field. Apply the filter. Did it work as you expected it would?

7. Try some other likely filter expressions to see how they work.

8. Click the Filter by Form button again to return to the form. Add the filters "1970" in Birth Year and "M" in Sex. Apply the filter. Note that this filter is an "AND" query.

6

9. Return to the Filter by Form form by clicking the appropriate button. Note the Or tab in the lower-left corner of your screen.

10. Click the Or tab and enter **1969** for an additional criterion in `Birth Year`. Apply the filter. Did things work as you anticipated?

11. Open the View menu and choose SQL view. Notice that the criterion is part of the actual query.

12. Construct a criterion for `Surname` that will return only those records where the birth year is before 1940, and the surname ends in the letter *s*.

DAY 7

Basic Reports

This lesson covers the report basics. Because there are many similarities between form design and report design, this lesson skips lightly over some basics, assuming that you learned them in Day 5, "Simple Forms." This prevents a lot of repetition for those reading this book sequentially. If you're not familiar with the material on forms, this is a good time to at least skim over that lesson.

Today You Will Learn

A report generally is a printed version of the information in the tables in your database. Sometimes this information needs to be summarized, grouped, or presented differently than what the user can see directly within the tables. This lesson touches on the necessary basics to get you started in finding all about reports. Specifically you will learn about:

- The use of reports within Access
- The AutoReport Wizard (again)
- The Standard Report Wizard
- Using the report design view
- Grouping within a report

- Summing in a group
- Keeping a report running sum
- Subtotaling on reports
- Sorting in one or multiple levels within a report
- Viewing one or multiple pages of a report
- Report sections
- Manipulating group properties to your advantage
- Cutting, copying, and pasting controls on reports

Reports in Access

Reports tend to be forms idealized for non-current display. By non-current, I don't mean the data is dated, but that it isn't needed in real time. For example, if a customer calls up wanting to know the status of his order, a form would be the way to go about giving him the information even though a report could contain the same information. If the sales manager of your firm wants to know sales by region and by salesperson, a report would be the way to go even though a form could work.

Reports also differ from forms by being weighted to perform well with output devices such as Web pages or printers, while forms work best on screen. The Web has changed this slightly, where reports do duty as display-only pages while forms do double duty as display and edit/entry Web pages. For example, if you want to display your company's earnings over the Web you would most likely choose a report. If you want to take customer orders, your first choice would have to be a form.

Tip

Forms can display or accept user input such as edits. Reports are read-only objects.

Access does blur the line somewhat between reports and forms. For example, there's a Form Wizard for a pivot table form (cross tab) and pivot chart. These are display devices requiring no user input. Similarly forms can contain graphics or the entire form can be a graphic—again a non-input or edit use for a form. In no cases can a report accept user input, however.

Tip

I encourage you to create your reports using a wizard and then customizing them later on. Most folks find modifying the basic layout of a report wizard is shorter than making a report from scratch.

The AutoReport Wizard

The AutoReport Wizard behaves identically to the AutoForm Wizard although obviously the output is a report, not a form. Here's how it works.

Note

The following material, like in the past, is somewhat of a repeat of the material in Day 3, "Automatic Access." It's presented here for clarity of context and in a step-by-step rather than a survey form. Merrily skip over this stuff if it seems simple or repetitive to you.

Task: Using the AutoReport Wizard

1. Launch Access and open the Day 7 database. This database is part of the CD. Click the Queries button in the Object bar. Locate the table qryVoterAddresses. Click that object, but don't open it.

2. Locate the New Object button on the standard toolbar. That's the button that has something that looks like an icon with a lightning strike.

3. Click the button to open the combo box. Locate the AutoReport entry and click it. Access creates a report using this query as a record source. Your screen should resemble Figure 7.1.

FIGURE 7.1

The AutoReport quickly generates a very simple report.

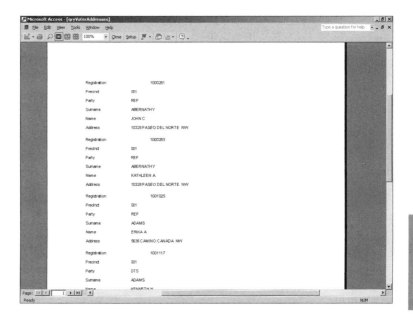

4. Save this report by choosing File, Save As from the main menu giving it the name **rptVoters** if you want to overwrite the sample objects or give it a name of your own choosing if you don't want to.

5. Close the report. Click the Reports button in the Object bar (if necessary) and note that your new form is now part of the report objects in Access.

> **Note**
>
> The reports in this lesson are based on a table of real voter data. The DTS for party affiliation means "did not state" party.

That's all there is to the AutoReport wizard. If you want to open this report in design view, you'll see how simple it is.

Report Wizard

The AutoReport is a wizard without options. There is also a general-purpose Report Wizard that's quite capable. The following task runs through a wizard session. Note that the facilities offered within this wizard should make your report-designing chores easier no matter what your level of expertise within Access.

Task: Using the Report Wizard

1. Launch Access and open the Day 7 database. This database is part of the CD. Click the Reports button in the Object bar.

2. Locate the New button on the database view toolbar. That's the button that has something that looks like a book with a star. Click that button to start a new report.

3. Choose Report Wizard from the main list box. Open the combo box at the bottom of the dialog box and choose the query qryVoterAddresses for this report. Your screen should resemble Figure 7.2.

4. Click OK to start the actual wizard process. The first dialog box is the familiar one where you specify which fields to include in the report. Choose them all. Click Next. The subsequent dialog box allows you to specify what if any fields to group on. Choose the Precinct field. Your screen should resemble Figure 7.3. Click Next.

> **Note**
>
> The meaning of a group within a report will become clear when this report is done and you preview it.

▼

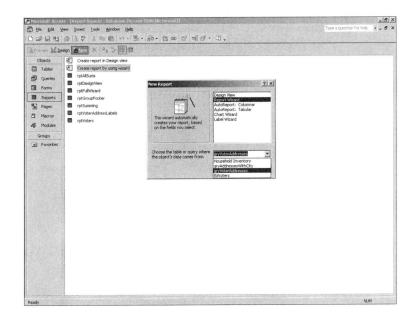

FIGURE 7.2

When you start the Report Wizard you start out by binding it to a table or query.

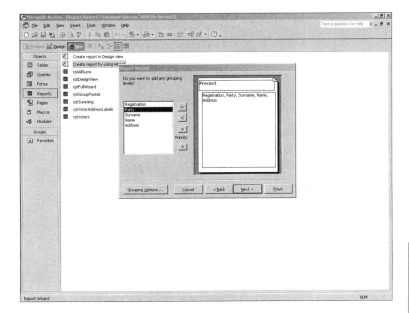

FIGURE 7.3

The full Report Wizard includes the ability to group on one or more fields.

7

▼ 5. Don't specify any sort order at this point. Although you will most likely want a sort order in a report of this nature, the purpose of this Task is to demonstrate the Report Wizard's nature. Sorting only slows down the previewing of this report. Click Next and the layout step is shown.

6. Choose Outline 1 for your report's layout. Leave all other fields at the default. Your screen should resemble Figure 7.4. Click Next to move on.

FIGURE 7.4

The wizard offers layouts suitable for almost any style of report.

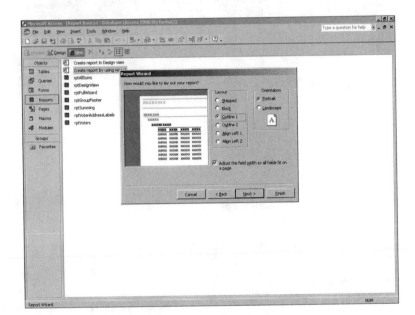

7. This example uses Soft Gray as a style for the report. Use that or one you prefer. The reason I used Soft Gray is that it reproduces well in a grayscale book. Click Next.

8. Name the report **rptBookDisplay**. Click Finish to preview your report. A report preview is a screen view of how your report will look on the Web (approximately)

▼ or from a printer. Figure 7.5. shows this report in Preview view.

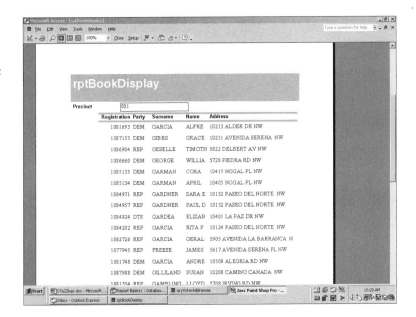

FIGURE 7.5

*Print Preview is a
screen rendition of
how a report will look
when printed.*

Report Preview Details

The report that you just generated groups voters under their precinct number and then
lists them in the order of their registration number. The registration number is the primary key for the table tblVoters. That is the table qryVoterAddresses uses. Because there
are no specified sort orders in either the query or the report, Access preserves this order
(but within the groups) for this report.

To see more than one report page at a time, locate the Two Pages or Multiple Pages buttons on the report toolbar. Click the Multiple Pages button and choose the 1×3 selection
in the first row to the far right. Your screen should resemble Figure 7.6.

To see a page in detail from the multi-page view, click the page with the cursor/
magnifying glass. Doing so zooms you to the page.

By examining this report, you can see the result of a report group. Remember you
grouped according to Precinct number. This sorts the precincts in ascending order (starting with 001) and groups every record belonging in that group under it sorted, in this
case, by its default sort order (primary key field).

7

FIGURE 7.6

You can see more than one page at a time. Depending on your monitor size and screen resolution, you might not have much detail in these multiple-page views.

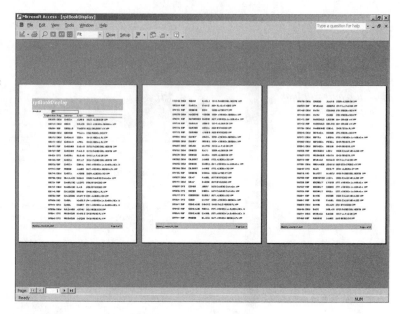

Similar uses of groups are

- To group employees under department number or supervisor
- To group customers under ZIP code or area code
- To group sales under salesmen
- To group customers under sales territory

I'm sure you can think up some other specific uses for groups in reports depending on your specific needs.

Note

This report might open very slowly on some machines. This is due to the need for Access to group the records. Grouping in a large dataset like the tblVoters requires a lot of processing power and disk read/write.

This report isn't perfect or even acceptable at this stage. Here are the major problems with this wizard-generated report:

- The Name field is too short to display all the letters in the first name. This might not be correctable due to the need to fit the entire report on a single $8^{1}/_{2} \times 11$ page.

- The header for this report is the same as the report name in the database view (I've created a special name for the screen shot example). This name (with convention) makes sense for developers to see in the database and other developer views, but makes for a poor header in a report for public display.

The next section addresses these issues.

The Report Design View

The report design view is similar, but not identical, to the form design view. All the skills learned in one view are fully transferable to the other. If you're unfamiliar with the form design view fundamentals covered in Day 5, this is a good time to review that material.

Without further ado, it's time to jump in and fix those elements of the report wizard that need addressing.

Task: Using Report Design View

1. Launch Access and open the Day 7 database. This database is part of the CD. Click the Reports button in the Object bar.

2. Locate the report called rptFullWizard, which is part of the sample data. I've further made this report look bad by reducing the party field to two characters. If you're using the report you just made, switch to design view and skip the part about modifying the party field width. If you're in the database view, highlight the report and click the Design button on the database view toolbar. This launches the report in design view. Your screen should resemble Figure 7.7.

3. Take a moment to look at this report in design view. Although it's a bit more complex than the forms yesterday, you should have a good idea of what's going on. The only totally new concepts are within the Page Footer section. You'll note two fields in that section one containing the function NOW(), on the left, and the objects Page and Pages on the right. The function NOW() places the current system date or time on a form, report or other object. The Page and Pages keywords display the current and total pages in a report or form respectively. So the NOW() function puts the current system date and time on the page footer of the report while the expression on the left displays the current page number and how many pages are in the entire report. Figure 7.8 shows the bottom of the first page of this report in Print Preview. Note that there are many pages in the entire report so don't try to print it unless you're ready for a long print run.

7

FIGURE 7.7

The report design view looks similar to form design view.

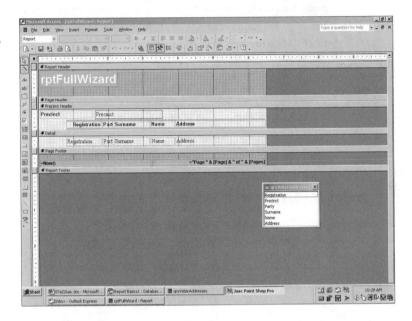

FIGURE 7.8

The built-in Access functions NOW( ), Page, *and* Pages *find good use in footers or headers for reports and forms.*

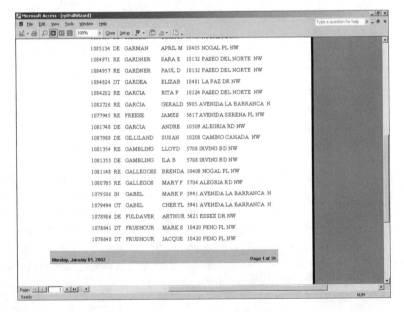

▼   4. The first thing to correct in this report is the field length for the two short fields.
        Right now the report goes to the right edge of the page so you can't just stretch
        these fields or you'll end up beyond the margins of this report. Doing so causes
        Access to print a left and right part of each page, making this report twice as many
        pages. Worse, with each logical page spread over two physical pages, the report
        loses cohesion. Here are the strategies you can do to address the field short fall.

        • Choose File, Page Setup to alter the size of the paper setup size, stretch the
          right page side, stretch the two short fields, and then print to the wider paper.

        • Choose File, Page Setup and reduce the margins of the page, thus giving you
          more room on the page, widen the right side of the report, and stretch the
          fields.

        • Choose File, Page Setup, and change the report from portrait to landscape
          layout.

        • Reduce the Address field and put the increase in the Party and Name fields.
          This works, but might truncate the addresses.

        • Move all the fields within the group to the left reducing the indent of the
          report and use the added room to make larger fields.

     5. This Task uses the last strategy, as it's the best approach in this case, but it might
        not be in all. The important concept here is not to disturb the relative position of
        the fields and their labels as you move them. The key to doing this is multiple
        selection.

     6. Click and drag to select all the fields and labels that need to be moved left.

Note | The labels for the fields are those above the Detail section. The fields or con-
       trols are those inside the Detail section.

        Look carefully at Figure 7.9 to see which fields need selecting. You can use either
        marquee select (click and drag) or the Shift+click method to choose multiple fields
        and labels.

     7. Drag the group of controls to the left about .5 inches (1 cm). When you're done,
        click away from the highlighted group to deselect it. Now select the Address field
        and label and drag it back to the right margin. Be careful not to drag it beyond the
        current right margin. Then select the gray line just above the field labels and
        extend it to cover the new span of the fields and their labels. Your screen should
▼   resemble Figure 7.10.

7

FIGURE 7.9

*Either marquee or
shift+click will select
multiple controls on a
report or form.*

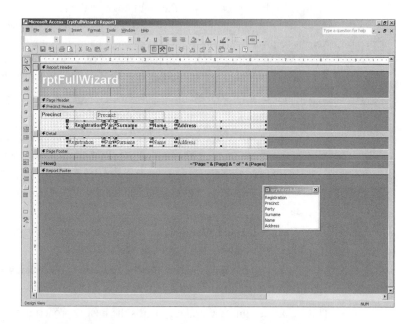

FIGURE 7.10

*Make sure when drag-
ging to move the field
and its label at the
same time to preserve
their relative positions.
You can restore their
positions if they get out
of sync, but that's an
extra step.*

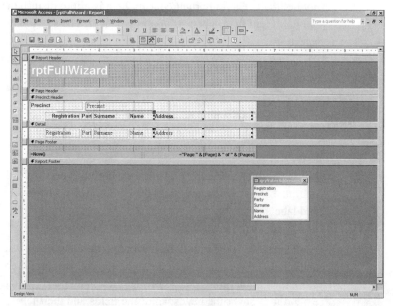

▼

Tip

There are many ways to ease your report and form design chores. While most folks and Microsoft prefer using the mouse to move fields, I like to use the cursor arrow keys. Instead of dragging the fields in step 6, try using the left arrow key.

Another way I like to ease my report writing woes is to highlight both the label and the field control when moving one to keep them indexed. You can move them independently by having the report properties snap to grid or by using the cursor keys, but why take the extra trouble if they're currently aligned and only need to be moved?

8. The next step requires a fine touch. You might also need to cycle between design and preview view to adjust the fields to the optimal width. Here's what needs to be done.

Tip

If you make a mistake when sizing or moving fields on a report, remember Ctrl+Z undoes your last action.

- Widen the Name field and label to the same width and then move them right until they abut against the Address field. You should use as much space as available for the Name field except for one character space reserved for widening the Party field (next step).
- Widen the Party field and label to accommodate the needed three characters for party affiliation. After you're done, your screen should resemble Figure 7.11.

Tip

Here's an easy way to adjust the position and size of report objects such as lines. Select the object, then open the Properties list box. Click the Format tab and note the position and size properties. Adjusting these numbers is easier than dragging these objects to the size and place you want them.

9. Save this report optionally using a new name (File, Save As). This example used the name rptDesignView for the save name. The completed example on the CD also replaced the double gray lines of the wizard (the ones above and below the field labels) with single double-width lines.

7

▼

FIGURE 7.11

The final step is to widen the Party *field to accommodate three-letter abbreviations.*

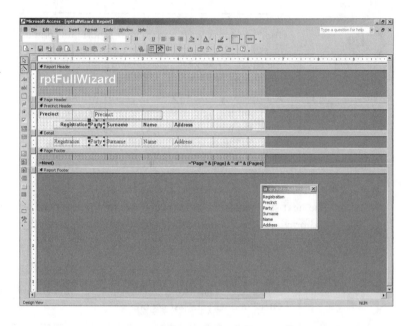

FIGURE 7.12

When run, this report now has more room for the Name *field and displays the full party label.*

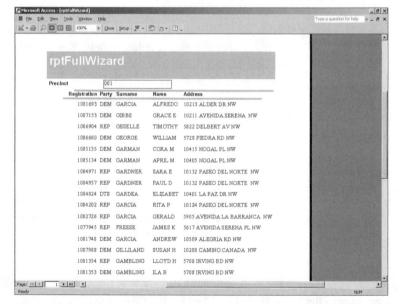

10. Switch your view to Print Preview by clicking that selection on the View button of the toolbar. Your screen should resemble Figure 7.12.

11. Return to design view. Adjust any fields that need adjustment. Click the label in the Report Header section. Open the Properties list box if it's not currently open.

12. Locate the Format tab in the Properties list box and click it. Locate the Caption property and edit it to **Voters by Precinct**. Your screen should resemble Figure 7.13.

FIGURE 7.13

You can edit a label either directly in the label box or from the Properties list box.

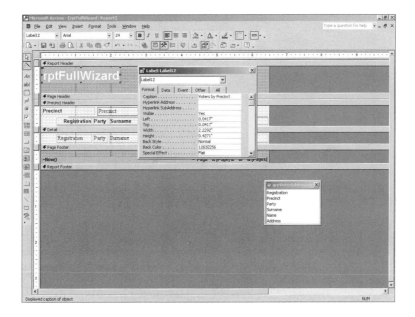

13. Tab (or press Enter) out of the Caption field. The new caption appears in the label. You'll need to widen the label to accommodate the new caption. Switch back to Print Preview. Your screen should resemble Figure 7.14.

Note

The report still isn't cosmetically perfect because, unless you also moved the dividing lines along with the fields, the soft gray dividing lines now aren't aligned with each other or with the fields. You move or size lines like you do any other object in report design view. Figure 7.14 shows the line misaligned. The sample data rptDesignView shows them in the right position.

7

FIGURE 7.14

The report now displays the fields properly and has a more reasonable report header name (caption).

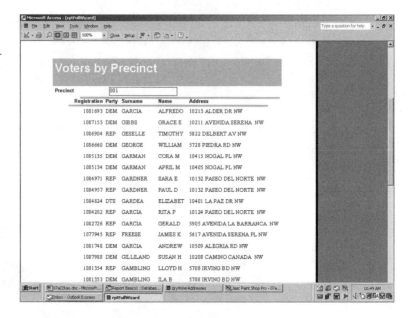

Grouping in Reports

The wizard took care of grouping all the voters within their precincts, but you could have easily done this yourself. Manually creating a group consists of three steps:

1. Open the Sorting and Grouping dialog box to specify the field to group on and a sort order for that field. You can open the Sorting and Grouping dialog by clicking the Sorting and Grouping button on the standard toolbar. It's the button with the two equal signs with a couple of parenthesis on it.

2. Set the properties for the group.

3. Make any header or footer entries for the group.

As usual, these steps are fairly easy to grasp after seeing them in an example. To see how a grouping works, locate the report called `rptDesignView` in the sample data. You might have saved this report under a name of your own choosing. Use either your report or the one that's part of the sample data. Open it in design view. Click the Sorting and Grouping button on the toolbar. Your screen should resemble Figure 7.15.

FIGURE 7.15

The Sorting and Grouping dialog box has two columns and a very important section for group properties.

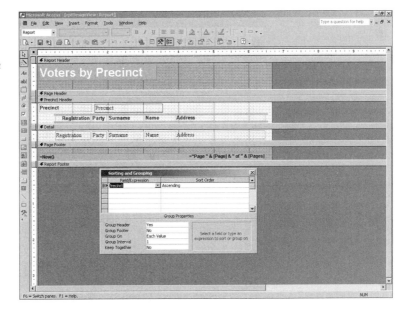

Note that you can enter (or select using the combo box) a field or an expression to group on. That's the left column. The right column lets you specify if you want to sort the groups in ascending (lowest first) or descending order.

 Note

You must specify a sort order for groups. Access does not permit you to use a random order for report groups.

The Group

Click in the Field/Expression column. Open the combo box and choose Party for a group criterion. Return to Print Preview. Because you've not changed the header information (precinct), you'll find you've grouped by party for each precinct. Figure 7.16 shows the results of using Party for a group.

Return to design view and likewise return the group criterion to Precinct.

7

FIGURE 7.16

If you really want to change the group to Party *instead of* Precinct, *you should also change the header or footer information. However, this example serves well as a grouping demonstration.*

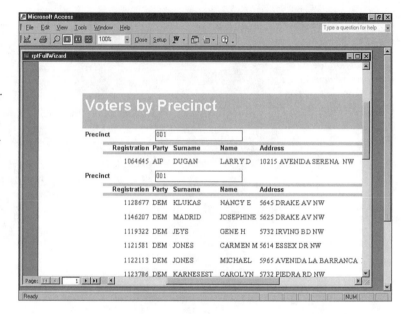

Properties

It's vital you understand and set the group properties correctly to get the results you want. Here are the properties along with an explanation of what each does:

- Group Header—Does the group get a header section for itself? If you say yes, you'll have a place to enter a label or labels telling your users what each group represents. Access groups just fine without a header, but the results might not be obvious to your users.

- Group Footer—Like a header, a footer is useful for delimiting and labeling groups. Footers also serve for holding expressions that subtotal or otherwise display summary information about a group. To give you an idea how handy this facility is, try the task that follows this listing.

- Group On—Selects the criterion to start a new group. In other words, what breaks a grouping? There are different options depending on the underlying data type of the field. For more information look at the context help by selecting the Group On property and then pressing the F1 key.

- Group Interval—Selects the number of characters Access should examine to decide whether a string is a group. Let's say you have data entries such as Ford Explorer, Ford Ranger, and Ford Expedition. You'd want Access to go beyond the word Ford to decide when a group starts.

- Keep Together—Selects whether Access should keep groups together on a page. In many cases this is impossible, because all the information in a group might not take only one page. In this case, the group will be broken up on to as many pages as needed.

Task: Counting Voters by Precinct

1. Open the report `rptDesignView` in design view. Choose File, Save As and give the report a distinct name. This example uses `rptGroupFooter`.

2. Open the Sorting and Group dialog box. Click in the Precinct entry in the Field/Expression column. Locate the `Group Footer` property in the Group Properties pane. Double-click that property to toggle it to Yes. Close the Sorting and Grouping dialog box by clicking its button in the toolbar (toggle).

> **Note**
>
> The purpose in saving a report right after opening is to prevent over writing the sample data. If you don't care about this (and it's not a big deal since you can restore from the CD), you can skip saving the files in each task.

3. Locate the Text Box tool in the toolbox. If the toolbox isn't open, you can open it by clicking on the View, Toolbox menu. Click the Text Box tool. Click anywhere over to the right of the group footer to insert an unbound text box in the report footer section. Open the Properties list box (if necessary) and enter

   `=Count([Precinct])`

   for a `Control Source` for this text box. Edit the label for this text box by clicking it and editing its `Caption` property to read something like **Precinct Count** or another entry of your preference. Your screen should resemble Figure 7.17.

FIGURE 7.17

This group footer includes a function to count voters within precincts and report the results in the group footer section.

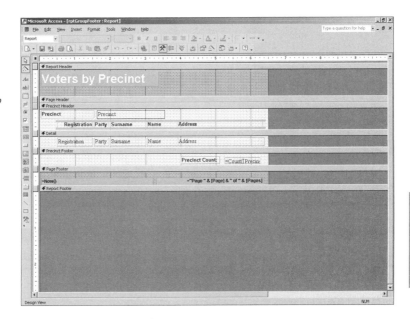

7

> **Tip**
>
> This task is moving along quickly. If you feel a bit lost, open up the report `rptGroupFooter` and examine the Sorting and Grouping dialog box, along with the two new entries in the Group footer section.

4. Return to Print Preview. Move to the end of the report (the query has been limited to only precinct 001) by clicking the last record VCR button at the bottom of the screen. After the last entry you'll see an entry with your label and a count of the voters in this precinct. Your screen should resemble Figure 7.18.

FIGURE 7.18

At the end of each group, Access gives you a count of the members of the group.

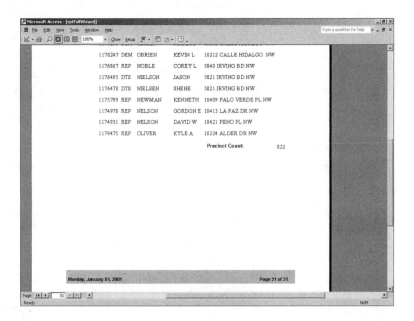

5. Close this report, optionally saving changes. If you want to see the counting function better presented, open up the query `qryVoterAddresses` in design view, remove the criterion for the `Precinct` field, and then rerun the report in print preview. Scroll through the report, noting how many voters exist in each precinct.

> **Note**
>
> The expression in the unbound text box is based on a built-in function of Access, `Count()`. The entire expression, `=Count([Precinct])`, tells Access to place the count (number) of occurrences for Precinct in the Group footer section. Access assumes you want to count the number of occurrences in

each group. Had you placed the expression in a text box in the page footer section, you would have gotten a count of entries on each page. If you would have placed the expression in a text box in the report footer or header, Access would have returned a count of all the occurrences in the entire report.

Mailing Labels

Access 2002 has built into it a wizard for making mailing labels. Essentially this wizard creates a label layout using the fields within a table or the query you want to use and then formats the report to a page size that fits a particular label or sheet of labels. Unlike other report wizards, the mailing label wizard turns out a report that requires no modification.

Note

Due to the built-in information of mailing label size in the wizard, almost all Access developers use the Label Wizard to design their mailing labels. In some instances, you'll want to modify the wizard's output, but not nearly as often as with other wizard-generated reports.

The following task takes you through the Mailing Label Wizard.

Task: Using the Mailing Label Wizard

1. Launch Access if necessary. Click the Reports button in the Object bar of the database view. Click New to start a new report. Choose the Label Wizard for a Report Wizard and the query `qryAddressesWithCity` for a query to bind the report to. Your screen should resemble Figure 7.19.

Tip

You might want to examine this query and its bound table in both views before proceeding. The query has one field created by an expression while another non-displayed field limits the query's return to a single precinct. The reason for limiting the query's selection is to make the query and the report run faster.

2. Click OK to start the wizard. The first dialog box requires you to specify a label by number and vendor or by size. The combo box at the bottom right lets you select a vendor. The large list box at the center allows you to choose from the vendor's selection. If your vendor or label isn't listed, choose the closest based on layout and size. This example uses a Herma 5074 and English measure. Click Next to move on.

7

FIGURE 7.19

The Label Wizard requires a bound table or query before it can run.

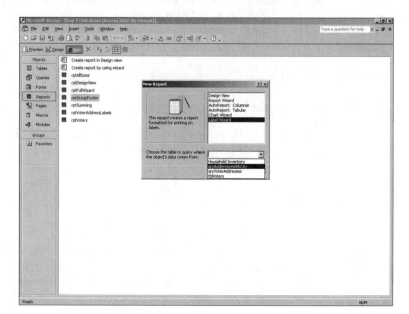

3. The next dialog box allows you to specify a font and its characteristics. Unless you have a good reason not to, leave this information at default as they work well for labels.

4. Click Next to move on to the only tricky part of the Label Wizard. Here you have to lay out the label itself. Don't just put all fields over to be included in the label as that puts them all on one line. You need to specify which fields you want on the label (in this case, all of them) and where they go. To move a field from the Available Fields list to the label, highlight it and then click the Move (caret) button. To move to a new line in the label, press Enter. You enter punctuation such as spaces or commas by literally entering those characters using your keyboard. Figure 7.20 shows the finished label. Note there is no separate field for State. That's because this field has been included in the City field. While this is improper database design, it makes no difference in this context.

5. After your label looks similar to Figure 7.20, click Next to move on. In the next dialog box choose to sort on Surname. Click Next.

6. Give the report the name **rptVoterAddressLabels** or one of your own choosing if you don't want to overwrite the sample data. Click Finish to see your label. Your screen should resemble Figure 7.21.

FIGURE 7.20

The Label Wizard asks you to not only include fields, but to lay them out as you want to see them in the finished label.

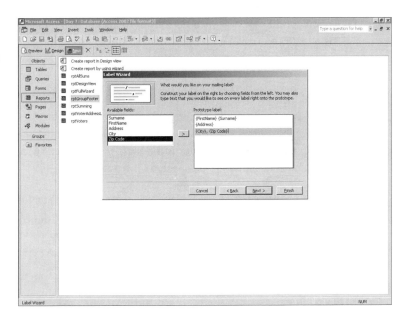

FIGURE 7.21

The current mailing label works fine although it's not aesthetically perfect.

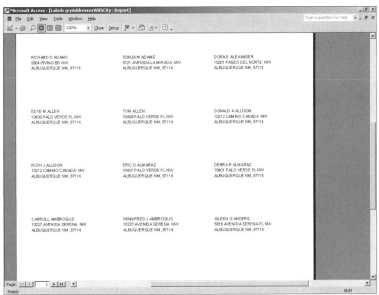

7. Switch to design view for this report. Note that the first line and third lines of the label are expressions.

Expression Details Explained

Take a look at the expressions used for the fields in the mailing label report. The first field is a text box control with the Control Source:

```
= [FirstName]&" "&[Surname]
```

The equal sign (=) tells Access that what follows is an expression.

After the FirstName field (including the square brackets), the next character is the ampersand. That concatenates the FirstName field to the next character, a " ". The double quotes mean the next character is a literal, in this case a space. The next character is an ampersand concatenating the space with the Surname field.

 Note   Previous versions of Access required the Trim() function to format the mailing labels correctly. Access 2002 has Trim() implied for each field.

Page Layout Settings

Critical to the success of any report is the page layout setting for that report. Launch Access, load the Day 7 database, click the Reports button in the Object bar, and then click report rptVoters part of the sample data. Click the entry File, Page Setup from the main menu. Review the three tabs for page layout, noting the type of data each hold. The entries are self-explanatory.

Close the Page Layout dialog box either by clicking OK or Cancel. Highlight the report rptVoterAddressLabels, also part of the sample data. Again open the File, Page Setup dialog box. The critical part of this setup is in the Columns tab.

 Note   You can't choose another report for the Page Setup dialog box while the dialog box is open because the box is modal. Modal means that it grabs the entire attention of the application or even the system preventing the focus from going anywhere else. The Print Setup dialog box is application modal. As long as it's open, nothing else in Access accepts the focus.

Click that tab and note the precise settings for the two columns that make up the report. Similarly, the Labels Wizard has assigned precise margin data for this report. The combination of the two make for a label report that hits the labels sheet after sheet without lag or creep.

Note Newcomers to Access often try to format a page the size of a label and print the report to that size, figuring that by defining a page as having the dimensions of a label they center the data on the label. While this does work after a fashion, it means that you'll end up with one label per page rather than the desired multi-label for each page (8.5×11" in the US).

Tip If your Access reports shoot out extra pages—either blank or with only a few characters on them—you've created a report that's bigger than the net size of the page. The net size of a page is the actual page size minus the sum of the opposing margins. A page that is 8.5" wide with 1" margins left and right has a 6.5" maximum print area. Print Preview shows you if you'll be seeing extra pages. Always run Print Preview for a few pages (at least) before committing a report to a printer.

Sums, Subtotals, and Running Sums

Many reports require you to sum or subtotal a field or fields. Naturally you can only sum on a numeric field such as those formatted as a Number or Currency data types.

There are several ways to sum in a report:

- Sum for a section such a page or group
- Sum for an entire report
- Keep a running sum of sections or groups

The key function to summing in Access is the SUM() function. Here's how to use that function as well as how to do the various summing chores.

Task: Using Sum Functions in Reports

1. Launch Access if necessary. Click the Reports button in the Object bar of the database view. Locate the report rptSumming and open it in Print Preview. Your screen should resemble Figure 7.22.

2. Switch to design view for this report. Save it using a different name than it currently has. This example uses the name rptAllSums, but you should use a different name if you don't want to overwrite the sample data.

3. Open the Sorting and Grouping dialog box by clicking its button in the toolbar. Locate the Category Name group at the top and then click it. Then locate the Group Footer property in the Group Properties pane at the bottom, and toggle this to Yes. Close the Grouping and Sorting dialog box to get it out of the way.

7

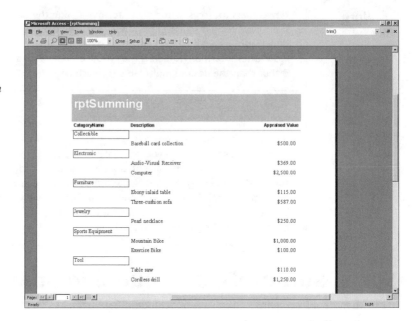

FIGURE 7.22

Here is the basic report complete with groups, but without any summing function as of now.

4. Click the text box control in the toolbox. If the toolbox isn't visible, drop down the View menu and toggle it to be visible. Click in the CategoryName footer section to insert an unbound text box control there. Your screen should resemble Figure 7.23.

FIGURE 7.23

This unbound control has a summing function as part of its Control Source.

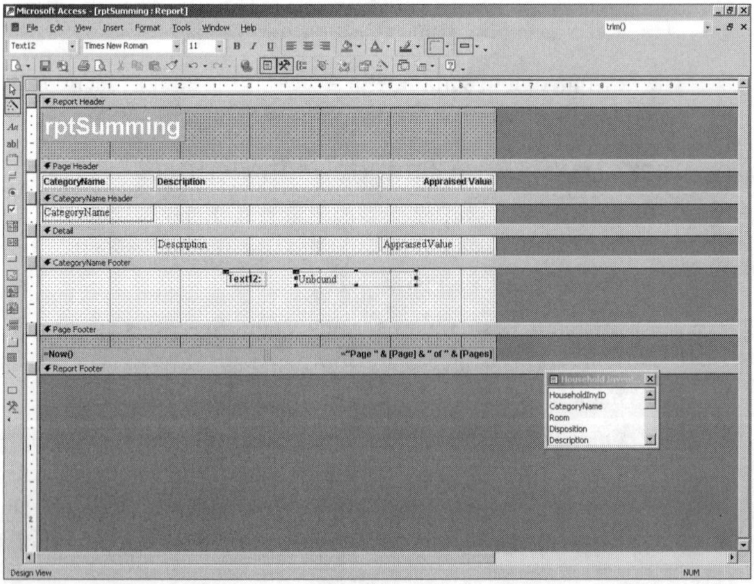

Tip   Widen the Group Footer section to make this part of the task easier.

5. Open the Properties list box if necessary. Click the Data tab and click in the
    `Control Source` property. Press Shift+F2 to open the Zoom box for this property.

Tip   You can open a Zoom box for many areas in Access including any property
          list box and the query design grid.

6. Enter the expression

    `=Sum([AppraisedValue])`

    for this property. Your screen should resemble Figure 7.24.

FIGURE 7.24

*Entering an expression
using the Zoom box is
a lot easier on the eyes
than squinting at the
Properties list box.*

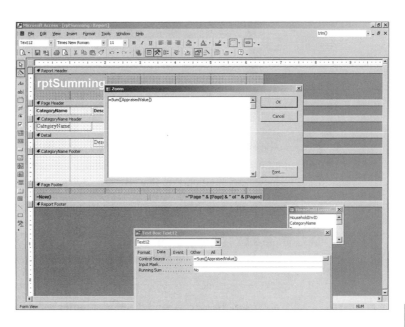

Tip   Clicking the Font button in the Zoom box allows you to specify a font and
          font size for your Zoom box.

7

▼   7. Click OK to close the Zoom box. Click the label area of the unbound text box.
       Click the Format tab of the Properties list box. Locate the property `Caption` and
       edit that to read **Group Sum** or anything you prefer. Switch to Print Preview and
       note that you now have a sum for every group on the report. Your screen should
       resemble Figure 7.25.

FIGURE 7.25

*Getting a subtotal for
every group or catego-
ry was as simple as
adding a function to
the section.*

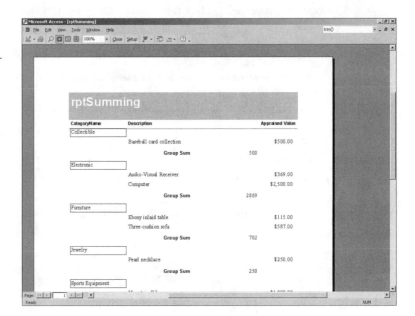

   8. Return to design view. Click the unbound text control and locate the Format tab in
      the Properties list box. Locate the Format entry, pull down the combo box, locate
      the Currency entry, and choose that. Return to Print Preview.

   9. Return to Design view. Marquee select the unbound text control from the previous
      steps and press Ctrl+C to copy it to the clipboard. Click in the Report Footer sec-
      tion and press Ctrl+V to paste this control to that section. Alter the label to read
      Report Sum. Your screen should resemble Figure 7.26.

Note

You might have to expand the Report footer section to be visible or wide
enough to accept the new controls.

▼ 10. Return to Print Preview. Scroll to the bottom of the report and note that you not
       only have sums for each group, but the entire report.

FIGURE 7.26

Adding the same controls to the Report footer section summed the entire report instead of a group.

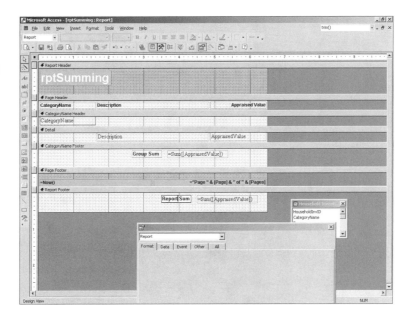

Note

The reason the controls summed differently is that Access sums across the span or influence of the section in which the control is placed. Placing the SUM( ) function in the group section summed the group. Placing it in the Report Footer section summed the report.

11. This gets a bit tricky. Widen the group section to accommodate another control. Highlight both the Group Sum text box and its label. Choose Edit, Copy from the menu. Choose Edit, Paste from the menu to paste a new copy of the old control into the same section. Edit the label to read **Running Sum**. Your screen should resemble Figure 7.27.

12. Click the data part of the control (as opposed to the label). Locate the property Running Sum in the Data tab of the Properties dialog box. Change the value from No to Over All.

13. Return to Print Preview. You now have a report that sums for every group (subtotal), keeps a running sum for all groups, and gives you a grand sum for the entire report. Your screen should resemble Figure 7.28.

7

FIGURE 7.27

A simple property change alters this control from a duplicate of an existing one into a running sum control.

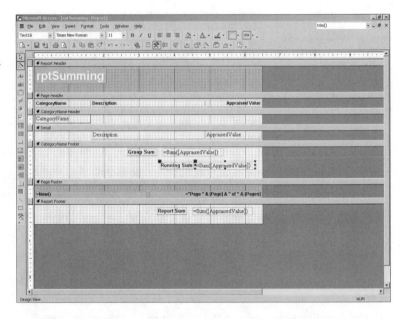

FIGURE 7.28

The report is now replete with sums of all sorts or, to put it another way, all sorts of sums.

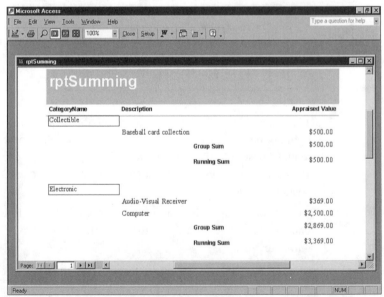

Tip

If you want to put the finishing touches on this report, align the fields appropriately, select all the unbound fields, open the Properties dialog box, locate the Format tab, pull down the Format property, and choose the Currency format. If you want to see the results of these operations, open the report `rptAllSums` in any view. I've done it for you.

Summary

Reports are to printers what forms are to screens. That's a bit of a simplification, but it does make the point of what each specializes in. The chief difference operationally between a report and a form is that a report has no way to edit or enter data while a form does.

The skills you learn in report design or form design are almost entirely transferable from one to the other. Each object has an adjustable design grid, controls that can be bound or unbound, a toolbox, and the critical Properties list box for controls and other objects compromising the report. Additionally, both objects are constructed of sections.

You can use built-in (or user defined) functions in unbound controls in reports similar to how you can use them in forms. The function, when applicable, operates differently depending on the section it's located within. For example, a control with the COUNT() function in a group section counts occurrences over the group.

Q&A

Q. If a report has one page, is there any difference between the SUM() function in the page and report section?

A. Technically they behave differently, but in practice, they return the same values.

Q. Can I sum within the Detail section?

A. Sure. Your results will be the sum of the objects contained within that section.

Q. Can I subtract, multiply and divide in an expression?

A. Yes. For example, the expression

```
=[SalesPrice]-[Cost]
```

subtracts the value of SalesPrice from Cost or gives you the gross margin. Similarly you can group using standard algebraic notation. For example,

```
=([SalesPrice]-[Cost])/Count([Widgets])
```

figures the gross margin and then divides by the number of widgets.

7

Q. Do you need to use [] for every field in an expression?

A. Technically no, but you do for any field with a space in the Name (Control Name for those old VB hands). If you do use [] for field names, Access never makes an error, whereas it might without those brackets. They also immediately identify a field from a function to the developer. Use them always.

Q. Can I use color in reports?

A. Sure and there are a few Microsoft-supplied styles in the wizard that use color.

Q. Can I include pictures in a report?

A. Yes. There are bound and unbound image controls available for reports just as there are for forms.

Workshop

The Workshop helps you solidify the skills you learned in this lesson. Answers to the quiz appear in Appendix A, "Answers to Quizzes."

Quiz

1. How can you customize which fields the AutoReport Wizard includes in a report?
2. Is there any difference binding a report to a query versus a table?
3. What does the `Keep Together` property of a group do?
4. What does the `[Pages]` return in the report header?
5. What does the white space in between the double quotes in the following expression do?

   `=[Name]&" "&[LastName]`

Exercises

1. Open the report `rptAllSums` in design view.
2. Widen the Pager Footer section to accommodate a new field.
3. Copy the control along with its label that yields the sum of each group (not the running sum).
4. Paste that control into the Page footer section. Edit the label to be sensible for a page summation rather than a group summation.
5. Switch to print preview. Is the control working as you expected?
6. Return to design view.
7. Paste the control into the Report Header section. Edit the label accordingly.
8. Return to Print Preview. Is the value in the header the same as the footer?
9. Close the report optionally saving changes.

WEEK 1

In Review

This week you learned about how relationships exist between data. You learned that Access stores data in tables, and you can use forms, reports, and queries to turn data into information. You already know enough about Access to begin developing your own databases. You know how to create forms and reports to present information to users of your database and how to use queries to present select records or combination of records to users. However, Access is a powerful database tool, and to realize the full potential of Access, there is much more to learn.

1

2

3

4

5

6

7

WEEK 2

At a Glance

Week 2 will get you started building on the skills you gained in Week 1. You already know the basics of tables, forms, and reports. This week you will learn to make more sophisticated ones.

Day 8, "A Macro Primer," you will learn how to create Access macros and how they have a valuable place in developing databases. You will learn under what situations they are best used and when you should turn to another alternative.

Day 9, "Refining Your Tables," you will learn how imperative it is that you correctly construct your data tables. You will learn just how much the design of tables can enhance or inhibit your database. You will learn how effective Access can be at insuring data integrity with validation rules and input masks.

Day 10, "Improving Your Forms," will show you how to make your forms both intuitive and interesting for users. The more intuitive and interesting your products are, the more users will like and use them.

Day 11, "Manipulating Queries," will show you how to join multiple tables together to present a complete picture of information to users.

Day 12, "Getting Reports Right," you will see how to create reports to present complex information to your users. You will learn that the presentation of information is directly related to how easily it is understood. Your users might not fully appreciate a really good report, but they can recognize a poor, useless one.

8

9

10

11

12

13

14

Day 13, "Learning Structured Query Language or SQL," will show you how Access is built on an SQL foundation. You don't need to learn or use SQL directly to use Access even up to a fairly high level, but you do need to use SQL to take full advantage of Access.

Day 14, "Special Query Uses," you will explore some of the more advanced query capabilities available in Access 2002. You won't use these types of queries every day, but at some point you'll need them.

DAY 8

A Macro Primer

If you've been reading the book sequentially, you'll note that I've been going over material more or less (one big exception) in the order objects appear in the database view. Here I'm going to skip data access pages and go right to macros.

Today You Will Learn

From working with people who use Access, I found that (contrary to what major trade magazines want you to believe) macros are put to good use for a variety of tasks. There are several good reasons for this, and in this lesson, you will learn the basics in order to put them to use in your database application. Specifically in this lesson you will learn

- What macros do in Access
- When to use macros
- The elements of macros
- How to use macros with events
- How to group macros into one macro object
- How to create macros that run conditionally

Although macros are not the answer to every problem in Access, they enable you to extend your database application easily. This is especially true if you don't have a background in programming. In fact, many professional developers started out programming their database applications with macros. So, let's see what we can learn in this lesson that you can put to good use in your database applications.

Macros and Access

Macros, in the form of recorded and then played-back keystrokes, acted like a simple programming language in the first popular program for IBM-compatible PCs—Lotus 1-2-3 for DOS version 1. Later, advanced users of 1-2-3 started using commands along with recorded keystrokes to write rudimentary programs for that three-in-one program.

"Real" computer programmers, those who used Turbo Pascal or BASICA, despised these macro programmers for invading their turf with this "fake" programming system. Yet the popularity of 1-2-3's macro language and the ease with which untrained personnel could get results, assured the widespread use of this system, not only in 1-2-3, but other successor spreadsheets such as Excel.

Now, twenty years later, little has changed. Access includes both a macro language that incorporates commands and a keystroke player. It also sports a BASIC programming language, Visual Basic for Applications (VBA). Programmers of the BASIC persuasion, usually sporting either a lot of self-training or formal education in computers, look down upon macros, as well as those who use them. However the popularity of macros, their ease of use, and their utility hasn't been lost on either Microsoft or the millions of people who automate their applications using this system.

In a bit of irony, there are certain things that only macros, and not pure VBA, can do. The existence of these tasks, marked by the VBA keyword

```
DoCmd
```

remains a sore point for the VBA-only cadres.

And The Point Is?

The reason I've gone into this longish introduction about macros is that many users will encounter anti-macro attitudes during their career. While in theory, the arguments made against macros (such as their lack of any error traps) is valid, what's equally valid is that there are tens of millions of applications running macros with no difficulties whatsoever.

Keep in mind several points about macros and VBA:

8

- Use macros sparingly, only when there isn't a way to do the task in VBA, and only when you're reasonably sure the blind running method of macros won't harm your application.

- Most developers find that VBA-launched macros via the DoCmd keyword are easier to debug than macros created using the macro design view.

- Don't use macros if you believe there is a reasonable chance that they might put your application in an error condition.

- Avoid using SendKeys whenever possible. While this macro keystroke playback facility is the only way to do certain things, the nature of its run profile makes it very easy for it to land your application in trouble.

> **Note**
> The concepts of keyword, event, error trap, and others used in this lesson might not be clear to you at this point. Just try to get a general sense of things now and come back to this section later after learning about macros and VBA in subsequent lessons. By then, it'll all make sense if it doesn't now.

> **Note**
> Microsoft has tried to address both the desires of Access developers who like macros and those who fear them due to their lack of error traps by creating, for forms and reports, an On Error event that can trigger a macro or VBA code that can then respond to that error.

Elements of a Macro

Back at Day 2, "Learning the Basics to Develop an Access Database Application," you saw how a simple macro could react to a mouse cursor moving over an area of the screen (the mouse corral). There are four elements to a macro, one of which is optional:

- **Event**—The reason the macro "fires" or runs. Some event examples are a form control gaining or losing focus, a mouse cursor moving over an area, a keystroke, or a form load.

- **Action**—What the macro roughly does. Some actions are load object, close object, requery, launch another application, or delete object.

- **Action arguments (properties)**—To what specifics the action applies to. For example, when you use Access to create a macro that opens the form frmDataEntry, the action is to open a form while the property of that action is the form frmDataEntry.

- **Conditions**—You can program your macros to only fire (or run) when certain conditions (such as a field having a specific value) exist. The conditional ability of macros is considerably less developed than in VBA, but still useful as you'll see later in this lesson.

The Macro Design Grid

The macro design view is similar to other design views you've seen in previous lessons. Figure 8.1 shows this grid.

FIGURE 8.1

The macro design view is a grid with a context-sensitive Action Arguments list section at its bottom.

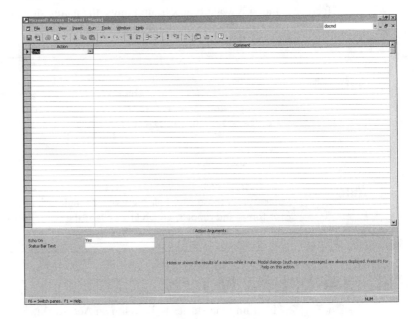

> **Note**
>
> The Conditions column doesn't appear in Figure 8.1. If you want to see it, click its toggle button in the toolbar. You'll also see a Macro Names toggle button in this toolbar. This toggles a column to group macros under a single macro name.

A Very Simple Macro

The following exercise results in a free-standing macro that displays a special type of dialog box called a message box. Windows uses various styles of message boxes to display messages upon the occurrence of certain events.

The point of this task is to familiarize you with the Actions and Action Arguments areas of the macro design view.

Task: Using the Message Box Macro

1. Launch Access and open the Day 8 database. This database is part of the CD. Click the Macros button in the Object bar. Click New in the database view toolbar to start a new macro. Your screen should resemble Figure 8.1, but have no entry in the Action column yet.

Note   I put an action in for Figure 8.1 to open up the Action Arguments area of the macro design grid.

2. Click in the Action column at the first row. This changes the row into a combo box. Pull down (expand) the combo box. Scroll down to find the action called MsgBox. Your screen should resemble Figure 8.2.

FIGURE 8.2

The list of actions for macros is part of a combo box. You can enter values directly or pick them from a list.

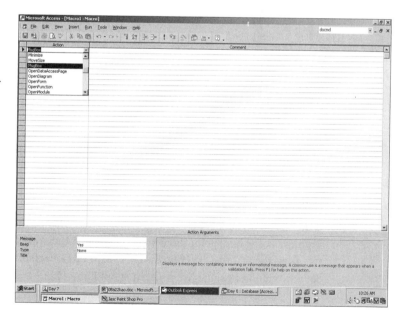

Tip   When you click in the Action area, press the first letter of the action you want to use (in this case m). Access scrolls to the first action that starts with *m*. This is the express train to finding actions on the list.

▼   3. Locate the Message line in the Action Arguments section of the design grid. Enter
       a message—for example

       Overdrawn at the memory bank!

       or any message of your preference. The specific message is unimportant.

    4. Locate the Title line in Action Arguments and type

       Message from your RAM

       or any other title for the message box you prefer. As with the message above, the
       specific wording is unimportant. Your screen should resemble Figure 8.3.

FIGURE 8.3

*You can customize
what your message is
like using the Action
Arguments section of
the macro design view.*

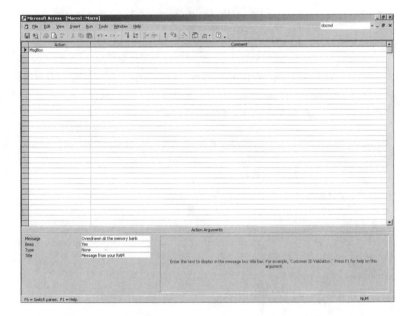

    5. Click the Run button on the toolbar. Access prompts you to save this macro. Do so
       using the name **mcrFirst** if you are alright over writing the sample data or another
       if you're not. After saving, Access displays your new message box with your cus-
       tom message and title. If your computer is sound-enabled, you also hear the
▼   default Windows sound. Your screen should resemble Figure 8.4.

FIGURE 8.4

Creating a message box with a custom message takes only a few seconds.

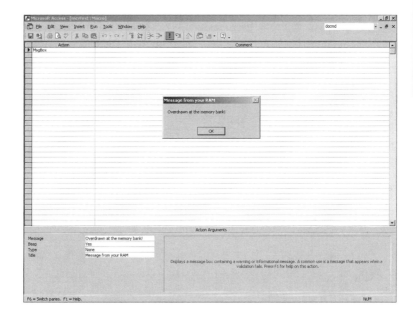

Actions in a macro execute sequentially from the top of the design view to the bottom unless a condition prevents them from occurring at all. To see this in action for yourself, open the macro mcrFirst in design view, and then add another message box action along with a different title and message. Figure 8.5 shows the design view of such a macro.

FIGURE 8.5

Macros execute actions sequentially from top to bottom unless a condition prevents execution of one or more actions.

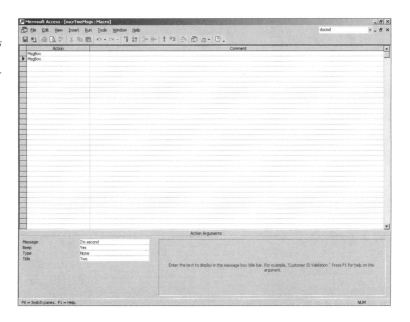

Run the macro. Access prompts you to save the macro. Do so and the macro runs. As soon as you clear the first message box, the second one appears. Figure 8.6 shows the second macro action executing. This rather silly macro is part of your sample data under the name `mcrTwoMsgs`.

FIGURE 8.6

As soon as you clear the first action, the second executes.

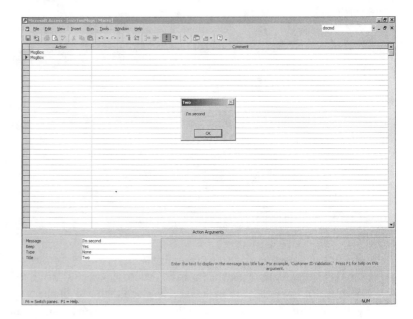

Note

Again, as in earlier lessons, I often use impractical examples to make a point. I can't think of why you'd have an unconditional macro that displays two message boxes in sequence in a real application, but the purpose of this demonstration was to show the default execution order of macros.

Deleting and Inserting Macro Actions

The next task isn't helped at all by having two macro actions, so it's time to remove the second. To do so, highlight the entire line where the action appears by clicking the gray square that's the equivalent of the record selector. This is directly to the left of the Action entry. When you hit the right spot, the entire macro line is highlighted.

Figure 8.7 shows the line highlighted with the cursor over the area you must click to make it so.

FIGURE 8.7

To delete or insert a line, you highlight a row in the macro design view.

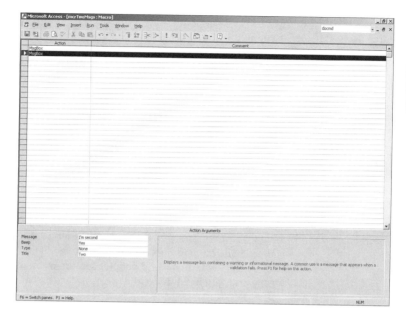

Press the Delete (or Del) key to remove this line. You also can choose Delete from the Edit menu to remove a row.

If you wanted to insert a macro action in between two existing ones, highlight the lower one and then press the Insert (or Ins) key. You can also click in the row where you want a row to be inserted above, and choose Insert, Rows from the main menu.

Shift+click and Ctrl+click work for multiple selections in the macro design grid as well. You can use these techniques to insert or delete multiple rows.

Macros and Events

The macro mcrFirst is interesting, but useless unless it conveys a worthwhile message. For a message box to do so, it must appear at a required or desired time.

A macro's execution should always be triggered by a specific event. A successful Access developer not only does a good job designing macros (or VBA code), but also attaches those macros to the proper event. It takes a bit of thinking and experience before you can reliably find the correct event for your macros and VBA code.

For example, take the two events for a text box, After Update and On Lost Focus. You might decide you want a macro to execute after a user makes an entry in a text box. Logically, you understand that after users make an entry, they'll move out of the field either using the Tab key, the Enter key, or a mouse click. That causes the text box control to lose focus so you might attach the macro to the On Lost Focus event.

That wouldn't be right simply because a person can cause the loss of focus on a control without making any data entry or edits. The right event for execution after a user makes a data entry is the After Update.

> The key to knowing if your macros are attached to the right event is testing. There are always unpredictable user actions you must, as a developer, account for. Testing using real people, other than your own predictable self, is the right way to make sure your application works in the field as you envisioned it would when you designed it.
>
> Using the example in this section, the On Lost Focus event would work just fine if you were sure that every time the user gave a field the focus, he'd edit or update it and then move on. However, field-testing proves that that's not the case with real world people. Because of the inconvenience of the real world, you need to use the After Update event.

The following section gives you a few ideas of events and how they work with different form controls. The specifics in this section apply to reports as well as forms.

> The Help system for Access is extremely useful for learning about Events. In fact, most Access developers use Help extensively when designing their applications. To see a short note on any event, click in the Event's line and look at the Status bar. To see full help text on an Event, click in its area in Properties and press F1.

Task: Associating Events and Macros

1. Launch Access and open the Day 8 database. This database is on the CD in the Day 8 folder. Click the Forms button in the Object bar. Note the location of the form frmEventPractice. This form has several controls ready for macro attachment. Each example uses the macro mcrFirst for a macro to attach or bind to an event.

2. Highlight the form frmEventPractice and click Design in the database view toolbar to open it in design view. Your screen should resemble Figure 8.8.

3. Click the command button bearing the label "Click Me". If necessary, open the Properties list box by choosing it from the toolbar or the View menu.

FIGURE **8.8**

*The sample data has a
form ready for some
macro practice.*

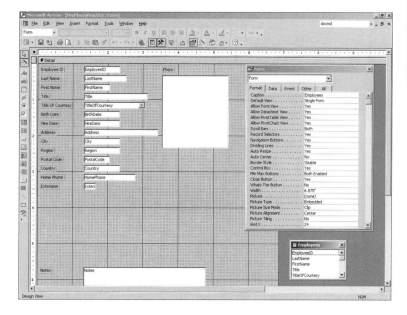

4. Click the Event tab in the Properties list box. Locate the property On Click. Click
   in the area to the right of the Event label. This converts the line to a combo box.
   The entries in the combo box are macros that are defined in your database. Pull
   down the combo box and choose mcrFirst from the list. Figure 8.9 shows what
   your screen should look like after you finish this operation.

5. Switch to form view by clicking the View button in the toolbar. Click the Click Me
   button. Your screen should resemble Figure 8.10.

6. Clear the message box and return to design view. Clear the On Click event from
   the command button's Event listing. Click in the purple area of the rectangle that
   says "I'm a Box."

Tip

The "I'm a Box" control consists of a label control inserted over a rectangle
control. Both have a 3D characteristic added and sport different colors. You
can achieve the stacked effect for controls by, well, stacking them in this
manner.

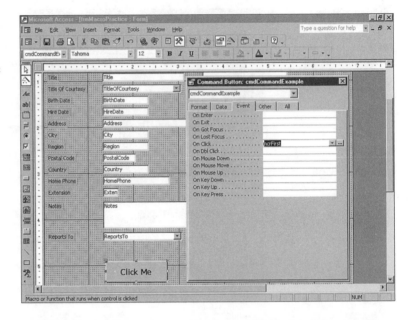

FIGURE 8.9

To associate a macro with a specific event, you can choose it from the drop-down list.

FIGURE 8.10

Now each time you click the command button, the macro fires.

7. Locate the `Mouse Move` event in the Properties list box, pull down the combo box, and then choose `mcrFirst` from the list. Return to form view. Move your mouse around, but not over the rectangle control. Move the mouse over this control. The macro fires. Return to design view.

8. Clear the `Mouse Move` event for the rectangle control. Click in the unbound text box control below the command button. Add the macro to the `On Got Focus` event of the text box. Return to form view. The macro executes immediately because the unbound text control is first in Tab Order so gets the focus on form open. Clear the message box.

9. Click the command button. Nothing should happen if you've cleared the event from this control. Click back in the unbound text control. The macro again executes as the control regains the focus.

10. Return to design view. Remove the macro from the `On Got Focus` event and add it to the `After Update` event. Return to form view.

11. This time the macro doesn't fire on form open, because there hasn't been an update to the control. Click the command button. Click back in the text control. Add any entry (such as the letter *d*) to the control. Tab away from the text box. The macro fires as you can see in Figure 8.11.

FIGURE 8.11

You can enter and exit the unbound control indefinitely without the macro firing. However, if you do any updates to the control, the macro fires upon the loss of focus.

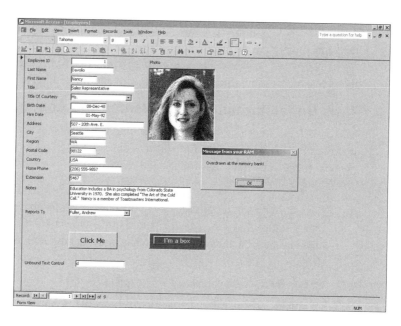

▼
▲

12. Experiment with other events. Feel free to add different controls to this form to practice with their events, too. When you're done, close the form discarding changes. If you want to preserve the modified form as a learning experience, you can always save it using a different name.

Macro Names

The most common actions for macros is to open and close objects (usually forms or reports), to display message boxes, and to go to controls. If you created a macro object for every event that you needed to respond to, you could have scores of macro objects in your database view. Macro Names take care of this by letting you group sets of macro actions within the same macro object. For example, if you create several macros for one of your forms, you can combine them into one macro object. This keeps you better organized and, with some care in naming that macro object, you can tell just by looking at the name where those macros are used.

What makes macro names so confusing is that they have nothing to do with the naming of the macro object that you see in the database view. Microsoft, in all its wisdom, didn't name this column Macro Groups, which is what I would have named it. If you think of "Macro Group" instead of "Macro Name," you'll be less confused.

The following task shows you how to combine multiple macro objects into one that does the same thing but uses macro names. The macro objects mcrOpenImOpen and mcrCloseImOpen open and close the form frmImOpen. You can use the same techniques to open and close any object (or do any macro action) within Access.

Task: Understanding Macro Names and Common Actions

This task demonstrates how to combine multiple macro objects into one macro object that does exactly what the multiple macros did. We are going to take the macro objects mcrOpenImOpen and mcrCloseImOpen and move the macro actions into a new macro object.

1. Launch Access and open the Day 8 database. This database is on the CD under the Day 8 folder. Click the Macros button in the Object bar. Create a macro object by clicking the New button on the toolbar in the database view. This new macro name defaults to Macro1.

2. Switch back to the database view by pressing the F11 key.

3. Locate the mcrOpenImOpen macro and highlight it. Click the Design button on the toolbar in the database view.

4. Locate the mcrCloseImOpen macro and highlight it. Click the Design button on the toolbar in the database view.

▼

▼   5. Position your open design view windows so that you can see all three at the same
       time. An easy way to do this is to click on Windows, Tile Horizontally from the
       menu and the Minimize the database view. Your screen should look similar to the
       one shown in Figure 8.12.

FIGURE 8.12

*The macros are open
in design view.*

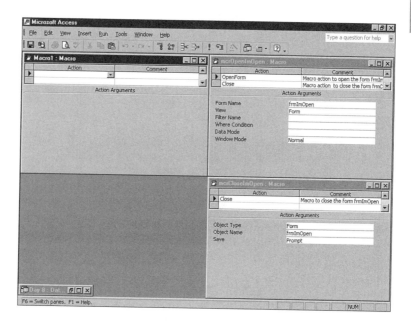

6. Click the mcrOpenImOpen macro design window to select it. Select the first row.

7. Shift-right-click the second row and select Copy from the context menu.

8. Click on the Macro1 macro design window to select it. Right-click in the first row
   and select Paste from the context menu. Your screen should now look like the one
   in Figure 8.13.

9. Click on the mcrCloseImOpen macro design window to select it. Copy the first row
   by selecting the row. Right-click and select Copy from the context menu.

10. Click back on the Macro1 macro design window to select it. Right-click in the
    third row and select Paste from the context menu. Close both mcrOpenImOpen and
    the mcrCloseImOpen macro. Your screen should now look like the one in Figure
    8.14.

       Notice that we now have a problem. If you were to map out the steps of the
       macro as it is, you would notice that the form, frmImOpen gets opened in the
       first step, but gets closed in the third action. It's a good thing we aren't fin-
       ished yet, because this macro doesn't do what it needs to do. We need to sep-
▼   arate the actions by using macro names.

FIGURE 8.13

The mcrOpenImOpen macro actions copied into the new macro.

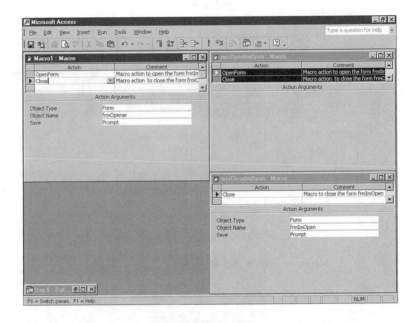

FIGURE 8.14

Both the mcrOpenImOpen and mcrCloseImOpen macro actions copied into the new macro.

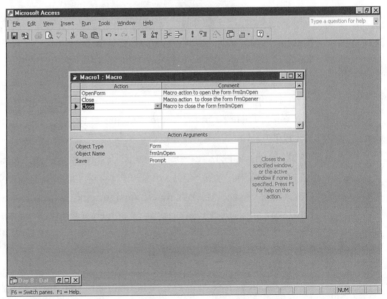

▼ 11. If you don't have a Macro Name column in the design view, locate and click the Macro Names button on the standard toolbar. If you have trouble locating the Macro Names button, click View, Macro Names from the menu.

12. Click in the Macro Names column in the first row and type **OpenImOpen**. All the actions will still be executed but we will remedy that in the next step.

13. Click in the Macro Names column in the third row and type **CloseImOpen**. Your screen should look like the one in Figure 8.15.

FIGURE 8.15

You now have two sub-macros.

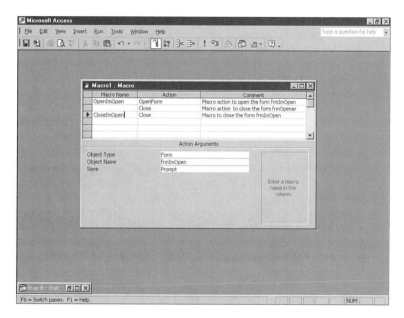

You now have created two separate sub-macros with the one macro object. We still have to reattach the events so that the correct macro is called.

14. Save the macro by clicking on the Save button on the standard toolbar. Save the macro as mcrOpenAndClose. Close the design view of the macro.

15. Press the F11 key to locate and bring up the database view. Click the Forms button in the Object bar and locate and click on the frmOpener form to highlight it. Click the Design button on the toolbar in the database view to open the form in design view.

16. Locate and click on the Command0 button. If the Properties window isn't open, right-click the button and select Properties from the context menu. Go to the Event
▼ tab in the Properties window. Your screen should look like Figure 8.16.

▼

FIGURE 8.16

The properties window open to Event tab for the Command0 *button on the* frmOpener *form.*

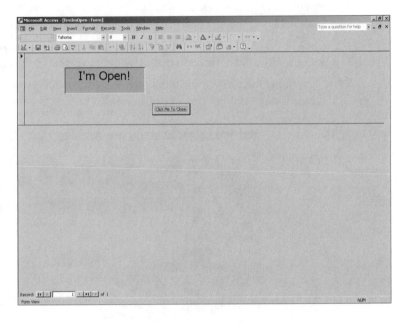

17. Locate and open the combo box in the On Click event. Currently the value that is in the On Click event is the old mcrOpenImOpen macro. Select the mcrOpenandClose.OpenImOpen value. Your screen should look like Figure 8.17.

FIGURE 8.17

The mcrOpenandClose. OpenImOpen *will execute instead of the* mcrOpenImOpen *macro.*

▼

▼ 18. Close the form frmOpener accepting to save the changes. Open the form
frmImOpen in design view. Click the command button and examine its On Click
event. It contains the macro mcrCloseImOpen.

19. Change this macro to point to mcrOpenandClose.CloseImOpen. Again refer to this
sub-macro and you'll see that when you click the button, you close the currently
open form, frmImOpen.

20. Try putting our changes into action. Close the form frmImOpen accepting to
save the changes. Back at the database view, double-click the form frmOpener.
Your screen should resemble Figure 8.18.

FIGURE 8.18

The form frmOpener *is
ready to execute the
first macro*
mcrOpenandClose.
OpenImOpen.

21. Click on the Click Me to Open a Form button on the frmOpener form. The form
frmImOpen opens and then closes the frmOpener form. Your screen should resemble Figure 8.19.

FIGURE 8.19

The form frmImOpen
*was opened by the
event generated when
you clicked the button.*

22. Click the Click Me to Close button. You have now replaced the functionality of the
two macros with the new macro. You can now delete the mcrOpenImOpen and
▲ mcrCloseImOpen macros.

More About Macro Actions

There are many additional macro actions available to you using either the macro design
grid or through VBA. Most, if not all, of the actions are self-explanatory by their names.
Keep in mind that you have two excellent sources for information about macro actions
including examples for their use.

The first line of explanation is the status bar of the macro design view. Open the Action combo box, choose an action, and you'll get a short explanation of how that action operates. Additionally, the Action Arguments exposed contextually when you choose an action gives you a good hint as to what sort of objects or behaviors you can expect from that action.

Finally, there is online help. Microsoft has assembled a rather exhaustive reference type help for developers. Help won't teach you how to use Access, but it works as a reference type resource for details most developers, if not all, don't want to commit to memory.

Even the most accomplished developers don't want to memorize all the macro actions, much less the Action Arguments for each action. They use online help regularly. Now that you have a feel for how to create a macro and how to associate the macro action with its Action Arguments and an event, you're ready to explore the various actions and how they operate in a full Access project.

Only one topic remains: conditional macros. The next section covers that.

Conditional Macros

A conditional macro tests for a condition and then fires when that condition is true. Truth in macros, as in all computer topics, doesn't refer to metaphysics or some obscure brand of anti-existentialism, but to the fundament of truth—whether a statement matches a condition.

To create a conditional macro, you only need to add the step of constructing a conditional statement, and then associating it with a macro. Associating the macro with an event automatically also associates the conditional statement to the event.

A conditional statement is an expression with a logical component that's either explicit or implicit. You've seen statements before in previous lessons. For example, this is an expression:

```
Sum([Sales])
```

Add a logical conditional part like this:

```
Sum([Sales]) < 500
```

And what you're really saying is, "If the total sales are less than 500."

The condition creates a program branch. A branch is an essential, perhaps the essential, element in computer programming. The computer tests for a condition and then executes one way if the condition is met, another if the condition isn't met. Failing to execute is a way of executing, just as not deciding an issue is a decision to accept the default situation.

8

The variety of conditional branching within the macro world is much less than in VBA. While macros do a good job of firing this way if a condition is true, or not firing (or firing a different way) if the condition is false or different, once your conditional needs grow slightly complex, you should investigate using VBA instead of macros.

This doesn't mean, as some VBA purists would have you believe, that using conditional macros is a bad idea, but like any shortcut, macros should be used only when appropriate.

 Tip

Use VBA for branching if you, as a developer, believe there is any reasonable chance for an error condition to exist or develop over the course of the branch. Remember, you can trap and handle errors using VBA while the errors trap you in the macro world.

The following task creates a conditional macro and uses it in a simple, but illustrative, way as a check to make sure your users enter data in a required field. This is one way to make sure your users enter data. Another way is to make the field have the `Required` property in table design view.

However, this method has certain advantages that make it more desirable to you in some circumstances. It's also a good demonstration of a fairly complex macro with a conditional branch.

Task: Specifying Conditions in Your Macro

▼ TASK

1. Launch Access and open the `Day 8` database. This database is on the CD in the Day 8 folder. Click the Forms button in the Object bar. Note the location of the form `frmMyTwoFields`. Open this form in design view. Your screen should resemble Figure 8.20. Note it has two controls, both text boxes. One is `txtName` and the other `txtSurname` along with their labels. These controls are unbound, but the task would work the same were they bound to a table or report. Close the form once you're familiar with it.

 Tip

You can keep this form open (active) and switch to the macro design grid by pressing F11 and choosing Macros from the Object bar of the database view. The reason this book closes and then opens views is to keep things simple and focused. You can either do like the book, or differently, if you choose. Your outcomes won't differ.

▼

FIGURE 8.20

*This simple form is the
test bed for a condi-
tional macro.*

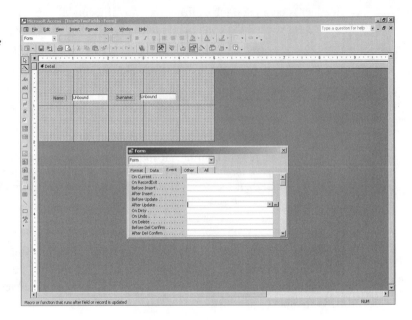

2. Click the Macros button in the database view Object bar and choose New to start a
   new macro.

3. Choose as the first Action your old friend `MsgBox`. Enter the following for a
   `Message` property:

   You need to enter a name

   For the `Title` property:

   Empty Field Warning

   Change the `Type` property to the following:

   Warning!

4. Click the Conditions button on the toolbar to expose the Conditions column (if
   necessary). Type the following on the same row as the message box action:

   IsNull([txtName])

   Your screen should resemble Figure 8.21.

5. Save the macro giving it the name `mcrConditions`, or one of your own choosing if
   you don't want to overwrite the sample data.

8

FIGURE 8.21

The completed conditional macro as of this point.

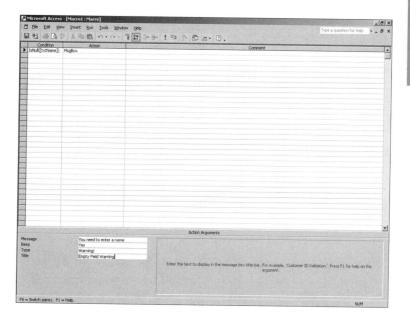

Note

If you try running this macro, nothing occurs. This is because the condition can't be met. Access tells you it can't find the object you're testing to see if it's Null.

6. Close the macro design grid. Open the form frmMyTwoFields in design view. Associate the macro you just created with the On Lost Focus event of the txtName field. Your screen should resemble Figure 8.22.

7. Switch to form view. Enter some data in the Name field. Tab away to the Surname field. Nothing should occur other than the cursor moves.

8. Click back into the Name field. Remove any entry in this field thus making it null (empty or void). Tab away again. This time your message box appears.

9. However, there is a problem at this point from a developer view. The cursor remains in the Surname field after you clear the message box. The desirable action for this macro is to not only tell the user that there is a need for an entry in Name, but to also take him back there to make sure he does so. Close the form saving changes or saving under a new name if you want to preserve the original form from the sample data.

FIGURE 8.22

The stage is now set to test the new conditional macro.

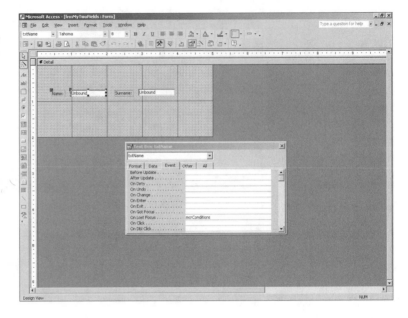

10. Return to the macro mcrConditions in design view. Click in the Conditions row below the existing condition and enter an ellipsis (...).

11. Enter an action GoToControl and enter a property to have the cursor skip to the control txtSurname. Repeat these two steps again but adding the property txtName as the second property.

12. The ellipsis continues the condition to the next line and the GoToControl skips the cursor to the control specified in the Action Argument. Now when you leave the Name field null (empty), you'll see a message box advising you of your entry error and find the focus back in the Name field ready for data entry.

Summary

Macros are, in general, the most controversial section of Access. A significant number of Access "super experts" would have Microsoft eliminate macros from the program, thus forcing everybody into using VBA for programming chores.

These people make a good case in theory. Macros can't handle error conditions as VBA can and their operation is similar to "close your eyes and fire." That's the theory. The fact is that the vast majority of Access developers use macros—often extensively—with good

8

result. The truth is that you shouldn't be afraid of using macros. If you find that in some circumstances they lead your users into error conditions they can't easily recover from, then modify your use of macros for those circumstances.

Also keep in mind that you can't stretch Access' programming possibilities to their utter extent using macros alone. As cool as macros are for doing simple chores like opening or closing forms, knowing macros isn't a substitute for learning VBA if you're determined to become a proficient Access developer.

You create a macro by opening the macro design grid, specifying a macro action and filling in the Action Arguments. You can optionally specify a macro name to group macros under one name in the database view. You also can specify conditions for the macro to execute.

The final step to creating a macro is to associate an event (usually in a report or form) with a macro.

Tip

> A macro named Autoexec at the database view fires automatically upon an application's startup. The name must be Autoexec, not mcrAutoexec, because that is the name that Access was programmed to look for.

Q&A

Q. Can I call a macro from VBA or VBA from a macro?

A. The DoCmd VBA statement is a call to a macro. The RunCode macro action can call a VBA sub or function. So the answer is yes and yes.

Q. Can a macro control the entries in a set of controls?

A. The SetValue action, usually accompanied by a condition can do this. Before using SetValue with conditional statements to examine and set a series of values, take a look at the Select-Case statement for VBA.

Q. Can I set an expression as a macro action?

A. Yes. Precede the expression with the equal sign (=).

Q. Why did you warn against the SendKeys action earlier in the lesson?

A. SendKeys blindly sends keystrokes (hard interrupts) to the application. If an unanticipated object has or gains focus during this macro action, your results could be anywhere from odd to disastrous. Use with care.

Q. Can I use macros to suppress spurious error message boxes?

A. The SetWarnings macro action can do this. Set the action to SetWarnings and the Action Argument to **No**. Be sure to bracket your action by reactivating warnings later when you want them to reappear.

Q. How can I eliminate the flash and boom of a long series of macro actions executing?

A. Set the macro action to Echo and the Echo On argument to **No**. You also can set a text for the status bar to display while you're suppressing the macro flash display. Be sure to bracket the Echo statement when you want to show the macro display again.

Workshop

The Workshop helps you solidify the skills you learned in this lesson. Answers to the quiz and exercises appear in Appendix A, "Answers to Quizzes."

Quiz

1. What constitutes properties for a macro action?
2. Do entries in the macro Name column appear in the database view?
3. Do you need to precede a condition with an equal sign?
4. What does the following condition mean?

   [City]<>"New York"

5. Is the following expression valid?

   Between #4/5/98# and #4/5/99#

Exercises

1. Open the form frmMacroPractice (in the Day 8 database) in form and design view to familiarize yourself with it.
2. Start a new macro.
3. Create a macro action to go to a new record for this form. Hint: you need to set the Action to GoToRecord, set the object type, the object name, and the record to go to all in Action Arguments.
4. Save the macro using a name of your own choosing. The sample data saved this macro using the name mcrDay8.

5. Open the form `frmMacroPractice` in design view.

6. Set this macro to fire when the form opens. You need to make the form the object addressed and locate the `On Open` event to do this.

7. Switch to form view. The form should now open with a new record displayed instead of record number 1 as it did in step 1.

8. Remove the macro from the event. Again switch to form view. Note the effect of the macro.

9. Close the form optionally saving changes.

8

Refining Your Tables

You, as a developer, need to control the quality of the data entered in to your application. This applies not only to applications distributed to far-flung places, but to applications you will use yourself.

As I write this lesson, I'm working with a large medical provider who, at this point, can't report its research findings to its granting agency. The reason is that the designer of the database where the research was supposed to be compiled failed to institute good data validation procedures. The resulting chaos caused by questionable data is costing this provider a lot of money (my fees) plus is putting its grant in jeopardy. Ignore this part of database design only at your extreme peril.

Today You Will Learn

Tables are the fundamental elements within Access. You were introduced to tables in Day 4, "The Data Foundation—The Table," but today we are going to build on that foundation by learning about the data that goes in to your tables. Specifically you will learn

- Why you need data integrity
- The fundamental rule for data representation
- The data validation property
- How to use expressions to ensure data integrity
- How to use lookup tables for data validation
- What input masks are for
- How to create input masks with a wizard
- Symbols used for input masks
- How to include OLE objects in tables
- How to include hyperlink objects in tables
- How to include hyperlinks outside of the dataset
- How to present table data in Web format
- Special considerations for editing hyperlink data

Tables and Data Integrity

The reason to control data input is to be assured of data output. Take a look at Figure 9.1. The `tblInvalidData` table is part of your sample data in the Day 9 database of the CD.

FIGURE 9.1

This tiny table is full of (often silly) examples of what can occur to a table's data if a developer doesn't take care in designing data input validation.

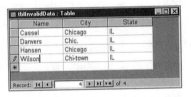

As you can see, there are several spellings and abbreviations for the city Chicago and the state Illinois. Most people familiar with the U.S. would understand that the entries

```
Chicago
Chic.
Chi-town
```

all refer to Chicago. However the database isn't nearly as intelligent or experienced with U.S. cities and their abbreviations or slang names. Similarly, a person not familiar with U.S. cities and slang might guess that *Chic.* is an abbreviation for Chicago, but would

likely miss Chi-town. In fact, a person familiar with U.S. cities might assume the word
Chic. is an error for the town Chino or another town named China.

It gets worse when you consider filters and queries as applied to multiple entries for the
same data. A reasonable person, when trying to select records where Chicago is the city,
might use Chicago as the city field criterion.

However using that criterion on this table would miss all but one Chicago record. If you
changed the criterion to one that selects all these records, such as the following:

```
Like "Ch*"
```

then you'd also select

```
China
Chico
Chirucuaha
```

and so forth.

The rule for data entry is that any datum must be represented in one and only one way in
a database. It matters little if you choose to represent the city of Chicago as

```
Chic.
Chi-town
Chicago
```

Just use one and stick to it. That way when you select or filter using a criterion, you'll
know that not only have you selected all the records matching that criterion, but you
haven't selected records not meeting your criterion.

Remember that when using the datasets in this book, you can visually examine the data
to make sure that it's as you want it to be. However in the real world of databases, your
datasets will grow well beyond your ability to scan them for accuracy.

For example, let's say you're in charge of record keep for a political party's fund raising
efforts. You have a database that has, among its tables, contributors along with their
addresses. Your boss asks you to give him a list of all contributors from Chicago. You run
a `Select` query using Chicago as a criterion. Your return is 10,348 records.

You likely aren't familiar enough with your data to know if that's right. You have to trust
your database engine and your data so you know to an utter certainty that you do have
10,348 contributors who have addresses in Chicago. Hoping and guessing just won't do
in this and other similar instances.

The first part of this lesson covers how you can design your tables to be sure they represent data uniformly.

Data Validation Using Table Expressions

You've already seen several expressions in use for queries, forms, and reports. Some data validation techniques rely on expressions as well.

> **Tip**
>
> The easiest data validation trick is to use a default value when you have a field that can contain identical values such as city. Users can override the default value of course, but having such values for often repeated field values not only creates a validation for data entry, but saves data input time.

The expressions for data validation look just like those expressions that might appear in a query as a criterion. For example, the expression,

```
"CIA" or "AFL-CIO"
```

only allows the values "CIA" or "AFL-CIO" to be entered in a field with that validation so defined.

The following task takes you through a sample data validation.

Task: Implementing Data Validation Using Table Expressions

1. Start Access if necessary and locate the database, Day 9 on the CD. Locate the table tblFirstValidation and open it in design view.

2. This table was made using the Mailing List table wizard, but only uses a few of the available fields. Click the OrganizationName field and locate the Validation Rule entry in the Field Properties list box. Enter

   ```
   CIA Or AFL-CIO
   ```

   for an entry. Tab out of the field. Your screen should resemble Figure 9.2.

3. Save the table using a new name (File, Save As), if you don't want to overwrite the sample data. The finished version of this table is part of the sample data under the name tblFirstValidation-done. Switch to Datasheet View after the save. Locate the field with the Caption Organization Name, enter any value other than CIA or AFL-CIO, and then tab out of the field. Your screen should resemble Figure 9.3.

4. Click OK to clear the message box and enter CIA for a value in the Organization Name field. Tab out again. This time the table accepts your entry as it meets the criterion for the Validation Rule property.

FIGURE 9.2

The Validation Rule property for the OrganizationName *field requires that the value must be* **CIA** *or* **AFL-CIO**.

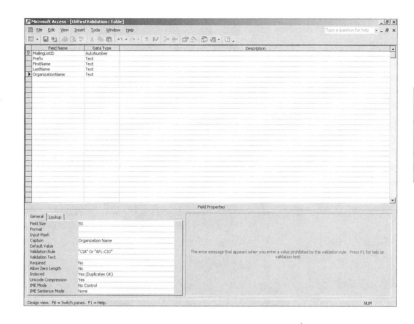

9

FIGURE 9.3

Access rejects any entry that doesn't match the field's validiation rule.

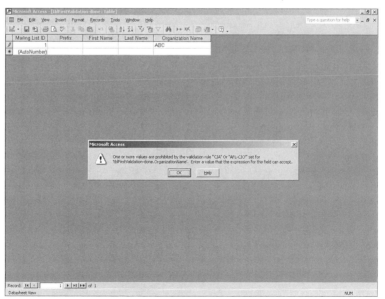

▼ 5. While the new validation entry does a fine job of requiring the user to enter one of the two values specified, the text of the error/warning message box isn't terribly informative, especially for beginners. Switch back to design view.

6. Locate the field Validation Text under Field Properties. Enter the following as a property:

```
Please enter AFL-CIO or CIA.
```

Your screen should resemble Figure 9.4.

FIGURE 9.4

Yes, you can create custom message boxes in lieu of the standard Access boxes.

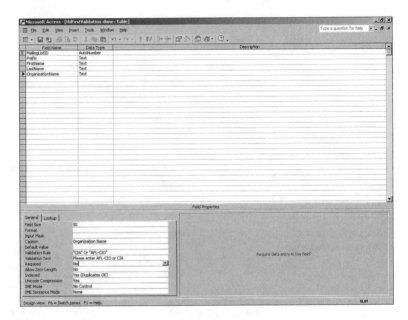

7. Save the table and return to Datasheet View. Click in the Organization Name field and enter an invalid value such as

```
FBI
```

8. Tab away from the field and now your custom dialog box should resemble Figure 9.5.

9. This technique works as long as you only have a few criteria and don't want users to be able to modify those criteria. When your needs grow more complex, you ▼ need to use a lookup facility. That's coming right up.

FIGURE 9.5

Here is a custom message box (specialized type of dialog box) created by your validation text property.

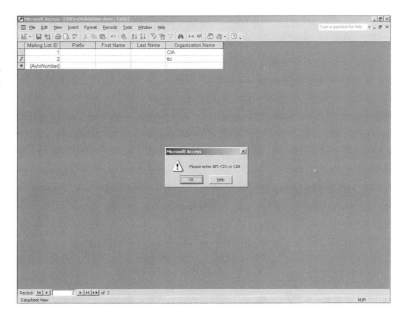

Data Lookup in Tables

You can create combo boxes in your tables that look up data from other tables. This allows you as a developer, to restrict your data entry to values existing in another table.

There are several advantages to doing this. First you can have your users (optionally) edit the looked-up table to alter its contents, thus letting users decide what is valid for entries. Second, you can list many values (thousands if necessary) for your lookups without having to enter those same values as a validation rule.

Generally speaking, you shouldn't have a large table (in number of records) for data validation. However, you might be looking up from a large table when, for example, you want to only enter records in the many-side of a relationship where an entry already exists in the one-side. You can force users to only add records to the many-side where a one-side record already exists by enforcing referential integrity when establishing the link. However if a user tries entering a nonexistent many-side record he'll only get an error message.

If you create a lookup system for record entry on the many-side (such as orders for exist-ing customers), you'll greatly speed up data entry in any system where the data entry person hasn't memorized the values in the link fields (most systems are too big for the memorization).

Creating the lookup is quite simple; once you've seen the method for doing one, you know this method for all.

Task: Creating Field Lookup Validation

1. Start Access if necessary and locate the database Day 9 on the CD. Locate the tables, tblLookUpValidation and tblCityLookUp. The first table is the one where a combo box looks to the second table for its data.

2. Open the table tblLookUpValidation in design view. Click in the City field. Your screen should resemble Figure 9.6.

FIGURE 9.6

Again this simple table structure makes the point of this task clear-er than a complex table where the trees might get lost due to the size of the forest.

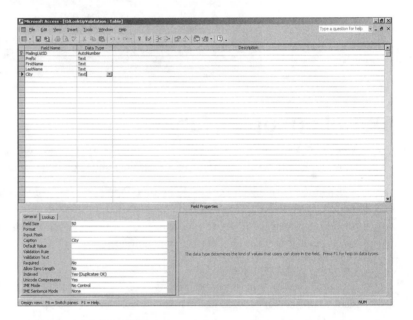

3. Note the Lookup tab behind the General tab in the Field Properties pane.

4. Click the Lookup tab to open that property sheet. Open the Display Control combo box (a lot of combo boxes!) and choose Combo Box for the display control.

5. Locate the Row Source property. Open its combo box and place the table tblCityLookUp as the Row Source for this control. Change the Limit to List property to Yes. When set to Yes, the Limit to List property ensures that only what is in the list is chosen or entered. Your screen should resemble Figure 9.7.

FIGURE **9.7**

*This Lookup tab set
limits the entries in
one table's fields to
values in another
table.*

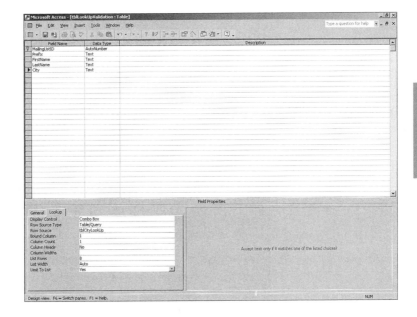

9

> **Tip**
>
> Keep your eye on the rectangle to the right of the Field Properties list box
> to see pointers and tips about the property that currently has focus.

6. Save the table using a new name if you want to preserve the sample data in its
   original form. This example uses the name `tblLookupFinished` for a save name.
   Switch to Datasheet View. Move to the `City` field and open the combo box that
   forms when the field has focus. Your screen should resemble Figure 9.8.

7. Well, this is a fine kettle of fish we're in. The entry for Miami is spelled *Maimi* and
   we're limited to the entries on this list for the `City` field. The lesson to learn here is
   that if you use tight data validation, make sure your data is valid. In this case, during normal use, the users would enter **Maimi** for every entry where the city was
   really Miami.

> **Tip**
>
> If you find yourself with a set of bad data such as a city named Maimi
> instead of Miami, don't despair. You can fix the error using an Update query
> covered later in this book. You can also use Find and Replace to alter

> values in a table. If, due to audit considerations, you don't want to alter table data, you can link the values in `tblCityLookUp` to another table holding the correct values and use that link in your queries/forms/reports.

FIGURE 9.8

You're now limited to using the city name on this list. However, one entry seems to be spelled oddly.

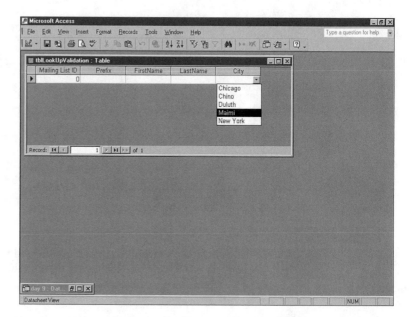

Input Masks

An input mask is a template of how you want your data to appear or be entered in to your project. For example, the date displayed as

12/12/01

has a template of

##/##/##

where the character # holds the place for a number. Similarly, the common U.S. phone display of

(302)555-8827

uses a template of

(###)###-####

again using the # character as a placeholder for where numbers go.

Keeping this in mind, you can construct input masks to work alone or in conjunction with data validation expressions to further enforce validation or control display.

| Tip | Input masks use wildcards as placeholders. This allows you to use them to specify the length or form of input without using the specific strings required in a data validation expression. |

9

Like so many things in small computing, input masks are easy to understand once you've created one or two, as the next task does.

Task: Creating Input Masks

1. Start Access if necessary and locate the database Day 9 on the CD. Locate the table tblMaskMe. Open it in design view. Your screen should resemble Figure 9.9.

2. Switch to Datasheet View. Enter a date for the Date of Birth field. Access formats the date to reflect the entry in the Format property for this field. This first mask creates a template for date entry in this field.

FIGURE 9.9

Here is another very simple table perfect for practicing on.

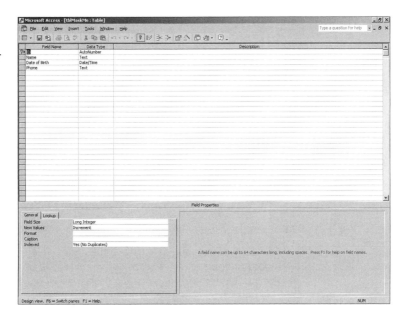

3. Switch back to design view. Click in the Date of Birth field to bring up the properties for this field.

4. Click in the Input Mask area of the Field Properties. You can manually enter a mask or use a wizard to build a mask for commonly masked field types. This task uses the wizard.

Note

New for Access 2002 is the editing ability to the predefined input masks supplied with the program. Feel free to experiment with this facility (seen in the first dialog box of the wizard) after you've created a mask or two to familiarize yourself with the terminology of these masks.

5. Click the ellipsis (Build button) to launch the Input Mask Wizard. Your screen should resemble Figure 9.10.

FIGURE 9.10

The Input Mask Wizard has several predefined masks for various data types. This is the predefined list for the Date/Time data type.

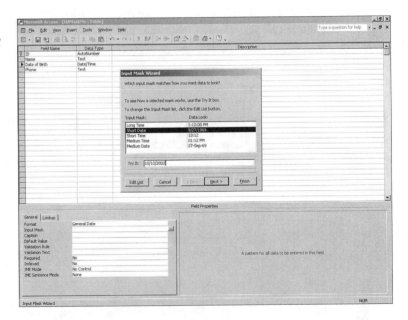

Note

Access stores time and date data in the same numeric format. You can choose to display time, date, or both by changing the display characteristics. The Input Mask Wizard uses this universal date/time storage method to display time, date, or both.

6. The first dialog box gives you a choice of various templates or masks to display the information in this field. Click Short Date and then click the Try It section below to see how your mask works.

7. Click Next to move on, leaving Short Date as the mask type. The next screen allows you to directly change the mask details. You also can change the type of placeholder your mask displays to indicate to your users that the mask is looking for input. Open the Placeholder character combo box and choose the # symbol for a placeholder. Your screen should resemble Figure 9.11.

FIGURE 9.11

Open the Placeholder character combo box and choose the # symbol.

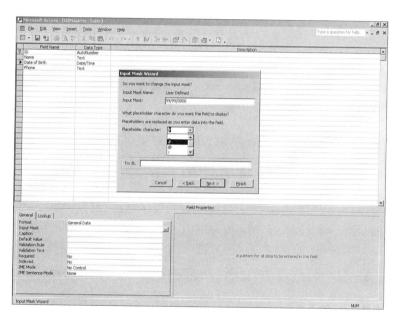

8. Click Next to move on. That's it for the Input Mask Wizard. Click Finish (as you could have done in the last dialog box) and you're done. Access creates the Input Mask to your specification and places it in the Input Mask Field Property. The mask for this field is

`99/99/00;0;#`

9. Here's an explanation of this mask. The character 9 is a key character that allows the user to enter either a number or a space. This allows both the dates 12/12/12 and 1/1/12 to be entered. The first two zeroes force the user to enter two numbers, preventing an entry such as 12/12/1. The zero after the semicolon tells Access to store the formatting characters (this time the slashes) with the data. The final character here is the placeholder.

▼   10. Save the table or save as using a new name if you don't want to overwrite the sample table. This example uses the final save name as `tblMaskMe-Finished`.

11. Switch to Datasheet View. Enter a date in the `Date of Birth` field. Enter only one digit in the year area and then tab away from the field. Access prevents you from entering such a date in your table.

12. Return to design view and replace the # symbol with an underscore for the last item in the mask. Save and return to Datasheet View. Note how that instead of underscores in the field, there are # symbols. Return to design view and then replace the underscore with the number symbol again.

13. Click in the `Phone` field and again click the Build button in the Input Mask field of Field Properties to start another wizard. Because the Text data type field is quite flexible, Access doesn't automatically know what type of data it's to deal with so it offers you a list of various masks it has predefined suitable for a text type field. Choose Phone Number, which should be the default choice anyway.

14. Click Next to move on to the input mask details screen. Leave the next screen at default and click Next. Feel free to run through this wizard time and again to experiment with other options. When the dialog box asks you if you want to store symbols with the data, choose not to. This dialog box with the proper option button chosen is shown in Figure 9.12.

FIGURE 9.12

This dialog box permits you to either include or exclude formatting characters from your dataset.

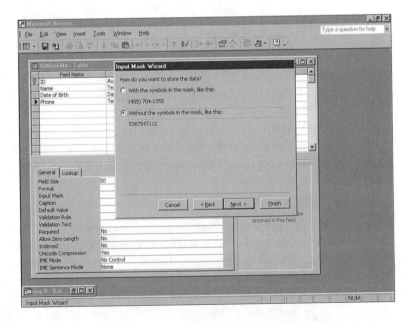

▼

▼ 15. Click Finish to end the wizard process. This takes you back to design view. Note the mask reads

`!(999) 000-0000;;_`

16. There's nothing between the two semicolons. This indicates that the formatting characters are not stored with the values entered in this field. Save the table and experiment with the `Phone` and `Date of Birth` field until you're satisfied with

▲   how they work. Table 9.1 is a complete table of input mask characters.

TABLE 9.1   Input Mask Characters

Character	Use in mask
`,`	Thousands separator or other character as specified by the regional settings for Windows
`/ :`	Date and time delimiters or other characters depending upon the regional settings for Windows
`\`	Regard next character as literal
`!`	Fill from left to right (default is right to left)
`"string"`	Show the values in between the double quotes literally in mask
`<`	Display as lowercase
`>`	Display as uppercase
`A`	Force alphanumeric
`a`	Optional alphanumeric
`&`	Force any entry including whitespace
`0`	Force any number
`9`	Optional any number
`#`	Digit, space (default), or operand
`L`	Force alpha
`?`	Optional character
`C`	Optional character or space
`.`	Decimal delimiter or other character as specified by the regional settings for Windows

Using OLE Objects and Hyperlinks in Tables

You can define a table field as having the Data Type `OLE Object`. An OLE object can be almost anything from a sound to a movie clip to a still picture. The specific objects available to you depend on your computer's configuration.

Open the Day 9 database and locate the table Employees. This is a table imported from
the Northwind database supplied with Access. Open Employees in design view. Locate
the Photo field and note that the Data Type is OLE Object.

Switch to Datasheet View and scroll over to see the field Photo. Note that this field
seems to have all the same entry: Bitmap Image. Right-clicking this field brings up a
context menu with the entries Edit and Open. These entries allow you to bring up the
picture in an editing environment, assuming you have a bitmap editor registered as part
of your Windows.

Even if you don't have such a registered program, you can display the images by choosing AutoForm from the New Object button on the toolbar. Figure 9.13 shows the table
Employees in Datasheet View. Figure 9.14 shows the same table after the AutoForm wizard creates a form for this table.

FIGURE 9.13

*The contents of an
OLE Object field might
all appear the same
because the contents
aren't literals, but a
description of the type
of object contained.*

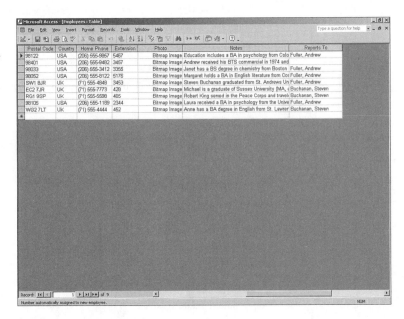

Inserting OLE Objects

To insert an OLE object into a field having the data type OLE Object choose the Insert,
Object menu choices. If you want to try this, you'll need an OLE object of some sort
available to you.

While this example uses a picture, you could also use a sound, a movie clip, or any other
object type your computer has registered.

FIGURE 9.14

There's little to be gained by showing OLE objects in tables, but they make for great-looking forms.

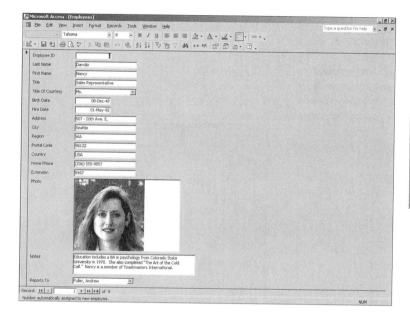

9

To insert a new OLE object, click in the field where you want to place the object. In Access, that field must have the data type `OLE Object`. This example uses the `Photo` field in the `Employees` tables. You can use this or the AutoForm as shown in Figure 9.14. This form is part of the sample data as `frmShowOLEObject`. Choose Insert, Object from the menu. This brings up a critical dialog box.

You can choose Create New for the object. If you choose this, you'll go to the application registered for that OLE object type so you can start creating. After you're done and exited, you'll have a chance to embed or link the new object to the table or form.

Note

To link or embed an object after creating it, choose the menu selections File, Exit from the program you used to create it and then follow the prompts. A linked object retains an updatable link to the creating program. An embedded object does not have such a link. That is, you can alter a linked object by invoking the creating application.

This example uses an existing picture, so choose Create from File, as shown in Figure 9.15, and browse for the file.

I've included a bitmap image of a happy face, `blinking face.gif`, on the CD in the Day 9 folder for you to use if you want to follow along.

FIGURE **9.15**

*This dialog box shows
the types of OLE appli-
cations registered on
your computer or
allows you to browse
for an existing object.*

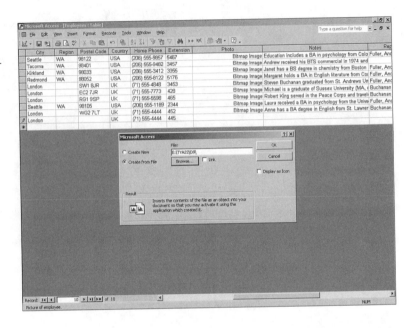

If you choose the Link checkbox, you won't embed the object in the table, but rather link
to an existing object. Linked objects don't expand the database too much, but you must
distribute the objects along with the application. Embedded objects, on the other hand,
become part of the data, but expand the database significantly.

After locating the object, click OK. Access updates the table with an indication that the
new picture or other object is now part of your data. Figure 9.16 shows the updated table.
Note that the object inserted (a picture) is registered in this workstation as a Paint Shop
Pro image.

The updated table is saved as tblUpdatedEmployees and part of the sample data. The
form bound to this table is saved as frmUpdatedEmployees. Open the form to see the
new object that's now part of this dataset. Figure 9.17 shows the new form with the
object on display.

Note

To display this picture correctly, the property Size Mode was changed from
the default of Clip to Zoom for this control.

FIGURE 9.16

Browse and click OK to insert (embed) the new OLE object in to the table.

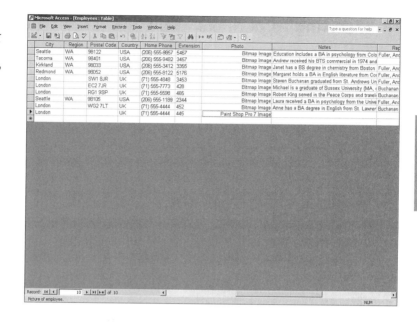

FIGURE 9.17

The picture Smiley is now part of the dataset.

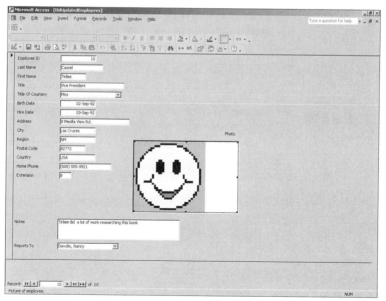

9

Inserting Hyperlinks

Hyperlinks are jumps to other documents. While hyperlinks predate the World Wide Web by quite a bit, the Web is the place most people first encounter them. You can include hyperlinks in Access forms, tables, and queries.

The basis for inserting a hyperlink in a table is to format the field as Data Type hyperlink. Open up the table tblUpdatedEmployees in design view. This table is part of the sample data. Note the last field in the table is called Web Page. This field isn't part of the original Employees table. The data type is Hyperlink. Switch to Datasheet View. Scroll to the field Web Page and click in a row that doesn't have a hyperlink.

You can enter a hyperlink either directly just like any other datum, or you can click the Insert Hyperlink button on the toolbar to access a dialog box to assist you with these insertions. By all means, use the Insert Hyperlink for any insertions other than the most simple as the richness of the invoked dialog box acts almost like a wizard for link insertions.

Tip

Right-click fanatics aren't left out here. You can also right-click the hyperlink field and choose Hyperlink, Edit Hyperlink from the context menu. I don't think that Edit Hyperlink is the same as Insert Hyperlink, but Microsoft seems to think so and they're in charge here.

Note

You can hyperlink not only to Internet Web pages, but intranet pages, unpublished pages, and files.

Figure 9.18 shows the Insert Hyperlink dialog box. If you are following along, your dialog box has different contents.

FIGURE 9.18

This complex dialog box allows various settings for hyperlinks as data.

Note that this dialog box has its own Object bar over at the left. You can include a lot
more than just Web links in a form or table. Click the Object in this Database button to
bring up a tree view similar to Explorer, that allows you to insert links to objects from
the database.

> **Tip**
>
> You don't need to use the Insert menu to insert a hyperlink anywhere in
> Access. If you know the address, such as www.microsoft.com (a familiar
> one to many) you can enter it directly.

9

Similarly, you can link to other files or drives on your computer or network.

Working Around the Hyperlink Edit Catch-22

Once you've entered a hyperlink in to a table, you have a problem trying to edit it. Other
kinds of data are easy to edit because they aren't hot (single-click) jumps. You can click
in a non-hyperlink field with your mouse and edit away. If you click in a hyperlink field
you'll end up either jumping to the link site or you'll get an error message.

The trick to editing a hyperlink value is the Tab or Enter key. Click in the field preceding
the hyperlink field (coming before in the tab order) and then press tab. This gives focus
to the hyperlink field.

Press either F2 to enter edit mode or Shift+F2 to enter zoom mode. Most people prefer
Shift+F2 for this task. After entering either zoom or edit mode, you can edit the hyperlink. If you're in edit mode, leaving the field restores the link facility. If you're in zoom
mode, clicking OK does so. Figure 9.19 shows the zoom mode method of editing a
hyperlink field.

> **Tip**
>
> You can also right-click the hyperlink and choose Hyperlink, Edit Hyperlink
> from the context menu to edit these fields. This is the method I greatly pre-
> fer, but others prefer the Shift+F2 method so I offer both to you. I find the
> Zoom box useful for other things in Access, such as editing query expres-
> sions, but not here. Also the Zoom box picks up the title text of the hyper-
> link, not the actual link which, to my way of thinking, is less than useful.

Using Free Floating Hyperlinks

Starting in about 1996, Microsoft went Internet crazy. Office 2002, of which Access
2002 is part, continues this tradition of internetworking everything.

FIGURE 9.19

Trying to edit a hyper-link using the usual methods only ends in frustration. You need to invoke either zoom or edit mode. Here is zoom mode.

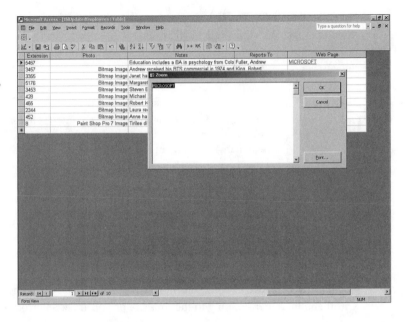

In the previous sections you've seen how you can insert hyperlinks as field data for tables. You can also create hyperlinks to drop on forms as free floating objects or another type of form controls.

This very short task takes you through the steps.

Task: Creating Free Floating Hyperlinks

1. Launch Access and the `Day 9` database if necessary. Locate the form `frmHyperlinks`. This form is bound to the `tblUpdatedEmployees`, but only includes three fields for simplicity.

2. Open the form in design view. Choose the menu selections Insert, Hyperlink or click the Insert Hyperlink button on the toolbar. The Insert Hyperlink dialog opens. Select a hyperlink of your own choosing or use `www.microsoft.com` as the example does. Enter

   Microsoft's Site

   for a Text to Display. Click the Screen Tip button and enter

   Visit Microsoft

   Your screen should resemble Figure 9.20.

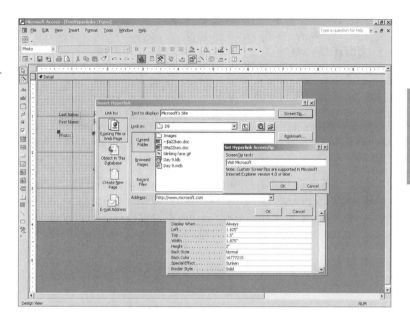

FIGURE 9.20

Enter a Screentip (a tooltip) to display when the mouse is hovered over the hyperlink.

9

3. Click OK in each dialog box to exit. Access drops a hyperlink somewhere on your form. Drag this link to the right of the Photo field. Your screen should resemble Figure 9.21.

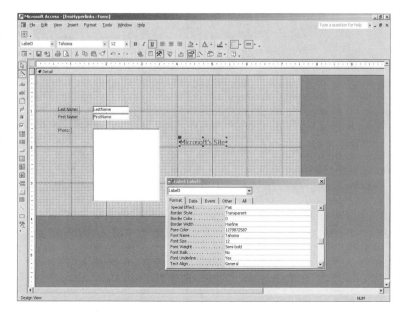

FIGURE 9.21

Access drops the newly created hyperlink somewhere on the form, but as the link isn't active in design view, you can easily drag and drop it to a location of your choosing.

▼

Note   I've edited the font size and font weight properties for this hyperlink field to show up better in the screen shot. You can modify these properties at will using the Format tab of the Properties list box for the hyperlink object.

4. Switch to form view. Move your cursor over the newly created link. The cursor switches to the jump cursor. You'll also see your Screen Tip pop up. If you click this link (and are connected to the Internet) you'll jump to the main Microsoft site.

5. Return to design view. Click the hyperlink field to give it focus. Open the Properties list box if necessary. Click the Format or All tab. Locate the two properties `Hyperlink Address` and `Hyperlink SubAddress`. Here is where you can manually enter the address for this link. A subaddress is a page at a site. Close the form optionally saving changes. This finished form with the hyperlink is part of the sample data under the name `frmHyperlinks-Finished`.

▲

Saving Tables as HTML

You can also save table data as an HTML page for use at a Web site or viewing for those who don't have Access. Doing so is fairly simple. At the database view, choose the table you want to convert to HTML, click to highlight it, and then choose File, Save As. This brings up the dialog box shown in Figure 9.22.

Choose Data Access Page from the pull-down (combo box) list under the As label. Click OK and you'll get a standard Save dialog box. Choose a name for the file but be sure to leave the extension at default.

Access creates not only the HTML page but also an ASP control for browsing through the records in the table. At this point, anybody loading the page into a browser or other enabled application (such as Word) can browse through the records of the table so saved.

Exporting tables is a much more flexible than using the save-as option. I can't say whether you'll ever use these options, but it is nice to know they are there if you're ever asked to supply Access data in different formats. Take a look at what Access can export to by selecting a table, then choosing File, Export from the menu system. Open the Save as Type combo box to see the huge list of export types available to you. You should also see a pure (well, fairly pure) HTML export option. You can even export to HTML using a template—an option you'll see when you choose this format.

FIGURE 9.22

The File, Save As dialog box for tables allows the exporting of that table to a format readable by browsers.

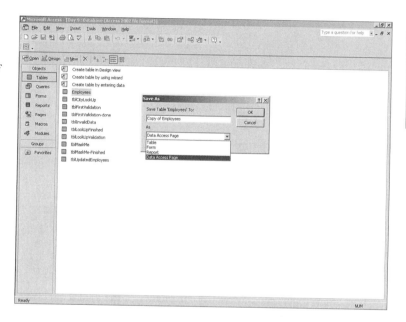

I've exported Employees to an HTML table and included the table in the Day 9 folder for you to check out. I used fairly standard export guidelines. Figure 9.23 shows this table in Internet Explorer. As you can see, this needs some work if you want to impress the boss, but it sure is nice to know that something is there for you.

Tip

Try exporting to various formats which you think you might need to learn how well Access does in these exports. This is something good to know now rather than after you've promised your boss' boss that you can come up with great-looking or acting formats foreign to Access.

FIGURE 9.23

The Employees *table exported to HTML.*

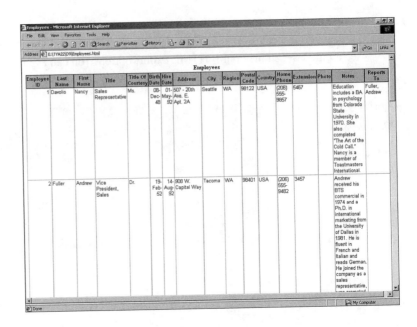

Summary

The material today built on the previous material about both tables and expressions. You, as a developer, need to control the quality of the data that can be added to your project. If some users enter the city Chicago as "Chicago" while others use "Chi" or other variants, your queries and finds won't work as you expect. When you have real-world datasets containing thousands or millions of records, you can't expect to validate the quality of the queries by inspection.

You can control the quality of data (data validation) at the table level using several tools. They are validation rules, input masks, and lookup tables. Most developers use all of these tools, mixing and matching depending on the need.

You can include hyperlinks as data by defining a table field as the Hyperlink Data Type. Similarly, you can include a hyperlink by dropping it anywhere on a form where it acts like an active label.

Access 2002 saves a table as a two-part HTML document called a Data Access Page or a plain HTML document. One part of a Data Access Page contains the actual HTML, the other an ASP control for browsing through the records in the table. Once saved, anybody with a sufficiently up-to-date browser can view the table records.

Q&A

Q. What use is a free-floating hyperlink on a form?

A. One common use is to link to a help or reference facility that applies to the entire set of data represented in the form.

Q. Can I view a Data Access Page from within Access?

A. Yes. There is even a macro action, `OpenDataAccessPage`, to automate this for you.

Q. Do I need to include the equals sign as a prefix for data validation expressions?

A. No, just enter the expression.

Q. How can I order the items in a lookup to be different from the order of the primary key of the underlying table?

A. You can base your lookup not only on a table, but a query too. Thus, you can sort on any field in the query and then use the sorted query as a lookup source.

Q. Can I show more than one field in a lookup?

A. Yes. Just change the `Column Count` property from the default of 1 to however many columns you want to display. Also examine the properties `Column Heads`, `Column Widths`, and `Bound Column` for related information.

Workshop

The Workshop helps you solidify the skills you learned in this lesson. Answers to the quiz appear in Appendix A, "Answers to Quizzes."

Quiz

1. Can you display a hyperlink using a label or a different display text?
2. Does the expression `In("Madrid","London")` as a validation rule allow the entry of the city Belfast?
3. Does the expression `In("Europe")` as a validation rule allow the entry of the city Belfast?
4. Do you need to use the built-in message boxes for Validation violations?
5. What does the expression "Not Denver" do as a validation rule?

Exercises

1. Open the form `frmHyperlinks`.

2. Create a hyperlink by pressing Ctrl-K. The Insert Hyperlink dialog box will appear. Enter `www.mrshowbiz.com` in the address field.

3. Enter `Visit Mr. Showbiz` in the Text to Display text box.

4. Click on the OK button to close the Insert Hyperlink dialog box.

5. You can position the newly inserted hyperlink on the form just as you do any other control.

6. Close the `frmHyperlinks` form after you are done experimenting with hyperlinks.

DAY 10

Improving Your Forms

In a typical Access database project, users interact with forms more than any other object. In fact, there are many Access databases in use where the users see nothing but forms on screen and reports from the printer.

Happy users are the key ingredient to a successful application. One way to make users happy is to make the objects they interact with, forms for the most part, comfortable to use and attractive to view.

Today You Will Learn

You've seen some of the elements available to you to dress up your forms, give them added function, or both. This lesson goes into details I somewhat glossed over earlier. Today you will learn:

- How to change colors in forms
- How to use a picture for a form background
- How to include a static picture for decoration
- How to use pictures on command buttons
- About 3D and other object effects

- The most commonly used form format objects
- About manual placement of controls
- How to change form views
- What multi-table forms (subforms) are
- What controls wizards do

Using Color to Enhance Forms

Access tends to default to gray, which is the dominant Windows color used for standard menus, toolbars, scroll bars, and status bars. There's nothing wrong with this color except it does get a bit old after a while. You can use color (sparingly) to dress up forms and to make features stand out. For example, a gray command button doesn't jump out if it's on a gray background, but it does if it's on a blue background. This isn't too important if your target users are young or have good eyesight, but older users, or those with visual limitations will greatly appreciate your efforts on their behalf.

 Note

This book is limited to grayscale screen shots. Due to this, some of the color detail in the screens will be difficult to discern, but you can see these changes by following along with the directions or viewing the sample data supplied on the CD.

Altering Object Color

There is no color property for the form overall. You need to change form color by section. Launch Access if necessary. Open up the database in the Day 10 folder on your CD. Click the Forms button in the Object bar and then choose to make a new form through design view.

Click in the Detail area to make that active. Open the Properties list box if necessary, and then click the Format tab. Locate the Back Color property. Note that it's a long number. This is how Access stores color information about its objects, but it's not terribly user friendly.

 Note

Access will not have a property for the back color of the form in general. You must click the specific area (such as detail) where you want to set the color. New Access users find this confusing.

> **Note**
>
> The color number is a decimal representation of the bits set for whatever color depth is available on the computer. If an application uses a color not available, Windows makes an intelligent guess about what color to substitute.

Click in the area where you'd enter a number and note the appearance of the Build button (an ellipsis). Click the button to bring up the standard Windows color picker dialog box. Your screen should resemble Figure 10.1.

FIGURE 10.1

The form color picker is the standard Windows control.

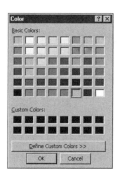

10

Choose another color. This example uses a light blue. Click OK; the dialog box closes, the number changes in the Properties list box, and when you click out of the property, the form appears in the new color.

Add a text box control to the form. Click the label part of the control and note that it too has a color assigned different from the form, but it appears to be the same color as the form. This is due to its Back Style property defaulting to Transparent. This property is directly above the Back Color property. Alter the Back Color property (this example uses red) using the Build button and then alter the Back Style to Normal. This displays the new color for the label.

The default text color is 0 or black. This doesn't show up too well with a red background, so locate the Fore Color property farther down the list, click the Build button and change the color to a bright yellow.

> **Note**
>
> The computer used for this lesson is set to display in True Color, or about 17,000,000 colors (2^24 colors). If you're set up for fewer, you won't have as wide a choice as you see in these screens.

Add another unbound text box control to the form. Again highlight the label part of the control and this time open the Fill/Back Color button from the standard toolbar, choosing Red again. Doing this not only adds the color to the control, but also switches the Back Style property to Normal.

Now open the Font/Fore Color button on the standard toolbar and choose yellow. There's no difference in your result between the two methods. Which way you choose to work is up to you. After you're done, your screen should resemble Figure 10.2.

FIGURE 10.2

You can change colors many ways.

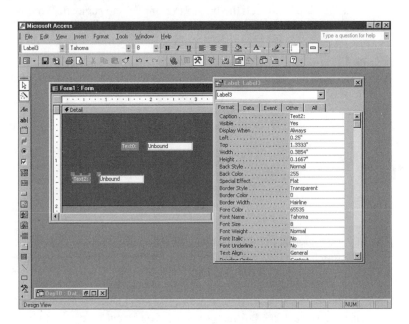

> **Note**
>
> There are thousands of combinations of formats you can use for form objects. There is no need for me to step you through each property in the Format tab—you can do that yourself. I encourage you to pause for a few minutes to experiment with these properties and their appearances. Just remember you can overdo this formatting to make a decent form look hideous by editing too many properties.

Adding Pictures to Form Objects

Earlier, you saw how the form wizard uses a graphic as a background for a form. You can duplicate this wizard facility and go it one better.

Click the form selection section of the form design grid. That's the gray square at the immediate upper-left corner of the grid (right under the toolbar). Or you can open the object selection combo box in the form design toolbar and choose Form. You also can open the Properties dialog box and select Form from the object combo box there.

Locate the `Picture` property in the Properties list box. Click in the field and then either enter a filename and path for a picture (a bitmap) or click the Build button and browse for it. Figure 10.3 shows a picture embedded in a form as well as the properties list box showing the property that included the picture.

FIGURE 10.3

This form now looks cluttered.

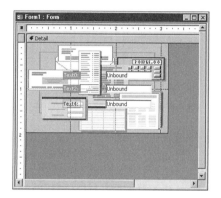

Although the picture in Figure 10.3 is attention getting, many might think it is too busy for a working form. While you can see the fields clearly, reading their contents isn't nearly as easy as before. The field (or control) labels aren't nearly as well defined as without the picture.

Note the other picture properties such as `Picture Type`, `Picture Size Mode`, `Picture Tiling`, and `Picture Alignment`. These control whether the picture becomes part of the database (embedded) or is linked, how Access handles a picture that has a different size or aspect ratio than the form can handle, whether the picture appears once or as tiles, and how the picture relates to the form. Feel free to experiment with these properties to see how they interact. For example, by altering the `Picture Size Mode` from Clip to Stretch, you can stretch the picture to fill the entire form. This will distort the picture if the form has a different aspect ratio from the form. Figure 10.4 shows a stretched picture.

If you want to see this form, it's part of the sample data saved under the name `frmLurid` in the `Day 10` database.

FIGURE **10.4**

*Make a few changes to
the format of the pic-
ture and you'll have an
entirely new look.*

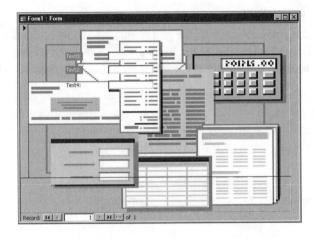

Note

Again, you can see for yourself the results of changing the picture format properties. I've included the picture called `expenses.gif` as part of the sample data so you can experiment too.

Adding Pictures to Command Buttons

You can also add a picture to a command button. You might have run into this earlier when you used the wizard to create a command button to exit a form. Like form pictures, you can create a command button picture without the wizard.

The routine is identical to adding a picture to a form. Create the command button, then locate the `Picture` property on the Format tab of the Properties list box, and finally specify either a file or path for your bitmap or browse using the Build button. In this case, the build button will bring up a fairly complex dialog box allowing you to browse for a file or choose from command button type pictures supplied with Access. Figure 10.5 shows this dialog box.

Figure 10.6 shows the command button added to the form (the picture from the last section has been deleted) with a picture added to the button.

There is no way you can include both a caption (or label) and a bitmap on a button, although many developers have requested such an ability. What you can do is include the label as part of a bitmap and use the bitmap or create a label for the command button.

If you wish to see this form and button, it's part of the sample data under the name `frmGirlButton`.

FIGURE 10.5

*The dialog box to
select your picture is
fairly complex.*

FIGURE 10.6

*You can have a picture
on a command button,
although this example
is a bit silly.*

10

Tip

Open the form `frmGirlButton` in form view. Click and hold on the command button to see the change in the bitmap when the button is pressed. Click and release the button several times to see the animation effect of this change. The bitmap change gives buttons equipped with pictures a strong visual clue when they're pressed. Keep this characteristic in mind if you create applications for visually impaired users.

Tip

You can include both text and a picture on a command button by including the text as part of the bitmap image.

Applying 3D Effects and Controlling Object Tab Order

By combining 3D effects you can create some spectacular effects or just get an object to stand out. The following Task will give you a taste of what you can do.

▲ TASK   Task: Exploring Special Effects for Forms

1. Launch Access and open the form frmRaiseLower in design view. The form is part of the sample data in the Day 10 database.

2. Locate the rectangle tool in the toolbox. Click it and draw a rectangle around the two form controls. If you lose view of the controls, locate the Back Style property in Properties and switch from Normal to Transparent.

3. Locate the Line/Border Width button on the toolbar. Pull down the button to see its selections and choose a width of 4. Rectangles and lines are useful for highlighting form areas. The wider the border, the more attention the highlight gets. Locate the Line/Border Color button and choose another color such as red. Your screen should resemble Figure 10.7.

FIGURE 10.7

You can create the 3D look through simple manipulations of form object properties.

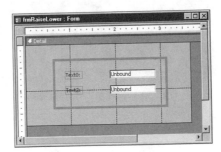

4. Select the form. You can choose to use a 3D effect to also highlight a form area. Locate the Special Effect button on the toolbar. Click it to show its content and then choose Sunken for an effect. You can tell which option is Sunken by hovering your mouse over the options in the Special Effect button. Applying a special effect to a form removes the old border because the special effects are created by using special borders that give the illusion of depth.

You can add many rectangles giving each a sunken or raised effect for an even more startling look to your forms. Figure 10.8 shows three rectangles all with a sunken effect. The cumulative effect is quite interesting.

FIGURE 10.8

Successive sunken rectangles can, when either offset or concentric, create an interesting effect.

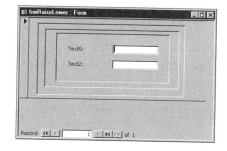

You can also change the effect to shadowed, chiseled or etched. Each will have a different look. Shadowed works well with most objects while chiseled and etched look best when applied to a series of data type controls such as text or combo boxes. If you want to see this form, it's part of the sample data saved as frmRaiseLower-Done.

Tip

Remember you can select multiple objects and simultaneously set their matching characteristics. For example, if you select all three rectangles in frmRaiseLower, you can then set all of them to any effect at the same time.

Formats and System Tools

There are two active form views, form and datasheet. The datasheet view looks like a table or query return. Most importantly, you can't have form objects such as command buttons appearing on a datasheet. On the other hand, datasheet form views are terrific for browsing a dataset.

If necessary, open the Day 10 database, locate the form frmEmployees, and open it in form view. Your screen should resemble Figure 10.9.

FIGURE 10.9

The now-familiar face of Nancy Davolio smiles at us from this simple form.

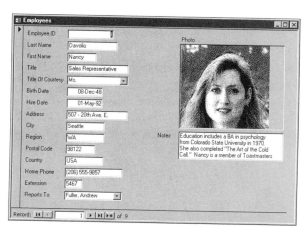

Pull down the View button and switch to Datasheet view. Browsing for an employee is a lot faster in this view. Locate the employee named Steve Buchanan, employee number 5. Click anywhere in that record. Note that the record selector at the extreme left of the screen shows a caret at the current record. Now switch back to Form View using the View menu. Now the current record isn't Davolio, but Buchanan.

From Form View, click the first record button. That's the VCR-like button at the bottom of the screen to the left. This jumps you back to Davolio. Now click in the record number field at the bottom of the screen. This currently shows a number 1 since that's Davolio's record number in this dataset. Highlight the number 1 and enter a number 5. Press Enter and Access takes you to record number 5. This go-to-record-number feature is handy if you know the record number of the data you seek—a rather rare thing in Access.

Tip

> Click in the Notes field for any record. Note how this activates a scroll bar allowing you to scroll through the entire contents of this field.

Record selectors don't do too much in form view. Alter the view for this form to design view, open the Properties list box if necessary, and locate the Record Selectors property in the Format tab. If you don't see this property, make sure you have the form itself selected, and not an object within the form.

Change this property to No. Locate the Navigation Buttons property and change this property to No. Return to form view. This gives you a much cleaner look without losing any functionality. Your screen should resemble Figure 10.10.

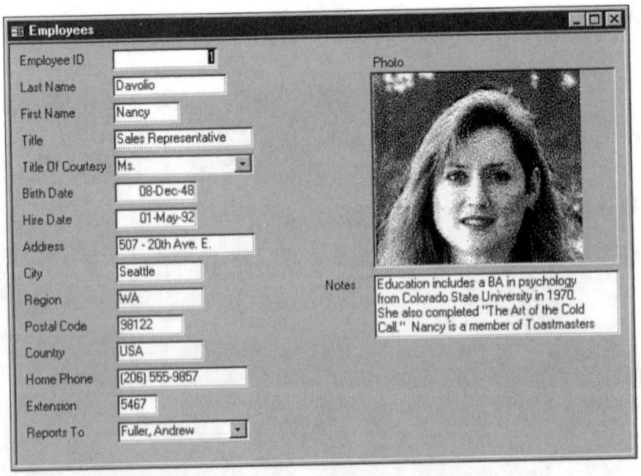

FIGURE 10.10

Removing record selectors from a form gives the form a much cleaner look without sacrificing any functionality.

Switch back to datasheet view. Note that the record selectors, now that you need them, reappear. There's no way to remove record selectors from datasheet view.

The other commonly used form formatting properties and their uses are in listed in Table 10.1.

TABLE 10.1 Commonly Used Form Formatting Properties

Property	Effect on Form
Caption	Specifies the text to appear in the title bar when the form is open
Default View	Specifies the view the form opens in
Allow Form view	Specifies if the user is allowed to change the form to Form view
Allow Datasheet view	Specifies if the user is allowed to change the form to Datasheet view
Allow PivotTable view	Specifies if the user is allowed to change the form to PivotTable view
Allow PivotChart view	Specifies if the user is allowed to change the form to PivotChart view
Scroll Bars	Specifies if the form will show vertical, horizontal or both sets of scroll bars
Record Selectors	Specifies if the form will show the record selectors in form view
Navigation Buttons	Specifies if the VCR buttons at the bottom of the form will display
Control Box	Specifies if the control menu (the menu at the upper left of the screen) will be available through this form
Min Max Buttons	Specifies if the minimize and maximize buttons (on the right of the screen) will be available through this form
Close Button	Specifies if the close button will be available for this form
Moveable	Specifies if the user can move the form
Auto Resize	Specifies if the form will resize itself to show a complete record if possible

While this isn't a comprehensive list, it does show the most commonly used form formatting tools.

Note

Microsoft has added many new form properties to Access 2002 when it upgraded the product from the last version. Even if you're familiar with the product from using a previous iteration, it will pay you dividends to browse through the Properties list box to see what's new. For example, there is a subtle, but significant change to the views allowed and how they're called.

10

A great deal of user satisfaction comes from the aesthetics of an application. Removing extraneous elements from your form, laying it out so the user can easily find information, and including easy-to-use command buttons for often used functions all are part of making your users happy with your project. For example, if you have a Close Form command button (and you should) on your form, you don't need a close button at the upper-right of your form. Removing this object not only makes your form look cleaner, but gives your application a custom look different from other Windows programs most of which sport such a button.

Adding Artwork

You can also add pictures or line drawings to forms. Figure 10.11 shows a variation of the frmEmployees with several changes.

FIGURE 10.11

Adding a picture to a form header can increase the effectiveness of a form.

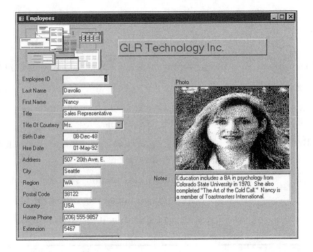

The following list includes the changes that have been made to the form to make it more interesting:

- Added a Form header by selecting View, Form header from the menu selection.
- A label with the Caption property set to GLR Technology Inc. was added to the header.
- The label was given a raised look and its text was made dark red.
- An Unbound Object Frame was added to the header portion.
- The file expenses.gif (part of the sample data) was added to the unbound object frame.
- Record Selectors and Navigation Buttons properties were set to no.

If you want to see this form, it's part of the sample data under the name frmEmployeesWithPicture. If you'd like to try your hand at making this form, start with the form frmEmployees and make the same changes listed. You will also need to move a few form controls to a new location if you want to show a full record on one screen. The latter consideration depends on your screen resolution.

Try scrolling through the records in this database using the navigation buttons. Note that the header remains static while the records change.

Creating Multi-Source Forms

You've had it pretty easy today, but that's about to change. The following topic is important because its quite common to use such forms in your data entry or display chores.

Remember the concept of one-to-many relationships in tables. For example, in a school enrollment database you might have a situation where more than one student is assigned to a class. The class data will appear in the one table while the students in the many table. They'll be linked by some key field—usually student ID or social security number (in the USA). How would you show that relationship on a simple form? The answer is that you really can't, but you can if you use a multi-source form or, in Access talk, a form and subform.

Access keeps the data coordinated using link fields which you'll find in the properties list box. Just to give you an idea of where you'll be headed soon, take a look at Figure 10.12. This is a form and subform from the Northwind database, part of the sample data from Microsoft that came bundled with Access 2002.

FIGURE 10.12

A form with two subforms.

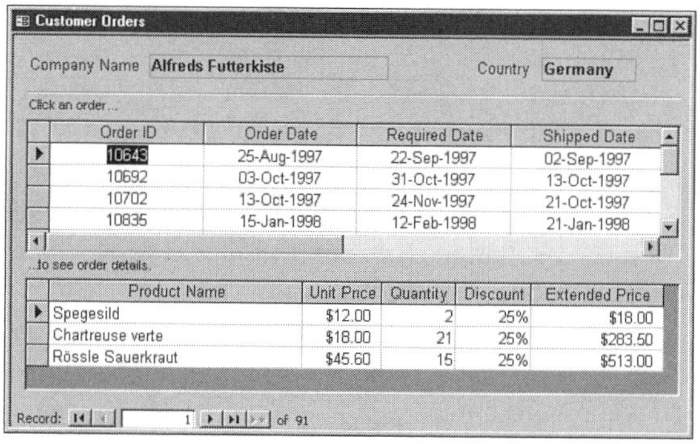

> **Tip**
>
> You will have to install Northwind if you chose the standard Office installation. For reasons known only to Microsoft, it chose to configure the typical Office XP installation without installing Access sample data.

The form shown in Figure 10.12 has two subforms. The top area shows the customer, the second area shows the order information, and the third area provides details of each order from the second area. Open this form, called Customer Orders, click an order in the second area and watch the detail in the third area change. Similarly if you enter another customer in the first area (at the top) then you'll see a change in the orders as Access selects only orders for that customer. To switch customers, use the VCR-like controls at the very bottom of your screen.

You can use two or more queries or tables in your form with a subform. Access doesn't care. Just remember that Access queries are live. Changes in the data affect the data in the bound tables. Folks accustomed to other database products where queries aren't live often make the mistake of thinking queries won't write to the underlying tables.

The following task takes you through the creation of a form with a subform. The underlying data, contained in two tables which are part of the sample data for today, are silly in the extreme. However, the reason for using such simple data is to keep you focused on the task. After you grasp the principles involved in making this form with a subform, using that knowledge with real-world data will be fairly simple.

Task: Creating Multi-Source Forms

1. Launch Access and open the Forms objects in the database view. I've created two simple forms using the autoform generator linked to the tables tblCD and tblSongs with respective names. Examine the forms frmCD and frmSongs, and the underlying tables to gain some familiarity with them.

2. Open the Relationships window by choosing Tools, Relationships from the menu. Note the one-to-many link between the two tables. This link instructs Access how to coordinate the two tables when in a form with a subform. Close the Relationships window.

 Note
All you really need do to get a form with a subform at this point is to use the Autoform on the table tblCD and Access will know to create a form with a subform. I'm taking things a bit more slowly so you can see the theory behind the action.

3. Open the form frmCD in design view. Move it so you can see it and the database view too. Your screen should resemble Figure 10.13.

4. Locate the form frmSongs in the database view. Click that object and drag it to the open form frmCD in design view. Drop the form frmSongs anywhere away from existing fields. Make sure the form you just dropped is selected. If not, click the

▼ gray rectangle at the upper-left corner of the subform to select the form. Locate the property Default View in the Format tab of the form Properties list box. Make sure it is set to Datasheet. Your screen should resemble Figure 10.14.

FIGURE **10.13**

Preparing to drag and drop your way to a subform.

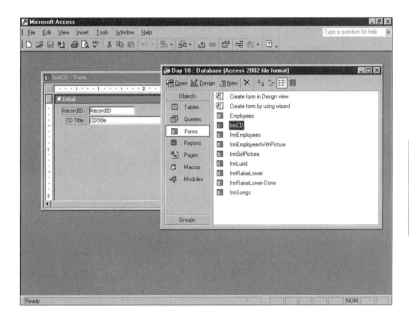

10

FIGURE **10.14**

And that's all there is to making a form with a subform.

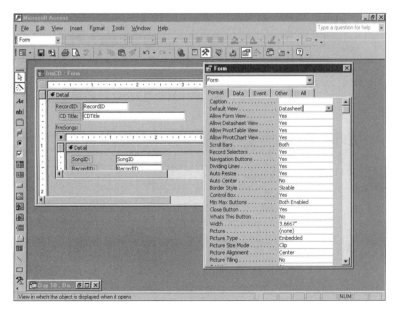

▼

▼   5. Switch to form view. Move through the record selectors at the bottom of the screen
        to switch CDs. Note how the songs change with each song only showing up for the
        appropriate CD. That's the magic of a form with a subform. Figure 10.15 shows
        this form in action.

FIGURE 10.15

*The songs and CDs
stay in synchronization
in a form with a sub-
form.*

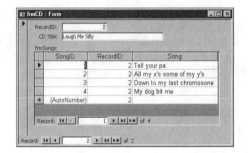

    6. Switch back to design view for this form. Click in the detail area of the subform.
        Examine the Data tab in the Properties list box. Note the two properties, Link
        Child Fields and Link Master Fields. They show the fields that are linked and illus-
        trated as such in the Relationships window. Even if there is a mismatch in the field
        names between the two tables, Access has no problems linking the fields to keep
        the form with a subform in synchronization. If you want to see this form in the
        sample data, it's saved as frmSub.

Note

Access isn't sensitive at all about the names of linked fields. If they are
linked in the Relationships window, they'll be linked in forms with subforms
regardless of the names.

▲

Note

I haven't bothered to clean up the form with a subform for this example,
but you might want to play around with it to do so. Here, for example, the
record selectors for the main form work well, but not the ones for the subform.

Tip

Before dragging a form that will become a subform onto the main form,
change its view to datasheet and then save. This works because in most
cases you want the subform in datasheet or table form anyway.

Control Wizards

Access 2002 uses several wizards to automate certain form controls. To activate the wizards, make sure you've selected the Control Wizards tool. This is the button in the toolbox with an icon that looks like a magic wand (complete with stars coming from it). Once activated, it looks like it's pressed. To deactivate, click the button again.

After you've turned on the Control Wizards tool, the corresponding wizard will activate when you place one of the following controls on the form:

- Command button
- Combo box (drop-down list box)
- List box
- Option group

10

If you get a "cannot start" wizard message when trying any of these controls, Office offers to install it. You'll need your circulation CD to do this unless you use a network install, in which case you'll need the location of installation files or the permission of your system administrator.

These wizards are simple to use. I encourage you to create a scratch form, activate the control wizard option, and then click one of the above controls. Click again anywhere on the form and then step through the associated wizard.

Summary

Aesthetics is important in forms not only to make your applications pleasing, but also to help users navigate. In short, a pleasing form is a good form.

Access provides many tools that you can use to spruce up your forms. You can add headers and footers as you've seen in previous lessons. You can color complete parts of or objects within a form, add lines and rectangles, and change the characteristics of any objects to make them seem indented, shadowed, raised, etched, or chiseled.

Access also contains a variety of options allowing you to change the functionality of a form. You can add or remove the minimize, maximize, control menu, record selectors, and similar objects on your forms.

The only real caution when experimenting with form formatting is not to go overboard. It's very easy to make your forms look like a circus clown or a ransom note. A little formatting goes a long way in Access.

You can make a form much more attractive by adding a header label or a picture. Doing so will enlarge your database, but the price is often worth the gain in attractiveness. Like other formatting elements, use pictures and colors sparingly.

Q&A

Q. How can I get my forms to open maximized?

A. You can create a small macro with the Action Maximize and then place it in the Form's `On Open` event.

Q. Can I make my forms modal?

A. Although you can, this powerful feature should be used sparingly. Under the Other tab for the form's properties you'll find a `Modal` property. The default is No. Change to Yes and you've done it.

Q. How can I restrict the Tab key's cursor movement to the current record?

A. Alter the `Cycle` property for the form's property to Current Record. The `Cycle` property is on the Other tab.

Q. Can I change lines from solid to dashed or do I need to add a new line for every dash?

A. The line and rectangle objects have the property `Border Style` that controls the solidity of the line or rectangle. You'll find this property on the Format tab.

Q. I'd like to make sure my pictures automatically size to fit the object frame. How do I do this?

A. Change the `Size Mode` property on the Format tab to Stretch and your pictures will fill all available space in the frame. This can distort pictures, however. Figure 10.11 shows Nancy Davolio's picture stretched to fit a frame. As you can see, the results aren't very attractive. You're better off including pictures of the same size and using a properly sized frame than altering this property to Stretch.

Workshop

The Workshop helps you solidify the skills you learned in this lesson. Answers to the quiz appear in Appendix A, "Answers to Quizzes."

Quiz

1. Can you alter one property to change background color for both the form footer and detail area?

2. Can you include a sunken rectangle object within a raised rectangle object?

3. Can you make some form design changes in form view?

4. If you don't have as many colors to choose from for form color as you wish, what can you do to increase your selection?

5. Can you change the identical property for several objects at the same time?

Exercises

1. Open the `frmEmployeesWithPicture` in design view.

2. Alter the bound object frame to an etched look.

3. Make sure the `Allow Design Changes` property for the form is set to All Views.

4. Switch to form view. If the Properties list box isn't open, open it. If necessary click the bound object frame so Bound Object Frame appears in the title bar of the list box.

5. Alter the Special Effect (use the toolbar button) for this object to Raised and then Shadowed. Which property do you prefer?

6. Try to resize the Bound Object Frame to be the exact size of the included picture.

7. Switch to design view and resize the Bound Object Frame to fit the table's pictures. Hint: Note the desired size of the photo to the picture in the unbound picture frame above it and use that as a guide for resizing.

8. Close the form optionally saving changes.

10

Manipulating Queries

Back in Day 4, "The Data Foundation—the Table," you saw some of the power
of select queries. Later, in Day 14, "Special Query Uses," you'll learn how easy
it is to manipulate your data and the database itself using action queries. Today,
you'll see how to use expressions in queries, the meaning of joins, and some
other highly useful, but often overlooked query abilities.

Today You Will Learn

Each of the features or techniques in this lesson is fairly short in length, so this
day tends to jump around quite a bit from one seemingly unrelated topic to
another. While it's true that these subjects have little in common other than
their use in queries, they do form a body of knowledge utterly vital to any serious Access developer:

- Details about the query design grid
- SQL view
- A start on complex queries
- Using expressions to create query fields

- Inner Joins
- Left Joins
- Right Joins
- Self Joins
- Theta Joins
- Using ranges in query expressions

> **Note** This lesson uses the tables from the Microsoft-supplied sample database Northwind, extensively. These, as well as other database objects, are all part of your sample data in the Day 11 folder.

Don't worry about memorizing each and every approach or method shown here in one exposure. Just get a feel for what you can do and keep in mind that you can always come back here when you need a refresh on specifics. For example, it's important to know that you can do date and time math in queries, but not important to memorize all the parameters of the expressions that do so.

> **Tip** An expression is an expression. The ones you see today to calculate totals, time, or other values work in forms and reports, as well as queries assuming the context is valid. Similarly, the expressions you saw as examples in form and report lessons will work in queries.

The Query Design Grid

Open any database or start a new one and go to the Queries objects. A good idea is to make a duplicate of Northwind (giving it another name such as New Northwind) and then using that for experimentation because it has many sample objects to experiment on. An easy way to duplicate the Northwind database is to use the New File Task Pane and select the hyperlink New from existing file, Choose file. The New from Existing dialog box opens, allowing you to select the database from which you want to create a copy. You can locate Northwind in the Samples directory where you installed Office.

Start a query by clicking the New button on the top of the database view and then choose Design view. The Show Table dialog opens. Just so you have something to work with, add a few tables or queries by clicking a table or query and pressing the Add button.

Right-click in a blank area of the query design grid above the actual grid where the tables or queries list boxes appear. Note that this brings up the Properties list box for the query. You also can get to this properties dialog box by choosing View, Properties from the menu. Some of these entries are duplicates of entries in the menu or toolbar (which are also duplicates), but some are unique to this list box. For example, the property Orientation affects how the query interacts with the printer. You also can restrict the query return to a certain number of records. Figure 11.1 shows the Properties list box for the query.

FIGURE 11.1

The Properties of the query.

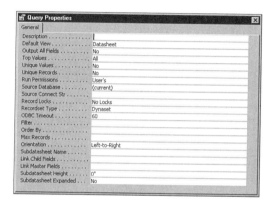

A very handy, but often overlooked, entry on the right-click menu is the entry Relationships. This is a duplicate of an entry in the Tools menu, but few seem to know that it's there. When designing a query, you'll often find it useful to know what relationships exist already, and this is the quick way to see that.

If you right-click the table (or query) list box, you'll see a short properties box containing a bit of information. The most useful part of this context menu is to delete the object from the query.

Tip

Remember you can query a query. If an existing query has a result close to where you want to go with a new query, that as a starting place instead of reinventing the whole business with one huge complex query.

Also note that there are two Properties for the entire query that deal with the source database for this query. Most queries use the current (or open) database for its sources, however Access allows you to query objects outside of the current database, even if they aren't currently imported or attached (linked).

To connect to a source other than the current database, say an Access database, enter the path to that database in Source Database. Say you want to connect to a database called `My Database.mdb` located in `C:\My Files`, enter

C:\My Files\My Database.mdb

for this property.

> **Note**
>
> The documentation for this property says you don't need to add the .mdb extension for Access databases. You do.

> **Note**
>
> You can link tables external to the current database by choosing the main menu options File, Get External Data, Link Tables. This makes these tables apparently part of the current database, when they really exist externally. You can link to objects which aren't in native Access format. For example, if you want to link to a dBASE table maintained in a dBASE dataset, this is the way to do it. Of course, you can always import into the Access database, but then it won't reflect changes made in dBASE where linking will.

One other area that's often a problem for folks with Access, or at least they often ask how to do this, is the `Top Values` properties. Here, you can have Access return only the most or least values in number or percentage.

A Quick Look at the SQL View

It's a good idea to start to get familiar with Structured Query Language (SQL). I encourage you to take a look at the SQL behind each query you encounter or make using the query design grid—also called the query-by-example format.

SQL isn't a very difficult language when it comes to syntax because it's pretty much standard English. You can take a look at the queries and get a good idea of what they're about even without a single idea of what SQL is.

Open the `Day 11` database and open the query `qrySimpleSQL` in design view. Locate the View button which is the one furthest left in the toolbar. Pull down the View button and choose SQL view. Note the SQL expression

```
SELECT Employees.LastName, Employees.FirstName, Employees.HireDate
FROM Employees
WHERE (((Employees.HireDate)>#1/1/1993#));
```

Now click the button to switch to datasheet view. You easily can see how this expression or query works. Also take a look at design view to see how Access translates the SQL into query by example. You can learn more in Day 14, "Special Query Uses."

Note

Access is SQL-based. It uses that language for its internal workings often showing you the pretty face of query by example (QBE) instead. It is vital that you learn SQL if you want to do advanced work in Access, because a pretty face isn't always available. For example, you can use SQL to populate a form field by entering the expression as the `Control Source` property on a form, but there is no QBE "face" to do this.

General Math in Queries

Access has many built-in functions such as the `Count()` function (which you've seen demonstrated in counting voters). You can use expressions to do various math calculations working across a query. For example, let's say you have a table (or query) with a column for price, and another with the percentage discount. You easily can create a third column showing the dollar value of the discount or the net cost to your customer.

Here's how.

11

Note

This example uses very simple tables for clarity. While the sample data is somewhat strained and not realistic in an actual operational scheme, the point is to show by example this aspect of Access queries and not to be a template for a real business.

▼ TASK Task: Using Expressions in Queries

1. Launch Access and open the Day 11 database. Start a new query using the design view. Include the two tables, `tblCustomerDiscounts` and `tblPrices`. You might want to examine the Relationships window and the two tables in both design and table view before proceeding to get an idea of these table's contents and their relationships.

2. Add `CustomerName` and `Discount` from `tblCustomerDiscounts` to the query design grid. Add the `Standard Price` field from `tblPrices` to the grid, too. Remember, you add fields to a query by clicking the field and dragging it to the query design grid. Your screen should resemble Figure 11.2.

▼

FIGURE 11.2

*The new query with
tblCustomerDiscount
and tblPrices tables
added.*

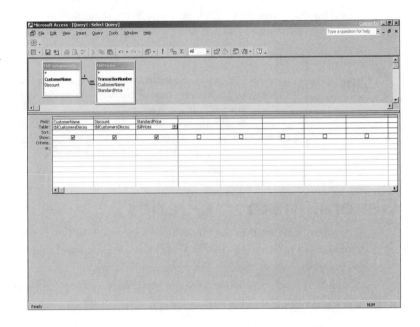

Tip

When making queries, more than almost any other Access objects, run them often as sanity checks to make sure all is running as it should. This prevents you from having to do a long and confusing debug if and when the query doesn't, in the end, work out the way it should have.

3. Switch to query view to make sure your query is working as it should. Your screen should resemble Figure 11.3.

FIGURE 11.3

*Run sanity checks
often when making
even slightly complex
queries.*

CustomerName	Discount	StandardPrice
Noisy Noses	2.00%	$56.00
Pip Boys	12.00%	$1,239.00
Value Stores	0.02%	$234.00
Zoom Discounte	2.30%	$948.00
*		

4. Return to design view. The first calculation to do is the discount amount. Click in the first empty column. Enter the expression

```
Dollar Discount: [Discount]*[StandardPrice]
```

5. This example uses the zoom window (Shift+F2) to enter the expression. You can see this operation in Figure 11.4.

FIGURE **11.4**

*The Zoom box is a
good place to edit
expressions.*

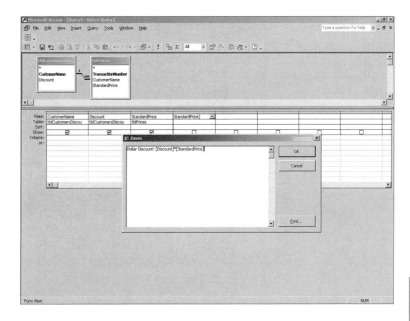

6. Switch to query view. Access uses the string to the left of the expression's colon as
   a column header while placing the requested calculation in the query return itself.
   Your screen should resemble Figure 11.5.

FIGURE **11.5**

*Works first time and
every time—well, sort
of works.*

CustomerName	Discount	StandardPrice	Dollar Discount
Noisy Noses	2.00%	$56.00	1.11999997497
Pip Boys	12.00%	$1,239.00	148.679996677
Value Stores	0.02%	$234.00	0.04679999882
Zoom Discounte	2.30%	$948.00	21.8040000424

7. This column now has the right amount, but much too precise. Return to design
   view, click in the column containing the expression, and then open the Properties
   list box by clicking the Properties button in the toolbar. Locate the Format property
   on the General tab. Pull down the combo box and enter the Currency entry for a
   value. Your screen should resemble Figure 11.6.

8. Switch to query view. The discount now appears appropriate to the values it holds.
   Return to design view. In the next empty column enter

   ```
   Net: [StandardPrice]-[Dollar Discount]
   ```

9. Switch to query view. Access now calculates the net amount based on the
   StandardPrice and the calculated discount amount. Your screen should resemble
   Figure 11.7.

FIGURE 11.6

There are properties lurking everywhere which are useful as can be.

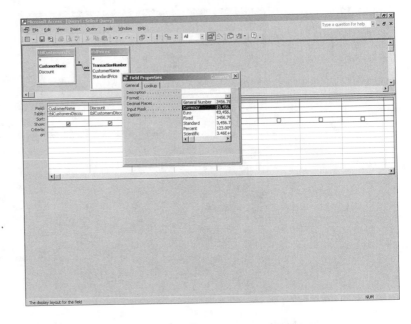

FIGURE 11.7

Access can calculate expressions quite well and quickly.

CustomerName	Discount	StandardPrice	Dollar Discount	Net
Noisy Noses	2.00%	$56.00	$1.12	$54.88
Pip Boys	12.00%	$1,239.00	$148.68	$1,090.32
Value Stores	0.02%	$234.00	$0.05	$233.95
Zoom Discounte	2.30%	$948.00	$21.80	$926.20

10. Save this query giving it a name of your choosing. This example uses the name `qryDiscountExpressions` which is supplied in the Day 11 database.

> **Note**
>
> Access uses the standard algebraic order of operation to perform its calculations. You can use nested parentheses to alter the order from the default.

Date and Time Math in Queries

Very likely, the most used math in queries is calculations of dates and times. Access, through built-in functions, can calculate not only time spans between two fields in a query, but also dynamically calculate time differentials between a field date and the current system date.

> **Note**
>
> This lesson, as with the ones before, uses the built-in functions exclusively. You, as a developer, also can create your own functions by using VBA. You'll see how to do this starting on Day 15, "Introduction to VBA Concepts," and throughout the second half of this book.

Task: Using Date Math in Queries

1. Launch Access and open the Day 11 database. Start a new query using the design view. Add the table Employees.

2. Create an expression

   ```
   Name: [TitleOfCourtesy] & " " & [FirstName] & " " & [LastName]
   ```

   and place it in the first column. This gives us a column with the label Name containing the courtesy title, plus the first and last names of all employees.

3. Switch to query view to make sure your query is working as it should.

4. Return to design view. This exercise creates an expression that calculates the approximate age of the employee at hire date. It uses the two fields containing the hire date and birth date as a basis for this calculation. So enter this expression into the next empty column:

   ```
   Age at Hire: DateDiff("yyyy",[BirthDate],[HireDate])
   ```

5. The DateDiff() function calculates the interval between two dates (or times) and returns the value in various forms. The "yyyy" parameter tells the function to return the interval in years. If you replace the parameter with "m", your return is in months. Switch to query view. Your screen should resemble Figure 11.8.

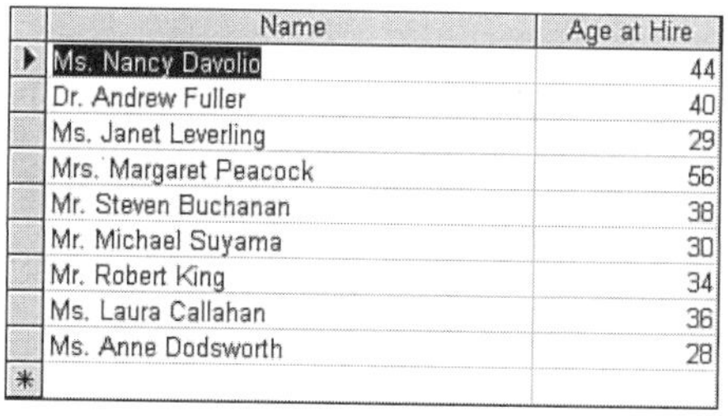

FIGURE 11.8

Here are the approximate ages of the employees at hire date.

Name	Age at Hire
Ms. Nancy Davolio	44
Dr. Andrew Fuller	40
Ms. Janet Leverling	29
Mrs. Margaret Peacock	56
Mr. Steven Buchanan	38
Mr. Michael Suyama	30
Mr. Robert King	34
Ms. Laura Callahan	36
Ms. Anne Dodsworth	28

6. Switch back to design view. Access has built-in functions for the current system time. This next expression uses one of these functions to calculate the approximate number of years the employee has been working for the company. Enter this expression into the next empty column:

   ```
   Seniority: DateDiff("yyyy", [HireDate], Date())
   ```

7. Return to query view and you'll see that the new field contains a value giving the approximate number of years an employee has been with the company. The number of years shown depends on your system date as the Date() function returns this value.

Note

> The Datediff() function is hardly perfect. In the above two examples, it uses calculations based on the year only. A person who hasn't yet met his yearly anniversary still gets credit for the year as if he had. While these examples serve well as approximates, if your date/time math needs are critical, such as calculating vesting, you'll need to either develop your own functions or create significantly more sophisticated expressions.

8. Save this query giving it a name of your choosing. This example uses the name qryDateMath. It is part of your sample data.

The two other significant built-in date functions are DateAdd() and DatePart(). The first calculates the value of adding time to a date or time. For example,

```
DateAdd("d",Date(),10)
```

returns the date 10 days from the current system date. If you enter the expression

```
DatePart("m",Date())
```

Access returns the current system month.

Sorting Values That Are Not Alphabetically Sequential

Access sorts, or orders, using fixed sort values. For example, depending on whether the sort order is ascending or descending, it sorts the following states like

```
California
Kansas
North Dakota
```

or

```
North Dakota
Kansas
California
```

There is no way you can convince Access, under usual circumstances that the order you want is

```
Kansas
California
North Dakota
```

Similarly, you can't get Access to sort in days of the week order, as the day names aren't alphabetically sequential. See Figure 11.9.

FIGURE 11.9

The alpha sorts that Access offers don't work too well with days of the week.

Many Access developers get around this problem by adding a number field to a table, adding a number to any data, and then sorting on the number field but leaving it out of the query return. Figure 11.10 shows such a query in design view.. This is the query `qryFalseData` which is part of your sample data.

FIGURE 11.10

Now the sort order is the same as the order of days in the week, but this is a clumsy technique.

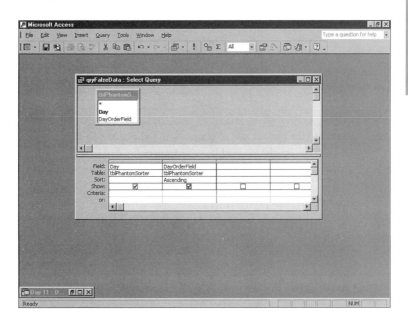

11

While this technique works, and is used quite often, it's inflexible. Also, not only does it add extraneous data to a table, but it requires either an extra (but related) table or additional data entry. If you want to see how this query works, it's part of the sample data using the name `qryFalseData`.

You also can use the `Switch()` function which is a superior way to solve this and similar dilemmas. Open the query `qryInvisibleSort` in query view. Note the default sort order is the order of the `autonumber` field. The boss wants to sort this query in the following order.

```
Colorado
Kansas
North Dakota
California
Arizona
```

Note there is no way to do this by sorting either ascending or descending on any of the data fields available in this table or query.

To accomplish this seemingly impossible task, add this expression to the first empty column in design view.

```
Switch(Office="Colorado",1,Office="Kansas",2,Office="North Dakota",
    3,Office="California",4,Office="Arizona",5)
```

Sort this column ascending by specifying `Ascending` in the Sort row. Your screen should resemble Figure 11.11.

FIGURE 11.11

Here is the `Switch()` *function working out in the open.*

OfficeNumber	Office	City	Expr1
3	Colorado	Durango	1
4	Kansas	Fizro	2
5	North Dakota	Fargo	3
1	California	Burbank	4
2	Arizona	Sedona	5
(AutoNumber)			

Switch to design view and uncheck the checkbox to exclude the last field from the query return. The checkbox enables you to specify whether that column shows up in the query returns. This is useful when you need to sort or filter on a particular column, but don't want to show it as part of the query results. Switch back to query view. Your screen should resemble Figure 11.12.

FIGURE 11.12

Eliminating the field from the display gives a much more elegant look to your query.

OfficeNumber	Office	City
3	Colorado	Durango
4	Kansas	Fizro
5	North Dakota	Fargo
1	California	Burbank
2	Arizona	Sedona
(AutoNumber)		

Using the identical technique, you can order table data any way you want without including phantom fields in the table to sort on.

The finished query shown in Figure 11.12 is part of your sample data for today saved under the name `qryInvisibleSort-Done`.

Joins

When querying two or more tables, you'll note that Access indicates the linked or joined fields by a line. There are several different characteristics of this join. While by far the most often used join is the one used by default (inner), you also should gain familiarity with outer joins as they do come in handy during the course of database development.

Table 11.1 explains the three common joins used between two tables. The section after the table gives examples to illustrate the short explanations for these concepts. All explanations use specifics from the query qryJoins.

TABLE 11.1 Join Types

Join	Description
Inner	Returns only records from both sides where the joined fields from both tables are equal.
Left Outer	Returns all the records from tblJoinSuppliers whether or not there are any corresponding records from tblJoinProducts.
Right Outer	Returns all the records from tblJoinProducts whether or not there are any corresponding records from tblJoinProducts.

Task: Experimenting with Three Joins Types

1. Launch Access and open the Day 11 database. Open the query qryJoins in query view. Your screen should resemble Figure 11.13. This query shows all the products that a particular supplier provides. This is accomplished by an inner join where there must be records from both tables (equal) for the query to return something in its selection.

FIGURE 11.13

Here is the most common join—inner.

	SupplierID	Suppliers	Products
▶	1	Boxing Ring	Widges
	1	Boxing Ring	Gigits
	1	Boxing Ring	Slamming Sammmies
	2	Ammo Dump	Whamos
*	(AutoNumber)		

2. Switch to design view. Double-click the line joining the two tables. This brings up the Join Properties dialog box as shown in Figure 11.14. Click the second option button for a left outer join, click OK to close the dialog box, and then return to query view to see the results. Your screen should resemble Figure 11.15.

▼

FIGURE **11.14**

The Join Properties dialog box allows you to change join types. It also gives an excellent description of the results of changing join types.

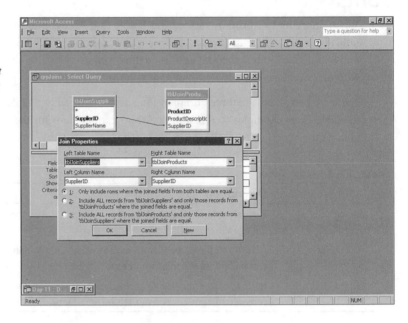

FIGURE **11.15**

A left outer join returns all suppliers even if they have no products entered in the table.

	SupplierID	Suppliers	Products
▶	1	Boxing Ring	Widges
	1	Boxing Ring	Gigits
	1	Boxing Ring	Slamming Sammmies
	2	Ammo Dump	Whamos
	3	Soccer Kick	
	4	Baseball Hit	
✱	(AutoNumber)		

 Note

In most situations, you'd establish a link in Tools, Relationships between tables holding supplier and product information. You'd also make sure, through referential integrity, that your users couldn't enter a product without a supplier. This example purposely leaves out this common (and usually required) link to demonstrate a right join.

3. Switch to design view. Again bring up the Join Properties list box, but this time switch to the third option by clicking the appropriate button. Close the dialog box and switch to query view. Your screen should resemble Figure 11.16.

▼ 4. Close the query, discarding changes.

FIGURE 11.16

A right outer join returns product even with no supplier.

SupplierID	Suppliers	Products
		No Supplier Mitts
1	Boxing Ring	Widges
1	Boxing Ring	Gigits
1	Boxing Ring	Slamming Sammmies
2	Ammo Dump	Whamos
(AutoNumber)		

Note

Some developers claim there are no such things as "outer" joins because the Access SQL statement for a left outer join can make do with just "left join," whereas the statement for a right outer join can make do with just "right join." Similarly, there are no "inner joins" as all common SQL dialects use the equal (=) sign so they are really equi-joins or equal joins. However people, when you're speaking descriptively, use the term *outer* to indicate all the records from the left or right table should be returned. SQL is not standard across all implementations. Most SQL dialects use the full syntax for a right or left join does include the word outer as in "left outer."

Self Join

11

You can join a table to itself in order to select data from the single table in the same way you would if the data were located in two tables. For example, say you have a table with commission and salary data in it. You want to see the salaries that are higher than a certain commission value. The self-join is a way to do this.

To construct a self-join, add the same table twice to the query design grid. Access adds a "_1" to the second table you add. If you want, you can right-click the table that you want to alias, and select the Properties button from the context menu. Change the Alias property to something else. In our example, I changed the table name to **Second Self**. From there on, you can refer to this table by its alias. Figure 11.17 shows the table properties list box with an alias added.

Tip

Cute tricks, such as adding aliases, seem like a lot of fun, and they are, but if they start getting so complex that you lose sight of what you're trying to do, cut the fun back some.

From here, what you do depends on your goal. For the most part, you'll drag to create a join on the two fields you want to join on, then use either an expression as criteria in an expression field or construct a SQL statement using the WHERE keyword.

FIGURE 11.17

*You can alias a table if
you don't like to use
the _1 nomenclature.*

FIGURE 11.17

*You can alias a table if
you don't like to use
the _1 nomenclature.*

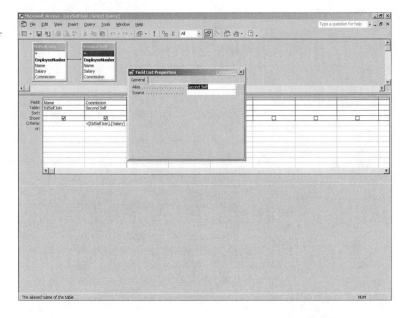

> **Tip**
>
> If you want to pause now and get a SQL primer, jump to later in this lesson
> or for a fuller treatment, skip ahead to Day 14.

For example, if you wanted to display records where the salary was higher than the commission and your two table instances were aliased `TableOne` and `TableTwo`, your `WHERE` statement would look like,

```
WHERE TableOne.Salary < TableTwo.Commission;
```

You also can enter a criteria expression that would look like

```
>TableOne.Salary
```

in the `Commission` field if you prefer entering expressions and letting Access create the SQL statement.

If you are confused, don't be alarmed. There is a query called `qrySelfJoin` that's part of the sample data for today. Open it in both design and query view to get an idea of how it works. Experiment with the expression in the `Commission` field to see how editing this changes things. Try especially changing the lesser than symbol for a greater than.

Although you won't hit the full lesson on SQL until Day 14, the statement for this query is

```
SELECT tblSelfJoin.Name, [Second Self].Commission
FROM tblSelfJoin INNER JOIN tblSelfJoin AS [Second Self] ON
➥    tblSelfJoin.EmployeeNumber = [Second Self].EmployeeNumber
WHERE ((([Second Self].Commission)<[tblSelfJoin].[Salary]));
```

If you're feeling adventurous, try editing the statement to include more fields or the WHERE statement. Remember, as long as you don't save the query under the same name, you can't "ruin" it. Just close without saving and reopen to start afresh or restore from the CD.

Figure 11.18 shows this query running, while Figure 11.19 shows the design view.

FIGURE 11.18

Here is the self join query (qrySelfJoin) *in action.*

Name	Commission
Jones	$1,200.00
Buechlein	$3,400.00

FIGURE 11.19

This is the design view for qrySelfJoin.

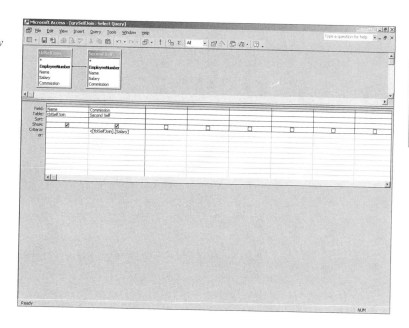

Inner to Theta Joins

The inner join is a specific case of the general case theta join (I sure do enjoy this terminology). An inner join returns records where the linked fields are equal. This makes sense when joining text fields such as the name of a supplier.

Theta joins are more flexible, allowing the return where linked fields are not only equal, but greater than or lesser than. While this doesn't have much, if any, use in true text-type data, it does when the data is numerical. This includes not only data types of numbers and currency, but also dates or time.

The easiest way to create such joins is to edit the SQL statement for an inner join to read another operator. To do this, follow these steps:

1. Create the inner join query using whichever technique you prefer.

2. Switch to SQL view using the View button on the toolbar.

3. Locate the equals sign (=) and edit to <, >, <=, or >=.

Using Ranges in Queries

By adding a simple expression, you can create queries that return a range of records. The following short task takes you through such a query.

Task: Creating a Range Query

1. Launch Access and open the Day 11 database. Start a new query using the design view. Include the tables Products and Suppliers. Add the CompanyName field from Suppliers and the ProductName and UnitPrice fields from Products. Switch to query view. Your screen should resemble Figure 11.20. Note that there are 77 records returned.

FIGURE 11.20

Sanity check time again at the old database ranch.

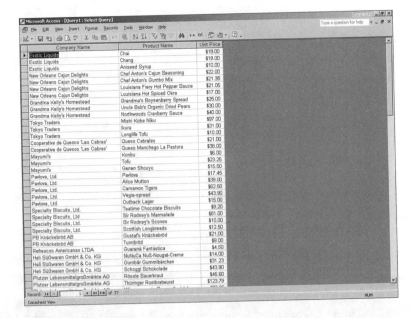

▼ 2. Return to design view. Create the following expression in the criteria row of the
      UnitPrice column:

   Between 34 and 100

   Return to query view. This time Access returns 17 records—only those where the
   price is between $34.00 and $100.00 inclusive.

   3. Return to design view. Delete the criteria for UnitPrice. Enter the following
      expression, in the criteria row of the CompanyName field:

   Between A* and C*

   This restricts the return to those suppliers with a name starting with A, B, or C.
   Switch to query view to see if it works as you expect it to.

   4. Return to design view. Edit the expression in CompanyName to read

   Between E* and F*

   Add the following criterion on the second criteria row of UnitPrice:

   >100

   Your screen should resemble Figure 11.21.

FIGURE 11.21

*Here, either of the
ranges results in a
return.*

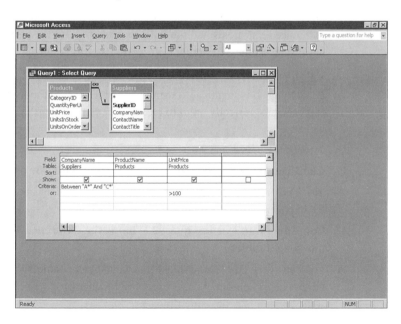

11

   5. Return to query view. Your return should be any record where the supplier's com-
      pany name begins with an *E* or an *F*, or where the UnitPrice is over $100.00. This
▲   is an example of using an OR criteria query with a range.

Summary

This lesson dealt with query issues, which were, for the most part, considerably more complex than previous lessons. Don't feel bad if the entire material hasn't sunk in yet. Knowing how to construct something like a self-join isn't intuitive at all. The important thing is to know such constructs exist. When you need them, you'll at least know what to look up either in this text or in online help.

Besides various joins, you saw how to construct a new field in a query using an expression. You also can create new fields based on other expression fields. Finally, you saw how to construct ranges in queries and combine them with other criteria which can be optionally ranged too.

Q&A

Q. Is it better to break data up so I never have to use a self-join?

A. Doing so is possible, but you'll then run the risk of "over-normalizing" your data. This is the process of breaking it into such small pieces that you inhibit the working of your database. For example, if you had salary and commission in two tables, you'd need link fields and the links to relate back to the employee. In this and similar instances, the extra table isn't worth the effort.

Q. Can I use dates in ranges?

A. Yes. Doing so is identical to using any numerical data. For example, the following expression is perfectly valid to return records from April 5, 1990 to April 5, 1999 inclusive:

```
Between #4/5/90# and #4/5/99#
```

Q. Can I construct expressions with product and divisor operands?

A. Yes. The product operand is an asterisk (*), the divisor operand is a slash (/), and the exponentiation operand is a carat (shift-6 or ^).

Q. Can I query an existing query? What is the difference between doing this and querying a table?

A. You can query an existing query just as you can a table. Operationally there is no difference. When run, Access executes the queries sequentially. This does take some additional processing time.

Workshop

The Workshop helps you solidify the skills you learned in this lesson. Answers to the quiz and exercises appear in Appendix A, "Answers to Quizzes."

Quiz

1. How does Access store date and time information?
2. Must you use only built-in functions for use in queries?
3. What is the most commonly used built-in Access function for calculating date or time intervals?
4. What use is the Switch() function?

Exercises

1. Open up the query qrySelfJoin in design view.
2. Alter either the expression or the SQL statement to return records where the commission is less than the salary. Switch to query view to see if it worked as you expect.
3. Close the qrySelfJoin discarding changes.
4. Create a new query using the Products and Suppliers tables. Have the query show the CompanyName, the ProductName, and the UnitPrice.
5. Create a criterion where the only records returned were those where the ProductName is in the range of the first letter starting with the letters *R, S, T,* or *U*. Move to query view to see if it worked as you expect.

Extra Credit for those who feel adventurous:

6. Remove the criterion from Step 5. Create a criterion returning only those records where the second letter of the CompanyName is an *e*. Hint: use the Mid() function.

11

DAY 12

Getting Your Reports Right

This lesson is all about getting what you need from your reports. Reports are the part of your database application that everyone else sees. More times than not, that everyone else is your boss or the boss's boss.

Even when you are the only one looking at a report, it is important to present your information in a concise and consistent manner. Information presented in this manner increases the chances of your audience recognizing trends and it speeds up the processing of information.

Today You Will Learn

With the Access report wizards, Microsoft makes it easy for anyone to create a report in a matter of seconds. What the wizards can't do for you, you can learn to do yourself. In this lesson you will learn some tricks and even a little philosophy that will help make your reports professional. Specifically you will learn:

- How to filter data for reports
- How to sort and group
- How to summarize information in crosstab reports

Creating Professional Reports

There are many types of reports, including detail, summary, and crosstab to name a few. Detail reports are the easiest report type to produce, while creating summary and crosstab reports require more mental resources.

It doesn't take much thought to create a detail report, simply because most of the time the report is a regurgitation of the data. The report wizards are great for creating detail reports. The sad fact is that most people will print out a long report and won't bother to look at anything after the first two pages because they don't have the patience to sort through it.

The good news is that most reports can be filtered down by some criteria to a manageable size. This could include date ranges for date sensitive information, dollar amounts for sales, and alphabet ranges for customer lists. You'll learn more about filtering and some useful techniques for doing so in "Filtering Data for Reports," later in this lesson.

For reports that can't be filtered down, you can present information in manageable sizes by sorting and grouping. Even though the same amount of information is in the report, it is presented better. You'll learn about these techniques in "Sorting and Grouping," later in this lesson.

Summary and crosstab reports are much more difficult to produce, because you need to know details of what you are trying to present. Maybe the boss wants to see how a particular product sold during a certain timeframe, or she wants to see how the department in the call center performed every month last year. You create summary and crosstab reports so you can see the "big picture" of your data. You'll learn more about crosstab reports, later in this lesson, in the section "Understanding Crosstab Reports."

Filtering Data for Reports

Access, with its report wizards, makes it easy to create huge reports quickly. Alternatively, the best way to produce useful reports is to include just enough information to get the subject matter to its intended audience. There are several ways that you can do this and I'll present them to you in this section. Because this might be unfamiliar territory for you, I've chosen to organize the material from the more simple solution to the increasingly difficult and more professional solution.

Filtering Reports by Changing the Underlying Query

When you are new to Access, the various wizards help you learn how to do different things within the application. Although Access report wizards can be useful, they don't help you filter the data down to the necessary information. When a report isn't filtered down to the precise subset of data, the report isn't very useful. At the very least, the report design can be improved on. Look at Figure 12.1 and the rptOrdersNotFiltered report in the Day 12 database.

FIGURE 12.1

The rptOrders NotFiltered report needs improvement.

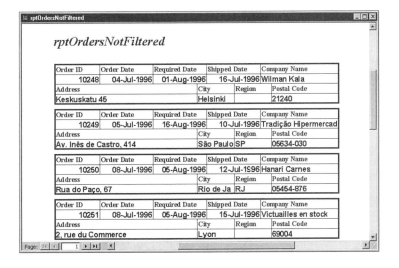

Note

By this time you are familiar with the reports in the Northwind sample database. Even though Northwind is a sample database, Microsoft recognizes that reports are only as relevant as the information shown. To make them more valuable and dynamic, all the reports in Northwind have some kind of criteria that filters the final output.

Notice that the information in rptOrdersNotFiltered ranges all the way back to 1996? This is great if you want to see how much business you had five years ago, but not at all pertinent for today. You must modify your report so that it only contains the necessary data.

You learned how to create reports in Day 7, "Basic Reports." You also learned how to filter data in queries on Day 11, "Manipulating Queries." In this next task you are going to apply the knowledge gained in Days 7 and 11, to creating a new report that only contains the needed information. You are going to get the information needed by modifying the underlying query for the report.

Task: Filtering by Changing the Underlying Query

1. Open the Day 12 database.

2. Click the Report button on the Object bar in the Database window.

3. Click the rptOrders2001byqry report to select it. This report is simply a copy of rptOrdersNotFiltered that I've included so you didn't have to copy it yourself.

4. Right-click the report and then select Design View from the shortcut menu. You could also click the Design View button on the Database window. Your screen will look similar to Figure 12.2.

FIGURE 12.2

The rptOrders2001 byqry report in design view, before you've changed the criteria.

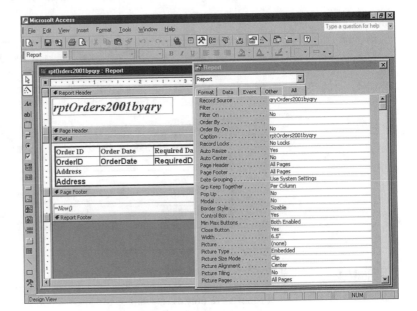

5. If the Properties list is not open, right-click the square in the upper-left corner of the report design window and select the Properties entry from the menu.

6. With the Properties list open, make sure the Report object is selected. If it is not, you can select the Report object from the drop-down at the top of the Properties list.

7. Locate the RecordSource property on the Data tab, and click in it to select it.

8. Notice the ellipsis button to the right of the RecordSource property and click it to take you to Design view of the qryOrders2001byqry query.

9. You want to filter the query for the report, so that it returns the subset of data in which you are interested. Find the OrderDate column and then click in the first Criteria row in that column.

▼   10. Enter the following expression into the first Criteria row:

Between #1/1/2001# And #12/31/2001#

Tip When entering dates in expressions, you could choose not to enter the "#'s." Access will modify your expression to include them. If the "#'s" weren't there, Access might try to interpret "1/1/2001" as 1 divided by 1 divided by 2001. So when using dates in expressions, always remember the "#'s".

11. Your query changes are complete. If you want to see the results of your handiwork, click the Run button (it's the red exclamation point) on the standard toolbar. Your query results will be similar to what is shown in Figure 12.3.

FIGURE 12.3

The qryOrders2001 byqry query in Datasheet view, after you've changed the criteria.

Order ID	Order Date	Required Date	Shipped Date	Company Name	Addre
11639	01-Jan-2001	29-Jan-2001	09-Jan-2001	Princesa Isabel Vinhos	Estrada da saúde n. 58
11640	01-Jan-2001	29-Jan-2001	07-Jan-2001	Wellington Importadora	Rua do Mercado, 12
11641	01-Jan-2001	29-Jan-2001	07-Jan-2001	Laughing Bacchus Wine Cellars	1900 Oak St.
11642	02-Jan-2001	30-Jan-2001	08-Jan-2001	LINO-Delicateses	Ave. 5 de Mayo Porlamar
11643	02-Jan-2001	30-Jan-2001	12-Jan-2001	Reggiani Caseifici	Strada Provinciale 124
11644	05-Jan-2001	02-Feb-2001	09-Jan-2001	Ricardo Adocicados	Av. Copacabana, 267
11645	05-Jan-2001	02-Feb-2001	14-Jan-2001	Victuailles en stock	2, rue du Commerce
11646	05-Jan-2001	02-Feb-2001	14-Jan-2001	Save-a-lot Markets	187 Suffolk Ln.
11647	06-Jan-2001	03-Feb-2001	04-Feb-2001	Great Lakes Food Market	2732 Baker Blvd.
11648	06-Jan-2001	20-Jan-2001	13-Jan-2001	Königlich Essen	Maubelstr. 90
11649	07-Jan-2001	04-Feb-2001	12-Jan-2001	Magazzini Alimentari Riuniti	Via Ludovico il Moro 22
11650	07-Jan-2001	04-Feb-2001	16-Jan-2001	Cactus Comidas para llevar	Cerrito 333
11651	07-Jan-2001	04-Feb-2001	13-Jan-2001	Rattlesnake Canyon Grocery	2817 Milton Dr.
11652	08-Jan-2001	05-Feb-2001	15-Jan-2001	Split Rail Beer & Ale	P.O. Box 555
11653	08-Jan-2001	05-Feb-2001	16-Jan-2001	Trail's Head Gourmet Provisioners	722 DaVinci Blvd.
11654	09-Jan-2001	06-Feb-2001	13-Jan-2001	LILA-Supermercado	Carrera 52 con Ave. Bolív
11655	09-Jan-2001	06-Feb-2001	30-Jan-2001	Folk och fä HB	Åkergatan 24
11656	09-Jan-2001	06-Feb-2001	14-Jan-2001	Drachenblut Delikatessen	Walserweg 21
11657	12-Jan-2001	09-Feb-2001	06-Feb-2001	Blondel père et fils	24, place Kléber
11658	12-Jan-2001	26-Jan-2001	06-Feb-2001	Bon app'	12, rue des Bouchers
11659	13-Jan-2001	27-Jan-2001	04-Feb-2001	Rancho grande	Av. del Libertador 900
11660	13-Jan-2001	10-Feb-2001	23-Jan-2001	Island Trading	Garden House
11661	13-Jan-2001	24-Feb-2001	21-Jan-2001	Tradição Hipermercados	Av. Inês de Castro, 414

Record: 14 ◄ | 1 | ► ►I ►* | of 270

12

12. Close the query by clicking the "X" button in the upper-right of the Datasheet view.

13. You will see a message box asking whether you want to save changes to the query and update the property. Click the Yes button. Note that this changes the query permanently if you click the Yes button.

14. Click the Print Preview button on the standard toolbar. Your screen will look similar to Figure 12.4.

▼

FIGURE 12.4

The rptOrders2001 byqry report in Print Preview, after you've changed the criteria for the underlying query.

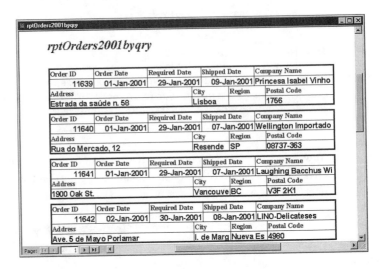

Now when you run the rptOrders2001byqry report you only get records where the OrderDate is in the year 2001.

Filtering Reports by Changing the Filter Properties

You can also filter the report by changing the Filter and Filter On properties on the report. To me this is more complicated than changing the query, but sometimes you might not have the luxury of changing the underlying query. For example, you might be working in one of the many third-party Access database applications and don't want to change the query.

There is a Filter property on each report that you can modify to get only the results you want. In this next task you are going to modify the Filter and Filter On properties to only get data where the OrderDate is in the year 2001.

Task: Filtering by Changing the Filter and Filter On Properties

1. If you didn't already open the Day 12 database in the task before, open the Day 12 database now.

2. Click the Report button on the Object bar in the Database window.

3. Click the rptOrders2001byprop report to select it.

▼ 4. Right-click Report and select Design view from the context menu. You could also click the Design view button on the toolbar in the Database window. Your screen will be similar to Figure 12.5.

FIGURE 12.5

The rptOrders2001 byprop report in Design view, before you've changed the Filter and the Filter On property.

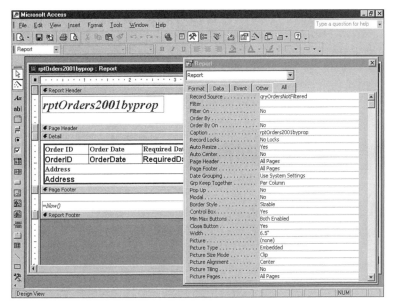

5. If the Properties list is not open, right-click the square in the upper-left corner of the report design window and select the Properties entry from the menu.

6. With the Properties list open, make sure the Report object is selected. If it is not, you can select the Report object from the drop-down at the top of the Properties list.

7. Locate the Filter property on the Data tab, and click in it to select it.

8. Enter the following expression exactly as shown:

   `[OrderDate] Between #1/1/2001# And #12/31/2001#`

   If you don't include the "#'s", Access doesn't know to treat the numbers as dates.

9. Locate the `Filter On` property on the Data tab, and change its value from No to Yes. Your screen will be similar to Figure 12.6.

▼ 10. Click the Print Preview button on the standard toolbar (see Figure 12.7).

12

FIGURE 12.6

The rptOrders2001
byprop report in
Design view, after
you've changed the
Filter and the Filter
On property.

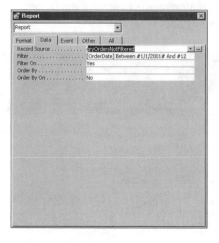

FIGURE 12.7

The rptOrders2001
byprop report in Print
Preview, filtered to
show records where
the OrderDate is in
2001.

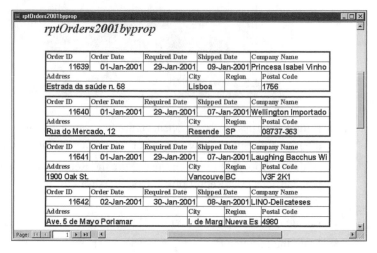

Your report is now filtered to show only records where the OrderDate is in the year
2001.

Making Report Criteria Dynamic—Using Parameters

Now that your reports are returning only the data for 2001, you have a problem. What
happens when you do want to see data for 2000? Do you make a new report with a new
query? You could, but doing this is a waste of resources and time. If you need to make a
change in the report, you would have to make the same change in all the similar reports.
Doing this could lead to inconsistencies, which will degrade how your reports are per-
ceived.

The better alternative would be to make your criteria dynamic so that you can choose what years or combination of criteria you need at that moment. Right now your reports are based on what is known as "hard-coded" criteria. In order to be more dynamic, you need to know about parameter queries.

When run, parameter queries prompt you for the values that need to be dynamic. For example, you could make a report based on a parameter query that prompts you for the starting and ending dates you want to include on that report.

Tip

> If you are interested in what else you could do with parameter queries and reports, look in the Microsoft Access Help, under the topic "About parameter queries that prompt for criteria." Alternatively you can study how Northwind uses parameter queries for all the reports.

In this next task, you will change the underlying query to prompt for the starting and ending dates you want the report to include.

Task: Filtering by Using Parameters

1. If you didn't already open the Day 12 database in the task before, open the Day 12 database now.
2. Click the Report button on the Object bar in the Database window.
3. Click the rptOrdersbyParam report to select it.
4. Right-click report and select Design view from the context menu. You could also click the Design view button on the toolbar in the Database window. Your screen will be similar to Figure 12.8.
5. If the Properties list is not open, right-click the square in the upper-left corner of the report design window and select the Properties entry from the menu.
6. With the Properties list open, make sure the Report object is selected. If it is not, you can select the Report object from the drop-down menu at the top of the Properties list.
7. Locate the RecordSource property on the Data tab and click in it to select it.
8. Notice the ellipsis button to the right of the RecordSource property and click it to take you to Design view of the qryOrdersbyParam query. Your screen will look similar to Figure 12.9.

12

FIGURE 12.8

The rptOrdersbyParam report in Design View, before the underlying query has been changed.

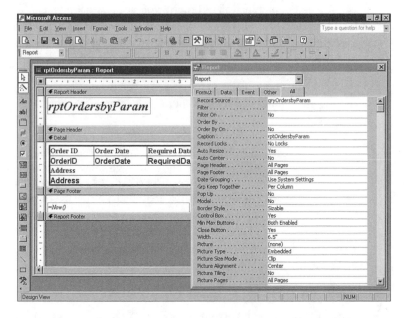

FIGURE 12.9

The qryOrdersbyParam query in Design View, before the parameters have been specified.

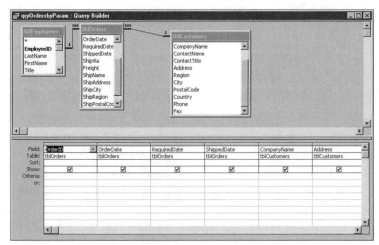

9. You want to filter the query dynamically when the report runs so that it returns the subset of data in which you are interested. Find the OrderDate column and then click in the first Criteria row in that column.

▼ 10. Enter the following expression exactly as shown, into the first Criteria row of the
        `OrderDate` column:

        `Between [Enter Start Date for Report] And [Enter End Date for Report]`

    11. You could stop here and run the query, but to be complete, you need to fill in the
        Query Parameters dialog box. Open the Query menu and click the Parameters
        menu entry. The Query Parameters dialog box will open.

    12. In the first row, first column, add **Enter Start Date for Report**. Notice that this
        is the same text without the square brackets. Select **Date/Time** for the Data Type.
        Selecting the Data Type tells Access that this parameter is going to be a date when
        the user runs the report or query.

    13. In the second row, first column, add **Enter End Date for Report**. Select
        Date/Time for the Data Type. Your Query Parameters dialog box will look similar
        to the one in Figure 12.10.

FIGURE 12.10

*The Query Parameters
dialog box filled out
with the two dynamic
parameters.*

    14. Close the Query Parameters dialog box by clicking the Ok button. Your query
        changes are complete. Close the query by clicking on the "X" button in the upper-
        right of the Query Design view.

    15. You will see a message box asking whether you want to save changes to the query
        and update the property. Click the Yes button. Note that clicking the Yes button
        changes the query permanently.

    16. Click the Print Preview button on the standard toolbar. When you run the report,
        you will be prompted for the first parameter. In this case it is the "[Enter Start Date
        for Report]" parameter. The criteria dialog box is seen in Figure 12.11.

▼ 17. Enter **6/1/2000** in the first criteria dialog box and click the OK button. Enter
        12/31/2000 in the second criteria dialog box. Your results will be similar to what is
        shown in Figure 12.12.

12

▼

FIGURE 12.11

The criteria dialog box prompting for the start date.

FIGURE 12.12

The rptOrdersbyParam report filtered down to show only Orders with the OrderDate between 6/1/2000 and 12/31/2000.

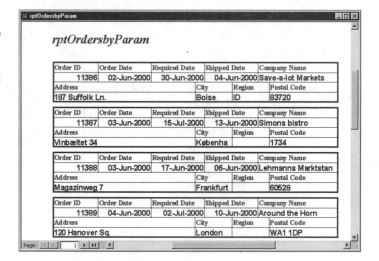

▲

You now can filter your report on any start date and any end date that you desire, without having to change the query or the filter properties.

Sorting and Grouping

In instances when you can't use filtering to create precise reports, you need to use sorting and grouping to organize your report. Sorting and grouping is a way to organize your reports vertically down the page. On Day 7, you learned about sorting and grouping, but this lesson shows you how to modify reports so that your information is presented logically and is precise.

Tip

Sorting and grouping is not new to you. If you need a refresher on each property of the Sorting and Grouping dialog box, refer to Day 7.

Sorting

The simplest way to organize your report vertically is sorting. Sorting on a field or fields helps the reader of your report to see related information. Figure 12.13 shows an example of the `rptCustomerDirectoryNotSorted` report that isn't sorted.

FIGURE 12.13

The rptCustomer DirectoryNotSorted report in Print Preview view is hard to read because it is not sorted.

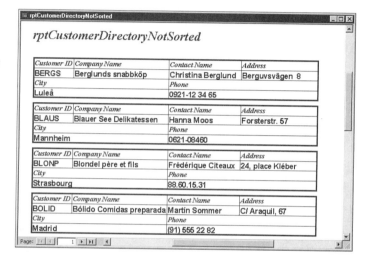

This report is hard to read and the reader needs more time to process the information contained in the report. If the reader needs to find a particular customer, he would have to look through at each line on every page. Obviously this is not ideal. This can be fixed simply by specifying a sort order.

This next task shows you how to specify a sort order on your Customer Directory so that each customer's company name can be located alphabetically.

▼ TASK

Task: Specifying a Sort Order for a Report

1. If you don't already have the Day 12 database open, do so now.

2. Click the Reports button on the Object bar in the Database window.

3. Locate the `rptCustomerDirectory` report and click it to select it.

4. Right-click the report and select Design View from the context menu.

5. Click the Sorting and Grouping button to open the Sorting and Grouping dialog box. (It's the button that has two equal signs and a couple of parenthesis.) Your screen should resemble Figure 12.14.

▼

12

FIGURE 12.14

The Sorting and Grouping dialog box.

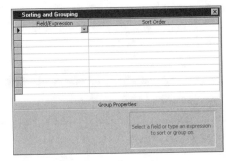

6. In the first column, first row, open the field drop-down menu and select CompanyName.

7. Close the Sorting and Grouping dialog box by clicking the "X" button.

8. Click the Print Preview button on the standard toolbar to view your results. Your results will be similar to what is shown in Figure 12.15.

FIGURE 12.15

The rptCustomerDirectory report sorted by company name, shown in Print Preview.

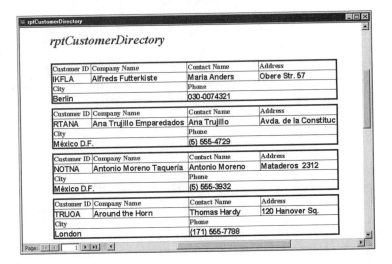

The rptCustomerdirectory report is now sorted by the CompanyName field.

Grouping

Grouping is a little more complex than sorting mainly because there are many options that influence how your report looks. Grouping allows you to vertically separate related information into sections. This proves useful in customer lists, ranking reports, region sales figures, and many other such lists.

While I can't show you an example of the possibilities I named, I *will* show you how to create a customer list that looks like a directory. Armed with what you learn in this lesson, you should be able to apply this concept to other possible uses.

Even though you specified a sort order in the last section, the Customer Directory needs more help. What you want for this report is to show every customer grouped by the first letter of their company name. For example, you want all the companies where the company name starts with "A" in the same group and so on.

Task: Grouping by the First Letter of the Company Name

1. If you don't already have the Day 12 database open, do so now.

2. If you already have the rptCustomerDirectory report open, skip to step 5. If not, click the Reports button on the Object bar in the Database window.

3. Locate the rptCustomerDirectory report and click it to select it.

4. Right-click the report and select Design View from the context menu.

5. Click the Sorting and Grouping button to open the Sorting and Grouping dialog box. (It's the button that has two equal signs and a couple of parentheses.)

6. If you didn't follow the steps above for sorting, click the first row and select the CompanyName field from the drop-down menu. If you followed the steps for sorting, your report will already have this set. If so, go to step 7.

7. In the Group Properties pane, change Group Header to **Yes** and the Group Footer to **Yes**. This creates two new sections—a header section and a footer section—in the report.

8. Change the Group On property to **Prefix Characters**. This allows you to group on a particular number of characters. In this case, you only want to group on 1. Keep the Group Interval property at **1**. Your screen should resemble Figure 12.16.

FIGURE 12.16

The Sorting and Grouping dialog box with the properties set to group on the first character of the CompanyName field.

9. Change the Keep Together property to **Whole Group**. Specifying this property tells Access to try to keep everything (the header, the detail, and the footer) on one page if possible.

▼   10. Click the "X" button to close the Sorting and Grouping dialog box.

     11. Click the Print Preview button on the standard toolbar to preview the report. Your
         report will look like Figure 12.17.

FIGURE 12.17

*The rptCustomer
Directory report with
the new grouping.*

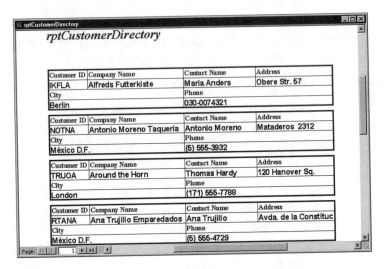

▲

The customer directory is not quite done. You need to put on the finishing touches by
placing a single block letter that indicates what group is being printed. With the block
letter, you can quickly scan to the correct subset of data. For example, if you're looking
for "Smith," you want to quickly scan the report looking for the letter "S." This next task
adds the block letter to the header of each group.

Task: Adding Sort Labels to Finish the Customer Directory

1. Click the Design view button.

2. Locate the CompanyName Header section and click it to select it.

3. Locate the Textbox tool in the Toolbox and select it.

4. Create a text box in the CompanyName Header section.

5. Select the corresponding label of the newly created text box and press the Delete
   key. (You don't need the label.)

6. Select the text box. Change the Font size to 16, by selecting **16** from the Font Size
   button on the standard toolbar. Change the Font weight to Bold, by selecting **B**
   from Bold button on the standard toolbar.

7. If it's not already opened, open the Properties list by right-clicking Textbox and
▼   selecting the Properties entry.

▼   8. On the Data tab of the Properties list, locate and change the Control Source
        property to **=Left$([CompanyName], 1)**. Your screen should look similar to
        Figure 12.18.

FIGURE 12.18

*The rptCustomer
Directory in Design
view with the newly
added Textbox control.*

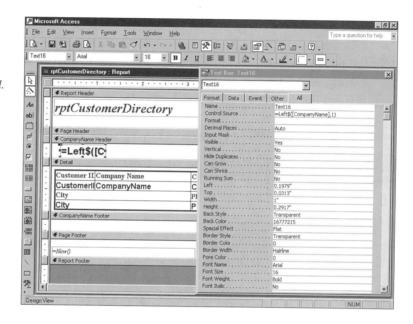

    9. Click the Print Preview button on the standard toolbar to preview the report. Your
       screen should resemble Figure 12.19.

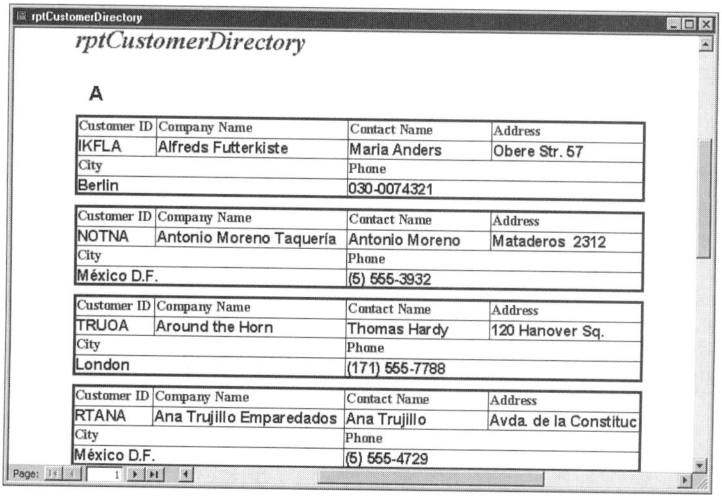

FIGURE 12.19

*The completed
rptCustomerDirectory
report.*

12

Notice with just a little bit of extra time you have greatly increased the value of this report. Your report is much more user friendly than it was before.

Understanding Crosstab Reports

Crosstab reports are a way to horizontally organize your information across the page so you can compare between logical categories. For example, you want to see all the sales for each quarter of the year so you can see what quarter is the strongest. See Figure 12.20 for an example of this kind of report.

FIGURE 12.20

The rptOrderDetails Crosstab report in Print Preview view.

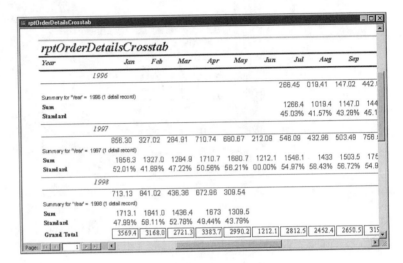

Even though I just showed you a crosstab report, Access really doesn't have anything called a "crosstab report." What Access does have is a crosstab query which you use as the underlying query for your report. When I mention crosstab report, realize I mean a report based on a crosstab query.

Each crosstab query has three major parts: Row Heading, Column Heading, and the Value. The difficulty with crosstab queries is figuring out what information goes in each of the three parts. Although learning how to create a crosstab query on your own is a difficult task, Access has a crosstab query wizard that helps you.

This next task shows you how to create the crosstab query for the crosstab report that you will create later. You want a report that summarizes the total dollars spent in each quarter for each year.

Note

To make this task simpler I've provided the qryOrderDetailsExtended query that separates the year of the order into its own field and totals all the orders. Doing this makes it easier to work with the Crosstab Query Wizard.

TASK ▼

Task: Creating the Crosstab Query

1. If you didn't already open the Day 12 database in the task before, open the Day 12 database now.

2. Click the Queries button on the Object bar in the Database window.

3. Click the New button on the toolbar in the Database window to start the Query Wizard. The New Query dialog box will open.

4. Select the Crosstab Query Wizard entry and then click the OK button.

5. In the first step of the Crosstab Query Wizard, select Queries from the View options.

6. Locate the qryOrderDetailsExtended entry and click it to select it. Your screen should resemble Figure 12.21.

FIGURE 12.21

The first step of the Crosstab Query Wizard with the qryOrderDetails Extended query selected.

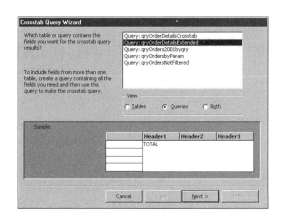

12

7. Click the Next button to go to the next step.

8. In this step you select the field that will be used as the Row Heading. Select the Year entry from the Available Fields listbox (on the left). Click the ">" button to move the Year field to the Selected Field listbox.

9. Click the Next button.

10. In this step, you select the field that will be used for the Column Headings part. Select the OrderDate entry.

▼   11. Click the Next button.

12. The Crosstab query recognizes that the OrderDate field is a date, so it presents a list of possible values that you might select. To keep this task and the next task simple, select the Quarter entry.

13. Click the Next button.

14. In this step, you select the field that is being summarized. In this case it is the Subtotal field. Select the Subtotal entry.

15. On the right is a list of possible functions. In this case you want the sum of the total number of sales. Select the Sum entry from the listbox on the right. Your screen will resemble Figure 12.22.

FIGURE 12.22

The second-to-last step of the Crosstab Query Wizard where the Value part is specified.

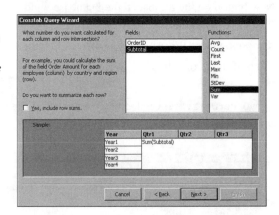

16. Locate the Yes, include row sums checkbox and uncheck it.

17. Click the Next button.

18. In this step, you name your Crosstab query. Name it qryOrdersSummaryCrosstab.

▲   19. Click the OK button, then close the query by clicking on the "X" button of the Datasheet view.

There! The hard work is done. Now that you've created the crosstab query, you can make a simple report to display the results for each quarter.

Task: Creating the Crosstab Report

1. If you didn't already open the Day 12 database in the task before, open the Day 12 database now. Note that you need to complete the Creating the Crosstab Query task before doing this task.

2. Click the Reports button on the Object bar in the Database window.

▼   3. Click the New button on the toolbar in the Database window to start the Report
        Wizard. The New Report dialog box will open.

     4. Click the AutoReport: Tabular entry to select it.

     5. Choose the query you just created (qryOrdersSummaryCrosstab) from the drop-
        down menu.

     6. Click the OK button.

     7. Access will create a simple report (see Figure 12.23).

Figure 12.23

*The finished
qryOrdersSummary
Crosstab report.*

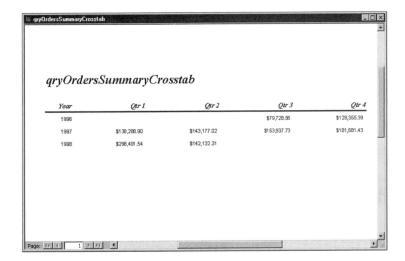

Year	Qtr 1	Qtr 2	Qtr 3	Qtr 4
1996			$79,728.56	$128,355.39
1997	$138,288.90	$143,177.02	$153,937.73	$181,681.43
1998	$298,491.54	$142,132.31		

▲

You've created a report that is precise in the information needed. You know exactly the
total sum of all orders for each quarter, broken out by year.

Summary

This lesson dealt with getting your reports right. It taught you how to filter your reports
based on changing the underlying query. It also showed you how to filter based on the
changing the filter properties.

This lesson also taught you that when you can't filter, you can organize information vertically by sorting and grouping.

Finally this lesson taught you to organize your information horizontally in crosstab
reports.

The most important lesson learned in Day 12 is that you should never give your audience
more than they need or want.

12

Q&A

Q. **What if my reports are based on an underlying table instead of a query as your examples showed in the Sorting and Grouping section?**

A. You can still filter using the methods shown. However, there are some differences when changing the RecordSource property. If you change the criteria, Access will update the RecordSource property with a SQL string.

Q. **Now that my reports are filtered down, I can't tell what's been filtered. Is there some way to display, for example, a date range that is included in the report?**

A. Yes, you can do this by making the parameters fields in your query. Then you can create a text box on your report that uses those fields as the ControlSource property.

Q. **Crosstab queries and reports seem difficult to understand and to master. Isn't it easier to just export the data out and do the summarizing and grouping in Excel?**

A. Yes, but this may not always be an option for your users.

Workshop

The Workshop helps you solidify the skills you learned in this lesson. Answers to the quiz appear in Appendix A, "Answers to Quizzes."

Quiz

1. If you need to organize the information in your report vertically down the page, what technique do you use?

2. Name one method that allows you to show a subset of information in your report.

3. In the Sorting and Grouping dialog box, what does the Keep Together property do?

4. When specifying dates in Access, why do you need to specify the "#" symbol around each date?

5. There are three parts to a Crosstab query: the Column Heading, the Value, and the _____.

DAY **13**

Learning Structured Query Language or SQL

Structured Query Language or SQL—pronounced "ess cue ell" instead of the often heard, but not really correct, "sequel"—is the underlying language behind Access queries. SQL is the standard language for users to interact with databases. All the major database programs, such as Microsoft's own SQL Server, Oracle, DB2 (from IBM), Ingres, and others, including (of course), Access, include an SQL interpreter (or engine) to process this language.

Today You Will Learn

You don't need to learn or use SQL directly to use Access even up to a fairly high level. You do need to use SQL to take full advantage of Access. It is necessary to use SQL for some less often used queries, but even here you can use it in a cookbook fashion. If you want to consider yourself a database professional, you will need to learn this language quite well—beyond the scope of this short lesson actually. This lesson will give you the necessary foundation to begin to learn what SQL is all about. Specifically, in this lesson you will learn:

- What is SQL?
- Where SQL is used
- About the SELECT statement
- How to select more than one field
- How to add criteria using SQL
- How to make a multitable SQL query
- How to eliminate duplicate query returns using SQL
- How to use aggregate and math functions in SQL

What Is SQL?

It was mentioned at the beginning of this lesson, but it bears repeating—SQL is the underlying language behind Access queries. The places where SQL is used in Access are

- In constructing a query
- In populating a form or report control

In the latter case, the statement almost always follows this syntax:

```
Select... From... Where
```

If you learn how to fill in the blanks in that SQL statement, you'll be on your way to knowing what you need to know about SQL and Access. This lesson simply gives you a start in using this language. You'll learn more in Day 14, "Special Query Uses," which provides examples of queries where you need to use SQL directly to make them work at all.

 Note
Although SQL is supposed to be a standard, like all standards in this industry, it tends to vary slightly from implementation to implementation. This isn't a serious concern. If you learn the Microsoft implementation of SQL in any of its products, you can quickly and easily switch to any other database that uses SQL—at least as far as knowing the language.

When I say "use SQL directly," I mean enter SQL statements. Access uses SQL for all queries, so any time you make a query or apply a filter to a dataset, you're using SQL, but not directly. The query by example (QBE) grid in Access—that is, the query design view—puts a non-language interface on SQL, but the query still operates using that language.

Using the SELECT Statement

SQL is as close to plain English as it can get and still function. When you see an SQL keyword, such as SELECT, take a good guess as to what it does and you'll almost always be right. SELECT, well, selects data from tables. The general syntax for the SELECT is

```
SELECT [something or somethings] FROM [somewhere]
```

In this case, the [something] is columns or field names. So if you want to see the first names of all employees where that data is in a field called FirstName, the start of the statement would be

```
SELECT FirstName
```

However, that's not enough as it stands because Access doesn't know where to look for the FirstName field or column (there can be more than one in a database, too). In this case, the data is in the Northwind-supplied table Employees which is part of the sample data on your CD under the name Day 13.

The next thing to do is to include the FROM so Access knows what table (or query) to look in. So here's the second part of the statement.

```
SELECT FirstName FROM Employees
```

Try it yourself.

Task: Constructing the SQL Query

1. Launch Access and open the Day 13 database. This database is on the CD in the Day 13 folder. Start a new query in design view. Close the Show Table dialog without including any tables or queries.

2. Click the View button at the far left of the toolbar. It should read SQL. This brings up the SQL language window.

3. Enter the following statement in the window:

   SELECT FirstName FROM Employees

   Your screen should resemble Figure 13.1.

4. Click the View button again to switch to datasheet view. Your query return should be like Figure 13.2.

13

FIGURE 13.1

Welcome to the major leagues. You're now constructing queries using SQL only.

FIGURE 13.2

The statement pulled the data into your query.

5. Switch to design view for this query and you'll note that Access has populated the QBE grid including adding the table to the grid.

> **Note**
>
> SQL convention is that its keywords are shown in all uppercase, and the rest of the query in mixed-case or lowercase letters. This book follows that convention, although the SQL interpreter in Access is not case-sensitive. Even though Access isn't case-sensitive, you should make all the keywords uppercase because, at the very least, it improves the readability of the SQL.

There is one further refinement in this query. Although Access pulled the correct data in this case, it's a good idea to make sure Access knows exactly what field in what table you want to pull from. To remove any possible ambiguity from the statement, use this syntax:

```
SELECT Employees.FirstName FROM Employees
```

This syntax, of course, leaves nothing to the imagination.

Here you can see the value of using naming conventions for your database objects. It would be a lot clearer if the earlier statement read like this:

```
SELECT tblEmployees.FirstName FROM tblEmployees
```

Minor attention to detail can make your life as an Access professional a lot more pleasant.

Selecting Multiple Columns or Fields

Selecting one field or column is simple. So then, how tough is it to include more than one column? The answer is that it's just as simple. Start a new query again, and again close the Show Table dialog box without including any selections. Go to the SQL view and enter

```
SELECT * FROM Employees
```

Then click the datasheet view. Your screen should resemble Figure 13.3.

FIGURE 13.3

The asterisk works like a wildcard pulling in all fields.

Employee ID	Last Name	First Name	Title	Title Of C	Birth Date	Hire Date	Address	City	Region	Postal Code
1	Davolio	Nancy	Sales Representative	Ms.	08-Dec-1968	01-May-1992	507 - 20th Ave. E.	Seattle	WA	98122
2	Fuller	Andrew	Vice President, Sales	Dr.	19-Feb-1952	14-Aug-1992	908 W. Capital Way	Tacoma	WA	96401
3	Leverling	Janet	Sales Representative	Ms.	30-Aug-1963	01-Apr-1992	722 Moss Bay Blvd.	Kirkland	WA	98033
4	Peacock	Margaret	Sales Representative	Mrs.	19-Sep-1958	03-May-1993	4110 Old Redmond Rd.	Redmond	WA	98052
5	Buchanan	Steven	Sales Manager	Mr.	04-Mar-1955	17-Oct-1993	14 Garrett Hill	London		SW1 8JR
6	Suyama	Michael	Sales Representative	Mr.	02-Jul-1963	17-Oct-1993	Coventry House	London		EC2 7JR
7	King	Robert	Sales Representative	Mr.	29-May-1960	02-Jan-1994	Edgeham Hollow	London		RG1 9SP
8	Callahan	Laura	Inside Sales Coordinator	Ms.	09-Jan-1958	05-Mar-1994	4726 - 11th Ave. N.E.	Seattle	WA	98105
9	Dodsworth	Anne	Sales Representative	Ms.	02-Jul-1969	15-Nov-1994	7 Houndstooth Rd.	London		WG2 7LT
*	(AutoNumber)									

Note

> If you think this topic is going to grow more difficult, you'll be disappointed. This is pretty easy material to master for the purposes of use in Access.

The next option is to include more than one field, but not all. Let's include both the first and last name fields. Here's how to do it:

```
SELECT Employees.FirstName, Employees.LastName FROM Employees;
```

Note two things. First, the comma is the delimiter between two or more fields or columns. Second, I've thrown in a semicolon at the end of the statement. While Access doesn't require the semicolon, it's standard SQL practice to end a statement with one, so I'll start doing that now. Some forms of SQL, such as Oracle's, require the semicolon at the end of a statement or it won't execute.

Selecting Multiple Tables

Doing these kinds of queries using SQL directly isn't difficult, but it gets a bit tedious and exacting. SQL is relentlessly logical and somewhat insistent on proper statement constructions for predictable results. Remember to use the comma as a delimiter and remember the differences between various joins. If you need a refresher, skip back to Day 11, "Manipulating Queries."

When Access (or SQL) selects data from two or more tables, it needs to know two things:

- The linked field with which to coordinate data
- How to join the tables

The sample database for today has two tables, `tblSuppliers` and `tblProducts` linked on the `SupplierID` field.

13

Note   tblSupplier and tblProducts are the same tables as the Northwind Supplier and Products tables. I've renamed them for this lesson to make the SQL statements easier to understand.

The general statement is this

```
SELECT [something]
FROM [Something] JOIN [to something] ON [linked fields]
```

Let's start taking things slowly. Say we want to display all products from the table tblProducts along with their suppliers from the table tblSuppliers.

The first thing we need is to tell SQL what fields we want. Don't try running the query yet, but here is the incomplete statement for that task.

```
SELECT tblSuppliers.CompanyName, tblProducts.ProductName
```

Note that this is the first statement where the tables differ. This is where the following syntax becomes mandatory:

```
Table.Field
```

The next stage is to tell Access how to link the tables to have the products matched up correctly with their suppliers. This statement is a bit longer:

```
FROM tblSuppliers INNER JOIN tblProducts
  lON tblSuppliers.SupplierID = tblProducts.SupplierID;
```

This clause reads from left to right with the more important keywords to the left. So FROM reads from the entire phrase to its right up to the semicolon. The JOIN is an INNER join meaning the return will be only those fields where there is a match in both tables. The ON statement is telling the interpreter which fields are linked. To expand this statement into pseudo code,

```
Take FROM the tblSupplers using an INNER JOIN to tblProducts
        ➥which is linked to tblSuppliers ON the fields
        ➥SupplierID in tblSuppliers and SupplierID
        ➥in the table tblProducts.
```

The results of the query statement can be seen in Figure 13.4.

SQL doesn't use the keyword OUTER for an outer join. An outer join selects all records from one table whether or not there are joins to the other table. SQL uses the words LEFT and RIGHT to tell which table to select all the records from. So to take all records from tblSuppliers, modify the statement to read,

```
FROM tblSuppliers LEFT JOIN tblProducts
        ON tblSuppliers.SupplierID = tblProducts.SupplierID;
```

Or just the opposite (RIGHT) to pull all records from tblProducts.

FIGURE 13.4

All the suppliers and their products.

Company Name	Product Name
Exotic Liquids	Chai
Exotic Liquids	Chang
Exotic Liquids	Aniseed Syrup
New Orleans Cajun Delights	Chef Anton's Cajun Seasoning
New Orleans Cajun Delights	Chef Anton's Gumbo Mix
New Orleans Cajun Delights	Louisiana Fiery Hot Pepper Sauce
New Orleans Cajun Delights	Louisiana Hot Spiced Okra
Grandma Kelly's Homestead	Grandma's Boysenberry Spread
Grandma Kelly's Homestead	Uncle Bob's Organic Dried Pears
Grandma Kelly's Homestead	Northwoods Cranberry Sauce
Tokyo Traders	Mishi Kobe Niku
Tokyo Traders	Ikura
Tokyo Traders	Longlife Tofu
Cooperativa de Quesos 'Las Cabras'	Queso Cabrales
Cooperativa de Quesos 'Las Cabras'	Queso Manchego La Pastora
Mayumi's	Konbu
Mayumi's	Tofu
Mayumi's	Genen Shouyu
Pavlova, Ltd.	Pavlova
Pavlova, Ltd.	Alice Mutton
Pavlova, Ltd.	Carnarvon Tigers
Pavlova, Ltd.	Vegie-spread
Pavlova, Ltd.	Outback Lager
Specialty Biscuits, Ltd.	Teatime Chocolate Biscuits
Specialty Biscuits, Ltd.	Sir Rodney's Marmalade
Specialty Biscuits, Ltd.	Sir Rodney's Scones
Specialty Biscuits, Ltd.	Scottish Longbreads
PB Knäckebröd AB	Gustaf's Knäckebröd
PB Knäckebröd AB	Tunnbröd
Refrescos Americanas LTDA	Guaraná Fantástica
Heli Süßwaren GmbH & Co. KG	NuNuCa Nuß-Nougat-Creme
Heli Süßwaren GmbH & Co. KG	Gumbär Gummibärchen
Heli Süßwaren GmbH & Co. KG	Schoggi Schokolade
Plutzer Lebensmittelgroßmärkte AG	Rössle Sauerkraut
Plutzer Lebensmittelgroßmärkte AG	Thüringer Rostbratwurst

Adding the WHERE Clause

It's time for things to get, if not technically difficult, at least a bit more complex. So far, the selections have pulled all records from any selected column. That's about to end.

Note

I use the terms column and field somewhat haphazardly and randomly in this lesson because Access tends to use the term *field*, whereas SQL documentation uses the term *column*. They mean the same thing.

Clause Versus Statement

Why is the WHERE keyword a "clause" and not a "statement" like the SELECT keyword? There actually is a good answer for this. The SELECT keyword can be used by itself to retrieve values, whereas the WHERE keyword must be used in conjunction with another SQL statement keyword, like the SELECT keyword.

13

The WHERE clause selects specific data, not just all records from the specified columns. Recall the last example that I gave you of an SQL statement:

```
SELECT Employees.FirstName, Employees.LastName FROM Employees;
```

You can add a WHERE clause like the following:

```
WHERE (Employees.LastName)="Davolio";
```

This makes a complete statement, that instructs SQL to: "Give me the first and last name of every employee with the last name, Davolio."

Make sure you remove the semicolon from after the table name Employees, and then run the query. Your results should be the same as in Figure 13.5.

FIGURE **13.5**

The results of using the
WHERE *clause on the*
Employees *table.*

Again, you can use the skills you learned in the QBE to add to this statement or modify it.

 Note | The parentheses in the WHERE clauses aren't necessary thus far, but work well to present the statement for the human eye. In other more complex statements, you'll need to use these or the interpreter will find it impossible to parse your statement.

To pull all last names with the letter D, change the WHERE clause to read as follows:

```
SELECT Employees.FirstName, Employees.LastName FROM Employees
WHERE (Employees.LastName Like "D*");
```

You also can use OR and the AND statements. For example, to show all employees with the last names beginning with D or S, try this:

```
SELECT Employees.FirstName, Employees.LastName FROM Employees
WHERE (Employees.LastName Like "D*")
    OR (Employees.LastName Like "S*");
```

You can use other criteria from Access, such as the BETWEEN and IN keywords. For example, to list first and last names of all employees with a birthday between January 1, 1950, and January 1, 1960, enter the following:

```
SELECT Employees.FirstName, Employees.LastName FROM Employees
WHERE (Employees.BirthDate) Between #1/1/1950# And #1/1/1960#;
```

Adding to SELECT

Here are a few more often used keywords for select queries. The ORDER BY will sort. To sort (or order on) a field, include this clause,

```
ORDER BY [something]
```

So to order the previous multitable query on Products, add the following syntax to the end of the query:

```
ORDER BY tblProducts.ProductName;
```

To sort in descending order, add the DESC keyword.

```
ORDER BY tblProducts.ProductName DESC;
```

Make sure to move the semicolon to the end of the statement as you edit away.

The GROUP BY keyword is used to aggregate records. You usually use this in Access for summarizing data. Say you want to display all suppliers and count the number of products they vend to your company using the two tables tblProducts and tblSuppliers. This tends to be a bit of an adventure, but it's obvious in retrospect. First, we need to say what we want to display in our answer which is the name of the supplier and a count of its products. This statement looks like this:

```
SELECT tblSuppliers.CompanyName, Count(tblProducts.UnitPrice) AS [Number]
```

Now you need to tell Access from where to pull the data using the FROM (where the data is located) statement:

```
FROM tblSuppliers INNER JOIN tblProducts
     ON tblSuppliers.SupplierID = tblProducts.SupplierID
```

Finally, tell Access to group by the company name field:

```
GROUP BY tblSuppliers.CompanyName;
```

The complete statement for the query is:

```
SELECT tblSuppliers.CompanyName,
[Count(tblProducts.UnitPrice) AS [Number]
FROM tblSuppliers INNER JOIN tblProducts
ON tblSuppliers.SupplierID = tblProducts.SupplierID
GROUP BY tblSuppliers.CompanyName;
```

The result of this query is shown in Figure 13.6.

13

 Note

The field label Number appears in brackets because that's an SQL keyword. Without the brackets, SQL would try to interpret this as a keyword and fail in the query. It's a good policy to always use brackets for these labels even if they aren't keywords. The worst you'll do is make it more obvious to yourself that these are field labels.

Figure 13.6

Here is the SQL count aggregation function in full bloom.

Company Name	Number
Aux joyeux ecclésiastiques	2
Bigfoot Breweries	3
Cooperativa de Quesos 'Las Cabras'	2
Escargots Nouveaux	1
Exotic Liquids	3
Forêts d'érables	2
Formaggi Fortini s.r.l.	3
Gai pâturage	2
G'day, Mate	3
Grandma Kelly's Homestead	3
Heli Süßwaren GmbH & Co. KG	3
Karkki Oy	3
Leka Trading	3
Lyngbysild	2
Ma Maison	2
Mayumi's	3
New England Seafood Cannery	2
New Orleans Cajun Delights	4
Nord-Ost-Fisch Handelsgesellschaft mbH	1
Norske Meierier	3
Pasta Buttini s.r.l.	2
Pavlova, Ltd.	5
PB Knäckebröd AB	2
Plutzer Lebensmittelgroßmärkte AG	5
Refrescos Americanas LTDA	1
Specialty Biscuits, Ltd.	4
Svensk Sjöföda AB	3
Tokyo Traders	3
Zaanse Snoepfabriek	2

This query is saved under the name `qryCount` and is part of your sample data for today.

> **Tip**
>
> You can use any and all of the Boolean operatives within SQL. So for example, if you want to return only records in a table with an Age field where the age is over 20, use the `WHERE Age > 20` clause in your query.

You can use the `HAVING` keyword to filter aggregated records as much as the `WHERE` statement filters on unaggregated records. The `HAVING` keyword is used in conjunction with the `GROUP BY` keyword. Start with a standard aggregate query:

```
SELECT tblProducts.ProductName, Sum(tblProducts.UnitPrice) AS SumOfUnitPrice
FROM tblProducts
GROUP BY tblProducts.ProductName;
```

This query sums up the cost of all of a company's product offerings, as seen in the `SumOfUnitPrice` column. Now we are only interested in companies where their `SumOfUnitPrice` is greater than $20. Add a `HAVING` clause to the statement, as shown in the following:

```
SELECT tblProducts.ProductName, Sum(tblProducts.UnitPrice) AS SumOfUnitPrice
FROM tblProducts
GROUP BY tblProducts.ProductName
HAVING Sum(tblProducts.UnitPrice)>20;
```

Run the query, and you will see that, in fact, you only have companies where the sum of their product offering is greater than $20.

You also can have both the `WHERE` clause and the `HAVING` clause in the same statement. In this case, the `WHERE` clause filters records before the grouping happens in the `GROUP BY` clause, whereas the `HAVING` clause filters on the grouped records. What if you only want companies whose name began with "A" all the way to "M," and whose sum of their product offerings was greater than $20? Look at the following query statement:

```
SELECT tblProducts.ProductName, Sum(tblProducts.UnitPrice) AS SumOfUnitPrice
FROM tblProducts
WHERE tblProducts.ProductName Between "A*" and "M*"
GROUP BY tblProducts.ProductName
HAVING Sum(tblProducts.UnitPrice)>20;
```

If you run the query, you can see that is what you will get.

Eliminating Duplicate Returns

Unwanted duplicate returns in queries are one of those great frustrations for folks starting out in any database. The SQL keywords to eliminate duplicates are DISTINCT and DISTINCTROW. Let's look at them in action.

Task: Preventing Duplicate Returns Using SQL

1. Launch Access and open the Day 13 database. Start a new query by choosing design view, but adding no tables or queries to the QBE.

2. Enter the SQL statement:

   SELECT Orders.EmployeeID FROM Orders;

3. Switch to datasheet view. Figure 13.7 shows what your return should be:

FIGURE 13.7

There are plenty of duplicates to prevent here.

4. Return to SQL view and edit the statement to read

   SELECT DISTINCT Orders.EmployeeID FROM Orders;

5. Return to datasheet view. Note only one entry for each Employee.

The DISTINCT keyword eliminates duplicate rows based on only those fields explicitly included in the query. DISTINCTROW works on all fields including those in the included tables, but not explicitly included in the query.

The QBE has the equivalent of DISTINCT and DISTINCTROW in the properties Unique Values and Unique Records, respectively. You can find those properties in the Properties list box for the query.

Getting Practical with SQL

You've probably concluded about this time that this lesson is a bit silly. There doesn't seem to be anything you can do with SQL that you can't do with QBE, which is much easier to use (especially to use without errors). You'll learn in the next lesson that this isn't strictly true because there are certain queries that can't be constructed in the QBE, so it requires using SQL directly.

The major reason to know SQL is to use it in forms. You can, for example, use these statements as a row source in combo boxes. I've created a trivial form to illustrate this. Go to your sample data, Day 13 on the CD. Locate the form frmSQL. This is a form with one control. Open in design view and open, if necessary, the properties list box. Click the combo box control (not its label) and locate the Row Source property on the Data tab. To see the contents of the property better, you can press Shift + F2 to bring up the Zoom dialog box.

The value of this property is

```
SELECT Employees.LastName FROM Employees
```

What do you suppose this will do? Change to form view. Now pull down the combo box to see what's in it. Switch back to design view again. Now edit the SQL statement to limit the list to only those employees with the last name Davolio. Here's how:

```
SELECT Employees.LastName FROM Employees WHERE Employees.LastName="Davolio";
```

Now return to form view and see how your changes have developed.

Summary

SQL is the underlying language behind Access and also powers other parts of the database program. SQL is almost universally used in other relational database products such as Microsoft's SQL Server and Oracle, to name a few.

Much of what you can do in the SQL window part of the query design grid, you also can do in the query by example (QBE) grid, but using SQL, you can construct some special queries as well as fine tuning those initially done in the QBE. Most Access developers use QBE and use the SQL view only for special purposes (which we'll discuss in Day 14), for fine tuning, or for use in areas outside of the query design grid, such as combo boxes on forms.

Q&A

Q. Is this all there is to SQL?

A. No, from a keyword view, this lesson only scratched the surface. It would take a whole book (there are many) to cover the subject in depth. This lesson covered the keywords used most often (by a wide margin) in Access.

Q. Is `Count()` the only function I can use in SQL?

A. No, you can use all the aggregate functions, such as `SUM()`, `MIN()`, and `MAX()`.

Q. Does the Access interpreter support all the SQL keywords?

A. Sadly, no, and it's missing some good ones too. For example, Access does not accept the keyword `MINUS`, which returns only values from one query not found in another. At last count, Access is missing about 200 keywords found in standard (ANSI) SQL.

Q. Does a query run better if written in SQL instead of the QBE?

A. All Access queries are converted to SQL and then run, so, no, it makes no difference.

Workshop

The Workshop helps you solidify the skills you learned in this lesson. Answers to the quiz and exercises appear in Appendix A, "Answers to Quizzes."

Quiz

1. Do you need to add a table to the QBE before constructing an SQL query?
2. Can you query queries using SQL or are you restricted to tables? Hint: Open the query `qryCountTheCounter` from the sample data and switch to SQL view.
3. What does the `WHERE` statement do?
4. Does Access SQL require keywords to appear in all caps?
5. Can you use Boolean operators such as >, <, and = in SQL?

13

Exercises

1. Start a new query. Add no tables or queries.

2. Using the SQL view, select all fields from the query qryWorkShop.

3. Switch to query view. Note the contents of this query.

4. Alter the SQL statement to include only those employees with nine years or more of service.

5. Open the query qryWorkShop.

6. Examine the SQL view. Note the combination of SQL and built-in Access functions, such as DateDiff().

DAY **14**

Special Query Uses

In earlier days you learned all about how to create queries and use their results. Today, you'll explore some of the more advanced query capabilities available in Access 2002. You won't use these types of queries every day, but at some point you'll find the need for them.

Today You Will Learn

- How to create and use action queries
- How to analyze data with crosstab queries
- What SQL-specific queries accomplish
- How to parameterize your queries
- How to reference form entries in your queries
- How queries can be useful for refining data
- Everything you ever wanted to know about query properties

Action Queries

As the name implies, an action query performs an action on your database. These actions can be taken on data within your tables, they can add data to or remove data from tables, and they can even create brand new tables.

The four action queries discussed today are the Update query, the Delete query, the Append query, and the Make Table query. The Update query is used to update data in a table. The Delete query deletes rows from a table while the Append query adds rows to a table. Finally, the Make Table query creates a brand new table within the database.

Adding Queries to Your Toolbar

You can use action queries in maintenance tasks or they can be standard operations for your users. To make it easy for a user to invoke action queries, you can attach them to form buttons, menu items, or toolbar buttons.

To add an existing query to a toolbar or menu bar, right-click the Access toolbar area and select Customize to invoke the Customize dialog box. If you're adding the query to a new toolbar or menu, you'll first need to create the new toolbar or menu on the Toolbars tab. When the toolbar you're adding the query to is visible, switch to the Commands tab and scroll the Categories list until you see the All Queries entry. Click this entry to display the existing queries in the Commands list. Finally, drag and drop your query from the Commands list to its destination toolbar or menu. Now when that toolbar button or menu item is used, the action query will be executed.

Update Query

The first action query I'll examine is the Update query. This query is one of the most important types of queries when it comes to data integrity and clean-up, a necessary evil for almost every database that gets any real use.

An Update query modifies the values of particular fields for particular records within your database. In fact, this is the only action query that operates on individual fields—all other action queries act only on rows in a table.

You'll use Update queries when you need to change the value of a set of fields for a set of records. For example, let's say you own a bookstore and have a database to track your inventory and order requests. One of the tables in this database is undoubtedly a `Publications` table that lists all of the works you carry or currently have on order. Suppose a publisher goes out of business (perish the thought!). You'll probably need to update all of the works produced by that publisher to mark them as no longer available.

Now, you could, if you were bored, open the `Publications` table in datasheet view, locate each work by this publisher, and set its `Available` field to `No` manually. But there is a better way! This is the exact task that Update queries are intended to automate.

The following task walks you through the steps involved in creating and running an Update query. Following the example in the two previous paragraphs, you'll create a query that will update all the publications from a single publisher to mark them as no longer available. The database you'll use has tables for the publishers and the publications. In the publications table there's a field named `Available` that you need to update.

Task: Creating an Update Query

1. Start Access if necessary and locate the database `Day 14` on the CD. This database contains several tables useful for tracking a book store inventory, including a `Publishers` and a `Publications` table.

2. Activate the Database window and make sure the Objects bar is active. Click the Queries button.

3. Click the New button on the Database window's toolbar. The New Query dialog box shown in Figure 14.1 appears.

FIGURE 14.1

The New query window.

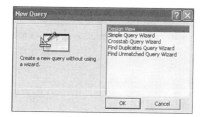

4. Leaving Design View selected, click the OK button. The Show Table dialog box appears.

5. Double-click the `Publishers` and `Publications` table. This will add these tables to the query's design view. Click the Close button to close the Show Table dialog box.

6. Use the Query, Update Query menu item to change this query to an Update query. The query window should now resemble Figure 14.2.

7. As you can see from Figure 14.2, there is already a link created between the two tables. We know the name of the publisher that has gone out of business, and we know that the field we want to update is the `Available` field. These fields need to be specified in the query, so double-click the Available field in the `Publications` table and the `PublisherName` field in the `Publishers` table to add the fields to the query grid.

14

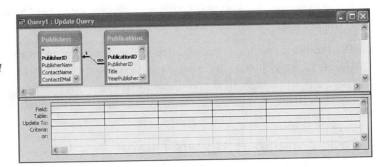

FIGURE 14.2

The query window after the appropriate tables have been added and the query type has been changed to an Update query.

8. In the query designer grid, click in the Update To row for the Available column. This cell is used to specify the value that should be placed in the fields being updated. For this task, enter **No** (the Available field is a Yes/No field). For this task, the Available field is the only one to be updated. If there were more fields that needed to have their data updated, you would simply add them to the query designer grid and specify the new value in the Update To cell.

> **Note**
>
> If you want to remove the value from a field, you should enter the word Null in the Update To cell. If the field's Required property is set to Yes, though, you'll create data validation errors when you execute the query.

9. Click in the Criteria row for the PublisherName column. The Criteria cell is used to identify which rows from the database will be updated. The publisher that has gone out of business is named JimBob Publishing. Enter that name here in the Criteria cell. Your screen should look similar to Figure 14.3.

> **Note**
>
> Although you entered a specific publisher name in Step 9, you typically wouldn't hard-code a query criteria this way. Instead, you'd create a more generic query using query parameters. These will be discussed later today.

10. Believe it or not, you're finished! All that's left to do is execute the query. Action queries are executed using the Run button on the toolbar or with the Query, Run menu item (if you switch to the datasheet view for the query, the query will not be executed). Access will display a confirmation dialog box, informing you of the number of records which will be updated, if any. Click Yes on this dialog box to perform the update; click No to cancel the update.

FIGURE 14.3

The query window after adding the fields and the necessary values.

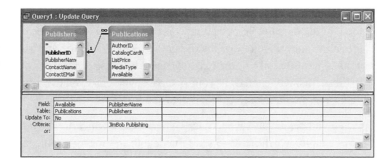

For educational purposes, let's take a closer looker at what you've done. Click the View toolbar button's down arrow and select the SQL View. This will show you the SQL statement that will be executed to accomplish the data update. See Figure 14.4.

FIGURE 14.4

The query window's SQL View, showing the statement that will be executed.

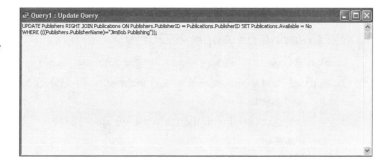

Let's break down the components of the SQL statement that the query designer has produced. The statement reads:

```
UPDATE Publishers RIGHT JOIN Publications
ON Publishers.PublisherID = Publications.PublisherID
SET Publications.Available = No
WHERE (((Publishers.PublisherName)="JimBob Publishing"));
```

The first word specifies that this is an Update action query. Following UPDATE is the table specification. In this case, we're joining the Publishers and the Publications tables, and using the PublisherID field from the two tables as the key. After the tables are specified, we have the SET keyword. This indicates that what follows will be the fields to be updated and the values to which to set those fields. Here we're only updating a single field, but if we were updating multiple fields they would be separated with commas. Finally comes the WHERE clause, which is used to choose the records to be updated.

14

Append Query

The Append action query grabs rows from other tables or a query's results and appends them to the target table, which must exist prior to executing the query. The existing rows are left as they were before the query is executed, and the appended rows are independent copies, not links to the existing rows. Because Access gives you the ability to attach to tables that are external to your database, you can even use append queries to extract data from or add data to external data sources.

When you create an Append query, you'll select which fields to grab the data from in the source table, which fields to send the data to in the target table, and which rows in the source table to use.

As an example of how to use an append query, suppose that you wanted to keep an archive of your no longer available publications in another table. You could easily construct an append query which grabs the rows where Available equals No and add them to a second table, as you'll do in the task to follow. After you've archived the rows into the archive table, you can delete them from the original table.

Task: Creating an Append Query

▼ TASK

1. Start Access if necessary and locate the database, Day 14 on the CD.

2. Activate the Database window and make sure the Object bar is active. Click the Queries button.

3. Click the New button on the Database window's toolbar. The New Query dialog box appears.

4. Leaving Design View selected, click the OK button. The Show Table dialog box appears. Because we're using the Publications table as our source table, double-click it and then click the Close button.

5. Because we're going to copy all of the fields to our archive table, double-click the asterisk in the Publications table's field list. If you only wanted to copy certain data to the other table, you would select the individual fields.

> **Tip**
>
> When you double-click or drag the asterisk from a table's Field list box into the query designer grid, Access automatically includes all of the fields from that table.

6. Next, because not all of the rows are to be appended to the target table, you need to tell Access which rows from the source table to use. You'll do this by double-clicking Available in the field list. Then enter No into the Criteria cell in the query designer grid for this field.

▼

7. To see that you're selecting the proper rows, go ahead and run this query now (it's still a select query). If anything looks suspicious, double-check your work above. Return to the design view when you're satisfied that the correct results are returned.

8. Change the query type to an Append query using the Query, Append Query menu item. The Append dialog box appears. Here is where you tell Access which table you're using as your target table. As you can see from Figure 14.5, you can also specify another database as the home of the target table.

FIGURE 14.5

The Append dialog box used in the construction of an Append action query.

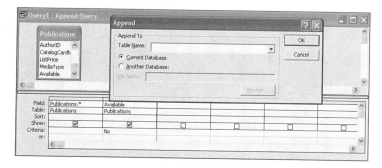

9. Leave the Current Database radio button selected and select ArchivedPubs from the Table Name dropdown list box. Click the OK button to close the dialog box. Your screen should now resemble Figure 14.6.

FIGURE 14.6

The query window for the Append action query.

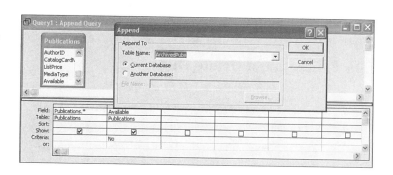

Caution

Although Access will gladly allow you to type a nonexistent table into the Table Name text box, and even let you close the dialog box without any warnings, you will receive an error message when you attempt to execute an Append action query that uses a nonexistent table as its target. If the table doesn't yet exist, use the Make Table action query discussed in the next section.

14

▼ 10. For the `Available` field, remove the text in the Append To cell of the query design-
       er grid. Access puts this text into the row automatically when you switch to an
       Append query. If left in place, Access will attempt to append this field twice to the
       target table and will display an error message. Be sure to leave the Criteria cell set
       to **No**.

    11. To execute the append query, click the Run button on the toolbar. Access will dis-
       play the confirmation dialog box informing you of the number of rows that will be
       added to the target table and asking you to confirm that you want to do so. Click
       Yes to continue.

    12. With absolutely no fanfare, Access adds the rows to the `ArchivedPubs` table. To
       verify this, open the table in datasheet view. You can now safely delete these rows
▲   using the steps outlined in the previous section.

Delete Query

You've already learned one way to delete records from a table: Open a table or query in
datasheet view, highlight the record or records you want to delete, and click the Delete
key. But just as the Update action query provides an automated way to update a set of
records, there's a Delete action query, which automates the removal of records.

Let's say, for example, that at some point you decide it's time to remove all of the
unavailable publications from the `Publications` table. You could open the table (or run a
query to retrieve only the records marked as unavailable) and delete each record by hand.
But suppose you wanted to run this process every couple of months? It would be better
to automate it, and the Delete action query, created in the next task, is the way to go
(remember, you can save the query and attach it to a toolbar or menu for easy access).

Task: Creating a Delete Query

TASK ▼

1. Start Access if necessary and locate the database, `Day 14` on the CD.

2. Activate the Database window and make sure the Objects bar is active. Click the
   Queries button.

3. Click the New button on the Database window's toolbar. The New Query dialog
   box appears.

4. Leaving Design View selected, click the OK button. The Show Table dialog box
   appears.

5. Double-click the `Publications` table. This will add the table to the query's design
   view. Click the Close button to close the Show Table dialog box.

6. The records to be deleted are those with the `Available` field set to No. Double-
   click the `Available` field in the `Publications` table's field list. This will add the
▼   field to the query designer's grid.

▼ 7. Click in the Criteria cell for the Available field. Enter **No**. Your screen should resemble Figure 14.7.

FIGURE 14.7

The query window set to determine the Publications which aren't available.

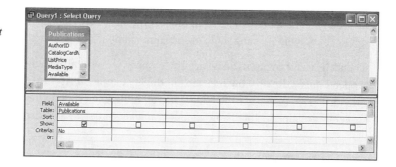

8. To make sure you've entered the criteria correctly, it's a good idea to run the query and check the returned records. Add the Title field to the query and click the Run button on the toolbar. All the returned records should have the Available checkbox cleared. If not, return to the design view and double-check Steps 6 and 7. It's very important to verify that you're selecting the correct records, because once they're deleted you can't get them back!

9. Use the Query, Delete Query menu item to change this query to a Delete action query. After the query has been changed to a Delete action query, the window title bar changes and a Delete line will replace the Sort line in the query designer grid.

▲ 10. Click the Run button on the toolbar. Access will display a confirmation message displaying the number of records to be deleted and informing you that the operation cannot be undone. Click Yes to delete the rows.

To verify that the rows have been deleted, you can either open the Publications table or change the query type back to a select query (use the Query, Select Query menu item).

Let's take a look at the SQL statement that the query designer generated. With the query designer active, use the View toolbar button to select the SQL View. The SQL statement is as follows:

```
DELETE Publications.Available, Publications.Title
FROM Publications WHERE (((Publications.Available)=No));
```

Like the Update query, the Delete query starts with the keyword DELETE. Following that is a list of fields. These fields are immaterial to what's going to be deleted, because the delete acts upon a full row. The FROM keyword indicates that what follows is the table (or tables) whose rows will be deleted. Finally, the WHERE clause indicates how Access will identify those rows.

14

Make Table Query

The previous section discussed the Append action query, which relies on an existing table as the target for the data. The Make Table action query, on the other hand, will create a new table and append data to it in one operation. However, it will always create a new table, deleting an existing table of the same name if necessary.

The steps to follow to use a Make Table query are virtually identical to those for the Append query. Just follow the steps in the "Creating an Append Query" task found in the previous section, but use the Query, Make-Table Query menu item instead. And don't forget to use a new table name unless you want to delete an existing table!

Crosstab Queries

Another powerful type of query is the crosstab query. Crosstab is short for "cross tabulation," which means that data will be tabulated across a set of rows. More technically, the result of a crosstab query is a two-dimensional matrix with a mathematical operation performed at each intersection.

For example, you might want to discover how many works each publisher produces in each category. The Publications table contains the information that you need to derive the results (the publisher and the category of the work), but this data can only be viewed in a list format. The summation of the data isn't immediately available. You could group the Publications table based on publisher and category, but you still wouldn't have a direct summary of the data such as that shown in Figure 14.8.

FIGURE 14.8

The results of a crosstab query: number of works by publisher and category.

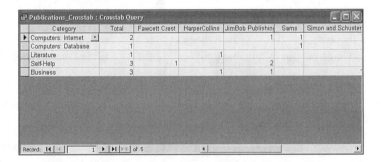

Using the Crosstab Query Wizard

It is about as difficult to construct a crosstab query as it is to understand exactly what they accomplish. For this reason, Microsoft Access provides an easy-to-use wizard to guide you through the steps. The following task demonstrates how to use the crosstab query wizard.

Task: Creating a Crosstab Query

1. Start Access if necessary and locate the database, Day 14 on the CD.

2. Activate the Database window and make sure the Object bar is active. Click the Queries button.

3. Click the New button on the Database window's toolbar. The New Query dialog box appears.

4. Click Crosstab Query Wizard and click OK. The first dialog box of the wizard, shown in Figure 14.9, appears.

FIGURE 14.9

The initial dialog box of the crosstab query wizard, where you'll choose the table upon which to base the query.

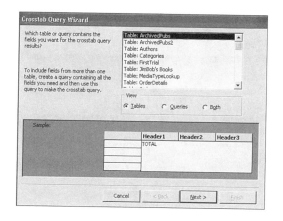

5. Click the Table: Publications entry and click Next.

6. On the dialog box that appears, you'll choose which fields to use as your row headings. Because you want to know how many works each publisher produces in each category, you'll use the categories for the row headers. Double-click CategoryID in the Available Fields list. Because this is the only field needed for the row headers, you can continue by clicking Next.

7. On the dialog box that appears you specify the field to use as the column header. You want the publisher's name to show up in the header, but in this database that's kept in a separate table. The link between the Publications table and Publishers table is the PublisherID field, so select that field in this dialog box. Your screen should appear similar to Figure 14.10. Click Next.

8. The dialog box that appears next is shown in Figure 14.11. On this dialog box select the PublicationID in the Fields list. Because we're going to do a count of records, you should use the primary key field. If you were going to do an average of list prices across publishers and category, you would choose the ListPrice field. Also, select Count in the Functions list. Leave the Yes, include row sums

14

▼   checkbox checked and Access will add a column that is the total number of works in each category. Click Next to continue to the final dialog box.

FIGURE **14.10**

The dialog box of the crosstab query wizard where you specified the field to use as the column header.

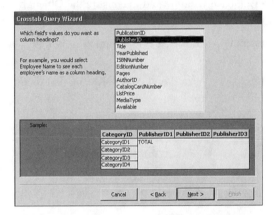

FIGURE **14.11**

The dialog box of the crosstab query wizard where you specify the operation to perform, the field on which to operate, and whether or not you want a sum for each row.

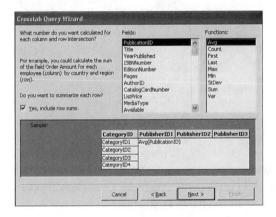

9. On the final dialog box, you provide a name for the query and specify whether or not you want to view the query's results or modify its design. Enter a name here, or use the default, and leave View the query selected. Click Finish to display the

▲   query results.

Did you notice that the results appear a little bit different from Figure 14.8? The wizard has gotten you started, but there's still some tweaking to be done. The next section discusses how to refine what the wizard produces.

Refining the Wizard's Output

The Crosstab query the wizard generates is pretty close to the results we wanted. But we still need to make a change or two to get the real results. And there are also some other tasks you can perform using the query design view; we'll look at those as well.

First and foremost, let's get the column headers to display the publisher name instead of the publisher's ID value. Although the Publications table is set up with a lookup combo box (see Day 9, "Refining Your Tables," for more details on how to set up lookup fields), this does not carry to the column headers in a crosstab query. The row header does obey the lookup field, but that's because it's inside the datasheet. In the following task, you'll add the publisher's name to the row header.

Note The following task cannot be completed unless you have completed the previous task in this section.

Task: Adding the Publisher's Name to the Row Header

1. Switch to the Design view for the query using the View, Design View toolbar button.

2. Click the Show Table toolbar button. Double-click the Publishers table and then click the Close button.

3. Locate the column in the query design grid which has PublisherID in the Field row. This column should also have Group By in the Total row and Column Heading in the Crosstab row. In the Table row, use the dropdown to select Publishers. Then, in the Field row select PublisherName.

4. Click the View, Datasheet View toolbar button. Your results should now resemble Figure 14.8, with the actual publishers' names in the column headers of the datasheet.

Next, let's look at what else we can do with this Crosstab query. Some of the examples that I'm about to show you are quite nonsensical given our current table (a publications table), but they do demonstrate some of the power of crosstab queries.

The first major change we'll make is to swap the row and column headers. We'll put publishers in the rows and categories in the columns.

Note The following task cannot be completed unless you have completed the previous tasks in this section.

14

Task: Swapping the Row Header with the Column Header

1. In the `CategoryID` column, change the Crosstab row to Column Heading.

2. In the `PublisherName` column, change the Crosstab row to Row Header.

3. Click the View, Datasheet View toolbar button. Your screen should resemble Figure 14.12.

FIGURE 14.12

The Datasheet view of the crosstab query with the column and row headers swapped.

Publisher	Total Of Publica	2	3	5	6	7
Fawcett Crest	1				1	
HarperCollins	2			1		1
JimBob Publishing	4	1			2	1
Sams	2	1	1			
Simon and Schuster	1					1

Record: 14 ◄ [1] ► ►I ►* of 5

4. Once again the column headers are out of whack. Save the query at this point with the name `exercise-ct`. You'll fix this in one of the Exercises at the end of the lesson.

Next, let's look at some of the other functions you can use in a Crosstab query. There's a field in the `Publications` table for the list price of a publication, so let's arrange our results to display the average list price for each publisher in each category. It doesn't matter whether the category name is the row or column header, so we'll just go with what's shown in Figure 14.12.

Note   The following task cannot be completed unless you have completed the previous tasks in this section.

Task: Adding a Data Value to the Query Results

1. Return to Design view. Find the column with Value in the Crosstab row. This is the column that defines what operation is performed to derive each non-header cell in the table.

2. We want to perform some calculation on the `ListPrice` field, so select that in this column's Field row.

3. The function we want to perform is to take an average of the list price. In the Total row for this column, you'll find all of the available functions. Select Avg.

▲ 4. Click the View, Datasheet View toolbar button to see the results.

Finally, let's add some limiting factors to our query. If you'll recall from previous sections today, we have a field in the Publications table that indicates whether a publication is currently available. In some cases you probably don't want to include unavailable books. The following steps show you how to limit the rows that will be used in constructing the crosstab.

> **Note**   The following task cannot be completed unless you have completed the previous tasks in this section.

Task: Limiting the Rows in the Query Results

1. Return to Design view. Double-click the Available field in the Publications field list.

2. A new column is added to the query design grid for the Available field. In the Total row, select Where from the dropdown list. Leave the Crosstab cell empty, and enter **Yes** in the Criteria cell.

3. Make sure there are some publications which are marked as not available (open the Publications table in datasheet view and uncheck several publications' Available box).

▲ 4. Click the View, Datasheet View toolbar button to see the results.

SQL-Specific Queries

Another set of advanced queries available in Access are the "SQL-specific" queries. These queries don't have a Design View available. Instead, you must enter and edit these queries with the query designer's SQL View. There are three SQL-specific query types: Union, pass-through, and data definition.

> **Caution**   If you have any existing query definition in Design View and you change the query type to one of the SQL-specific types, the existing definition will be completely lost. The same goes if you switch from a SQL-specific query to a different type of query.

14

Union Queries

A Union query is used to combine rows from two or more Select queries into a single result set. The number and data types of fields returned by the union query must be identical for each Select query being combined, with the exception being that Number and Text fields can be interchanged.

The following task walks you through creating a Union query.

Task: Creating a Union Query

1. Start Access if necessary and locate the database, Day 14 on the CD.

2. Activate the Database window and make sure the Object bar is active. Click the Queries button.

3. Click the New button on the Database window's toolbar. The New Query dialog box appears. Leave Design View selected and click OK.

4. Close the Show Table dialog box. Because you cannot use the Design View to create SQL-specific queries, don't add any tables. Close the Show Table dialog box.

5. Use the Query, SQL Specific, Union menu item to start the UNION query. The Design View will be replaced with the SQL View.

6. Enter the following SQL statement:

```
SELECT FirstName + " " + LastName AS Name FROM Authors
    UNION
SELECT PublisherName AS Name FROM Publishers
```

7. Run the query. The results should resemble Figure 14.13. Notice that authors and publishers are intermixed within the results, and that the results are sorted in ascending order.

FIGURE 14.13

The Datasheet view of the UNION *query displaying authors and publishers in a single list.*

8. To sort the results in descending order, return to the SQL view and enter **ORDER BY Name DESC** on a new line after the second SELECT statement. Run the query again to verify that the results are now sorted in reverse order.

Note

For Union queries there is only a single ORDER BY clause, and it goes after the end of last SELECT statement.

Tip

If you need to differentiate which row came from which SELECT within a Union query, you can do so by adding a hard-coded field to the SELECT statements. For example:

```
SELECT FirstName + " " + LastName AS Name, "Author" FROM Authors
UNION
SELECT PublisherName AS Name, "Publisher" FROM Publishers
```

Data-definition Queries

Data-definition queries use a data-definition language (DDL) query to create or alter objects within the database. In Microsoft Access, you can create new tables, add a field or a constraint to an existing table, delete a table, and create and delete indexes.

Data-definition queries have a syntax all their own. Table 14.1 shows the statements you can use.

TABLE 14.1 Data-definition Query Statements

Keyword	Purpose
CREATE TABLE	Creates a new table
ALTER TABLE	Modifies a table by adding a field or a constraint
DROP	Deletes a table or index
CREATE INDEX	Creates a new index

For example, the CREATE TABLE query looks like this:

```
CREATE TABLE Orders
([OrderID] COUNTER,
[OrderDate] DATETIME,
[ShipName] TEXT(50),
[ShipAddress] TEXT,
[ShipCity] TEXT(50),
[ShipState] TEXT(50),
[ShipPostalCode] TEXT(50),
[ShipDate] DATETIME,
[FreightCharge] CURRENCY,
CONSTRAINT [Index1] PRIMARY KEY ([OrderID]));
```

14

The new table will be named **Orders**. It will have a field named **OrderID** which will be an AutoNumber field (the syntax in the DDL for this is **COUNTER**). There will be several Text fields. Most will have a Field Size of **50** except for **ShipAddress**. This field will get the default Text field size of **255**. There will be two Date/Time fields and a Currency field. The **OrderID** field will be the table's primary key.

For more information on syntax, available data types, and so on, check out the Microsoft Knowledgebase article Q180841 at `http://support.microsoft.com/support/kb/arti-cles/Q180/8/41.ASP`. There you'll find several examples of the CREATE TABLE, CREATE INDEX, and ALTER TABLE queries.

Pass-Through Queries

The SQL-specific pass-through query is used to act directly on an ODBC-compliant data source. For all other query types, the Microsoft Jet database engine processes the query and results. In the case of the pass-through query, you're working directly on the tables on the ODBC database and you'll use the query syntax of the data source (as opposed to Microsoft Access' query syntax).

The following task walks you through creating a pass-through query. Note that pass-through queries and the ODBC connection settings are highly specific to the server you're accessing. What follows is merely a guide to how you would set up a pass-through query and could change drastically depending on your server. Check the server's documentation for details on setting up pass-through queries.

Task: Creating a Pass-Through Query

▼ TASK

1. In the Database window, click the Queries button. Click the New button.

2. On the New Query dialog box, leave Design View selected and click OK. When the Show Table dialog box appears, click the Close button.

3. Use the Query, SQL Specific, Pass-Through menu item to change the query to the pass-through query type.

4. Click the Properties button on the toolbar to display the Query Properties dialog box (see Figure 14.14).

5. Set the ODBC Connect Str property to specify the connection information necessary to connect to the ODBC data source. If you leave the default setting of "ODBC;" then Access will prompt the user for the connection information each time the query is executed. You can also use the Build button to use the ODBC Select Data Source dialog box to obtain the connection information.

▼ 6. If the query does not return any records, set Returns Records to No.

FIGURE 14.14

The Query Properties dialog box for a pass-through query.

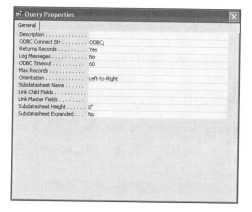

7. If the query returns messages in addition to data, turn Log Messages on by setting the property to Yes. Doing so will cause Access to create a new table each time the query is run to hold any returned messages. The table name will start with the user's login name, a hyphen, and then a sequential number starting with "00" (for example, "Admin-00," "Admin-01," and so on).

8. Close the Query Properties dialog box and enter the SQL for the query in the SQL Pass-Through Query window. See the data source's documentation for details on the query syntax necessary.

9. To run the query, click the Run button on the toolbar. If it's a query that returns records, you can also switch to the Datasheet view to see the results.

Using External Criteria in Queries

So far the queries you've seen today are fairly static and hard-coded. What if your query needs to change based on user input or data on a form? You can make your queries dynamic through the use of parameterized queries.

This section describes how to create two different types of dynamic queries. One is a query which will prompt the user for the values to use in the query. The other uses data on a form as the parameter value.

Parameterized Queries

When you have a query which needs to extract data based on a varying value of a particular field or fields, you have a candidate for a parameterized query. For example, if you

14

have a publications database and need to retrieve the books written by a particular author you can use a parameterized query.

In the following task you'll learn how to create parameterized queries using both the Design View window and the SQL View window. The task begins by demonstrating how to use the Design View. Then you'll see how the query is represented in the SQL View window.

Task: Creating a Parameterized Query

▲ TASK ▼

1. In the Database window, click the Queries button. Click the New button.

2. Leave Design View selected in the list box of the New Query dialog box. Click the OK button.

3. On the Show Table dialog box, click Authors in the list and click the Add button. Do the same for the Publications table. Click the Close button.

4. Double-click the asterisk item in the Publications table field list. This will add all of the fields to the query's output.

5. For this query, we'll be searching for books based on the author's last name. Double-click LastName in the Authors table field list (see Figure 14.15).

FIGURE 14.15

The new query after adding the LastName field.

6. In the Criteria row for the LastName column, enter **[Last Name]**. Because you entered the square brackets, Access considers this to be a field name. And because this field does not exist in the tables used in the query (because there's a space between Last and Name and the field name is LastName without the space), Access considers this to be a parameter for the query. The text you enter here will be displayed in a prompt dialog box when the query is executed, so make the text as meaningful as possible. The prompt dialog box will not display the characters in square brackets.

7. Save the query using the Save button on the toolbar. Enter a meaningful name when prompted.

▼   8. Execute the query by clicking the Run button on the toolbar. Access will prompt
         you for the last name of the author for whose books you're looking for (see Figure
         14.16). Enter a value (use Eddy if you're using the sample database) and click OK
         (clicking Cancel will simply return you to the Design View window).

FIGURE 14.16

*When you execute the
query, Access will
prompt you for the
parameter value.*

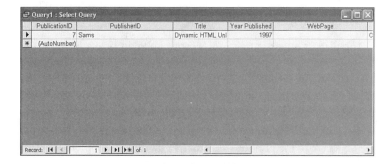

      9. The Datasheet View window shows you any rows for the author whose last name
         you entered in the parameter.

> **Note**   If you have more than one parameter in the query's design, Access will dis-
>   play one dialog box for each parameter.

      10. Now let's look at the SQL Design window. Use the View, SQL View menu item.
          The SQL Design window is shown in Figure 14.17. As you can see, the SQL
          WHERE clause for a parameterized query is no different than the WHERE clause for
          any other query, with the exception of the fact that the value after the equal sign is
▲   a nonexistent field.

FIGURE 14.17

*The SQL statement for
a parameterized query.*

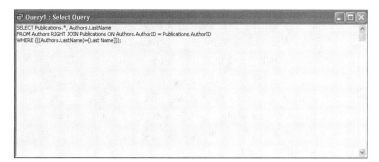

14

Query Criteria from Form Entries

Parameterized queries certainly are handy, but what if you have a lot of parameters for your user to enter? As mentioned in a note in the previous section, Access will display a dialog box to the user for each parameter. This can be tedious for the user, obviously. Access provides a way to get around this problem using a combination of forms and special query syntax.

The plan of attack is to create a form with edit boxes for each of the parameters to be used in the query and then to reference those edit boxes from the query. The following task explains how it's done.

Task: Using Form Entries for Query Criteria

1. In the Database window, click the Queries button. Click the query saved from the task in the previous section (if you didn't complete that task, please do so now—it won't take long!) and use the Edit, Copy menu item. Then use Edit, Paste and provide the name FormQuery as the new query name.

2. In the Database window, click the Forms button. Click the New button.

3. On the New Form dialog box, leave Design View selected and don't select anything in the dropdown list at the bottom of the dialog box. Click the OK button.

4. On the Form Design window, add a Text Box control using the Toolbox. Name the text box txtLastName and set its visual properties to match Figure 14.18.

> **Note**   For more information on creating and editing forms, see Day 5, "Simple Forms," and Day 10, "Improving Your Forms."

5. Make sure the Control Wizards button in the Toolbox is active (it should be outlined). If it's not, click the Control Wizards button in the Toolbox. If you don't see the Toolbox, use the View, Toolbox menu item to display it. Add a button to the form. When the Command Button wizard displays, select Miscellaneous in the Categories list and Run Query in the Actions list. Click Next.

6. On the next dialog box, select FormQuery from the list of available queries and click Next. On the next dialog box, select the Text radio button and change the caption if you wish. Click Finish (the final dialog box in this wizard allows you to rename the control, and we don't really need to in this example). Your form should look like Figure 14.18.

FIGURE 14.18

The parameter form in Design View.

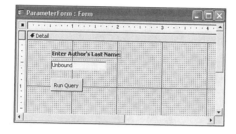

Note

If you had additional parameters in your query, you would add additional edit boxes for them. Make sure you give the edit boxes meaningful names.

7. Save the form with the name `ParameterForm`. Return to the Database window and click the Queries button. Click `FormQuery` and then click the Design button.

8. Replace `[Last Name]` with `[Forms]![ParameterForm].[txtLastName]` (note all those square brackets). Save the query and close the window.

9. Return to the form design window and switch to Form View. Enter an author's last name (use Eddy) in the edit box and click the Run Query button. The query should execute and display the same rows as the previous task's query, assuming you entered the same last name of course.

The most important step in the previous task is step 8. It is imperative that you properly specify the form field in the query criteria. Otherwise, the query will not execute and will likely cause Access to display cryptic error messages. The `[Forms]!` portion specifies that what follows is a form name (`ParameterForm` in this case). The form name is followed by a period, specifying that what follows is a control name (`txtLastName` in this case).

Summary

Today you've learned quite a bit about some fairly advanced query capabilities. The day started with a discussion of the various action queries, named because they "act" on data and tables within the database. The action queries discussed were the Update query, the Append query, the Delete query, and the Make Table query.

Next we looked at Crosstab queries. These queries create summaries of data within your database and are quite powerful. As you saw, they are very easy to customize in order to retrieve the information you're looking for.

14

We then looked at several SQL-Specific queries, including Union, pass-through, and data definition queries. Finally, you learned how to make your queries more useful by making them dynamic. This was done through the use of parameterized queries, which prompt the user for WHERE clause values each time they're executed, and through the use of form element values within a query's WHERE clause.

Q&A

Q. **When I modify the query associated with a subform and click the Refresh button (or Requery the subform), the updated query doesn't seem to be used (see the section "Query Criteria from Form Entries"). What's the deal?**

A. If you modify a query used as the basis for a subform while the subform is running, even refreshing the subform will not pick up the new query. You need to close and reopen the form in order for it to use the updated query.

Workshop

The Workshop helps you solidify the skills you learned in this lesson. Answers to the quiz appear in Appendix A, "Answers to Quizzes."

Quiz

1. Instead of using the table Datasheet View, what's a more efficient way to modify the field values of a known group of records?

2. When you execute a Delete query, can the deletions be undone?

3. Can you create a table by writing a query?

4. How does Access determine what's a parameter in a query's WHERE clause?

5. How do you reference a form field from within a query?

Exercises

For further practice working with queries, perform the tasks in this exercise. If you have not performed the tasks in the "Crosstab Queries" section you need to do so before continuing with the Exercises.

First, let's fix the Category Header in the Crosstab Query.

1. Open the query you created in the task "Creating a Crosstab Query" in design view. If you need a reminder of the problem at hand, switch to datasheet view. The column headers display a numeric value (the CategoryID) instead of the category name. Return to design view.

2. The category names are stored in the Categories table. Add this table to the query (use the Show Table button).

3. Find the query grid column for the Row Header (it's the one with CategoryID as the Field). Change the Table value specified to `Categories`.

4. Change the Field value to `Category`.

5. Switch to the datasheet view. Now the column headers have category names. Save the query.

Now, let's eliminate unavailable publications.

1. Open the `Crosstab` query you created in the task "Creating a Crosstab Query" in design view (if you've just completed the previous exercise, just switch back to design view).

2. Because we don't really want to include publications that are not available, we need to add a criterion to the query to only include those rows from the Publications table where the Available field is set to `Yes`. Double-click `Available` in the Publications field list.

3. The default value for the Total row in the query grid is `Group By`, but we only need the Available field for the query criteria. So change the Total row in the Available column to `Where`.

4. Click in the Criteria row for the Available column. Enter `Yes`.

   Switch to the datasheet view. The quantities will be changed if you have any unavailable publications in the Publications table. If it hasn't changed, open the Publications table in datasheet view and change the value of the Available field for several rows. Then rerun the query to see the changes.

14

WEEK 2

In Review

Most of the additional information on forms, reports, tables, and queries presented this week were just extensions of the basics you learned in the first week. The more you use Access, the easier you will find it is to implement what you learned this week. The material on SQL was more complex, but even this information will become clearer as you begin using it in your development work. Don't hesitate to return to the lessons of this week when you encounter the need to hone your Access programming and development skills.

8

9

10

11

12

13

14

WEEK 3

At a Glance

Week 3 will get you started using VBA to directly access your data. You will learn to polish the applications you build and to prepare them for distribution.

Day 15, "Introduction to VBA Concepts," you will learn the fundamentals of Visual Basic for Applications (VBA). In addition, you will see how Access is event-driven and how you can use these events most effectively.

Day 16, "VBA Language Elements—Part 1," you will begin using VBA. You will learn about using modules, procedures, and variables. You will see how important they are to replicating code.

Day 17, "VBA Programming—Part 2," brings you to the next step in VBA. You need to learn about operators, branching, and looping in order to make VBA work for you. If you are new to programming, you will need to follow this lesson carefully.

Day 18, "Objects and Collections," introduces you to objects and collections in Access. You will discover how important they are to harnessing the power of Access.

Day 19, "Extending Access Using VBA," you will see how to use ActiveX Data Objects to enhance your database. You will learn how to develop with multiple developers and how to prepare your database for distribution.

20

Day 20, "Maintaining and Securing Access Databases," you will learn how to repair and compact your databases and how important these tasks are to maintaining a complex application. You will see how to secure your database from unwanted viewing or tampering.

Finally, Day 21, "Access on the Web," shows you the features allowing you to publish data via XML and how to publish static and dynamic HTML files or Active Server Pages from your tables. Day 21 also introduces you to Data Access Pages.

DAY 15

Introduction to VBA Concepts

During Day 14, "Special Query Uses," you learned how to use queries to both manipulate large amounts of data at once and to create or modify tables within the database. Beginning today and continuing through Day 19, "Extending Access Using VBA," you'll learn how to perform these same activities, plus many, many more, using Microsoft's Visual Basic for Applications (VBA). VBA is a programming language that is based on Microsoft's BASIC language and provides you with direct access to the data and structure of the current database and beyond.

Today you'll be introduced to VBA: where it came from, where it can be used, and the basics of VBA as it relates to Microsoft Access. The day starts off with an introduction to VBA and its uses. Next comes a more historical perspective: Where did VBA get its origins? Then you get into the meat of the learning with introductions to event-driven programming, objects, collections, and modules. Finally, you'll get an introduction to the Visual Basic Editor (VBE). This is the tool where your learning will be put to use.

Future days provide more "meat" to the topic of programming in Microsoft Access. Day 16, "VBA Language Elements—Part 1," gets you started actually using the language and introduces the various building blocks of VBA programming. During Day 17, "VBA Programming—Part 2," you'll learn some more advanced programming techniques, including ways to control the "flow" of the VBA routines you're writing.

Day 18, "Objects and Collections," teaches you how to use and create "objects" and how to use the Windows API (application programming interface) which provides you with a library of commonly used routines. Finally, Day 19, "Extending Access Using VBA," introduces more advanced concepts which can be used to create powerful applications within Microsoft Access.

Today You Will Learn

- What VBA is and does
- The history of the Visual Basic programming language
- How event-driven programming works and how to write code for events in Access
- What object-oriented programming is all about
- How to work with VBA code in Access

What Is VBA and Why Should You Learn It?

During Day 8, "A Macro Primer," you learned about automating functionality through the use of macros. VBA is similar in concept: You write VBA code to automate some functionality, making the user's tasks easier to accomplish. There are vast differences, however, between what can be accomplished with macros and what you can do using VBA.

The biggest difference is that macros provide only a "hard-coded" list of functionality. If there's not an existing macro to accomplish the task at hand, you're out of luck. In some cases you can combine different macros to perform the task, but you're still very limited as to what you can do. Using VBA, however, opens the entire world of Access and the database to your manipulations.

Whereas macros must be chosen from a predefined set of actions, VBA allows you to create routines to accomplish just about any task you need to perform. A subset of the Microsoft BASIC programming language and access to the database's "object model" (more on this in the section "Introducing Objects") combine to provide you with a plat-form upon which you can write extensive data and user interface manipulation routines.

> **Note**
>
> For more differences between macros and VBA, see the section "Should I use a macro or Visual Basic?" in the Microsoft Access Help file.

If your database is to be more than just a mere repository of data, you'll need to add some VBA knowledge to your repertoire. Using VBA you can make forms more interactive, manipulate data behind the scenes, display error messages, and utilize external and third-party components and objects within your programming code.

VBA is based on Microsoft's very successful Visual Basic programming language. Its constructs and syntax are straightforward and easy to learn and use. VBA code is also highly "portable" because it is built in to all of the Microsoft Office suite's applications and in to several other applications as well (such as Visio). You can take helper functions and other code written within VBE for Microsoft Access and copy and paste them into Microsoft Word's VBA editor, for example.

And best of all, once you learn VBA in Microsoft Access, you can easily utilize its power in Microsoft Excel, Microsoft Word, and other applications. Simply learn the object model provided by the application in question and you're off and running!

The BASIC Programming Language

First things first: the acronym. You've probably noticed that when people write BASIC they write it in all caps (or at least they should) instead of in sentence caps (that is, "Basic"). So, is the language a basic language, or is the word an acronym for something complicated? Well, the language is a basic, easy-to-learn language, as you'll see. But the name of the language is actually an acronym (and hence the caps) for Beginner's All Purpose Instruction Code (BASIC).

So how did the BASIC language come to be, and is VBA something radically different? You'll explore those two topics in this section.

Historical Perspective

Most programmers today think that BASIC was born when Bill Gates and Paul Allen created the BASIC language on the Altair (the world's first personal computer). However, the language was actually created in 1964 at Dartmouth College's Department of Mathematics. John Kemeny, chairman of the department, and Professor Thomas Kurtz created the language as a stepping stone to help students progress to more complicated languages such as FORTRAN (FORmula TRANslation) or ALGOL (ALGOrithmic Language).

According to the "Jones Telecommunications and Multimedia Encyclopedia" (`http://www.digitalcentury.com/encyclo/update/BASIC.html`), Kemeny and Kurtz had eight goals in mind for their new language. BASIC had to be

- Easy for beginners
- General-purpose (as opposed to FORTRAN, which was aimed at the scientific community)
- Allow for advanced features to be added to the language
- Interactive
- User-friendly when it came to error messages
- Fast and responsive
- Usable without a knowledge of the computer's hardware (as opposed to assembly language which often requires an intimate knowledge of the inner workings of the hardware)
- Usable without having to deal with the computer's operating system

In a testimony to how easy BASIC was (and is) to use, "... Kemeny and Kurtz felt a student should be able to write a program after only three classroom lecture sessions. Students, however, thought the third lecture was a waste of time, so it was eliminated" (`http://www.digitalcentury.com/encyclo/update/BASIC.html`).

In 1974, the American National Standards Institute (ANSI) began work to create a standardized version of the language. However, in that same year the first personal computers (in the form of kits for home building) began shipping. Obviously, these computers needed to provide some means for the owner to make their new computer do something, so the manufacturers included some version of BASIC. However, because a standard had not yet come out of ANSI, each brand shipped with a slightly different version of BASIC and thus programs written on one machine could not be used directly on another.

Gates and Allen created their version of BASIC for the MITS Altair (another kit computer) in 1975. Whereas the previous versions of BASIC were compiled languages (meaning that the lines of code were run through a compiler to produce a program which you could execute), the Microsoft version of BASIC was an interpreted language (meaning that as you entered lines of code you could execute them immediately). Gates and Allen felt that by using an interpreted language they could provide more and better feedback to the programmer about the syntax and results of what they entered.

Without a doubt, the Microsoft version of BASIC, which eventually morphed into today's wildly popular Visual Basic programming language, was responsible for a revolution in programming.

15

> **Note**   Interestingly, Kemeny and Kurtz were not entirely happy with the version of BASIC produced by Microsoft. They were concerned that in the name of compromising for ease-of-use, many mistakes were made.

Visual Basic for Applications Versus Visual Basic

Building on the fantastic success of its Visual Basic (VB) product, Microsoft decided to leverage the language in to its Office suite of applications. There are two reasons this made sense: First, the vast number of programmers who claimed VB knowledge could bring their efforts to bear customizing Office applications and, second, the language was perfectly suited to become the scripting language of choice for Office applications.

There are really only two major differences between Visual Basic and VBA:

- Visual Basic can be used to create stand-alone applications, ActiveX controls, and COM components; VBA must be used from within a host application such as Access.

- The application hosting VBA typically makes available a set of objects which make automating the application straightforward. For example, Access provides your VBA code with a built-in object named `CurrentDb` which represents the current database.

Introducing Event-Driven Programming

Now that the introduction to BASIC is out of the way, it's time to jump in to the heart of the beast. This section will introduce you to event-driven programming. If you've done any programming in the Windows environment before, you're probably very familiar with events and event-driven programming. Feel free to proceed to the next section.

There are two main styles of programming: procedural and event-driven. Procedure programs "proceed" from one line to the next (albeit with some branching allowed) in a march-step fashion. The course the program will take is based on the input data and the logic in the programming code. Given a specific set of inputs, you can trace through the code in an orderly, predictable manner (bugs notwithstanding, of course).

Event-driven programming, however, relies on outside influences to direct the flow of the program code. Every Windows application is written in an event-driven model. Even applications with no user interface are still event-driven, although the event that triggers the code might only be a timer tick. In event-driven programming you write code that responds to the various events about which you're expecting Windows (or the host application in the case of VBA) to inform you (in the parlance, an event is said to be "raised" to the application).

So there are two things you need to know when you're going to write event-driven programs: What events the program respond to and what that response will entail. One of the nice things about programming in Windows is that you don't have to respond to every single event that occurs. Windows provides default event handlers for almost every event.

For example, there are events that are raised when you press down a key and when you release a key. Obviously in the vast majority of programs you don't really care that a key (or a mouse button) is in the down state. What you care about is when the user releases that key (or releases the mouse button). There's nothing to prevent you from handling the KeyDown event, but if you don't handle it you won't miss the KeyPress event!

Events in Access

When programming in Access, you'll respond to events that are raised by forms and their controls, in response to a macro that executes, or when reports are displayed. Figure 15.1 shows you a subset of the events available for a form. Note that these events are for the form itself, not for any controls which might be on the form.

FIGURE 15.1

Some of the events available for a form in Access.

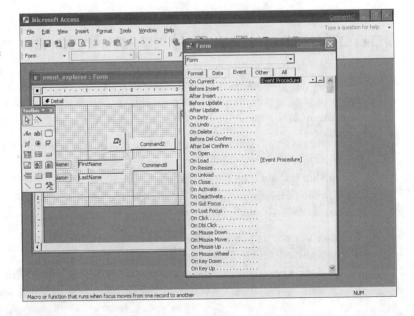

As you can see from Figure 15.1, the list is quite extensive, and this is just for the form object. Any control worth its salt will have its own list of events. So how do you know what all of these events are supposed to represent? One way is to use the onscreen tips Access provides. If you click in the edit box next to an event's name in the Properties window, the status bar at the bottom of the Access window will display text describing the event. Pressing the Help key (F1) opens the Microsoft Access Help file with a much more verbose description of the event.

How do you specify what to do in response to an event? Obviously there's an edit box next to the event name and you could just type something. But what? Well, Access provides you with the help you need. When you have the focus on the event's edit box, you'll notice a dropdown button and a "builder" button (the one with the ellipsis).

If you click the dropdown button you'll see an [Event Procedure] entry, plus entries for any macros that exist in the database. If you click the [Event Procedure] entry, nothing happens. That was helpful? Now click the "builder" button and you'll be transported to the Visual Basic Editor window and placed within the event procedure for the event with which you're working (more on what you do next, later).

You can also use the "builder" button directly (with nothing entered in the edit box). Doing so will display the Choose Builder dialog box shown in Figure 15.2.

FIGURE 15.2

The Choose Builder dialog box where you specify how to respond to an event.

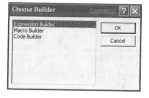

Selecting Expression Builder and clicking OK will display the Expression Builder dialog box. In most cases, this dialog box is not very useful for responding to events.

Selecting Macro Builder will display a new Macro window where you can create a macro. This is useful for tasks that you know are already provided by a macro action, such as OpenForm, PrintOut, and so on.

Selecting Code Builder will display the VB editor as if you had chosen [Event Procedure] in the event's edit box and then clicked the "builder" button.

In the following section you'll go through a task to explore the basics of using events in Microsoft Access.

Exercise: The "Events" Explorer

In this section you'll get a quick introduction to a few events and when they're raised. This is by no means an exhaustive or complete introduction, but when you finish this exercise you'll be familiar with how to specify the response to an event. You'll also get an introduction to the Visual Basic Editor built in to Access.

Task: Exploring Events

1. Start Access 2002. Open the database **Day 15** from the CD included with this book. The database has some of the tables, macros, and code modules referenced in this task.

2. Activate the Database window and click the Forms button in the Object bar. Click New. On the New Form dialog box, leave Design View selected in the list and select Authors in the dropdown list. Click OK.

3. If the Toolbox is not visible (that's the little tool window with buttons for each form control), use the View, Toolbox menu item to display the Toolbox. At the top-right of the Toolbox is the Control Wizards toggle button. If there isn't a highlight around the button, typically in the form of a blue outline but sometimes with a different background than the other buttons, click it. This will turn on the Control Wizards.

4. On the Toolbox, click on Command Button and then click anywhere on the form. The Command Button Wizard appears. This wizard sets up the command button's event procedure for you. On the first screen, select Miscellaneous in the list on the left and Run Macro in the list on the right. Click Next.

5. The next screen of the wizard allows you to select the macro to be run when the new command button is clicked. Select EventMacro in the list and click Next. The next screen lets you choose how the button will look. Select the options you wish and click Next. Leave the defaults on the final screen and click Finish.

6. To see what you've done, open the Properties window (press F4) and click on the command button you just added. In the Properties window, go to the Event tab. Notice that the On Click event has text in it. Click in the edit box and click the "builder" button to its right. You'll be whisked to the Visual Basic Editor where you can see the code that will run when you click the button. See Figure 15.3.

Note Notice that the Command Button Wizard runs the macro by executing VBA code even though the macro is available in the dropdown list next to the On Click event in the Properties window. This is because the Command Button

15

> Wizard has a standard way of causing all its different actions to happen. If
> you had chosen something other than Run Macro in Step 4, you'd see some-
> thing very similar in the event procedure code.

FIGURE 15.3

*The Visual Basic
Editor for the com-
mand button's Click
event.*

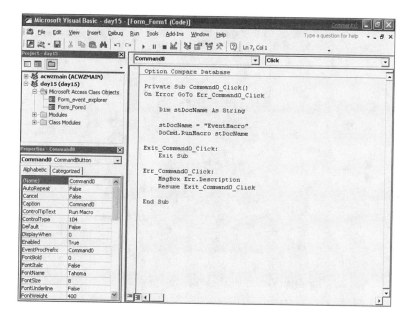

7. Close the Visual Basic Editor and return to the form Design window. Click the
Control Wizards button in the Toolbox to disable the Control Wizards. Add another
command button to the form.

8. The Properties window should still be active and on the Event tab but if not, activate it by clicking the new command button and pressing F4. On the Event tab,
click in the On Click edit box and click the dropdown arrow to its right. Select
EventMacro from the dropdown list.

9. Switch to Form View and click each button. Notice that despite the different methods used to run the macro, the same effect occurs.

10. Return to Design View and click on the form. In the Properties window you should
see Form in the dropdown list at the top of the window (if not, select it there).
Again, make sure the Event tab is active. Click in the On Load event's edit box and
then click the builder button. When the Choose Builder dialog box appears, select
Code Builder and click OK.

▼   11. The Visual Basic Editor appears again. You'll find the cursor within a procedure
         named Form_Load(). Type **MsgBox "Form_Load event procedure"** and press the
         Enter key. Your screen should resemble Figure 15.4.

FIGURE 15.4

*The Visual Basic
Editor for the form's
Load event.*

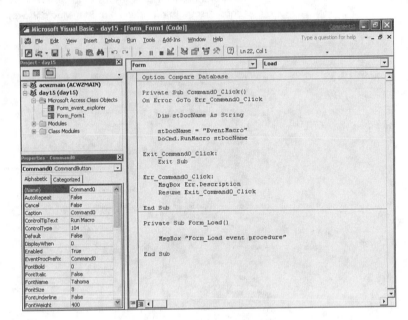

    12. Close the Visual Basic Editor and switch to the Form View. When you do this you
         should see the Form_Load event procedure message box. Click OK on this dialog
         box and the form is now waiting for your input, for its next event to be raised.
         Return to the Design View.

    13. Open the Field List window if it's not already in sight. Drag the FirstName field to
         the form. Select the field, open the Properties window, switch to the Event tab, and
         click in the GotFocus event. This event is raised when the control receives the
         input focus from Windows. Click the builder button, select Code Builder and click
         OK. In the Visual Basic Editor, enter **MsgBox "FirstName_GotFocus event
         procedure."** Close the editor, switch to Form View (click OK on the message box
         that appears because of the Form_Load event procedure), and click in the First
▲   Name field. You should see the message box.

To see more events in action, open the frmEventExplorer form included in the day's
database. This form has VBA code for many of the events. The code adds the event
name to the list box on the right-hand side of the form. Move the focus between the
fields, click the buttons, and change to a different record.

By examining the order of the events in the list box, you'll be able to tell when particular events are raised. The usual confusion is when the user is switching the focus between fields: Which comes first, GotFocus on the new field or LostFocus on the previous one? You can use this technique whenever you're debugging a form's event code and you're not sure what's what.

Also, update one of the fields, switch records, and take note of the order of the BeforeUpdate and AfterUpdate events and the LostFocus event for the field you updated. As you can tell, the LostFocus event does not fire until after the update events. This means that data validation in the LostFocus event might not be effective. Any data validation code should also be placed in the BeforeUpdate event.

Introducing Objects

The previous section discussed event-driven programming, the "behind-the-scenes" activity of all Windows-based programs. This section will introduce you to object-oriented programming, the methodology used most often in Access to make things happen.

Everything's an Object

In object-oriented programming, almost everything is represented as an *object*. The definition of an object is "a self-contained entity that consists of both data and procedures to manipulate the data" (http://www.webopedia.com/TERM/o/object.html). The data describes the object (a car's color, a book's page count, and so on) while the procedures define what actions the object is capable of performing.

The classic examples used when describing object-oriented programming are cars or animals. Both have attributes that are the data (known as *properties* in object-oriented terms) and both can perform actions which may or may not manipulate the data (these are known as *methods*). In the case of a car, its properties could include Color and CurrentSpeed. The methods could be SwitchGears, Accelerate, and Decelerate (or SlamOnTheBrakes in case I'm behind the wheel).

Additionally, some objects can themselves perform actions which the environment (your program) can react to (these would be *events* raised by the object). For example, a car might overheat and raise its Overheating event. You can choose to ignore the event (as you saw in the Event Explorer example earlier in the lesson, there are many, many events which get ignored) or you can write some code to react to it (which is advisable in the case of Overheating).

Encapsulating Functionality

One of the great benefits of using object-oriented programming is that once you have defined an object to represent an item (a Database object, for example) you can use that object in the same manner from many different pieces of code.

Many objects also present a consistent interface. Because the auto industry has decided to standardize the pedal arrangement, you can pretty much count on the order of the pedals no matter what brand of car you're driving: brake on the left, gas on the right.

Referencing Objects, Properties, and Methods

Like all elements of programming languages, objects are used with a standard set of language constructs. These constructs obviously can differ for each language, but in general they follow the pattern described here.

First, objects have what are known as instances. An instance of an object is a specific occurrence of that object. The instance contains data that is specific to it alone. When you act on an object, you must act on an instance of that object. In other words, the object is abstract but the instance is not.

When you reference an instance, you use a variable name to represent it. For example, Access provides a global variable (meaning that it's always available) named CurrentDb that represents the current database. You can use this and other global variables or you might need to create your own variables to represent instances of other objects.

You can use properties just like any other value or variable. Some properties are read/write meaning you can both set and read their values. Others are read-only meaning you cannot set the value of the property directly. Another seldom-used variety are write-only properties, but these should be avoided. The reason you should avoid write-only properties is that the nature of object-oriented programming is such that an object's properties should inform whatever is using the object about the current state of the object. Write-only properties obviously cannot inform the outside world about state. Instead of a write-only property, use a method to set the internal value that the write-only property controlled.

To use a property in VBA (and most other languages), you specify the instance variable name, a period, and then the property name. For example:

```
MsgBox CurrentDb.Name
```

displays the name of the current database in a message box dialog box. To set the value of a read/write property, you would use

```
CurrentDb.Connect = "MyDatasource"
```

15

To invoke a method (procedure) of an object instance, you use a syntax similar to accessing a property:

```
CurrentDb.Close()
```

The parentheses can enclose parameters which the method needs. These would be data which is passed to the method. The number and data type of the parameters depends on how the method is defined.

Another concept supported by some, but not all, object-oriented languages is the concept of a "default" property or method. In Visual Basic and VBA, if an object has defined a default property or method, you can access that property or method with simply the variable name of the instance.

For example, suppose we have an object whose default property is its `Name` property. If we have an instance of that object in a variable named `foo` we can display the name property with either

```
MsgBox foo.Name
```

or

```
MsgBox foo
```

Using default properties and methods is a way to shortcut some of your code, but you should balance this shortcut with the fact that your code might be less "self-documenting" in some cases. The previous example is one case where I would advocate using the long-hand method. When we talk about object collections in the next section, you'll see a case where it's probably better to use the short-hand method.

Introducing Object Collections

Another common concept in object-oriented programming is the concept of collections. A collection is a set of instances which you can act upon as a whole or individually.

Collections of Objects

By itself, a collection object is a true object that has properties (`Count` is a typical one) and methods (`Clear()` or `AddItem()` for example). Most of these properties and methods act upon the collection itself.

There will also be one or more properties or methods you can use to retrieve individual, specific members of the collection. Typically this property or method is named something like `Items()` and it is the default property or method for the collection object.

Because it's the default property, you can access it with merely the collections name and a specifier for the item to retrieve. In some cases items are specified with an integer index. In other cases items might be specified with a character string that uniquely identifies items. Which type of specifier is used depends upon the collection being accessed.

Once you've retrieved a particular instance from the collection, you can act on it or access its properties.

Collection Objects In Access

Access provides many, many collections which you can use to manipulate the various items in the current database. The available collections include objects like `AllTables`, `AllForms`, and `AllQueries`. These collections are accessed via the global variable `CurrentData` (note that this is different from `CurrentDb()` discussed earlier) and are generic in nature.

Each of these collections contains the same set of properties: `Application`, `Count`, `Item`, and `Parent`. The `Item` property is the default property of the collection.

Other collection objects are more specific to the various types of objects within Access. These include `TableDefs` which defines the tables within the database and `QueryDefs` which defines queries within the database. These collection objects are accessed using the global `CurrentDb()` property.

Introducing VBA Modules

Like other types of objects within a database, Access provides a place to store Visual Basic code. These are called Modules. There are two different styles of modules: those associated with forms and reports and generic modules.

You can create generic sets of code using the Modules section of the Database window. The modules associated with forms and reports are not displayed within the Database window. These are managed by the forms and reports with which they are associated. When you launch the VB Editor, though, you'll see these modules within the editor's Project window.

This section discusses the two types of generic VBA modules: standard modules and class modules. Standard modules are simply containers for generic VBA code which, once created, can be called from any other code within the database. Class modules allow you to create classes (which are objects in object-oriented programming) which can be accessed similarly.

Note Both standard modules and class modules will be displayed on the Database window.

Standard Modules

Standard modules can be used to store global functions and procedures as well as global variables. Because these are global, they can be accessed from any code within the current database. In the case of functions and procedures, this includes running from a macro.

Modules have two major sections. One is the Declarations section. This is where you will define any global variables as well as variables that will be available only to code within the module (known as private variables).

Note To define a global variable, begin the declaration with the keyword `Public`. To define a private variable, use the keyword `Private`.

The other major section is the section containing all of the procedures and functions within the module.

Class Modules

Class modules are used to create objects (remember, an object is an encapsulation of data and functions to operate on that data). You create the object's properties and methods by writing code in the class module.

When you create a Public Procedure or Function in a class module, it becomes a method of the object. When you create a Public variable within the class module's Declarations section, it becomes a read/write property of the object. To create a read-only (or a write-only) property, or to have more control over what happens when a property value is set or retrieved, you'll need to use the editor's Add Procedure dialog box to create the property procedures for you. This dialog box is discussed later in the section "Adding Procedures, Functions, and Properties."

Classes have two specially defined procedures which can be useful. One is called `Initialize` and is called whenever your class is first instantiated (that is, whenever a variable that is defined to be of your class's object type). You can put code inside this procedure to initialize local variables or to perform any other start-up tasks that are necessary. The other procedure is called `Terminate` and this is called when the Visual Basic runtime determines that the instance of your class is no longer being used. You would place code here to clean up any memory you've allocated manually (VBA handles most memory allocation for you) or to close any files you've opened, and so on.

Introducing the Access VBE (Visual Basic Editor)

VBA code for event procedures and modules is edited using the Visual Basic Editor (VBE). Although the VBE is a full-featured Visual Basic code editor, this section will introduce just a few of the features which are the most useful when dealing with Access forms.

Note

Because the user interface for your code is handled by Access forms, reports, and so on, the user interface editing features are hidden from the Access Visual Basic editor (with the exception of the Properties window, which is still visible mainly to handle the few properties of modules and class modules).

The Visual Basic Editor is shown in Figure 15.5, with the code module for the frmEventExplorer form described earlier.

FIGURE 15.5

The Visual Basic Editor.

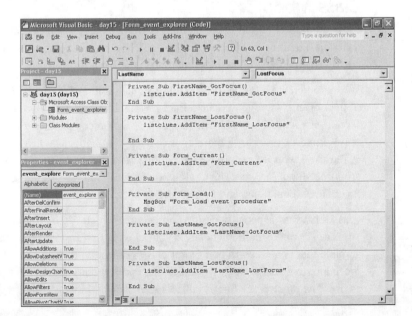

The editor consists of three main parts. The Project window at the top-left corner lists all the available code modules within the current database. Using the tree control in this window you can move between the various modules. Double-click an entry in the tree to open the Code window for that module. You can also use the context for items in the Project window to perform various tasks such as printing the module.

The Code window is where most of the action takes place. This is where you'll enter the VBA code that does all of the work. For modules associated with forms and reports, the dropdown list at the top-left of the Code window selects a control or section from the form or report. Once a selection is made in this list, the contents of the dropdown at top-right changes to list the available events for the selected control. If (General) is selected in the left-hand dropdown, the contents of the right-hand dropdown will be (Declarations), representing the section of code where you define global or module-level variables, and an entry for each procedure or function defined in the module.

For standard modules, the left-hand dropdown only contains (General), unless you've defined a variable for an object that raises events (see the Note that follows), and the right-hand dropdown contains a list of the procedures and functions in the module.

For class modules, the left-hand dropdown will also contain a Class entry with corresponding Initialize and Terminate procedures. These procedures were discussed in the previous section, "Introducing VBA Modules."

Note

In addition to the items just mentioned, it is possible to create a variable which is an instance of an object that raises events. This topic is beyond the scope of this book.

The third part of interest is the Properties window. When the current item in the Project window is a form's event module, the Properties window will allow you to modify properties of the form's sections and controls. When the selected item is a standard module, you'll be able to modify the module's Name property. For a class module, you'll be able to modify the Name and the "instancing" property. Instancing is a way of specifying the scope of the class. In Access VBA, a class module can be either Private or PublicNotCreatable.

Another useful portion of the editor is the toolbar. The toolbar shown in Figure 15.5 looks pretty cluttered. That's because all of the main toolbars are enabled (if your toolbar looks different, right-click over the toolbar area and activate both the Standard and the Debug toolbars). To see what each button does, hover the mouse pointer over the button and wait for the little "tooltip" to pop up. The important buttons are

- Find—Use this button to search for a string within your code modules.
- Object Browser—This button invokes the Object Browser window which is discussed later in the section "The Object Browser Window."
- Toggle Breakpoint—Use this to set a "breakpoint" in your code, meaning that when that line is about to be executed, the debugger will halt execution and open the VBE with that line highlighted. You can then perform some debugging on the code, check the values of various variables, and so on.
- Comment Block/Uncomment Block—This button will comment or uncomment a line or a set of selected lines of code. This is useful when you want to remove sections of code that are suspect.
- Toggle Bookmark, et al—Use the bookmarks to mark particular lines of code. Once a bookmark is set, you can return to it by repeatedly clicking the Next Bookmark or Previous Bookmark until the line you're looking for is found.
- Locals Window—When running through code, use the Locals window to view the contents of local variables (variables available only to the current procedure).
- Immediate Window—While you're debugging your code you can set a breakpoint. When you encounter a breakpoint, you can open the Immediate window and use it to run code snippets, examine the value of variables, and so on. To see the value of a variable, type `Print theVariable`, for example.
- Watch Window—Using the Watch window, you can place a "watch" on specific variables and even have the debugger "break" (stop) execution when an expression is True or when a variable's value changes.

Adding Procedures, Functions, and Properties

As you saw in the `frmEventExplorer` task earlier in the day, the procedure headers for form and control events are put in to the modules automatically by the form editor. However, if you are adding your own procedures or functions to a form's code module or you're creating a standard or class module, you'll need to add these yourself. The Visual Basic Editor provides a handy Add Procedure dialog box to help you do this.

 Note | Throughout the remainder of this section, the word procedure will be used generically to mean a procedure, function, or property.

To invoke the Add Procedure dialog box, open the code module where the procedure will be added. Then use the Insert, Procedure menu item. The Add Procedure dialog box, shown in Figure 15.6 appears.

FIGURE 15.6

The Visual Basic Editor's Add Procedure dialog box, used to add procedures, functions, and properties to the active code module.

15

This dialog box is fairly easy to use. Enter a name for the procedure in the Name edit box. Make sure the name is descriptive, particularly if you're creating a property. This will aid you when you need to reference the new procedure and will be invaluable should others need to review or maintain your code.

The radio buttons in the Type frame specify which type of procedure you're creating: a procedure (listed in the dialog as Sub, short for Subroutine which is another name for Procedure), a function, or a property. Finally, the radio buttons in the Scope frame determine whether or not you can access the new procedure outside of the current code module. If you choose Public, the procedure can be accessed from outside the current code module. Not surprisingly, choosing Private will restrict access to the procedure to the current code module.

Once the dialog box is filled in, click the OK button to add the procedure's wrapper code to the code module. The wrapper will consist of the VBA code used to delineate the beginning and ending of the procedure, function, or property. The code will be placed at the bottom of the code module, but the order of code within a module is irrelevant.

The Object Browser Window

The Visual Basic Editor provides a wonderful little window called the Object Browser (see Figure 15.7), which you can use to explore the various objects, properties, and methods available to your VBA code. You can learn a tremendous amount using this window and I recommend that you refer to it often.

To open the Object Browser window, either press the F2 key or use the View, Object Browser menu item. To use the window, click a class name in the Classes list on the left. The right-hand list will change to display the members (properties and methods) of the select item. Clicking one of the members will display some documentation in the bottom panel.

FIGURE 15.7

*The Visual Basic
Editor's Object
Browser window,
which provides lists of
the available objects,
properties, and
methods.*

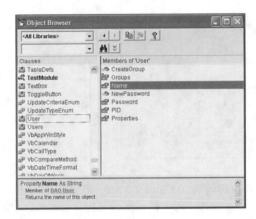

Within that descriptive panel at the bottom of the window you'll see underlined text. This text is a hyperlink to another class. Click it and the Object Browser will take you to that class. You can then use the Go Back or Go Forward buttons found at the top of the window to navigate (similar to the navigation within a Web browser).

The Object Browser also provides a search feature. Type something into the edit box to the left of the Search (binocular) button and hit Enter or click the Search button. A search results pane will appear. Click an entry in the results list and that entry will be highlighted in the bottom of the window.

VBE's Intellisense Feature

Another handy feature provided by the editor is Intellisense. As you type code, the editor window will provide as much assistance as it can to help you complete the statement you're typing. This can be a great time-saver when you've got a lot of code to enter.

Intellisense comes in a couple of forms. If you type in the name of a procedure or function that takes parameters, Intellisense will display a little tooltip window with the parameters listed. As you enter the parameters in to the editor, the tooltip window will highlight the parameter you're currently typing.

A second Intellisense feature is the ability to list the properties and methods available for an object whenever you're using an instance of that object. For example, if you were to type CurrentDb. into the editor, as soon as you typed the period, a list of the properties and methods available on the CurrentDb object would appear. You can scroll this list and click on the method or property you're after. The editor will type the name of the selected item for you.

Another more obscure feature is word completion. If you type Msg and then press Ctrl+Space, the editor will finish the word for you and you'll be left with MsgBox. If the editor cannot come up with a specific word for the completion, you'll be presented with a list box of all the possible matches. Keep typing and the selected item in the list will change to match what you've typed. Press the spacebar when the one you're after is selected and it will be entered for you.

Using Online Help

As with the rest of Microsoft Access, the Visual Basic Editor provides a complete set of online help. You can get help in any of several ways:

- The F1 Key—This key provides context-sensitive help. The Access Help file will be opened to a page that contains information about the word near the cursor, about the property currently selected in the Properties window, or about the active element on the screen.

- Using the Help menu—The Help menu has an item for the F1 key and an item labeled MSDN on the Web. This menu item will open your Web browser and browse to the Microsoft Developer Network Web site. Here you can search on any number of topics related to Microsoft Access or VBA coding.

- The Help dropdown—At the top-right of the VBE is a dropdown combo box. If you type a question or a topic in the edit box there and press the Enter key, the Access Help file will open and search for the words entered.

Note The Help dropdown is only available if the Access application window is sized large enough to accommodate its display. If the dropdown is not available, use the Help, Microsoft Access Help menu item or press the F1 key.

Summary

Using Microsoft's VBA, which is built in to all of the Office applications, you can perform a lot of tasks from forms, reports, and macros. This can help to automate your database for the user.

VBA provides you with the ability to create standard procedures as well as class objects. Class objects encapsulate both data about the object and functionality to operate upon the object.

Access provides you with the Visual Basic Editor built into the application. Using this editor you can easily create the VBA code to perform the tasks your database needs to perform. In addition to a plain text editor, the Visual Basic Editor provides several tools which make your programming job less onerous.

Q&A

Q. When should I create an application in Visual Basic as opposed to doing everything within Access?

A. If performance is a concern, you should definitely use Visual Basic to create an executable. You can still use all of the database features of Access, including tables and queries. There is also the issue of how much you want to have to distribute to your users; you'll have fewer requirements if you create a Visual Basic application.

Q. Why not just use class modules for everything and not worry about standard modules?

A. To call code in a class module you have to create an "instance" of variable which has the class as its type. While there's not anything particularly difficult about this, it does add overhead both to your code and to the execution time. If you simply need to call a utility function, there's no need to have the overhead of a class wrapping that function.

Q. What's the difference between a procedure and a function?

A. A function is a procedure which returns a value. A procedure is simply a piece of code which gets executed and does not return a value to the calling code. The calling code does not have to use a function's return value and in fact, can invoke the function just like it would a procedure.

Q. Sometimes when using the Object Browser I click on a member that doesn't have any descriptive text associated with it. Why is this?

A. The descriptive text (such as "Returns the name of this object" seen in Figure 15.7), is placed in to the object when the class is compiled. If the author of the code does not provide such documentation, it won't be displayed. To add descriptive text to the procedures, properties, and methods you've defined in your code modules, find them in the Object Browser, right-click and select Properties from the context menu. A small dialog box containing a Description edit box will appear. Fill in the description and click OK.

15

Workshop

The Workshop helps you solidify the skills you learned in this lesson. Answers to the quiz appear in Appendix A, "Answers to Quizzes."

Quiz

1. What are the three types of code modules?
2. Objects have the following:
    a. Properties
    b. Methods
    c. Events
    d. All of the Above
3. Was Bill Gates the inventor of BASIC?
4. Can you use a macro to execute a Visual Basic procedure?

Exercise

1. Open the Day 15 file and create a new form. Add a text box (name it **txtSecondValue**), a label (name it **lblResult**), and a command button to this form.

2. Add the following code to the command button Click event handler:

```
Dim oClass as New ExerciseClass
Dim iResult as Integer
Dim iSecond as Integer

If Not( IsNumeric(txtSecondValue) ) Then
     MsgBox "Please enter a numeric value."
     Exit Sub
End If

iSecond = CInt(txtSecondValue)

iResult = oClass.AddUp(iSecond)

lblResult.Caption = CStr(iResult)
```

3. Return to the form and switch to Form View. Enter **3** into the text box and click the button. Do you see **6** as a result?

4. To see how this code works, return to the command button Click event procedure. Click on the line that begins with iResult = and press the Toggle Breakpoint button on the toolbar (it's the one with the hand palm facing). The left-hand margin

next to this line should display a red filled-in circle. This indicates that the line has a breakpoint set.

5. Return to the form and switch to Form View. Enter the value **5** in the text box and click the button. The Visual Basic Editor will display and the current line will be the one where the breakpoint was set. The line will be highlighted but it has not been executed yet.

6. Press the F8 key to "step into" the `AddUp()` method of `ExerciseClass`. Continue to press F8 until you return to the button click event.

7. Hover the cursor over `iResult` in the code window. It will display the current value of `iResult`. Does it display the value **8** in the tooltip? You can also activate the Immediate window, enter the code `Print iResult` and press the enter key to see the value of the variable.

DAY **16**

VBA Language Elements—Part 1

Our introduction to VBA in yesterday's lesson encompassed a lot of conceptual and foundational information. Today, you get to roll up your sleeves and actually start doing something with VBA.

Today You Will Learn

- What are Standard modules
- What are Class modules
- What is the basic structure of a module
- What are procedures
- How to pass arguments to procedures
- What are variables

Many of the concepts we're going to cover today and tomorrow can be very confusing if you've never done any programming before. We're also facing a "chicken-before-the-egg" problem in many cases, because it can be difficult to grasp one concept before learning another one we haven't yet covered. If you don't fully understand something we're covering at one point in the discussion, mark the page and put it aside for later review. Chances are the concept will make more sense a little later after we've covered another concept.

Understanding Modules

Modules are simply containers that hold your VBA programming source code. For example, when you use the wizard to insert a command button on a form, Access creates a code module that is attached to, or associated with, that form object. This is one common situation where Access automatically creates a VBA module for you.

Open the Day 16 database and open the form named frmFormAndCode in design mode. Now, select the button labeled Close Form. This button was created using the Command Button wizard. (Open the Properties list, if it's not already visible, by double-clicking the Close Form button or clicking the Properties icon on the toolbar.) Next, click on the Event tab of the Properties list. Your screen should resemble Figure 16.1.

FIGURE 16.1

frmFormAndCode *with the* Close Form *button selected in design mode.*

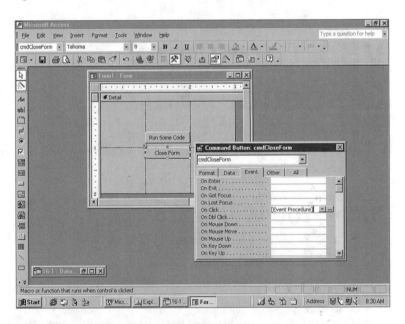

Note the "[Event Procedure]" entry indicated in the On Click event of the Properties list. This lets you know there is VBA code associated with this event that will be executed whenever a user clicks the command button. When you select that event by clicking it, you'll see a small ellipsis icon to the right of the event. Clicking the ellipsis opens the VB Editor and takes you to the associated event procedure in the form's code module.

> **Tip**
>
> When you used the command button wizard to create the "Close Form" button, you instructed the wizard to name the button cmdCloseForm.
>
> Never accept the generic default name that Access assigns to a new control you create on a form. It's much easier to identify the type and purpose of a control named cmdCloseForm than one named Command1. As you become more familiar with writing VBA code, you'll quickly discover that using a standardized naming convention for objects makes programming in VBA much less confusing. Naming conventions for controls are covered in tomorrow's lesson.

16

Now let's look at the code module for the cmdCloseForm command button, and while here, revisit a few points about the VB Editor. After opening the VB Editor, your screen should resemble Figure 16.2.

FIGURE 16.2

VBA procedure created by the command button wizard.

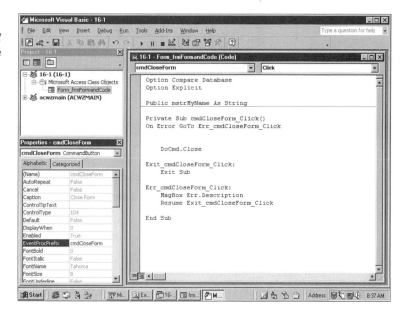

Class Modules

There are two kinds of modules, *class* modules and *standard* modules. Class modules are associated with some type of object—an Access form or report, for example.

The module associated with the cmdCloseForm command button is an example of a class module because it contains VBA code that is associated with an object—in this case, a control on your Access form.

Notice the two pull-down lists at the top of the Code Window. The one on the left is called the `Object ListBox`, and it lists all the objects that are associated with the current class object, in this case your `frmFormAndCode` form. Figure 16.3 show the expanded `Object ListBox` in the Code window.

FIGURE 16.3

Object Listbox show-
ing objects associated
with the
`frmFormAndCode` *class*
module.

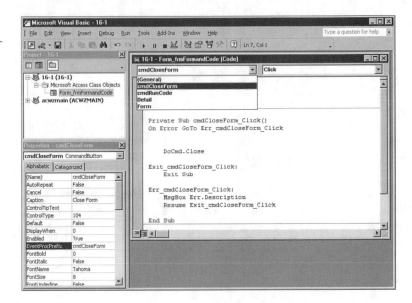

The pull-down list on the right is the `Procedure ListBox`. It shows all the events associated with, or exposed by, the object selected on the left. An event procedure listed in bold here means there's a code procedure in your module to handle the event. Figure 16.4 shows the event procedures associated with a button.

You might have notice that class modules associated with forms and reports are not listed on the Modules button of your Database window. All forms and reports inherently have a class module associated with them, unless you specifically set a form/report's `Has Module` property setting to No. If you don't need to run any code, you can set this property to No. To see the module associated with a form or report, open that form/report in design mode and click the Code toolbar button.

These are the most common types of class modules you'll be working with in Access—class modules associated with an Access form or report. Class modules are also used to define your own objects, which might or might not be related to any built-in Access objects.

FIGURE 16.4

Procedure Listbox *showing events for the* cmdCloseForm *button.*

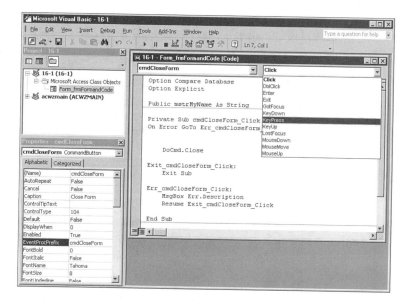

Standard Modules

Standard modules are containers for procedures and variable declarations which are used throughout your application. Standard modules are listed in the Modules button of your Database window.

To create a standard module, follow these steps:

1. Launch Access if necessary. Open the Day 16 database.
2. Click on Modules button on the Object bar.
3. Click the New button on the toolbar in Database view.

That's all you have to do. Access creates a new module; you remain in the VB Editor to add code to your new module. The structure of standard modules is pretty much the same as class modules but, unlike class modules, they are not linked to any specific object.

You can create as many separate standard modules as you want in your applications. It's smart to combine procedures with similar functionality together in a module named to indicate their purpose within your program. For example, I start every new project by creating several standard modules, such as GlobalVars, where I define all the variables and constants used *globally* in my program, and QueryProcs, a collection of procedures I often use to manage query-related tasks.

At times, things can get very complicated when you're programming, and anything you can do to logically organize your VBA code will help you keep things straight as your project grows.

Note

The word *globally* refers to the scope and lifetime of a variable, constant, or procedure. I'll cover scope and lifetime later in the chapter, but for now just know that a variable used *globally* can be seen and modified by any procedure in an application.

Structure of a Module

Every module contains two parts, a *declarations* section followed by one or more *procedures*. A module's declarations section is used to define, or *declare,* any variables, constants, or external procedures that you want accessible to all procedures in this specific module.

A variable declared in the declarations section of a module is said to have "module-level" scope. (Tomorrow's lesson covers scope in more detail.)

Figure 16.5 shows a standard module that contains a module-level declaration for a variable named gstrProgramVersion, which will contain *string* data.

FIGURE **16.5**

A standard VBA code module.

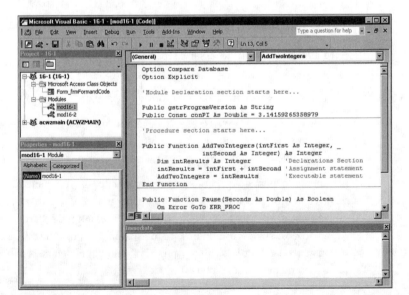

The VBA *String* data type holds alphanumeric text information, which you'll learn more about in the sections, "Variable Declaration" and "Data Types."

Understanding VBA Procedures

Procedures are the building blocks of computer programming. They are discrete collections of VBA code statements that perform some specific task in response to an event or when called from somewhere else in your application. Procedures help break up your programs into smaller, more manageable pieces.

There are three kinds of procedures: *sub* procedures, *function* procedures, and *property* procedures. Property procedures are used when creating your own class objects, an advanced topic beyond the scope of our discussion here.

The main difference between sub and function procedures is that function procedures *can,* but don't have to, return a value to the code that called it. Function calls, since they return a value, can also be included as part of an expression in an assignment statement. For example, the following statement uses the built-in VBA function, Now(), which returns the current date and time from your computer:

```
datOneWeekFromToday = Now() + 7
```

Seven days are added to the current date and the result is then assigned to the variable datOneWeekFromToday, which you would use in some further processing or assignment.

 Dozens and dozens of functions are built into VBA, and you can use any of these built-in functions as a part of your own procedures. We'll talk about some of VBA's built-in functions a little later in this lesson.

The basic structure of sub and function procedures are almost identical. When creating your own procedures to perform a task, it's usually preferable to define your procedure as a function. You'll explore this concept in more detail later in our discussion.

There are two basic types of sub procedures: event procedures and general procedures. Event procedures are triggered in response to some action related to an object. Access form and report event procedures are all defined as sub procedures. A general sub procedure is one that you create to handle a specific task, and are executed by calling that sub from another statement in your program in this format:

```
Call GetNextAvailableAppt lngUserID
```

16

The lngUserID following the sub procedure call is an argument being passed to the GetNextAvailableAppt procedure. Again, we'll be discussing *arguments* in more detail a little later.

Note

> The Call keyword used here is optional and seldom used in the real world.

Tip

> If you're looking at a block of code using the VB Editor and see a command you're unsure of, right-click the command and choose Definition from the context menu. If the command is a sub procedure defined somewhere else in your application, the VB Editor opens up that procedure for you to view.

As I mentioned before, it's usually smart to define your general-use procedures as functions, even if you don't foresee a need to use the function's result anywhere in an expression. You can define functions like this to return a *Boolean* value (true or false) to indicate the success of the procedure's code. That way, the previous example could be written as a function and called like this:

```
If GetNextAvailableAppt(lngUserID) = True Then
    'We got here, so we know the GetNextAvailableAppt function completed success-
fully
    ... {other VB statements}
End If
```

When a function is included in an expression like this, any arguments to the function must be enclosed within parentheses as shown.

If you don't care about the return value of a function, you can call it exactly the same way you would call a sub, and the return value will be discarded by VB:

```
GetNextAvailableAppt lngUserID
```

To reiterate, always define your general-use procedures as functions. They can then be called the same way you would a sub procedure, with several added benefits. It is often useful to use a function's return value as a True/False "flag" to let you know the procedure completed successfully. Further, Access allows you to use functions as part of your query definitions, and also enables you to call a function directly from the Properties list of any object. (We'll explore this ability shortly.)

Parentheses are optional if you're not actually sending arguments to a function, but including them makes your code more readable. Additionally, there are indications that the next version of VBA might *require* closing parentheses for function calls, and it would be smart to get in the habit of including them now.

Creating Reusable Code

Once you've defined and tested a code procedure, you can forget how it works internally. This is a very important concept to understand about programming: Once you've expended the time and effort to develop a code procedure that accomplishes a specific task, you can often reuse it in other programs without having to re-create the code from scratch.

Before you know it, you'll be creating and reusing your own code libraries—procedures you've written in the past or collected from other sources. Here's a useful procedure I developed some time ago, which I import into most of the applications I create today:

```
Public Function Pause(dblSeconds As Double) as Boolean
    Dim dblTime As Double
    On Error GoTo ERR_PROC
    dblTime = Timer() + dblSeconds
    Do While Timer < dblTime
        DoEvents
    Loop
    Pause = True
EXIT_PROC:
    Exit Function
ERR_PROC:
    Pause = False
    Resume EXIT_PROC
End Function
```

This procedure does one simple task: It pauses execution of the program for a specified time interval, which can be a fraction of a second. After you've imported this procedure into a standard code module in your application, you can cause a one-second pause, from anywhere in your program, by executing this code as follows:

```
Pause 1
```

Notice that I created this procedure as a function, even though I'll normally use it like a sub procedure. I won't go into all the details of how this procedure works right now—the reason I show it here is simply to illustrate the power of creating reusable code procedures. (And, by the way, feel free to use it in *your* future programs.)

Introducing Variables

Variables are used to temporarily store values in memory. Like procedures and objects, variables should be *declared* before they're used so VBA knows about them. Declaring a variable causes VBA to reserve space in memory to hold the values your variables will store.

VBA, by default, creates a variable the first time you use it in your code, and this is called Implicit Variable Declaration. Taking advantage of Implicit Variable Declaration is a poor programming practice and can result in frustrating programming errors that are hard to fix. For example, if you make a mistake while typing a variable's name in a statement, VBA assumes it's a new variable and automatically creates it as a different variable from the one you *thought* you were referring to in your statement.

Placing the statement `Option Explicit` at the top of any code module tells VBA to use Explicit Variable Declaration for that module. You can instruct VBA to use Explicit Variable Declaration for all new modules it creates, by ensuring "Require Variable Declaration" is checked in your VB Editor options, under Tools, Options, Editor. When set, VBA forces you to explicitly declare any variable before you can use it.

You'll be examining variables in detail later in this lesson. In the following examples just remember that variables are used to temporarily store values that you're manipulating with your VBA code.

Understanding the Structure of a Procedure

Procedures are made up of VBA code statements. A statement is a complete code instruction that contains VBA keywords, operators, variables, constants, and expressions. We'll be discussing these different elements in the rest of this lesson. Statements fall into three basic categories:

- Declaration statements, which define a variable, constant, or procedure before it's used in VBA.
- Assignment statements, which assign a value to a variable or constant.
- Executable statements that do something, such as calling a procedure, looping through blocks of code, or branching to other code depending on specific conditions.

Let's take a look at another simple function, one that adds two numbers together and returns the result to the procedure that called it. (You'll find this procedure in the mod16-1 module in the Day 16 database)

```
Public Function AddTwoIntegers(intFirst as Integer, intSecond as Integer) as
Integer
```

```
    Dim intResult as Integer          'Declarations Section
      intResult = intFirst + intSecond    'Assignment statement
    AddTwoIntegers = intResult        'Assignment statement
End Function
```

This function might be called from another section of an application using this format:

```
intSomeVariableName = AddTwoIntegers(15,22)
```

The first line of the function is the procedure declaration. The first word of the declaration, `Public`, sets the scope of this procedure. Declaring this procedure as having `Public` scope means it can be executed from anywhere in the program. If you had declared it as `Private`, then it could only be executed from code within this specific module. More on this later.

The second word is the VBA keyword `Function`, which tells VBA this is a function-type procedure and can return a value to the code that called it.

The third word is the actual name of the procedure, `AddTwoIntegers`, which defines how the procedure is executed, and is also used by functions to return values.

The values contained inside the parentheses are this procedure's *arguments*. Arguments are values that are passed into a procedure for processing. The names you give these arguments are used only within the procedure, and act as a private variable declaration for use within the procedure. The example function takes two arguments, `intFirst` and `intSecond`, both integer values.

> **Note**
>
> We'll be covering data types in more detail later, but for now just know that an `Integer` variable can store any whole number between –32,768 and 32,767.

The last part of the procedure declaration, `as Integer`, tells VBA what data type to return as the result of the function. For example, if the calling program executed this call to the function

```
intSomeVariableName = AddTwoIntegers(15,22)
```

the variable `intSomeVariableName` would contain 37 after the statement finished executing. The numbers 15 and 22 are passed into the function, which assigns them to the internal argument variables `intFirst` and `intSecond`. When the function's done executing, the return value of the function is then set to 37.

Now let's look at the VBA statements inside the function.

16

You'll notice that I've inserted comments at the end of each statement line. A VBA code comment is a line of code that starts with an apostrophe character. Comments are totally ignored by VBA when it checks or compiles your code. The VB Editor highlights them using a different font color, to help them stand out. VBA also considers any line beginning with `Rem` as a comment, for backward compatibility with previous versions of BASIC.

> **Note**
>
> Use comments generously when you write programming code! Even if nobody else ever sees your source code, the logic of your code—which makes perfect sense to you today—might be totally confusing to you six months from now. Trust me on this one....

> **Note**
>
> You'll notice that the variable names I chose in this example begin with the characters, `int`. Preceding a variable name with a three-character abbreviation of the variable's data type is an example of using variable *naming conventions*. Naming conventions for variables are covered in tomorrow's lesson.

The first line after the procedure declaration is a declaration statement:

```
Dim intResult as Integer
```

The keyword "Dim" tells VBA to create a *local* integer variable, named `intResult`, for use within this procedure. Local variables can only be accessed by code inside the procedure, and are "alive" only as long as the procedure is executing. After the procedure's finished, any local variables are destroyed, releasing the memory resources they required for other use. This variable has *procedure-level lifetime.*

The next statement adds the variables together and makes the assignment to the `intResult` variable. This statement does the function's actual processing:

```
intResult = intFirst + intSecond
```

This is a typical VBA *assignment* statement combined with an *expression*. When VBA executes this line of code, it evaluates the *expression* on the right side of the equals sign and performs whatever calculations are necessary to come up with a result. That result is then *assigned* to the variable on the left side of the equals sign.

Expressions in an assignment statement like this can sometimes be very complex. Regardless of the complexity, VBA evaluates the expression on the right side of the equals sign and assigns the final result to the variable on the left of the equals sign. (The equals sign is also used in logical comparison operations, where it really *does* mean "equals." We'll talk more about this later.)

The final statement inside the function is a simple assignment statement:

```
AddTwoIntegers = intResult
```

It assigns the value stored in `intResult` to the name of the function, thereby "setting" the return value for this function.

The final `End Function` statement simply tells VBA where the function definition ends.

Take a moment to try out your function. The easiest way to do this is from the Immediate window. If you press Ctrl+G you can bring up the Immediate window. Type the following line into the Immediate window and press Enter:

```
? AddTwoIntegers(15, 22)
```

The result, 37, should be displayed on the following line. (The ? is the Immediate window's shorthand for "Print" the result.) Now try replacing the 15 and 22 with different numbers.

Built-in Functions and Statements

You used the built-in function `Now()` in an earlier example. `Now()` is just one of dozens of functions built into VBA for you to use in your programs. Type the following command into your VBA Immediate Window and press Enter:

```
? Now()
```

VBA executes the statement and prints the result, the current date and time on your system, on the next line of your Immediate window. Click the word "Now" in the Immediate window, so the cursor appears somewhere within it and press your F1 key. The Visual Basic online help system opens up and displays the following about the `Now` function:

```
"Returns a Variant (Date) specifying the current date and
➥time according to your computer's system date and time."
```

Now, click the "Contents" table of the VB Help window and take a few minutes to explore the extensive list of functions built in to VBA. Each function is a specialized tool available for a specific purpose, and many of them are used infrequently.

You might never have a need to use many of these built-in functions, and you really never have to worry about memorizing details about any of them. Just remember that your F1 key is always ready to display everything you need to know about a function, when you need to know it, along with examples on how to use it.

I'll be introducing you to a number of useful built-in VBA functions in these VBA lessons; however, your best source for information is in the Online Help file.

Using Arguments in Procedures

You used two arguments in the AddTwoIntegers() function example. Now take a closer look at some details about arguments. Arguments are values that you pass into a sub or function procedure for use in its processing or calculations.

Arguments are defined in the Declaration statement for a specific procedure, and are inherently local in scope to that procedure. Let's take a look at the Pause() function once again:

```
Public Function Pause(dblSeconds As Double) as Boolean
    Dim dblTime As Double
    On Error GoTo ERR_PROC
    dblTime = Timer() + dblSeconds
    Do While Timer < dblTime
        DoEvents
    Loop
    Pause = True
EXIT_PROC:
    Exit Function
ERR_PROC:
    Pause = False
    Resume EXIT_PROC
End Function
```

The Pause() function takes one argument, dblSeconds, which is declared as a variable of the Double data type. Notice the similarity in the declaration of dblSeconds and dblTime, at the top of the function. The truth is, both these declarations identify variables that will be used inside the function. The real difference is that the value that gets assigned to the dblSeconds variable will be provided by whatever statement calls the function.

Arguments can either be passed by reference (ByRef) or by value (ByVal). The default method is ByRef if not otherwise specified.

Arguments passed ByRef are pointers to the actual data from the calling procedure, and those values can be changed from the procedure. Values passed ByVal are *copies* of the actual data in the calling procedure, so any changes you make to those values within your procedure do not affect the original values.

This is a little complicated, so I'll illustrate the point with a working example. You'll find the three procedures in Listing 16.1 in the module named mod16-2 in the Day 16 database.

LISTING 16.1   Module mod16-2 Illustrates the Effects of Passing Values ByRef and ByVal

```vba
Public Sub TestPassingValues()
    Dim intA As Integer
    Dim intB As Integer

    intA = 5
    intB = 7
    Debug.Print "----------------------"
    Debug.Print "Result of values after passing ByRef:"
    Debug.Print "Function Return = " & ChangeSomeNbrsByRef(intA, intB)
    Debug.Print "intA = " & intA
    Debug.Print "intB = " & intB

    'Reset variables to normal
    intA = 5
    intB = 7
    Debug.Print "----------------------"
    Debug.Print "Result of values after passing ByVal:"
    Debug.Print "Function Return = " & ChangeSomeNbrsByVal(intA, intB)
    Debug.Print "intA = " & intA
    Debug.Print "intB = " & intB
End Sub

Public Function ChangeSomeNbrsByRef(intNumber1 As Integer, _
                        intNumber2 As Integer) As Integer
    intNumber1 = intNumber1 + intNumber2
    ChangeSomeNbrsByRef = intNumber1
End Function

Public Function ChangeSomeNbrsByVal(ByVal intNumber1 As Integer, _
                        ByVal intNumber2 As Integer) As Integer
    intNumber1 = intNumber1 + intNumber2
    ChangeSomeNbrsByVal = intNumber1
End Function
```

The TestPassingValues function demonstrates the effects that passing ByVal has upon a variable. With the mod16-2 module open, enter **TestPassingValues** in the Immediate window and press Enter. You should see the following output after the line you typed in:

```
----------------------
Result of values after passing ByRef:
Function Returned = 12
intA = 12
intB = 7
----------------------
Result of values after passing ByVal:
```

```
Function Returned = 12
intA = 5
intB = 7
```

Passing the variable intA by reference to the first function allows that function to change its value in the calling procedure. Using ByVal in the second function preserves the original value of the variable. Understanding passing arguments ByRef and ByVal is very important. Although you'll often hear that only functions can return a value to the calling procedure, any sub or function can change any argument passed to it by reference.

Note

> Did you notice the underscore (_) character at the end of both function declaration statements? This is the VBA "line continuation" character, allowing you to break a single, long statement into multiple lines. When VBA sees a space followed by an underscore at the end of a line, it knows that you want to continue the statement on the next line. VBA always ignores spaces and tabs in your source code, unless they are enclosed by quote marks. This allows you to use spaces and indentation to make your code more readable.

Looking at a Real-World Procedure Example

Now let's take a look at a real-world example of using a procedure to do some real work in an Access application. In the Day 16 database, open the form named Customers in regular view mode. Press your "Caps Lock" and type something into the CompanyName field of the first row. Now press your Tab key to skip to the next field and observe how the text you just entered is converted to uppercase and lowercase characters.

Let's look a little closer at what happened. Switch to design mode and click the CompanyName text box. If it's not already displayed, open the Properties list and click its Event tab. Notice the "[Event Procedure]" entry in the After Update event? Highlight that entry and then click the ellipsis (or on the Code toolbar button) to open the VB Editor and look at that event procedure. Here's what you should see:

```
Private Sub CompanyName_AfterUpdate()
    Me.CompanyName = StrConv(Me.CompanyName, vbProperCase)
End Sub
```

Note

> Most Access objects have a default property, and the default property for a text box control is the text data contained within it. In this case, that data is "bound" to a field in the underlying recordset.

The Me that you see is a shortcut to refer to the object that defines the current module. You often use a control's AfterUpdate event in this fashion to check a user's entry and validate it or, as in this case, to convert it to a "proper case" uppercase and lowercase value. As you can see, this event procedure has only one statement, a call to a built-in function called StrConv() which takes two arguments, a reference to the variable or object containing string data, Me.CompanyName, and a *constant* that tells the StrConv() function what type of conversion to perform.

16

Note

> A constant is like a variable, but one that doesn't change its value during the execution of the program. Constants are used to make code easier to read. For example, the constant vbProperCase above actually represents the value 3, but StrConv(Me.CompanyName, 3) is not nearly as informative as using vbProperCase instead of 3. We'll be talking more about constants later.

You've added this same function to the AfterUpdate event of each alphanumeric control on this form, a total of six event sub procedures that each accomplish the same basic task. Anytime you find yourself repeating the same basic functions in multiple event procedures, there might be a better way to accomplish the task.

Calling Functions from the Properties List

Let's examine a way to accomplish the same functionality using only *one* procedure, a general function procedure that you'll call from the event procedure line for each control.

Note

> This might be a little advanced for some readers, so don't worry if it confuses you right now. It'll make more sense later on as you get more comfortable with VBA coding.

You can find the ToProperCase function by following these steps:

1. Launch Access if necessary. Open the Day 16 database.
2. Locate and click on the Forms button on the Object bar.
3. Locate and click on the Customers form to select it.
4. Locate and click the Code button on the standard toolbar. To help you locate it, hover your mouse over the standard toolbar and look for the word Code.

Access launches the VB Editor and places you in the module for the Customers form. You'll find the following function procedure at the end of the module attached to the Customers form:

```
Private Function ToProperCase() As Boolean
    Dim ctl As Control
    Set ctl = Me.ActiveControl
    ctl = StrConv(ctl, vbProperCase)
End Function
```

Now let's examine the details of the new ToProperCase() function. The first statement in the function declares a variable named ctl, which will store a reference to a control-type object. The next line, Set ctl = Me.ActiveControl, sets the ctl variable to whichever control is currently active on the form. (The Me is shorthand that refers to the current form, and ActiveControl is a property of the form that refers to the control that currently has the focus.)

The final statement, ctl = StrConv(ctl, vbProperCase), is the same executable statement you used before. The difference is that now you're passing a variable *referring to* a control, instead of the *actual* control reference you used before.

With the Customers form opened in design mode, select the top six controls by clicking and holding, dragging over the controls, and releasing the mouse button. Then click in the AfterUpdate line on the Properties list and replace the "[Event Procedure]" entry with the following:

```
=ToProperCase()
```

Figure 16.6 shows the results of placing the code in the AfterUpdate event.

You must adhere to a few rules to make a procedure call like this from within an object's Properties list. First, the procedure *must* be a function—another reason to create all your specialized procedures as functions instead of subs. Second, you must precede the function call with an equals sign, as shown above, and the function call *must* be followed by open/closed parentheses to indicate you're making a function call and not invoking an Access macro.

The AfterUpdate event line for all six controls should have changed, since you made the change with all six controls selected. Double-check this by selecting each control individually; make sure the AfterUpdate event line reads, =ToProperCase().

You've taken six event procedures and combined the functionality of all six into a single function call...one procedure to test instead of six...one procedure to cause problems instead of six. You get the idea, right?

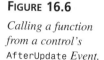

FIGURE 16.6

Calling a function from a control's AfterUpdate *Event.*

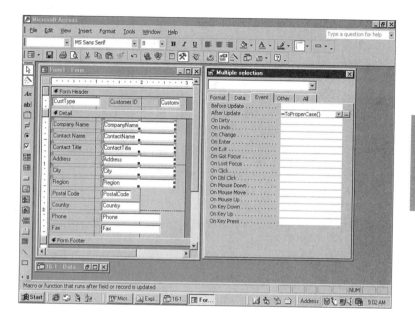

16

Understanding Variables

In simple terms, a variable is a temporary holding area for some value you want to remember and manipulate in your programs. You create them, assign values to them, change their assigned values, use them in expressions, pass them (or the values stored in them) as arguments to other procedures, and destroy them when you don't need them any more. Variables are one of the most powerful programming tools at your disposal.

You can create variables that live as long as the application is running (called *global variables*) or you can create variables that live only a split-second, during the execution of a specific procedure (called *local variables*).

Variable Declarations

You declare a variable, as you declare procedures, to let VBA know about it before you use it. VBA can create variables "implicitly" as you use them, but this is a very sloppy way to write programs—and will eventually cause you major grief.

The "right way" is to *explicitly* declare every variable that you're going to use, before you use it. To enlist VB's help in this regard, simply insert the following statement at the top of each of your modules:

```
Option Explicit
```

This tells VBA to check for undeclared variables when it compiles your module, and alert you with an error message if it finds any variables that have *not* been declared. You'll be surprised at how often VBA makes you aware of a typo in your code, where you typed in the wrong name of a variable. If you hadn't used `Option Explicit`, VBA would have simply created a new variable with the name that you misspelled, with the potential for numerous "logic errors" in your program.

Variables are either declared at the top of your modules, in the Declarations section, or in the Declaration section of individual procedures. Here are a few examples of legal variable declarations you might use in a code module:

```
Public gstrCompanyName as String
Private mcurIncome as Currency
Dim intAge as Integer
Static slngCumulativeRain as Long
```

The first keyword in a variable declaration—`Public`, `Private`, `Dim`, or `Static`—refers to the scope and lifetime of the variable, which we'll be discussing in the next lesson.

The second entry is the variable name. Choose descriptive names for your variables so it's obvious what the variable represents.

VBA Naming Rules

The following rules apply when choosing names for procedures, variables, constants, and arguments in a VBA module:

- The first character of the name must be a letter.
- You can't use a space, period, exclamation point, or the characters @, &, $, or # in any name.
- The name can't exceed 255 characters in length.
- Using a name that's the same as a built-in function, statement, or method is bad programming practice. Don't do it.
- You can't use the same name more than once within the same level of *scope*. In other words, you can't have two variables named "Birthday" in the same procedure, though you could have variables named "Birthday" declared separately in two different procedures.

The use of a standardized naming convention for your variables is an extension of this concept. For example, when I see a variable named `gstrCompanyName` in my code, the `gstr` prefix tells me that it's a string-type variable with global scope. We'll be talking about naming conventions tomorrow.

Data Types

Data types refer to the kind of data a variable will be storing. As you saw earlier, you also specify a data type for the return value from functions. Data types apply to many aspects of your programs and it's important that you have a basic understanding of what they are to use them effectively.

Table 16.1 provides in-depth information regarding the different data types used in VBA, including the actual amount of memory required for each and the range of values that can be stored in each. Take a moment now to become familiar with the information in the table.

16

TABLE 16.1   Data Types

Data Type	Storage Size	Range
Byte	1 byte	0 to 255
Boolean	2 bytes	True or False
Integer	2 bytes	–32,768 to 32,767
Long (long integer)	4 bytes	–2,147,483,648 to 2,147,483,647
Single (single-precision	4 bytes	–3.402823E38 to –1.401298E-45 for negative values; 1.401298E–45 to 3.402823E38 for positive values
Double (double-precision floating-point)	8 bytes	–1.79769313486231E308 to –4.94065645841247E–324 for negative values; 4.94065645841247E-324 to 1.79769313486232E308 for positive values
Currency (scaled integer)	8 bytes	–922,337,203,685,477.5808 to 922,337,203,685,477.5807
Decimal (sub-type of Variant)	14 bytes	+/–79,228,162,514,264, 337,593,543,950,335 with no decimal point; +/–7.9228162514264337593543950335 with 28 places to the right of the decimal; smallest non-zero number is +/–0.0000000000000000000000000001
Date	8 bytes	January 1, 100 to December 31, 9999

TABLE 16.1 continued

Data Type	Storage Size	Range
Object	4 bytes	Any Object reference
String (variable-length)	10 bytes + string length	0 to approximately 2 billion
String (fixed-length)	Length of string	1 to approximately 65,400
Variant (with numbers)	16 bytes	Any numeric value up to the range of a Double
Variant (with characters) String	22 bytes + string length	Same range as for variable-length
User-defined (using Type)	Number required by elements	The range of each element is the same as the range of its data type.

Boolean types store a simple True or False value, represented internally as –1 for True and 0 for False. The VBA keywords True and False are constants that equate to –1 and 0 respectively. You use Boolean variables to store a true/false or yes/no value, or to serve as a flag to control the flow of your programs.

Use the Integer type when the numbers you need to store will be a whole number in the range of –32,768 to 32,767. Integer variables are often used as counter variables in For...Next loops, which we'll explore in Day 17, "VBA Programming—Part 2."

The Long data type deserves special discussion. Longs are 32-bit values that can represent any number from –2,147,483,648 to 2,147,483,647 and, more importantly, are already in the format used internally by Windows, which is a 32-bit operating system. Because of this, VBA doesn't have to do any special conversion from its internal format, making it inherently more efficient for many operations.

Another good thing to know about Longs are that Autonumber key fields in tables are in Long format. If you need a variable to temporarily store this "ID" field in a table, declare your variable as a Long.

The Currency data type is a 32-bit integer formatted value that is scaled up to provide four decimal points of accuracy. It is optimized for money-related calculations and performs upward rounding to the fourth decimal. It can store up to 900 trillion values.

The way VBA and Access store date values is interesting. Dates and times are stored internally as an 8-byte floating-point number where the number left of the decimal point represents any date from 1/1/100 through 12/31/9999, and the number *right* of the decimal represents any time from 00:00:00 through 23:59:59. An hour is represented as 0.041666 and a minute is 0.0006944444. You can use the built-in conversion functions CDbl(datValue) and CDate(dblValue) to convert between these two data types, adding hours and minutes in the process.

VBA is very talented at deciphering legal date and time values. Use the pound sign (#) before and after date values in assignment statements. Here are some examples of legal date values that VBA will interpret correctly:

```
datNewYearsEve = #12/31/00#
datRightNow = #02/08/2001 12:59 pm#
datBirthday = #6-15-2001#
datStartTime = #3:15 PM#
datEndTime = #21:30#
```

16

VBA has a variety of built-in functions for manipulating date and time values. Check out the specifics for the following in the Visual Basic Online Help System:

```
Format()
```

```
Day()
```

```
Month()
```

```
Year()
```

```
Minute()Second()
```

```
TimeValue()
```

```
DatePart()
```

```
DateAdd()
```

```
DateDiff()
```

```
DateValue()
```

```
IsDate()
```

```
DateValue()
```

```
DateSerial()
```

```
FormatDateTime()
```

The String data type is used to store alphanumeric text data, and can be associated with the Text and Memo field types in table definitions.

You'll notice two entries for the String data type in Table 16.1, one for fixed-length Strings (which can store 65,4000 characters in length) and another for variable-length, or dynamic, String data (which can store around two billion characters.)

VBA works very efficiently with dynamic String data types, allocating the exact space that's needed for a specific String variable. Look at the following example code:

```
Dim strCompanyName as String
strCompanyName = "The XYZ Company, Inc."
'VB allocates 21 characters of available memory to store the assigned value

strCompanyName = "My Company"
'VB reallocates memory, and frees up 11 characters of memory it used before
```

Now let's compare the previous example with one that defines the `strCompanyName` variable as a fixed-length String data type:

```
Dim strCompanyName as String * 25
strCompanyName = "The XYZ Company, Inc."
'The string takes up 25 characters of space...

strCompanyName = "My Company"
'...regardless of how many you actually use
```

Notice the asterisk and 25 following the String declaration. This tells VBA to create the `strCompanyName` variable as a fixed-length string that can hold 25 characters. This is the way string variables used to be defined, back in "the olden days" of BASIC. There might be times when it makes sense to use a fixed-length string, but I can't think of a good reason right now.

A variable defined as an object data type stores a reference, called a pointer, to an actual object. Remember this function from the section on calling functions from the Properties list?

```
Private Function ToProperCase() As Boolean
    Dim ctl As Control
    Set ctl = Me.ActiveControl
    ctl = StrConv(ctl, vbProperCase)
End Function
```

The variable `ctl` is declared as type "Control", but nowhere in the list is there a VBA data type called "Control". This is actually an example of a typical object data type declaration. You could have specified, `As Object` in the variable declaration, but specifying it `As Control` tells VBA exactly what kind of object you're referencing. Here are some more examples of variable declarations using the object data type:

```
Dim frm as Form
Dim db as ADODB.Database
Dim rpt as Report
Dim rst as Recordset
Dim col as Collection
```

Though not readily apparent by the syntax, every one of these examples is defining an object data type variable that holds a pointer to some specific object with which you want to interface. Furthermore, I can't provide you with an exhaustive list of values you might see in an object variable declaration, because you could see literally anything specified as an object type.

Variants are the most flexible data types in your toolbox. They can be used to hold *any* type of data. Because of this, you might be tempted to use the variant data type exclusively, and many beginning programmers make this mistake. Fight the temptation....

You should use *strong typing* when declaring your variables. Strong typing is when you use the most specific data type for the intended purpose. For example, if you know a variable will never need to store a number higher than 255, declare it as a byte variable; and a variable meant to store monetary amounts would likely be declared as a currency variable.

You pay a heavy price for the flexibility of variants. VBA has to allocate extra space to store their values and your code takes longer to execute because VBA must frequently check each variant to determine exactly what kind of data it's storing. You also increase the risk of logic errors slipping into your programs, where using a strongly typed variable might have alerted you to a problem by generating an error during the testing phase of your project.

As a general rule, you should only declare a variable as a variant type when the variable *has* to have the capability to hold differing data types.

Our discussion of the variant data type would be incomplete with explaining a couple special values that a variant can hold, `Empty` and `Null`.

When a variant is declared, it is created and holds the value `Empty`, which can be tested for using the function `IsEmpty()`. A variant is the only data type that can hold this `Empty` value. Once a variant is assigned some other value, it never contains `Empty` again unless you specifically assign it back to `Empty`.

```
varName = Empty
```

`Null` is another special value that is most often associated with fields in a database table. `Null` generally indicates an unknown value in a field, and can only be assigned to a variant variable. The built-in function `IsNull(varName)` allows you to test for a `Null` value. The function `Nz()` is also very useful for dealing with errors that happen when assigning a potentially `Null` value to a non-variant data type. The `Nz()` function converts a `Null` value to the specified value.

Let's analyze the following code snippet, which opens a table called `Customers`, reads the first record in that table, and assigns the value in three fields to three procedure-level variables you've declared. This function, shown in Listing 16.2, contains a number of things you haven't covered yet, so be sure to read the comments within to help you understand what's happening:

LISTING 16.2   Function to Get the First Record

```
Public Function GetFirstRecord() as Boolean
    Dim db As DAO.Database      'Declares an object variable
    Dim rs as DAO.Recordset     'Declares an object variable
```

LISTING 16.2   continued

```
    Dim lngCompanyID As Long      'Three procedure-level variables
    Dim strCompanyName as String
    Dim lngPhoneNumber as Long

    Set db = CurrentDb()
    Set rs = db.OpenRecordset("Customers")      'Sets up rs to read from
Customers table

    rs.MoveFirst                   'Method of DAO object, points to 1st rec in table
    lngCompanyID = Nz(!CompanyID)          'Assigns value in CompanyID field to
local variable
    strCompanyName = Nz(!CompanyName)'Assigns value in CompanyName field to
local variable
    lngPhoneNumber = Nz(!PhoneNbr)    'Assigns value in PhoneNbr field to local
variable

    'We're done, now clean up after ourselves
    rs.Close : Set rs = Nothing         'Destroys the object variable and releases
memory
    db.Close    : Set db = Nothing  'Destroys the object variable and releases
memory

    'Function finished and the record fields are stored in our local variables
    'Of course, when the function ends, those local variables disappear!
    'If our variables were declared with global scope, the values would be
retained
    GetFirstRecord = True
End Function
```

Please note the function Nz() used in the variable assignments. When you're reading data from a recordset, that data is handled by VBA as a variant data type, which can very easily be a Null value. Attempting to assign Null to a non-variant variable will cause a runtime error, because only variants can hold Null values.

The built-in VBA function Nz() tests a variant value for a Null value and, if it does contain Null, returns a zero, a zero-length string, or another optional value you specify using this format:

```
lngVariableName = Nz(varVariantVariable, [Return Value if Null])
```

Again, you might be tempted to declare your variables as variants to avoid this runtime error, but I *strongly advise against it*. Strongly typing your variables is a much better programming practice, and will prevent many unforeseen problems in your future programs. The "right way" to handle this common type-conversion problem is to use the Nz() function to deal with data type conversion errors.

The User Defined Type (UDT) data type allows you to define their own special data types, which are made up of other built-in data types, objects, arrays, or even other UDTs. Before you can declare a variable as a specific UDT, you must define your UDT in the Declarations section of a module using the keyword Type. Here's an example of a UDT as you might see it used in a program:

```
Option Compare Database
Option Explicit

'The following Type definition must be in a module's Declaration section
Type CompanyInfo
    ID as Long
    Name as String * 20
    Address as String * 30
    City as String * 15
    Phone as String * 12
End Type

Public Sub AddACompany()
    Dim NewCompany as CompanyInfo     'Declares the variable
    NewCompany.ID = 12345
    NewCompany.Name = "Company ABC"
    NewCompany.Address = "1234 Anywhere Dr."
    NewCompany.City = "Albuqerque"
    NewCompany.Phone = "505-555-1234"
End Sub
```

The AddACompany Sub, adds a company using the UDT to hold the various pieces of data. As you can see, once a UDT is defined, the way you reference it in the code is very similar to the way you reference and work with objects. The individual elements of a UDT are sometimes referred to as the UDT's members.

Summary

This lesson introduced the various VBA language elements that help you to understand how to program an Access application. Modules permanently hold the programming code that make up an Access application. Procedures are the code and variables are building blocks that you use in the procedures to temporarily hold pieces of information in memory. Knowing how these three elements of the VBA language fit together will help you learn how to program. Combined with this lesson, the following lessons make your Access databases more powerful than you thought possible.

In the next lesson you'll learn some of the VBA language constructs, along with some good programming habits, that will make your procedures more powerful and your VBA code more readable.

16

Q&A

Q. Do I have to learn VBA in order to use Access?

A. No. Access is a powerful desktop database program by itself, but combined with VBA programming, you are able to do just about anything you can think of.

Q. Can I put all my code into one standard module?

A. Yes. It doesn't hurt anything if you do, but it is a good habit to follow to separate unrelated procedures into separate modules.

Q. Do I really need to know about data types?

A. Yes. Although you could declare everything as a variant, this could introduce hard to diagnose problems in your code.

Q. Do I really need to use Option Explicit and declare all the variables that I need to use?

A. Yes. Although it might seem like a pain to do so, but getting into the habit of declaring your variables will save you hours of time.

Q. Does this lesson teach me all I needed to know about VBA programming?

A. No. This lesson introduces important building blocks that will be used in the following lessons.

Workshop

The Workshop helps you solidify the skills you learned in this lesson. Answers to the quiz appear in Appendix A, "Answers to Quizzes."

Quiz

1. How do you ensure that every variable you use in your procedures is declared?
2. What data type would you use for a variable that you know will only store a whole number between −32,768 and 32,767?
3. What type of module is inherently attached to a form or report?
4. Where do you declare a local variable?
5. Which data type can store a null?
6. Which type of procedure can return a value: a sub or function?

Exercises

The following exercise is a contrived example, which demonstrates the importance of making sure that the Option Explicit line is at the top of every VBA module.

1. In your database create a new standard VBA module. Name it **basDataTypes**. You can create a Standard module by clicking the Modules button in the Database view. Click on the New button found on the toolbar in the Database view.

2. Delete the Option Explicit line from the top of the module.

3. Create a sub procedure and name it **TestOption**. Create the following code:

```
Sub TestOption()
    Dim x1 as Long
    xl = 20
    Msgbox x1
End Sub
```

Note that the declared variable is "x" with the *number* 1. On the second line note that the variable is "x" with the *letter* "l". Just by looking at the code, you would expect that the value in the message box would be 20, instead of the 0 that displays.

4. Now put the Option Explicit line back at the top of the module.

5. Rerun the code. Notice how you get an error.

6. Correct the error by changing the second line of code. Change the "xl" to "x1" and run the code. You should now get a message box that displays the value twenty.

16

DAY 17

VBA Programming— Part 2

Programming in VBA isn't just learning about variables and data types. If this was the case, you would be done and you wouldn't need this lesson. You need to learn about operators, branching, and looping in order to make VBA work for you. If you are new to programming, you will need to follow this lesson carefully. If you have programmed in other languages, these concepts will be familiar to you.

Today You Will Learn

In this lesson you will learn important concepts and structures that will make your programming powerful. Specifically you will learn:

- How to convert variables to different data types
- How Access evaluates expressions
- What operators are

- Looping
- Branching

Each topic in this lesson helps you put together the remaining pieces of the VBA programming puzzle.

Understanding Variables

Yesterday's lesson ended by introducing variables and data types. This lesson begins with more on variables, and then covers the following VBA topics:

- Decision structures (If...Then, Select...Case, IIF, Switch, and Choose)
- Looping structures (While...Wend, Do...Loop, For...Next, For...Each, and so on)
- Program flow statements (Goto, GoSub, and Call)

Converting Variables to Other Data Types

You learned in Day 16, "VBA Language Elements—Part 1," that variables will be of a specific data type. What do you do if you need to change data types? For example, your variable is a string but you really need that string to be a currency value. How do you get the variable to be a currency value? Well, VBA includes a number of built-in functions used specifically for converting one data type to another. Those listed in Table 17.1 are the functions recommended for converting data from one type to another.

TABLE 17.1 Type Conversion Functions

Function	Return Type
CBool (expression)	Boolean
CByte (expression)	Byte
CCur (expression)	Currency
CDate (expression)	Date
CDbl (expression)	Double
CDec (expression)	Decimal
CInt (expression)	Integer
CLng (expression)	Long
CSng (expression)	Single
CStr (expression)	String
CVar (expression)	Variant

Note: If the *expression* passed to the function is outside the range of the data type being converted to, a runtime error will occur.

For the example of a string value to a currency value I'll use the CCur() function. Look at the following code:

```
Dim strWithdraw As String
Dim curWant As Currency

strWithdraw = InputBox("How much money do you want?")
If IsNumeric(strWithdraw) Then
    curWant = CCur(strWithdraw)
Else
    curWant = 0
End If
MsgBox "You asked for " & curWant
```

The important concept is found in this line of the code:

```
curWant = CCur(strWithdraw)
```

The CCur() function converts the strWithdraw string variable to a currency data type.

17

Note

> These are just a few of VBA's built-in functions that you will use with variables; Microsoft recommends you use these for converting data types. Review your VB Online Help to learn about other useful functions.

Understanding Arrays

An array is a sequentially indexed set of variables of the same data type. The set of variables is referenced by the same variable name. In order to access a particular value, you specify the variable name by the index. Imagine you're a school teacher with five students, and during the course of a semester, each student has taken five tests. Now, you'd like to store the following test results using VBA data structures.

Nbr	Student	Test1	Test2	Test3	Test4	Final
1	Paul	85	83	75	77	92
2	Mary	77	88	82	96	87
3	Stuart	72	81	77	85	82
4	Louise	82	93	99	95	93
5	Marc	99	95	89	97	98

If you used standalone variables to store each value, your code would end up looking something like this:

```
intPaulsTest1 = 85
intPaulsTest2 = 83
intPaulsTest3 = 75
intPaulsTest4 = 77
intPaulsFinal = 92

intMarysTest1 = 77
'... etc.
```

You would have to name and declare a separate variable for every test and every student.

VBA supports a data structure called an array, which is designed for storing multiple related values like this.

You create an array by dimensioning it using parentheses in a variable's declaration, like this:

```
Dim aintTestScores(5) As Integer
```

This tells VBA to create a fixed-sized array, one that will hold six elements. No, that wasn't a typo; array elements are zero-based, and this is important to remember when dealing with arrays. The array is used in your code like this:

```
aintTestScores(1) = 85
aintTestScores(2) = 97
aintTestScores(3) = 100
aintTestScores(4) = 79
aintTestScores(5) = 88
```

The number used to refer an individual array element is called an index, and even if *you* are thinking in terms of from one to five test scores, VBA creates a zero element, `aintTestScores(0)`, whether or not you use it.

 Note

> You can instruct VBA to treat all arrays as "one-based" by adding the statement `Option Base 1` at the top of a module. This changes the default lower boundary for all arrays declared in that module. VBA defaults to `Option Base 0`.

The low and high index numbers in an array are called its *bounds*, short for boundaries. You can tell VBA to create an array with specific upper and lower boundaries by using an explicit declaration, as in the following:

```
Dim aintMonths(1 to 12) As Integer
Dim acurWeeks(26 to 52) As Currency
```

An array can be one-dimensional, as in the last example, or it can be multi-dimensional. For example, the original example of students and test scores would be better represented using a two-dimensional array, as shown in the example below:

```
Dim aintTestScores(5,5) As Integer
Dim intStudent As Integer
Dim intTest As Integer

For intStudent = 1 to 5
   For intTest = 1 to 5
       'Simply zeros out all test scores
       aintTestScores(intStudent, intTest) = 0
   Next intTest
Next intStudent
```

Note

I haven't covered For...Next loop statements yet, but the example above gives you a preview of two nested For...Next loops. The code is indented to indicate the inner and outer set of loops. I'll cover this in-depth later today.

17

Dynamic Arrays

There are many situations when you don't know exactly how many elements will be needed, or whether the number of elements will vary depending on other conditions. Dynamic arrays are tailored for use in this situation and can be redimensioned throughout your program to meet your needs. You declare a dynamic array almost the same way as you declare a fixed-length array:

```
Dim aintTestScores() As Integer
```

The open and closed parentheses after the variable name, with no specified bounds, tells VBA to handle this array as a dynamic array; one that it will size dynamically at runtime to hold a varying number of individual elements. Although the Dim statement identifies a dynamic array, it can't actually store any values until you tell VBA what its dimensions are to be. You do by this using the ReDim and ReDim Preserve statements. Take a look at Listing 17.1.

LISTING 17.1   ReDim and ReDim Preserve

```
Public Function DynamicArrayExample () As Boolean
    Dim aintTestScore () As Integer      'Dynamic Array declared
    Dim intStudent As Integer
    Dim intTest As Integer
```

LISTING 17.1 continued

```
'. . . . . . . . . . . . . . . . . . . . . . . . . . . . . . . . . . . . . . . . . . . . . . .
ReDim aintTestScore(5) As Integer

For intStudent = 1 To 5              'Loop 5 times
    aintTestScore(intStudent) =  100
Next intStudent


'. . . . . . . . . . . . . . . . . . . . . . . . . . . . . . . . . . . . . . . . . . . . . . .
ReDim aintTestScore(5,5)       'Redimension (throws away previous values)

For intStudent = 1 to 5
  For intTest = 1 to 5
      'Zero out all test scores
      aintTestScore(intStudent, intTest) = 0
   Next intTest

Next intStudent
'. . . . . . . . . . . . . . . . . . . . . . . . . . . . . . . . . . . . . . . . . . . . . . .
ReDim Preserve aintTestScore(5,6)
'Use ReDim Preserve to add elements to a dynamic
'array while preserving existing values
'Note: Some restrictions apply to redimensioning
'dynamic multidimensional arrays!

For intStudent = 1 to 5
   aintTestScore(intStudent, 6) = 0
Next intStudent

End Function
```

The same dynamic array is reused in all three sections of the procedure, simply redimensioning it to meet current needs. Using `ReDim Preserve` in the third section adds a sixth element to the array (another test) while preserving the previous values.

Look up Preserve in your online help for more information and restrictions on redimensioning multi-dimensional dynamic arrays.

Evaluating Expressions

You'll use expressions often in your VBA programs. An expression, sometimes called a formula, is a statement that combines numbers, variables, operators, functions calls, and keywords to create a new value. Here's an example:

```
VolumeTruncPyramid = dblHeight * (dblArea1 + dblArea2 +
➡Sqr(dblArea1) * Sqr(dblArea2)) / 3
```

This entire statement line is an assignment expression, and the part on the right side of the equals sign is actually a formula. Formulas are often mathematical in nature, as in the statement above, but are also commonly used to evaluate a True/False condition to control branching of our program code between two different logic paths.

We'll be talking about VBA's looping and branching statements later, so the following If...Then structure might be unfamiliar to you. Just consider it a preview of things to come. Here's an example of an expression statement that controls program flow:

```
If (Me.Form.Visible = True) And (gbooUserIsManager = True) Then
    'Execute the following statements if
    'the above expression evaluates as True
End If
```

Most programming languages, VBA included, use four different types of *operators*: arithmetic, concatenation, comparison, and logical. These arithmetic operators and their use should be familiar to you from high school math classes.

17

Arithmetic Operators

- +—Addition

  ```
  intTotal = intFirst + intSecond
  ```

- -—Subtraction

  ```
  intTotal = mintFirst - intSecond
  ```

- /—Division

  ```
  intTotal = lngFirst / lngSecond
  ```

- *—Multiplication

  ```
  intTotal = intFirst * intSecond
  ```

- \—Integer Division

  ```
  intTotal = dblFirst \ dblSecond
  ```

- Mod—Modulo

  ```
  intRemainder = dblFirst Mod dblSecond
  ```

- ^—Exponentiation

  ```
  dblTotal = dblFirst ^ intExponent
  ```

String Operator

There's only one String operator, and that's the concatenation operator, ampersand (&). Use this operator to join two string values together, as in the following:

```
strFullName = strFirstName & " " & strLastName
```

The strFullName variable is assigned to the combination of the value in strFirstName, a space and the value in strLastName.

Comparison Operators

These can be used with both numeric and string values, but if one value is numeric and the other is a string, the numeric value will evaluate as less than the string value.

- >—Greater than

  ```
  If curTotal > curMaxCredit Then
  ```

- <—Less than

  ```
  If curTotal < curMaxCredit Then
  ```

- <>—NOT equal to

  ```
  If curPriceSold <> curListPrice Then
  ```

- =>—Equal to or Greater than

  ```
  If curListPrice => curOrigCost Then
  ```

- <=—Less than or Equal to

  ```
  If curOrigCost <= curDiscountPrice Then
  ```

Standard Logical Operators

Logical operators are used to combine two Boolean expressions. The expressions being combined must return the values True, False, or even Null.

- And—Returns True if *both* expressions evaluate as True.
- Or—Returns True if *either* expression evaluates as True.
- Not—Reverses the True/False condition of the evaluated expression. For example, Me.Form.Visible = Not Me.Form.Visible, will toggle the value from True to False, or False to True.

Operator Precedence

It's important that you understand the order in which VBA evaluates complex expressions that contain multiple operators. This is called operator precedence. Grab a piece of paper or a nearby calculator and calculate this formula:

```
intAnswer = 15 + 25 * 2 - 3
```

If you came up with 62 as the answer, then congratulations. You remember what you learned in high school algebra. If you answered 77, then you simply ran each calculation from left to right, using the incorrect "order of precedence" per standard algebra rules.

When an expression includes multiple arithmetic or comparison operators, VBA evaluates the expression in the following order:

- Exponentiation—^
- Division and multiplication—/ and *
- Integer division—\
- Modulo arithmetic—Mod
- Addition and subtraction—+ and -
- Not
- And
- Or

There's a simple way to get around having to memorize these rules: Just use parentheses to tell VBA to indicate what part of an expression you want it to evaluate in which order. VBA evaluates formulas from the innermost set of parentheses to the outermost. For example, examine the various effects of using parentheses with the previous expression:

```
intAnswer = ((15 + 25) * 2) - 3    'intAnswer = 77
intAnswer = 15 + (25 * (2 - 3))    'intAnswer = -10
intAnswer = (15 + 25) * (2 - 3)    'intAnswer = -40
intAnswer = 15 + (25 * 2) - 3      'intAnswer = 62
```

Using parentheses not only frees you from worrying too much about order of precedence, it also helps make your VBA formulas and expressions more readable.

Constants

Constants are basically variables that don't change their value during program execution. The biggest advantage to using constants is that they make your code a lot more readable. Once you've assigned a value to a constant, you can use it the same as you would the actual value, in expressions and variable assignments, throughout your program. This is far more efficient, in both space requirements and execution speed, than using the actual values in assignment statements.

The AreaOfCircle() function example calculates the area of a circle given a radius. Look at this example and you'll see how constants can improve the readability of your code:

```
Public Function AreaOfCircle(dblRadius as Double) as Double
    Const conPI as Double = 3.14159265358979
    AreaOfCircle = conPI * dblRadius ^ 2
End Function
```

There are also many predefined constants built in to VBA, Access, and most other object libraries. You can use the Object Browser by pressing F2 from within the VB Editor to view constants associated with any object's properties or methods.

Here are a few examples showing how these built-in constants might look when used in your Access applications:

```
intResponse = MsgBox("Prompt", vbCritical + vbYesNo, "Title")
DoCmd.OpenForm "Form", acNormal, , , acFormReadOnly, acDialog
```

Constants associated with the VBA language normally use a vb prefix, whereas Access-related constants are prefixed with ac.

The generally accepted tag, or prefix, for your own user-defined constants is con. The format for declaring your own constant is

```
[Public|Private] Const conName As DataType = Value
```

When declaring a module-level constant, precede it with Public or Private to set its Scope within your program.

Understanding Scope and Lifetime

Scope refers to the range that a variable, constant, or procedure can be seen or referenced from another part of your program. Lifetime, as the name implies, refers to the period of time a variable actually exists in memory.

There are three levels of scope: global-level, module-level, and procedure-level. A variable's scope and lifetime are controlled by the way we declare it in VBA.

Global-Level Scope

A variable or constant has global scope when it's declared using the Public keyword in the Declarations section of a module or procedure. A global variable or constant can be read and modified by any other procedure in your application, as long as the module it's declared in is active. Here's an example of a global variable declaration:

```
'Declarations section of a module...
Public gvarMyVariantVariable as Variant
```

Note
You should try to limit the number of global variables you use within your programs. They can be modified from any code in your program, leading to potential logic errors that can be difficult to track down. Additionally, managing excessive numbers of global variables can become confusing as your programs grow more complex.

Module-Level Scope

If a variable needs to be accessible to all procedures within a module, but not to code in other modules, you should declare it as Private in the module's Declaration section.

Here's an example of how you might declare a module-level variable:

```
'Declarations section of a module...
Private mvarMyVariantVariable as Variant
```

Procedure-Level Scope

Variables have procedure-level scope when they're declared within a procedure using the `Private` keyword. Procedure-level variables and constants can't be seen or modified from outside the procedure in which they're declared.

```
'Declared within a procedure...
Private varMyVariantVariable as Variant
```

Lifetime

The concept of *lifetime* is closely tied to *scope*, and refers to the period of time a variable or constant actually exists. Global variables that are declared in a *standard* module are created the first time they're assigned a value and exist throughout the life of your application. At the other extreme, a procedure-level variable exists only while the procedure itself is running. When it finishes executing, VBA destroys its local variables and releases the memory they used. In this example, the variable `intDestroyWhenDone` is re-created each time the procedure runs:

```
Private Function MyFunction (intNumber As Integer) As Boolean
    Dim intDestroyWhenDone As Integer
    'intDestroyWhenDone will ALWAYS = 0 before adding intNumber
    intDestroyWhenDone = intDestroyWhenDone + intNumber
    MyFunction = intDestroyWhenDone
End Function
```

It is sometimes useful to retain the value of a procedure-level variable for use in further processing the next time that procedure is executed. You can create a special type of variable, which has procedure-level scope but module-level lifetime, by using the `Static` keyword when declaring the variable; for example,

```
Private Function DontForget(intNumber as Integer) As Boolean
    Static sintRemember As Integer
    'sintRemember will contain cumulative values from previous runs
    sintRemember = sintRemember + intNumber
    DontForget = sintRemember
End Function
```

You can instruct VBA to treat all variables in a procedure as `Static`, by declaring the procedure itself as `Static`:

```
Static Function DontForget(intNumber as Integer) As Boolean
    Dim intRemember As Integer
    intRemember = intRemember + intNumber
    DontForget = intRemember
End Function
```

17

The example above works exactly the same as the previous example, even though the `Dim intRemember As Integer` declaration implies a local variable whose value will be lost when the procedure is finished. Always strive to make your code clear by explicitly declaring variables as they'll actually be used.

> **Note**   You cannot use the keywords `Public` or `Private` when declaring variables or constants inside a procedure—use `Dim` or `Static`.

Variables with module-level scope have the same lifetime as the module they're in. Class modules, such as one attached to an Access form, live only as long as the class object exists. If you close a form, any module-level variables declared within it are destroyed.

Using a Standard Naming Convention

I've used the term "standardized naming conventions" throughout our discussion of VBA, and all the examples I've shown you have followed the "conventions" that I use when I write my programs. When you use naming conventions for your variables, constants, and objects, the name conveys information about that object and how you're using it. For example, which of these two equivalent statements makes more sense?

```
x = y * z
curSalePrice = gcurListPrice * gcurDiscount
```

The second example not only conveys the general meaning of each of our variables, it also conveys the data type and scope of each variable. Naming conventions are not a black-and-white rule; they're suggested guidelines to help you create programs that are self-documenting and easier to maintain and debug. The key thing to remember is that they're a tool to make your job easier, not to be a stone around your neck.

The Reddick Naming Conventions, named for author Greg Reddick, are probably the most commonly accepted in the Access/VB arena. Reddick states in the introduction to his conventions, "These conventions are intended as a guideline. If you disagree with a particular part of the conventions, simply replace that part with what you think works better."

I couldn't have said it better myself. Naming conventions are a helpful tool for you, the programmer, but shouldn't be so cumbersome that you're discouraged from using them. You can use them as religiously or casually as you find useful.

Personally, I use naming conventions religiously for my VBA variables and constants and am somewhat casual about applying them when naming my Access forms, reports, queries, and modules. (I purposely left out *macros* in the previous sentence because I almost *never* use stand-alone Access macros, and neither will you once you get comfortable writing your own VBA procedures.)

The complete Reddick VBA Naming Conventions document is around 19 printed pages, and has in-depth coverage on the topic. I'd like to thank Greg, and the many of contributors who helped him, for their hard work developing these suggested naming conventions.

Version 6.01 of Reddick's VBA Naming Conventions and VBA Coding Conventions is included on the CD-ROM you received with this book. You can also find the latest version online at Greg's Web site, `http://www.xoc.net`.

Here's a summary of the naming conventions that I typically use in my Access programs, a subset of Reddick's complete guide.

There are four parts to Reddick's Naming Conventions:

- A single-letter prefix to indicate the scope, as shown in Table 17.2.
- A "Tag" that indicates the type of object or variable, as shown in Table 17.3.
- A base name.
- An optional suffix that provides additional information about the meaning of the base name, when it makes sense to do so.

TABLE 17.2   Tags for Data Types

Tag	Object Referred To
(none)	Local (procedure-level) Scope
g	Global Scope
m	Module-level Scope
s	Static Lifetime

TABLE 17.3   Tags for Data Types

Tag	Refers To
bin	Binary
boo	Boolean
byt	Byte
cur	Currency
dat	Date

TABLE 17.3   continued

Tag	Refers To
dec	Decimal (Variant sub-type)
dbl	Double
int	Integer
lng	Long
obj	Object
sng	Single
str	String
var	Variant

TABLE 17.4   Tags for Various Access Objects

Tag	Object Refers To
app	Application
bas	Module
cbo	Combo Box
cmd	Command Button
ctl	Control
ctls	Controls
dap	Data Access Page
grp	Option Group Frame
frm	Form
frms	Forms
img	Image
lbl	Label
lin	Line
lst	ListBox
mcr	Macro
mem	Memo
mnu	Menu item
mod	Module
ocx	Custom Control
opt	Option Button

TABLE 17.4   continued

Tag	Object Refers To
qry	Query
rpt	Report
rpts	Reports
scr	Screen
sfrm	Sub-form
srpt	Sub-report
tab	Tab Control
tgl	Toggle Button
txt	Text Box

17

Here are some example variable names using these simple rules:

```
Dim gstrDayOfWeek As String            'Global-level String
Dim mlngRecordID As Long               'Module-level Long
Dim scurCumulativeBucks As Currency    'Static-scope Currency
Dim gfrmCustomers As Form              'Global-level Object (Form)
Dim ctl As Control                     'Local Object (Control)
Dim tabMenuForm As Control             'Local Object (Control)
```

The base name you choose for a variable or object should clearly describe what that variable or object represents in your program. It should also be formatted using uppercase and lowercase letters, without spaces, as presented in all the examples shown so far.

Access lets you name your forms, controls, reports, and so on, using spaces and characters that have special meaning in VBA, but then you have to use brackets when referring to those objects in your code, as shown in these examples:

```
strCompanyName = Me.[Company Name]     'a text box control on a form
frmCurrForm = Forms![User Lookup Table]   'a named form in your application
```

If you simply avoid spaces and VBA's "special" characters when naming your objects, you can write VBA code without having to train your fingers to find the "bracket" keys. Furthermore, your code will read much clearer.

```
strCompanyName = Me.CompanyName
frmCurrForm = Forms!UserLookupTable
```

Always remember, the reason for using a standard naming convention is to make your VBA code more "self-documenting" and you should adopt whatever makes most sense to you. For example, though the "accepted" Tag for Boolean data types is boo, I deviate from that standard and use yn, to indicate "Yes/No", in my programs. That's just a habit I developed before I first encountered Reddick's formal naming conventions. Naming conventions are *your* tool, to use in whatever way you choose.

Decision Structures

Our VBA programs wouldn't be very useful if they simply started at point "A" and ran in a straight line until they reached point "Z." You sometimes want to execute a section of code only if a certain condition is true at the time. You use the following conditional branching statements to control the execution of your VBA code.

If...Then...Else Statements

If...Then is the primary logic construct for performing conditional branching. Let's examine several examples of If...Then statements as they would be used in your programs. The syntax for a simple If...Then statement is as follows:

```
If [expression evaluates as True] Then [statement to execute]
```

Use a single-line If...Then statement, as above, if you only need to execute a simple statement depending on some condition:

```
If booAlarmSounded = True Then RingPolice     'Call sub RingPolice
```

The expression between the If and Then is evaluated as True or False. If the first expression evaluates to True, the VBA statement following Then is executed. If the first expression is False, the second statement is bypassed completely and program execution continues on the next line.

Note

Don't get confused over the two different ways to use the equals sign. In previous discussions, = has been used as an assignment operator, to assign a value to a variable. Now equals is used in its truest sense, to evaluate whether one value is equal to another.

You can also create multiple line If...Then conditional testing to handle more complex conditional branching. Multiple line If...Then statements are terminated with an End If statement.

```
If intTestScore >= 90 Then
    strMsg = "Fantastic! Your grade is an A!"
ElseIf intTestScore >= 80
    strMsg = "Not bad! Your grade is an B."
```

```
ElseIf intTestScore >= 70
    strMsg = "You passed... Your grade is an C."
ElseIf intTestScore >= 60
    strMsg = "You barely passed with a D."
Else        'Must be < 60 to reach here
    strMsg = "YOU FAILED! Please report to the Dean's office!"
End If
MsgBox strMsg
```

The keyword `ElseIf` let's you specify additional expressions, or conditions, to be evaluated.

When VBA evaluates a multiple line `If...Then` code block like this, it looks for the first condition that's true, executes the associated code block, and then exits the `If...Then` structure. If multiple conditions evaluate as `True`, only the first is recognized and acted upon.

Notice the `Else` check at the end of the above `If...Then` code block. VBA executes the statements following the `Else` line if none of the preceding conditional expressions evaluate to `True`.

You can also use `If...Then` statements inside other `If...Then` statements. This is called *nested* `If...Then` statements. Here's an example:

```
If intTestScore >= 90 Then
    If intStudentsAvg >= 90 Then
        strMsg = "Great like Always! Another A!"
    ElseIf intStudentsAvg >= 80 Then
        strMsg = "Congratulations! You pulled an A!"
    Else        'Students average must be < 80
        strMsg = "You got an A! Great work!"
    End If
ElseIf intTestScore >= 80 Then
    ... etc.
End If
```

There are times when nested `If...Then` statements can become complex and hard to follow. As you can see above, using indenting and line spacing helps make your programming logic a *lot* easier to follow.

Note

> Your code will be more readable if you write your `If...Then` statements using the multiple-line format, even when they could be written using the single-line format. Use indented spacing to spotlight the fact that a specific statement is *inside* an `If...Then` conditional check.

17

IIf() Function

The IIf() function stands for "Immediate If," and is useful when you need to perform a very simple test. Here's the syntax of the IIf() function:

```
IIf(Expression, Return Value if True, Return Value if False)
```

The IIf() function returns one of two results depending on whether *Expression* evaluates as True or False. Here's an example of how you might see it written in code:

```
strComputerSpeed = IIf(intCpuMhzSpeed > 600, "Fast Enough", "Too Slow")
```

The IIf statement above is equivalent to the following multiple line If...Then code structure:

```
If intCpuMhzSpeed > 600 Then
    strComputerSpeed = "Fast Enough"
Else
    strComputerSpeed = "Too Slow"
End If
```

Just about the only time you should consider using IIf statements, instead of an equivalent If...Then structure, is in queries and property sheets, where you *can't* insert multiple lines of VBA code. Not only are multiple lines easier to understand, it takes VBA longer to execute an IIf() function than an equivalent If...Then code block.

Another "gotcha" with the IIf() function is that VBA always evaluates all three arguments of the expression, even though one of them will never be executed.

Select...Case Statement

Select...Case is the preferred method for writing multi-line conditional statements involving three or more expressions. The following example takes our code from the example in If...Then and reformats it using a Select...Case structure.

```
Select Case intTestScore
    Case Is => 90
        strMsg = "Fantastic! Your grade is an A!"
    Case Is => 80
        strMsg = "Not bad! Your grade is an B."
    Case Is => 70
        strMsg = "You passed... Your grade is an C."
    Case Is => 60
        strMsg = "You barely passed with a D!"
    Case Else
        strMsg = "YOU FAILED! Please report to the Dean's office!"
End Select
MsgBox strMsg
```

Select...Case always executes blocks of code depending on the evaluation of a single expression—intTestScore in our example above. Using If...ElseIf...Then statements gives you the added ability to test different expressions at each ElseIf line.

As a general rule, if you're going to evaluate one or two conditional expressions, use an If...Then structure. If there are three or more, and you're evaluating a single expression, use Select...Case instead.

Switch() and Choose() Functions

The Switch() and Choose() functions also perform conditional testing, but are used less often than equivalent If...Then, IIf(), and Select...Case statements. Here is the syntax for the Switch() function:

```
Switch (Expression1, Value1 [Expression2, Value2, [Expression3, Value3 ...]])
```

The expressions inside the parentheses are evaluated from left to right, in pairs, until a True condition is found in "Expression." The function then returns the Value corresponding to that expression. Here's another real-world example:

```
strGrade = Switch(intTestScore >= 90, "A", intTestScore >= 80, "B", _
    intTestScore >= 70, "C", intTestScore >= 60, "D")
```

As with the IIf() function, VBA evaluates all expressions inside the parentheses, even though it only acts on the first True condition. This makes Switch() inherently slower than equivalent If...Then or Select...Case statements. Switch() is also less readable than a comparable If...Then or Select...Case structure. It does come in handy for use in queries and property sheets, however.

The Choose() function is a specialized function that's useful for assigning a value based on an indexed list of values. Here's the syntax of the Choose() function:

```
Choose(Index, Item1 [, Item2, ... [Item3]])
```

Index represents an ordinal value starting with 1. The function returns the corresponding item in the list following the Index or, if there's no corresponding item in the list, it returns Null. Below is a real-world example where using Choose() is especially useful, when using an Access option group, which utilizes an ordinal list of values.

```
Dim strAgeGroup As String

'Translates a corresponding Option Group
'into a String value for reports, etc.
strAgeGroup = Choose(Me.grpAgeGroups, "Under 18", "18-25",
➡"26-30", "31-40", "41-50", "Over 50")
```

17

The above statement checks the value of an option group grpAgeGroups, which evaluates to 1 through 6. It then assigns the text value matching that index to the string variable strAgeGroup.

Looping Structures

Looping statements allow you to run a specific block of code multiple times, either a pre-defined number of times or until some condition becomes true. You can use the looping structures listed in this section for a variety of tasks. You can use looping for applying a change to a property for all the controls on a form, for example.

For...Next

Use a For...Next loop when you know ahead of time how many times you want to loop through a block of code. For...Next uses a counter variable to track the number of times the loop has occurred. Here's the syntax for the For...Next statement:

For [*counter variable*] = [*starting value*] To [*ending value*] {Step [*value*]}

The optional Step keyword at the end allows you to increment the loop by a value other than 1. Examine these example For...Next statements in Listing 17.2, which you will find in the module named modForNextExample in example database Day 17:

LISTING 17.2   For...Next Statements in the modForNextExample Module

```
Public Sub TestForNext()
    Dim j As Integer

    'Example #1, Increment by 1
    For j = 1 To 5
        Debug.Print "j=" & j,
    Next j
    Debug.Print " Value after Loop = " & j

    'Example #2, Decrement by 1
    For j = 5 To 1 Step -1
        Debug.Print "j=" & j,
    Next j
    Debug.Print " Value after Loop = " & j

    'Example #3, Increment by 10
    For j = 10 To 50 Step 10
        Debug.Print "j=" & j,
    Next j
    Debug.Print " Value after Loop = " & j
```

LISTING 17.2   continued

```
     'Example #4, Decrement by 10
     For j = 50 To 10 Step -10
         Debug.Print "j=" & j,
     Next j
     Debug.Print " Value after Loop = " & j

     'Example #5, Inside line does not execute
     For j = 1 To 0
         Debug.Print "j=" & j,
     Next j
     Debug.Print " Value after Loop = " & j

  End Sub
```

Open the module in the example database and type **TestForNext** in the VB Editor's
Immediate window and then press Enter. The output displayed in your Immediate window should resemble the following:

```
j=1        j=2     j=3     j=4     j=5     Value after Loop = 6
j=5        j=4     j=3     j=2     j=1     Value after Loop = 0
j=10       j=20    j=30    j=40    j=50    Value after Loop = 60
j=50       j=40    j=30    j=20    j=10    Value after Loop = 0
Value after Loop = 1
```

Each of our example For...Next loops produces a single line of output in the Immediate
window by using the Debug.Print statement followed by a comma. (The Debug.Print
statement following each For...Next loop tells VBA to begin subsequent output on the
next line.)

Note

> A comma at the end of a Print statement causes the next value to be print-
> ed on the same line, separated by a tab from the preceding value. A semi-
> colon (;) at the end of a Print statement causes the next value to print
> immediately after the previous value.

Notice the ending value of "j" after each loop completes. You should never depend on
the ending value of a counter variable—it should only be used for the purpose of incrementing your For...Next loop. It's also poor programming practice to change the value
of your counter variable inside a For...Next loop, because it can cause logic errors that
are difficult to track down at runtime.

Notice that I used the single letter "j" as the name of my counter variable, instead of a
name that follows naming conventions, such as intCounter. This is fairly common when

17

a variable is being used for a simple For...Next loop and not much else. As a general rule, counter variables used in For...Next loops are usually specified as integers.

For Each...Next

For Each...Next loops are used to iterate through an unknown number of objects in a collection, or elements in an array. Here's the syntax for the For Each...Next statement:

```
For Each [object variable] In [collection of objects]
     ...statements
Next [object variable]
```

The For Each...Next statement implicitly assigns the next object in the collection to the object variable without using the Set statement.

The object variable must be defined as either an object or variant data type. If no objects are in the collection then program execution continues with the statements following the Next line; no statements inside the loop are executed.

Open the form frmForEachExample in example database Day 17 and switch to design mode. Click the code toolbar button, or on the View, Code menu item to open the VB Editor. Listing 17.3 shows the code that is attached to the Click event for the command button:

LISTING 17.3   The cmdLoopThruEachControl_Click() Sub in the frmForEachExample Form

```
Private Sub cmdLoopThruEachControl_Click()
    Dim ctl As Control

    'Controls collection of "Me", the current form
    For Each ctl In Me.Controls               'We only want text controls
        If ctl.ControlType = acTextBox Then            Debug.Print ctl.Name,
ctl.Value
        End If
    Next ctl

End Sub
```

Move from the VB Editor back to your Access form, and then switch to Form View. The form should resemble Figure 17.1.

FIGURE 17.1

*The
frmForEachExample
form example.*

Click the button labeled Loop using `For Each...Next` and then switch back to the VB Editor and you should see the following data output in your Immediate window:

```
CustomerID    ALFKI
CompanyName   Alfreds Futterkiste
ContactName   Maria Anders
ContactTitle  Sales Representative
Address       Obere Str. 57
City          Berlin
Region        Null
PostalCode    12209
Country       Germany
Phone         030-0074321
Fax           030-0076545
```

There are actually 23 controls on this form: 11 labels, 11 text boxes, and one command button. For our purposes here, we want to list only the names and contents of the 11 text boxes. Our procedure contains the following `If...Then` test to limit our actions to text boxes only:

```
'Ignore anything but Text Box controls
If ctl.ControlType = acTextBox Then
```

`ctl.Name` and `ctl.Value` are two of many properties we can read and manipulate for control objects. We could just as easily have locked specific controls depending on a user's security level, or perhaps changed a control's background color depending on the current value contained in it.

To see graphically why I included the `If...Then` test to limit our actions to text boxes, comment out the lines starting with `If...` and `End If`. (Type an apostrophe at the beginning of those lines.) Now try clicking on the form's command button again.

VBA reports runtime error 438, "Object doesn't support this property or method." This error occurs because label controls don't have the `.Value` property we're trying to output in our `Debug.Print` statement. For this reason, it's often necessary to test a control's `.ControlType` property when looping through controls on a form.

The `acTextBox` in our `If...Then` statement line is one of Access's built-in constants. Here are the other built-in constants that work with the `.ControlType` property:

AcBoundOjbectFrame	acCheckBox	AcListBox
AcCustomControl	acImage	acLabelacLine
AcComboBox	acCommandButton	acObjectFrame
acOptionGroup	AcPage	acPageBreak
acOptionButton	AcTabCtl	acTextBox
acRectangle	acSubform	acToggleButton

You can also use `For Each...Next` with arrays, but it's usually better to use a `For...Next` statement, coupled with the functions `UBound()` and `LBound()` to determine the upper and lower boundaries of the array.

While...Wend

Use the `While...Wend` loop statement when you want a block of code to execute repeatedly until some condition is met. Here's the syntax of the `While...Wend` statement:

```
While [expression equals True]
    ...statements
Wend
```

This looping statement tests an expression and, depending on its condition, either executes statements within the loop or skips those statements entirely. Listing 17.4 shows a real-world example, which you'll find in example database Day 17, in module `modWhileLoopExample`.

LISTING 17.4   The `WhileLoopExample` Subprocedure in the `modWhileLoopExample` Module

```
Public Sub WhileLoopExample()
    Dim db As DAO.Database          'Two DAO Object variables
    Dim rs As DAO.Recordset

    Set db = CurrentDb()            'Working with this database
    Set rs = db.OpenRecordset("Customers", dbOpenDynaset)

    While Not rs.EOF                'Loops until end-of-file is reached
        Debug.Print rs!CompanyName
        rs.MoveNext
```

LISTING 17.4   continued

```
     Wend

EXIT_PROC:
     rs.Close
     Set rs = Nothing
     db.Close
     Set db = Nothing
     Exit Sub
ERR_PROC:
     MsgBox Error$
     Resume EXIT_PROC
End Sub
```

There are a number of statements and concepts in this example that you haven't encountered yet, so let me explain what's happening. This is actually a very common use for the While...Wend statement, which you'll use when reading records from a table using ADO or DAO.

Note

ADO and DAO are object models used for manipulating data in attached tables, either within Access (or Jet, actually) or from some other data provider, such as Microsoft SQL. DAO stands for *Data Access Object* and has been in use for many years. ADO stands for *ActiveX Data Object* and is a newer standard which is beginning to replace DAO. I'll talk more about these later. I've used the older DAO method in this example because it's a little simpler to understand.

Our procedure opens the Customers table and then loops through the entire table, reading and printing the CompanyName field of each record. The important thing for you to understand in this procedure is the While...Wend loop. For the sake of clarity, here are what the other unfamiliar statements are doing:

The While Not rs.EOF line causes the loop to repeat until we've reached the end of the table (EOF stands for *end of file*).

The rs.MoveNext statement simply moves our pointer to the next record, so we'll either be ready to read the next record or, if we bypass the last record, will set the .EOF property.

The first four statements after the EXIT_PROC: label close the table connection and release memory used by the two variables.

Do...Loops

Do...Loop statements are similar to While...Wend loops, but have the added ability to test a condition at the end of the loop, for those times when you want the statements inside the loop to run at least once. Here's the syntax for Do...Loop statements:

```
Do [{While | Until} condition]
    ...statements
        [Exit Do]
    ...statements
Loop
```

The following syntax is also valid:

```
Do
    ...statements
        [Exit Do]
    ...statements
Loop [{While | Until} condition]
```

Listing 17.5 shows another example of a Do...Loop in actual use. You'll find this example procedure in module modDoLoopExample in example database Day 17:

LISTING 17.5 The DoLoopExample Subprocedure in the modDoLoopExample Module

```
Public Sub DoLoopExample()
    Dim varResponse As Variant
    Dim lngTotal As Long
    Dim strMessage As String

    strMessage = "Enter a number to add to the total, _
                 [or type 'Quit' to" & _
                 "stop this silliness." & vbCrLf & vbCrLf & _
                 "Total so far: "

    Do    'Begins our loop
        varResponse = InputBox(strMessage & lngTotal, _
        [ic:ccc}"Summing some numbers...")
        If UCase(varResponse) = "QUIT" Then
            Exit Do
        ElseIf varResponse = "" Then
            'Ignore empty entry, OK and Cancel, and ask again...
        Else
            lngTotal = lngTotal + varResponse
        End If

    Loop Until varResponse = "Quit"     'End of our loop

    MsgBox "You typed 'Quit'. Our final total was " & _
        [lngTotal, vbOKOnly, "All Done!"

End Sub
```

This code will loop until the varResponse variable is equal to "Quit." The way the loop is structured (with the condition check at the end of the loop) the loop will execute at least one time.

You can also structure a Do...Loop without checking a condition at the beginning or end, but you have to use an explicit Exit Do statement somewhere within the loop, or your code will get stuck in that loop (see Listing 17.6). To illustrate this point, run the EndlessDoLoop procedure in module modDoLoopExample in the Day 17 database. (Enter **EndlessDoLoop** in your Immediate window.)

LISTING 17.6 The EndlessDoLoop Subprocedure in the modDoLoopExample Module

```
Public Sub EndlessDoLoop()
    Dim intCounter As Integer
    Do
        Debug.Print intCounter
        intCounter = intCounter + 1
        'If intCounter > 2000 then Exit Do
    Loop
End Sub
```

When your code is stuck in an endless loop like this, simply hold down your Control key and press the Break (Pause) key to stop execution of your code. Now, "uncomment" the If intCounter... line by removing the leading apostrophe and rerun the procedure. This implements a conditional check within your Do...Loop and provides an exit from the loop.

Summary

In this lesson, you learned how to control your programs through program flow statements and loops. You also learned about operators and how Access evaluates expressions.

In addition, you learned about variable scope and lifetime and standard naming conventions. You will use every concept and structure many times, so come back and visit this lesson often.

Q&A

> **Q. I need a Do...Loop to execute at least one time. Where do I place the condition to achieve this behavior?**
>
> **A.** If you need the loop to execute once at the very least, you can place the condition at the end of the loop using this format:

```
Do
      ...statements
          [Exit Do]
      ...statements
Loop [{While | Until} condition]
```

Q. What does the `While...Wend` do for me that can't be accomplished with `Do...Loop`?

A. Nothing. In fact I rarely, if ever, use the `While...Wend` statement.

Q. Do I have to follow and use the naming conventions for my variable names?

A. There is nothing that says that you have to use the naming conventions set forth in this lesson. You will find that following naming conventions will make your code more readable.

Workshop

The Workshop helps you solidify the skills you learned in this lesson. Answers to the quiz appear in Appendix A, "Answers to Quizzes."

Quiz

1. What function would you use to convert a string variable to a currency variable?

2. If you were to follow the naming conventions that this book follows, what prefix do you use to notate a variable that is a string data type?

3. What does the name of the function `IIf()` stand for?

4. There are four types of operators. They are arithmetic, concatenation, comparison, and _____?

5. What VBA keyword do you use to resize a dynamic array?

6. The low and high index numbers in an array are called _____?

7. If you think your code is stuck in an endless loop, how do you stop it?

DAY **18**

Objects and Collections

Learning about objects and collections is important in your development as an Access developer. Many objects and collections of objects are built in to Access. You will need to learn about these to harness the power of Access.

Today You Will Learn

In this lesson, you will learn about the object-oriented implementation that Microsoft programmers used to create Access. You will also learn how to leverage these collections and their objects. Specifically you will learn the following:

- Understanding the basics of object-oriented programming
- Creating custom events
- Creating your own objects
- Creating properties and methods
- Creating collections

If this is your first exposure to objects and collections, some of the introductory material in this lesson might seem arcane. Don't despair if you don't understand this material after the first shot. You still will be able to use the built-in objects that Access provides even if you can't explain the concepts to someone else. As you get more experience with VBA programming, you will gain an understanding of all you need to know. So, let's get started.

Object-Oriented Programming

Object-oriented programming means different things to different programming languages, but as a VBA programmer, this isn't important. If you have benefitted from programming in other languages like C++, Java, or Smalltalk you might have a little difficulty translating how VBA can be object-oriented. It's okay if you do, because in the real world VBA is more often considered object-based.

The reason that it is object-based instead of object- oriented is that VBA doesn't fully support the definition of inheritance. In object-oriented programming, inheritance means that a new class can be based on an existing class, thereby gaining all its properties and methods. In addition to gaining its properties and classes, the new class can extend the base class by adding new properties and methods. This behavior is not supported yet in VBA. Stayed tuned because the next VBA versions promise changes in this area.

If you think about VBA programming being based on object orientation concepts and not as a pure object-oriented language, you shouldn't have any difficulty learning how VBA does objects and collections. As long as you learn how to use the objects and collections within Access, it doesn't matter whether you are a novice or a seasoned programmer. Know that for the sake of this lesson, references to object-oriented programming can be interchanged with object-based programming.

Understanding the Benefits of Using Objects

Code reuse is the most important benefit of using objects. In days gone by, before the advent of object-oriented programming, programmers would copy and paste code from existing applications to create new applications. Generally, code reuse was no more than that. Although the new application might have contained code from an already tested application, the developer would have to start the debug and testing cycle all over again for the new application.

To be efficient and meet ever-diminishing deadlines, developers realized that the functionality should be packaged into modules so that it could be dropped in to the new application without modification. Object-oriented programming was born from this realization.

Note

It's desirable to be able to completely reuse a module or object without modification, but unless it is designed correctly, this won't happen. For a more in-depth coverage of objects from a VBA/VB perspective read *Doing Objects in Visual Basic 6*, by Deborah Kurata.

You benefit from using objects, because you can reuse functionality in a matter of minutes. In addition to not having to develop needed functionality from scratch, you also benefit from hours of debugging and testing that Microsoft or other third-party companies have devoted to their objects.

In Windows or COM programming, which is Microsoft's standard for object interaction, objects are packaged into binary files, called DLLs (or Dynamic Link Libraries). Now the disadvantage of creating your objects within Access is that your code cannot be packaged separately into a DLL. You still would copy the original source to a new module within your database. Fortunately, as you'll see later in this lesson, you can reference other Access databases like you can DLLs. After you have referenced the database, you can use functions and classes defined in that database. To reduce confusion, I'll refer to any reference, whether it is a DLL or another Access database, as an object library.

I encourage you to take advantage of the resources Microsoft (and others, as we'll see later) offer by using their already built objects. For an example, in previous versions of Access, if you didn't want to (or couldn't) use the Common Dialog Control, you had to create and, of course, test and debug your own module that worked directly with the Windows API to locate and open files. Now Microsoft has provided this functionality via the FileDialog object in the *Microsoft Office 10.0 Library*, which you can use in your database application.

Interfacing with Other Objects

As mentioned already, in Windows, objects generally are packaged into DLLs. You can also create your own object library as shown later in this lesson. To gain access to these objects within your VBA project, you establish a reference in the VB Editor to that object library.

Open the Day 18 database. You can get to the VBE by clicking Tools, Macro, Visual Basic Editor or by pressing Alt+F11. Once you are in the VBE, you can go to Tools, References. This brings up the References dialog box as seen in Figure 18.1.

Note

You can also create objects from classes in your database. This is covered in this lesson, in the section "Creating Your Own Objects."

18

In the case of built-in objects, these object libraries are permanently referenced so you don't have to do anything further to use them. The permanently referenced libraries in Access are Visual Basic for Applications and the Microsoft Access 10.0 Object Library. You can see these permanently referenced object libraries in Figure 18.1.

FIGURE 18.1

Referenced object libraries.

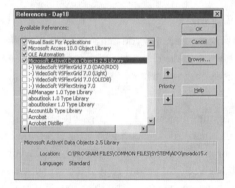

To establish a reference to an object library, you only need to click the checkbox beside the object library name. If you try to clear the checkbox of an in-use library, you will get a warning message as shown in Figure 18.2. You shouldn't try to remove or change the order of the first three entries in the Reference dialog box, because they are needed for Access to work correctly.

FIGURE 18.2

Error message box from trying to remove an in-use object library.

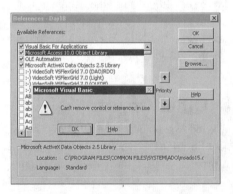

To use the FileDialog object, establish a reference to the *Microsoft Office 10.0 Object Library*. If you don't already have it up, bring up the References dialog box. Use the scrollbar to find *Microsoft Office 10.0 Object Library* and then check the checkbox to the left. When you are finished your screen should resemble Figure 18.3.

FIGURE 18.3

*Adding a new
reference.*

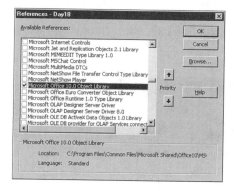

We'll use this reference throughout this lesson, so click the OK button to add the new reference to your VBA project.

Using the Object Browser

To find out what objects can be created from referenced object libraries, you can use the Object Browser. The Object Browser allows you to look at the classes, methods, properties, events, and constants supported by that object library. To open the Object Browser, open a class or standard module and then press F2. Your screen should resemble Figure 18.4.

18

FIGURE 18.4

The Object Browser.

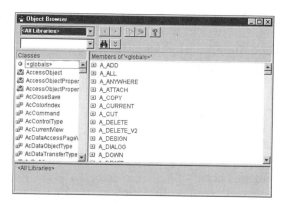

The Project/Library drop-down box, which is in the upper-left corner, allows you to select a specific object library. The Project/Library drop-down menu defaults to <All Libraries>. The Search Text drop-down box, which is under the Project/Library drop-down box, allows you to enter text to search the library. You can use wildcard characters in your search as shown in Figure 18.5. Also you can select previous search entries by clicking the down arrow. Once you have entered text for which to search, click the Search Button (the binoculars) or press Enter.

FIGURE 18.5

Wildcard search for "filed*".

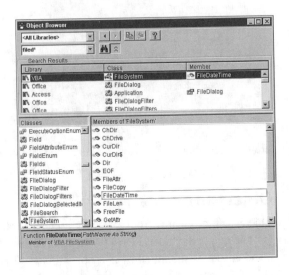

The Object Browser will make room for a search results pane, if its not already visible and show you the results of your search. When the Search Results pane is visible, the button just to the right of the Search Text drop-down box becomes the Hide Search Results button. You can click this button to toggle between showing and hiding the Search Results pane. The Search Results pane displays the Library, Class, and Member of the objects found.

Below the Search Results pane there are three more panes—the Classes pane, the Members of pane, and the Details pane. As you select items in the Classes pane, the members of the class are displayed in the Members of pane. Once you have selected an item in the Classes or the Search Results pane, you can click the help button (yellow question mark) for help on that item. For example, after I finished searching for filed*, I clicked on FileDialog in the Office library from the Search Results pane and then I clicked the help button. Look at Figure 18.6 for help on the FileDialog object.

If you select items in the Members of pane, you can see the definition of that member in the Details pane. This is helpful, because you can see what arguments a procedure takes, without actually going and looking at the definition.

There are two buttons to help you while working in the Object Browser. The Copy to Clipboard button in the Object Browser pastes the name of the item that you have selected in to the clipboard, so that you don't have to remember the exact spelling of that item.

Once you get used to using the objects, you probably won't need to use the Copy to Clipboard feature, but while you are learning them, it helps. The last button is the View Definition button, which is between the Copy to Clipboard button and the Help button. This button is only active when you have selected a member that is within your VBA project. Members that are within your VBA project are bold. Click the button to take you to the actual code that defines that member.

FIGURE 18.6

Help on the FileDialog object.

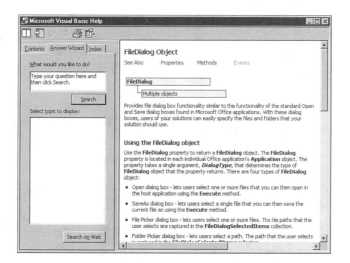

Creating Your Own Objects

Within Access you can create your own objects. There are many reasons for wanting to create your own objects. The list below will get you thinking about where you could use your own objects:

- Registry function wrapper
- Notifications

Understanding Classes: Object Templates

The key to understanding objects within Access is to think of a class as the pattern or the template for that object. A class contains the definition of the object. A much-used analogy you can use to help cement this concept in your mind is to think of a class as the cookie-cutter and the object as the cookie. Although this analogy is weak because it breaks down rapidly, it will suffice for the moment.

Each class is defined by the properties, methods, and events that make up that class. In a moment we'll create our own classes, but let's take a detailed look at the FileDialog object. If you haven't set a reference to the Microsoft Office 10.0 Library, do so now by following the directions in the "Interfacing with Other Objects" section earlier in the lesson.

When you are in the VBE, press F1 to bring up Help. Go to the Index tab, type the word **FileDialog**, and press Enter. Find and then click the FileDialog Object entry. Your help screen should look like Figure 18.6.

Notice that the Properties and Method hyperlinks are enabled, but the Events hyperlink is not. What this means is that there are Properties and Methods for the FileDialog object but there aren't any Events. Click the Properties hyperlink. A drop-down list displays all the available properties for that object. If you look at Figure 18.7, you will see that I'm about to select the DialogType property.

FIGURE 18.7

The properties shown for the FileDialog *object.*

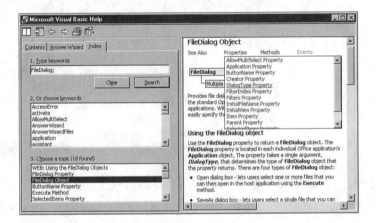

If you click the DialogType Property hyperlink, you can see what type of dialog box you can create from this object. Take a moment to peruse through the properties and the methods in the help file for the FileDialog object. All the properties and methods of the FileDialog object define what it can do and what it provides for you as a programmer.

Understanding Instantiation

How do you gain access to all this functionality? You just can't call the Show method of the FileDialog object, as you would on a standard class module. The following code would fail:

```
FileDialog.Show
```

You must declare a variable so Access can create the object in memory. When Access creates a representation of that variable in memory it is called *instantiation*. You can see this in Listing 18.1.

LISTING 18.1   Using the `FileDialog` Object to Select a File

```
 1: Function PickFile() As String
 2:     Dim objFileDialog As FileDialog
 3:     Dim lResults As Long
 4:
 5:     Set objFileDialog = Application.FileDialog(msoFileDialogFilePicker)
 6:     With objFileDialog
 7:         .ButtonName = "Pick it"
 8:         .Title = "Pick the correct file"
 9:         lResults = .Show
10:         If lResults = -1 Then
11:             PickFile = .SelectedItems(1)
12:             Debug.Print PickFile
13:         Else
14:             PickFile = ""
15:         End If
16:     End With
17: End Function
```

In Listing 18.1, the `FileDialog` object shows a dialog box that allows you to select a file. You can see that in line 2, the object variable is declared. In line 5, the object is created in memory (or instantiated) with the `Set` statement.

There are several ways that Access can instantiate object variables. Generally, the best way is to declare the object variable and then use the `Set` statement as shown in the following code:

```
Dim objFileDialog As FileDialog
Set objFileDialog = Application.FileDialog(msoFileDialogFilePicker)
```

For some objects, you can declare an objects variable and instruct VBA to instantiate the object on first use, without a `Set` statement. This call involves adding the `New` keyword to the declaration as shown in the following code:

```
Dim objPerson as New Person
```

Using this form of instantiation isn't as efficient as using a separate `Set` statement, because VBA has to check every reference you use in your code to see whether the object has been instantiated.

Introducing Properties, Methods, and Events

Properties, methods, and events, combined into one class, make up the definition for an object. You can create your own properties, methods, and events for your classes.

18

Properties

At its simplest, a property of an object is just a public variable declared in the general declaration section at the top of the class. For example, if you wanted to add a ZIP code property to a class, you would only need to declare a public string variable as shown:

```
Public strZip as String
```

Although this is the simplest way to define a property for an object, it is not the best way. Defining your properties this way robs you of the ability to control this property. To define a property for an object the correct way you need to learn a new way to declare procedures. Each property that you create for your object actually consists of two corresponding property procedures: a `Property Get` and a `Property Let`. A `Property Let` sets the value in the object and a corresponding `Property Get` procedure returns the value of the property.

The syntax for a property `Get` and `Let` procedure follows:

```
[Public | Private | Friend] [Static] Property Get name [(arglist)] [As type]
[statements]
[name = expression]
[Exit Property]
[statements]
[name = expression]
End Property

[Public | Private | Friend] [Static] Property Let name ([arglist,] value)
[statements]
[Exit Property]
[statements]
End Property
```

If you aren't used to looking at syntax, the previous code looks very confusing. So let's look at an example. In the Day 18 database, you will find three classes: `Person`, `PersonManager`, and `Telephone`. Each class illustrates an important concept. In the `Person` and the `Telephone` classes, you will find property procedures. For example, I've decided that a `Person` class has a `LastName`, `FirstName`, and a `Telephone` property.

Open the Day 18 database and press Alt+F11 to go to the VB Editor. Locate the `Person` class under the Class Modules entry in the Project window. Look at the pair of `Get` and `Let` procedures of the `LastName` property:

```
Public Property Get LastName() As String
    LastName = mstrLastName
End Property

Public Property Let LastName(ByVal vNewValue As String)
    mstrLastName = vNewValue
End Property
```

It's simple. Notice that the mstrLastName variable at the top is declared as a private variable. Now the only way that mstrLastName variable can be changed is if you change it yourself within your class. When you assign a value to the LastName of a Person object, the value is stored in the Private variable in the Let procedure. Conversely, when you want to retrieve the LastName, the property is assigned to the value of mstrLastName in the Get procedure. You should also note that each property procedure is declared as a public property. This allows code outside of your class to assign and get the values of these properties.

To cement in your mind how properties are created, let's add a social security number property to the Person class.

Task: Adding the SSNumber Property to the Person Class

1. Launch Access if necessary. Open the Day 18 database.
2. Open the VB Editor by pressing Alt-F11.
3. Locate the Person class in the Project Explorer. If the Project Explorer is not open, you can press Ctrl+R to open it.
4. Double-click the Person class to open it. Your screen should resemble Figure 18.8

18

Location where you will position
your cursor to add the
mstrSSNumber variable.

FIGURE 18.8

The Person class module ready to be edited.

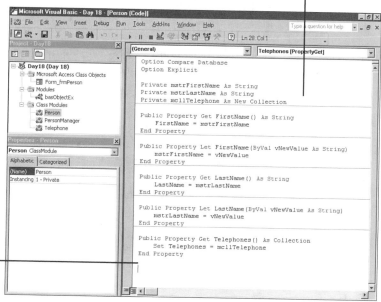

Location where you
will position your
cursor to add the
SSNumber property.

▼ 5. You need a private variable to hold your new property. Place your cursor at the location specified in Figure 18.8 (at the top of the window) to place the mstrSSNumber variable. Enter the following declaration:

```
Private mstrSSNumber as String
```

Your screen should resemble Figure 18.9.

FIGURE 18.9

The mstrSSNumber variable declared.

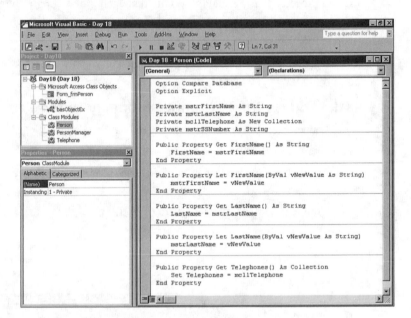

6. Now to add the SSNumber property, position your cursor at the location specified in Figure 18.8 (at the bottom of the window).

7. Now add the Property Get for the SSNumber as shown in the following code:

```
Public Property Get SSNumber() As String
    SSNumber = mstrSSNumber
End Property
```

8. Now add the Property Let procedure for the SSNumber as shown in the following code:

```
Public Property Let SSNumber(ByVal vNewValue As String)
    mstrSSNumber = vNewValue
▲   End Property
```

You now have added a new property to the Person class. In addition to the FirstName, LastName, and Telephones properties, you now have a SSNumber property.

Methods

Methods are procedures that the object contains. These functions or subroutines are written similarly to how you would write them in a standard module. The only exception would be that the method is only accessible through the object and generally is written specifically for that object. Listing 18.2 shows the code that is found in the PersonManager object:

LISTING 18.2 The CreatePerson Method Creates a Person Object

```
 1: Function CreatePerson(FirstName As String, _
 2:     LastName As String, _
 3:     Number As String, _
 4:     SSNumber As String) As Person
 5:
 6:     Dim objPerson As Person
 7:     Dim objTelephone As Telephone
 8:
 9:     Set objPerson = New Person
10:     Set objTelephone = New Telephone
11:
12:     objPerson.FirstName = FirstName
13:     objPerson.LastName = LastName
14:     objPerson.SSNumber = SSNumber
15:     objTelephone.Number = Number
16:     objTelephone.TeleUse = [1 - Home]
17:     objPerson.Telephones.Add objTelephone
18:
19:     Set CreatePerson = objPerson
20: End Function
```

18

In this function, a new Person object is created in memory and the FirstName and LastName properties are set. In addition a new telephone object is created in memory and the Number property is set. The CreatePerson returns the created person object to the calling code.

To shore up the concept of methods in object you are going to create a WhoAmI method. This is obviously a contrived example, but it will help illustrate how methods define the object.

Task: Adding the WhoAmI Method

▼ TASK

What you want to do is add a method that announces the object's properties when that method is called.

1. Launch Access if necessary. Open the Day 18 database.

2. Open the VB Editor by pressing Alt+F11.

▼   3. Locate the Person class in the Project Explorer. If the Project Explorer is not open,
         you can press Ctrl+R to open it.

      4. Double-click on the Person class to open it. Your screen should resemble Figure
         18.10.

FIGURE 18.10

The Person class opened and ready to add the WhoAmI method.

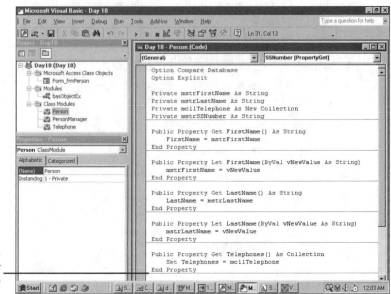

Location where you
will position your
cursor to add the
WhoAmI method.

      5. Position your cursor at the location shown in Figure 18.10.

      6. Press Enter to insert a blank line. There's no reason to do this except to make it
         easier to read.

      7. Now add the WhoAmI method as shown in the following code.

```
Public Sub WhoAmI()
    MsgBox "I am " & FirstName & " " & LastName & _
        vbCrLf & "My SSNumber is " & SSNumber
End Sub
```

When this method is called, a message box opens announcing the first name, last name,
and social security number of that Person object. Figure 18.11 shows this message box
in action.

FIGURE 18.11

The message box shown when the WhoAmI function is called.

▲

Events

As mentioned in Day 15, "Introduction to VBA Concepts," VBA programming revolves around responding to generated events. You can respond to many events within Access. For example, when you click a button, an event (the Click event) is generated. When you open a form, several events (Open, Load, Resize, Activate, and then Current, in that order) are generated. In fact, even when you move the mouse over the form, an event (MouseMove) is generated.

When you place code in event procedures, you are responding to an event that was generated. So far in this book, you have only written code to respond to events that the Access programmers decided you needed exposure to. In this section, you will create your own events for the objects that you create.

In the context of creating your own classes, custom events are usually used to provide notifications to another object. It's simple to define your own custom events. All you have to do is decide what your objects will need to raise. In the example seen later in this lesson, the Telephone object raises an event for every time the Number property is changed. You can think of your custom events as notifications to other objects.

You define a custom event by using the Event keyword as shown:

```
Event procedurename [(arglist)]
```

The statement consists of the Event keyword and a procedure definition. Note that you can only use the Event keyword in class modules. Access generates an error if you try to use it in a standard module. After you have defined the events for your object, you need to determine where in your object those events will be raised. To raise an event, you use the RaiseEvent keyword. Using the RaiseEvent keyword fires the event. For more information on the RaiseEvent keyword, see Help.

To see the notification or event, the consumer object contains a variable that is declared with the WithEvents keyword. The syntax is shown below:

```
Public | Private | Friend [WithEvents] varname[([subscripts])] [As [New] type]
➥[,[WithEvents] varname[([subscripts])] [As [New] type]]
```

Let's look at an example of events and using the WithEvents keyword. First, look at the Telephone class and the Event declaration:

```
Public Event NumberChanged(vNewValue As String)
```

This declaration is an event or notification that will be raised when the number changes. If you look at the Property Let Number procedure you can see where the event is raised:

18

```
Public Property Let Number(ByVal vNewValue As String)
    If vNewValue <> mstrNumber Then
        mstrNumber = vNewValue
        RaiseEvent NumberChanged(vNewValue)
    End If
End Property
```

The important part of this property is the `RaiseEvent` keyword. The pseudocode for this code is "If the number has changed, set the new number and then raise the `NumberChanged` event, passing the new number back." So any objects that are "listening" to the `Telephone` object's events will know that the number was changed without checking it.

You can check out the full example by opening the `frmPerson` form and changing the telephone number twice.

Defining Enumerated Types

Enumerations are long integer constants that can help you remember what values you can enter for a particular property or variable. The syntax of declaring an enumerated type is as follows:

```
[Public | Private] Enum name
membername [= constantexpression]
membername [= constantexpression]
. . .
End Enum
```

In our example database, you can see an enumerated type in the `Telephone` object. The enumerated type is used on the `TeleUse` property. The definition for our enumerated type follows:

```
Public Enum TeleUseEnum
    [1 - Home] = 1
    [2 - Office] = 2
End Enum
```

The enumerated type is declared as a `Public Enum`, so that it can be used on the `TeleUse` property. Although the values for our enumerated type are 1 for home and 2 for office, the value isn't checked to ensure that it is a 1 or a 2. In other words, any value that is a long could be assigned to the `TeleUse` property. If you use enumerated types and your properties must be those types, you should include code that ensures that the new value is one of the enumerations.

The use of enumerated types helps you while programming. If you have the `Auto List Members` Option turned on, if you try to assign a value to the `TeleUse` property, you will get a drop-down box that lists the enumerated types. See Figure 18.12 for an example of the drop-down box showing the enumerated types.

FIGURE 18.12

The enumerated types are shown in a drop-down menu.

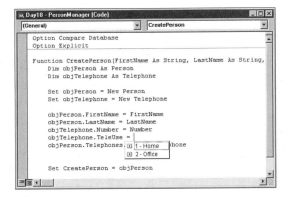

Creating Collections

Although you usually work with one object at a time, you might need to hold in-memory many objects. Collections are like arrays, in that they can hold many items. Collections trump arrays though, because collections can hold references to objects.

Although a single collection could contain disparate objects, generally you should keep only one type of object (like a `Telephone` object) in it. Keeping one type of object in a collection saves you from having to figure out by code, what is in the collection.

Understanding Collections

In the example, we decided that a `Person` could have multiple telephones. In particular, the telephones could be an office telephone and a home telephone. Okay, so you create two `Telephone` objects as shown below:

```
Dim objTeleHome as New Telephone
Dim objTeleOffice as New Telephone
objTeleHome.Number = "555-5432"
objTeleHome.TeleUse = [1 - Home]
objTeleOffice.Number = "333-5432"
objTeleOffice.TeleUse = [2 - Office]
```

Now whose `Telephone` objects are these? How do we associate these `Telephone` objects with a particular person? If you look at the `Person` object again, you will notice the `Property Get Telephones` returns a collection.

The `Telephones` property is how you assign the two telephone objects to a particular person. Each person object contains its own telephone collection as shown below:

```
Public Property Get Telephones() As Collection
    Set Telephones = mcllTelephone
End Property
```

18

In this example, you only deal with one, but they can have as many telephones as needed.

Understanding Collection Properties and Methods

Creating a collection is as simple as creating other objects. The following code is an example:

```
Dim cllNewCollection as New Collection
```

To add items to the `cllNewCollection` collection you call the `Add` method. For an example, if you want to add a `Person` object to the collection, you would call the following code:

```
cllNewCollection.Add mobjPerson
```

In addition to this simple call, you can specify other options. You can add a key and then retrieve the object by that key instead of the index number. You also can determine where in the order a particular object can go by specifying the `Before` or `After` arguments.

To remove the object, you would use the `Remove` method:

```
cllNewCollection.Remove 1
```

Note that these collections are 1-based, and by specifying **1** you remove that particular object from the collection.

The default method for a collection is the `Item` method. This method returns a particular item in the collection, by specifying the index or the key as the argument. To retrieve the seventh item from a collection, you would use code similar to the following:

```
Set objPerson = cllNewCollection.item(7)
```

Or, because `Item` is the default method you could use:

```
Set objPerson = cllNewCollection(7)
```

To determine how many items are in the collection you use the `Count` property as shown below:

```
Msgbox "There are " & cllNewCollection.Count & "
➥"items in the collection."
```

Summary

In this lesson, you learned about objects and their methods, events, and properties. You also learned about creating your own objects and properties that are a collection of objects.

Q&A

Q. Will I ever use objects and collections in Access?

A. Actually this answer depends more on you than anyone else. Objects and collections were introduced to help code reuse. It's up to you whether you use them.

Q. How do I create a read-only property for my object?

A. Instead of specifying both a Get and a Let property, just specify the Get Property.

Q. In the Day 18 database, the frmPerson form created and edited a Person record. Why wouldn't you just use a couple of tables instead?

A. You would just use tables, but the example was just that: an example intended to convey the concepts behind programming objects and collections.

Workshop

The Workshop helps you solidify the skills you learned in this lesson. Answers to the quiz appear in Appendix A, "Answers to Quizzes."

Quiz

1. An object is defined by what?
2. True or False. The Property Let is used when retrieving the value of the property.
3. Can you define more than one event in a class?
4. What keyword allows you to instantiate a variable without using the Set statement?
5. What keyword allows an object to "listen" to another object's events?
6. Is VBA programming object-oriented or object-based programming?
7. What method of the collection object would you use to get rid of an item in the collection?
8. What keyword do you use to gain access to Windows API functions?

Exercises

1. Add an event to the `Person` class that notifies "listening" objects that the `LastName` property has changed.

2. Add a `PersonKey` property to the `Person` class that is a Long and that can be written to only once.

DAY 19

Extending Access Using VBA

In the past few days, you've learned the basics of programming within Access. Today you'll learn how to put that knowledge to use with ActiveX Data Objects and Command Bars. Then we'll finish the subject of programming Access with a catch-all section of other considerations.

Today You Will Learn

In this lesson, you will learn how to extend Access 2002 using ActiveX Data Objects and how to make your database easier for others to use. Specifically you will learn

- What the ActiveX Data Objects (ADO) are
- How to use ADO within your database
- How to use command bars and menus
- How to develop with multiple developers

- How to hide the Database window
- How to distribute your database

ActiveX Data Objects (ADO)

Microsoft has a long history of producing programmable data access components. One of the latest and most effective is the ActiveX Data Objects (ADO). These components provide a consistent interface to a diverse set of data sources. In fact, these data sources can represent anything from your file system to the e-mails in your inbox. Regardless of the data source, using ADO you can count on a consistent way to retrieve and, possibly, modify that data.

Another advantage of ADO is an improvement in the object model over previous data access objects such as Microsoft's Data Access Objects (DAO) and Remote Data Objects (RDO). What were previously cumbersome tasks (because of all the various objects and methods you needed to use) have now been streamlined. ADO provides a small set of objects and a relatively flat object model.

To work with the current database, you should use the global `CurrentDb` object. This is a DAO object but does not require you to jump through the hoops of creating connection objects and connecting to them. You'll use ADO to work with data sources that are external to the current database, such as Microsoft Outlook, ODBC data sources, and so on.

This section introduces the ADO object model and provides the basics of how to work with it to retrieve data.

Avoiding Conflicts with DAO

Because ADO is the culmination of many different object models, it's possible that there will be some confusion. Indeed, many of the objects in the ADO model share the same name as similar objects in the other models, particularly the Data Access Objects (DAO). The DAO model was used extensively by previous versions of Microsoft Access.

Several objects from the DAO model remain within the Access 2002 object model. By default the DAO type library is not "referenced" by the Visual Basic Editor (see the section "Managing Library References" later in this lesson for more information on library references). However, if you need to utilize some of the DAO objects in your VBA code it might be necessary to add a reference to the DAO.

If you have referenced the DAO, it will be necessary to more fully specify which object model you're using for those objects with common names. This is the case when creating variables of type `Recordset`, for example. `Recordset` exists in both the ADO and the

DAO models. To differentiate the two versions of `Recordset` you need to add the library's name to the beginning of the data type. For example,

```
Dim ADOrecordset as ADODB.Recordset
Dim DAOrecordset as DAO.Recordset
```

creates a variable named `ADOrecordset` that is an ADO recordset object and `DAOrecordset` that is a DAO recordset object.

Note

> In general, it's always a good idea to add the library name to the data type. Your code will be more readable and doing so will prevent possible future ambiguity that could result if you add a library reference that contains an object with an identical name to one for which you've already created a variable.

Using ADO Objects

The ADO object model consists of only a few objects. There is no hierarchy to the model as there is in the Access `Application` object model. Instead, the model is flat but allows you to "attach" instances of objects to instances of another object. For example, you can create an instance of the `Connection` object and then use that instance multiple times when you create `Recordset` instances.

The ADO object model is shown in Figure 19.1. This section describes the major components of the model: `Connection`, `Recordset`, `Fields`, and `Field`.

FIGURE 19.1

The ADO object model.

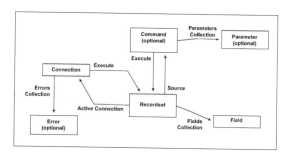

The Connection Object

The `Connection` object is used to gain access to the data source. You can run commands against the `Connection` object to either return a `Recordset` containing data or to act on the data source in some manner.

You open a connection to the data source using the `Open()` method. This method takes several optional parameters that are used by ADO to identify and locate the data source as well as provide any necessary login credentials. An example of using `Open()` is

```
oConnection.Open("Driver={Microsoft Access Driver (*.mdb)};" & _
                 "DBQ=day19.mdb;" &"DefaultDir=C:\samples;" & _
                 "Uid=Admin;Pwd=;", "Admin", "", 0
```

The first parameter is the `ConnectionString` parameter. This is the parameter that tells ADO where to find the data source. The second and third parameters are the `UserID` and `Password` login credentials that some data sources might require. Finally, there's a numeric (long integer) `Options` parameter that is passed to the data source. The values used for the `ConnectionString` and `Options` parameter depend on the data source. You'll need to consult the data source's documentation for what values to specify here.

Another property to keep in mind when opening the connection is the `Provider` property. Similar to `ConnectionString`, this property instructs the connection about how to open the connection. The default value for `Provider` is `MSDASQL` (the Microsoft OLE DB Provider for ODBC). Once again, you'll need to consult the data source's documentation to find out what value to use for the `Provider` property.

Once you have opened a connection, you can call the `Execute()` method with a command string to retrieve data from or act on the data source. If the command returns rows, a default `Recordset` will be returned. In some cases, you might want to create a more complex `Recordset` than that which is returned from the `Execute()` method. You will have to create a separate `Recordset` object, associate it with the `Connection` object, and then run the `Recordset`'s `Open()` method.

An example of the `Execute()` method follows:

```
Dim lRecordsAffected As Long
Dim oRecordset as ADODB.Recordset
Set oRecordset = oConnection.Execute "delete * from thetable", _
                 lRecordsAffected, 0
```

The parameters for the `Execute()` method are `CommandText` as `String`, an optional `RecordsAffected`, and an optional `Options` as `Long`. The `CommandText` specifies what you would like to do. For a data source related to an Access or a SQL Server database, this could be an SQL `SELECT` statement to return rows or an `UPDATE` statement that updates some data. If you pass a variable in the `RecordsAffected` parameter, the method will return the number of rows which were affected by an action query (such as `UPDATE`). Once again, the `Options` parameter's use depends on the data source and the command being executed.

Finally, when you've finished with the data source connection, call its `Close()` method (no parameters) to close the connection.

The `Recordset` Object

`Recordset` is the most complex object and the workhorse of the ADO object model. Using a recordset you can retrieve, update, add, and delete data from the data source. This assumes that the data source supports the activity in question, as data sources are not required to support updates, adds, and deletes.

Table 19.1 lists a subset of the more useful properties that the `Recordset` object provides.

TABLE 19.1 Properties of the `Recordset` Object

Property	Description
ActiveConnection	Sets or returns the currently active connection object. The meaning and usage depends on a convoluted set of rules. See the Access help file for details.
BOF as Boolean	Returns `True` if the current record pointer for the recordset is positioned before the first record.*
EOF as Boolean	Returns `True` if the current record pointer for the recordset is positioned after the last record.*
Bookmark as Variant	Sets or returns a unique bookmark value (when supported by the data source). You can use this value to "save your place" in the recordset.
EditMode as EditModeEnum	Indicates the editing status of the current record. Can be `adEditNone` (no edit in progress), `adEditInProgress` (current record modified but not saved), `adEditAdd` (AddNew method has been called but the record has not been saved), or `adEditDelete` (current record has been deleted).
Fields as Fields	The `Fields` collection is a collection of `Field` objects. Each column in the recordset has a corresponding `Field` instance in the `Fields` collection. More on this in the following section, "The Fields Collection."
MaxRecords as Long	Sets or returns the maximum number of records to be returned by the data source. A value or zero indicates that the data source should return all records. This property is read/write when the recordset is closed and read-only after it has been opened.

19

TABLE 19.1   continued

Property	Description
AbsolutePosition as Long	If supported by the data source, sets or returns a number from 1 to the recordset's RecordCount value that indicates the ordinal position of the current record. Note that the value for a particular record changes when records are deleted or when the recordset is re-sorted so it's not a good property to use when you want to indicate a particular record. Use the Bookmark property instead.
RecordCount as Long	Returns a Long indicating the number of records in the recordset, or -1 if ADO cannot determine the count.

If both BOF and EOF are True, there are no records in the recordset.

Table 19.2 lists the methods available on the Recordset object.

TABLE 19.2   Methods of the Recordset Object

Method	Description
AddNew [FieldList], [Values]	Adds a new record to the recordset, if the recordset is updateable. You can specify the values for fields using the FieldList and Values parameters.
CancelUpdate	Cancels changes made to the current row, whether the row is a new row or an updated row. If the current row has not been updated before you call CancelUpdate, an error is generated.
Clone([LockType as LockTypeEnum])	Clones the current recordset and returns a new recordset. See the section "Using a Recordset Clone" that follows.
Close()	Closes the recordset.
CompareBookmarks (Bookmark1,Bookmark2)	Compares two bookmarks and returns a value indicating the relative position of the two records being compared.
Delete [AffectRecords]	Deletes either the current record (by default) or the records specified by the AffectRecords parameter.
Find Criteria, [SkipRows], [SearchDirection], [Start]	Searches the recordset for a row that matches the specified criteria. See the Access Help file for details on constructing the criteria and on the other parameters
GetRows([Rows], [Start], [Fields]) as Array	Returns the rows from the recordset into a two-dimensional array.
GetString([Format], [NumRows], [ColDeliminator], [RowDeliminator],[NullExpr]) as String	Returns the recordset as a string.

TABLE 19.2 continued

Method	Description
Move NumRecords, [Start]	Moves the current record pointer to a new record based on the provided parameters.
MoveFirst	Moves to the first record in the recordset
MoveLast	Moves to the last record in the recordset
MoveNext	Moves to the next record in the recordset. If the current record is the last record, moves the current record after the last record and sets EOF to True. Subsequent calls to MoveNext will generate an error.
MovePrevious	Moves to the previous record in the recordset. If the current record is the first record, moves the current record to before the first record and sets BOF to True. Subsequent calls to MovePrevious will generate an error.
Open(various parameters)	Opens a recordset. See the following section, "Working with ADO Recordsets" for more details.
Requery([Options])	Refreshes the data in the recordset by reexecuting the query on which the recordset is based. Any records that have been added to the recordset will be available after a call to Requery.
Save([Filename], [PersistFormat])	Saves the recordset to the file specified. Details are in the section "Persisting Recordsets" which follows.
Supports(CursorOptions) as Boolean	Determines whether the recordset supports a particular functionality. The value passed in the CursorOptions parameter determines which piece of functionality is being referenced.
Update[FieldList], [Values]	Saves the changes that have been made to the current row. You can specify the values for fields using the FieldList and Values parameters.

The Fields Collection

As you can see in Figure 19.1, the Fields collection serves as the gateway between a recordset and the data columns it provides (in the form of a Field object). The Fields collection is populated when you open the recordset. You can also populate the collection prior to opening the recordset by calling the collection's Refresh() method.

Table 19.3 lists the properties and methods available on the Fields collection.

TABLE 19.3   Properties and Methods of the Fields Collection

Property or Method	Description
Count	Returns the number of fields in the collection.
Item(*Index*)	Returns a specific field in the collection. The Index parameter is either an integer ordinal (from 0 to the Count value minus 1) or a string value containing the name of the field.
Append	Adds a new field to the collection. There are two forms for Append. First, you can create a new Field object independent of the recordset and then pass it to the Append method. Second, you can pass the method parameters that specify how to create the field. See the Help file for the parameters to use.
CancelUpdate	Cancels any additions or removals of fields from the collection and also cancels any updates to the current record's data (see the recordset CancelUpdate method in the previous section).
Delete *Index*	Removes the specified field from the Fields collection. The Index parameter can either be the ordinal position of the field or the field's name.
Update	Saves any additions or deletions of fields to the data source.

The Field Object

The Field object corresponds to a data column in the recordset's underlying data source. The properties of the Field object provide information about the value of the column as well as metadata about how the column is defined (such as the column's data type, size, and so on).

Table 19.4 lists the more useful of the properties and methods of the Field object.

TABLE 19.4   Properties and Methods of the Field Object

Property or Method	Description
Name	Sets or returns the name of the column. Normally read-only, this property is read/write when you're adding a new Field object to the Fields collection.
Value	Sets or returns the value of the data column for the current record.
Type	Sets or returns a numeric value representing the data type of the column. For existing Field objects, this property is read-only. When you're adding a Field object to the Fields collection, the property is read/write.

TABLE 19.4   continued

Property or Method	Description
OriginalValue	Returns the value that existed in the field when the current record was retrieved from the database (before any updates were made to the record and prior to Update being called).
DefinedSize	Returns the data capacity of the field. For example, returns the maximum number of characters you can store in a character field.
ActualSize	Returns the actual length of a field's value. Unlike DefinedSize, the value of this property can change between two different records.

Creating Connections

The previous section described the main ADO objects and their properties and methods. It's now time to put that reference information to work.

> **Note**
>
> Although the Connection object is required to be initialized and opened prior to doing any real work with ADO, it is possible to create a Recordset object first and set some of its properties. Before you can retrieve or manipulate any data, however, you have to associate an opened Connection object with the Recordset.

The first step to creating a connection is to create an initialized instance variable. You can do so in either of two ways:

```
Dim oConnection as New ADODB.Connection
```

or

```
Dim oConnection as ADODB.Connection
Set oConnection = New ADODB.Connection
```

Once you've done this, you have a variable with which you can work. The next step is to call the Open() method:

```
oConnection.Open "connectstring", "userid", "password"
```

The "connectstring" parameter can instead be specified using the ConnectionString property and omitted when calling Open:

```
oConnection.ConnectionString = "connectstring"
oConnection.Open , "userid", "password"
```

19

The user ID and password parameters are optional as well. If your data source does not require that login credentials be provided, and you've set the ConnectionString property, you can call Open without any parameters.

If you have specified login credentials in both the ConnectionString property (or the connection string parameter of the Open() method) and as parameters to the Open() method, the parameter values will override the values in the ConnectionString.

The Open method does not return a value. If there is a problem opening the connection, an error will be raised. You should have error handlers active in order to know that you cannot proceed (see Day 17, "VBA Programming Elements—Part 2," for more details on error handlers). You can also check the State property of the connection to see if the connection has been opened.

Don't forget, when you're finished working with the connection, you need to close it using the Close() method. This will free up any system resources being used by the connection but won't remove it from memory or prevent you from changing its properties.

Working with ADO Recordsets

Now that you have an open Connection object, it's time to put it to work. There are two ways to open a recordset: using the Connection object's Execute method or the Recordset object's Open method.

The Execute method will return a recordset if the command executed is a row-returning query. For example:

```
Dim oRecordset as Recordset
Set oRecordset = oConnection.Execute "select * from thetable"
```

The recordset that is returned by the Execute method will be read-only and have a forward-only cursor (meaning that you can only move through the records in a forward direction). If you need a more powerful recordset, create and use a Recordset object.

To create a new Recordset object, use either

```
Dim oRecordset as New ADODB.Recordset
```

or

```
Dim oRecordset as ADODB.Recordset
Set oRecordset = New ADODB.Recordset
```

After you have an initialized Recordset object, you can open it using (for example)

```
oRecordset.Open "select column1,column2 from thetable", oConnection, _
        adOpenDynamic, adLockOptimistic
```

This will (if successful) return all rows from the table named `thetable`. The columns returned (as member's of the recordset's `Fields` collection) will be named `column1` and `column2`. The cursor type here is `adOpenDynamic`. This means that as other users make changes to the data in the recordset (including adding or deleting rows), the recordset's rows will reflect those changes. The lock type is set to `adLockOptimistic` which means that other users will not be prevented from editing the same record your code is currently editing except during the execution of the `Update` method from your code.

You can check to see if there are any rows by using the `BOF` and `EOF` properties:

```
If oRecordset.BOF And oRecordset.EOF Then
    MsgBox "There are no rows!"
End If
```

You can scroll through the rows using a `While` statement in combination with the `MoveNext` method and the `EOF` property:

```
While (oRecordset.EOF = False)
    MsgBox "Column1 = " & oRecordset("column1")
    oRecordset.MoveNext
Wend
```

Don't forget that call to `MoveNext`! If you do, you'll create an infinite loop and see the same value displayed each time the message box is shown. Although in this example there's not much code within the `While` loop, in most cases there will be a lot more work going on and it's easy to leave off the call `MoveNext`.

If you want to edit the value of one of the columns and save it back to the data source, you'd do something like

```
oRecordset("column2") = "Hello"
oRecordset.Update
```

This assumes that the record is editable and that `column2` is a character field. If either is not the case, an error will be raised.

To add a new record and set some values:

```
oRecordset.AddNew
oRecordset("column1") = 123
oRecordset("column2") = "Goodbye"
oRecordset.Update
```

To delete the current record:

```
While (oRecordset.EOF = False)
    If oRecordset("column2") = "Goodbye" Then
        oRecordset.Delete
    End If
    oRecordset.MoveNext
Wend
```

19

Finally, when you've finished working with the recordset, it's important to call its `Close()` method in order to release any resources it's using.

Using a Recordset Clone

There are times when you might want to work with two (or more) copies of a recordset. For example, you might want to keep track of more than one current record in a given set of records. To do this, the `Recordset` object provides the `Clone()` method. The `Clone()` method returns a `Recordset` object that is an exact copy of the original `Recordset` object. Using the `Clone()` method is much more efficient than opening a brand new recordset.

The first step in using clones is to determine whether the recordset supports bookmarks. You cannot clone a recordset that does not support bookmarks. To determine whether a recordset supports bookmarks, use the `Supports()` method:

```
If oRecordset.Supports(adBookmark) Then
    MsgBox "Recordset supports bookmarks!"
End If
```

Once you've verified that the recordset supports bookmarks, you can clone it:

```
Dim oClone as ADODB.Recordset
Set oClone = oRecordset.Clone()
```

There are some special properties of clones to keep in mind:

- Bookmark values from one recordset refer to the same rows in its cloned recordsets.
- Changes made in any of the recordsets are reflected in all of the clones.
- The current record of the new clone will be set to the first record, not the current record of the source recordset.
- Closing any of the clones or the original does not close any of the other clones. As an extension of this, you must explicitly close all of the clones manually.
- The clone will take on the lock type of the original recordset unless you pass the value `adLockReadOnly` as a parameter to the `Clone()` method. In this case, the clone will be read-only.

Persisting Recordsets

The final ADO feature we'll look at is persistence. It's possible to "persist" (store somewhere) a recordset and then load it again at a later time. You can save the recordset in XML, as an Advanced Data TableGram (ADTG), or in a provider-specific format.

To persist a recordset, it must already be open. If you have applied a filter to the recordset (filters allow you to limit the data in a recordset on-the-fly), only those rows returned by the filter will be saved. The rows will be saved starting with the first row in the recordset, and after the save operation has completed, the current row will be set to the first row. If you need to keep track of your current position when you save the recordset and the recordset supports bookmarks, store the bookmark for the current row into a Variant variable before saving the recordset.

To save the recordset, you use the Save() method. This method takes two parameters, both of which are optional. The first parameter is the destination. In most cases when using the Save() method within Access 2002 you'll specify a filename as the destination. The second parameter is a value that specifies which format to use when saving the recordset. The possible values are adPersistADTG, adPersistXML, and adPersistProviderSpecific. The default value should you omit this parameter is adPersistADTG; for example:

```
oRecordset.Save "c:\mydata.xml", adPersistXML
```

If you do not specify a destination when you call Save() for the first time on a recordset, the data will be saved to a file with it's name set to the value of the recordset's Source property.

After you call Save() the first time, you cannot call the method again using the same destination parameter until after you close the recordset. If you do use the same destination, an error will occur. The destination file is left open after calling Save(). Subsequent calls to Save() will update the data in the existing file unless you specify a different destination. The destination file (or files, if you've specified different locations when calling the Save() method multiple times) will not be closed until you close the recordset. (If you've cloned the recordset, closing the clones will not close the file. You must explicitly close the recordset instance used when you called Save().)

Introduction to Office Command Bars

Another way to extend Access is to use the Office Command Bars. The Command Bars encompass both toolbars and menu bars. You can programmatically add new toolbars and menu items using VBA code and the Command Bar objects. This section explores how you do so.

Note

The Office type library is not referenced in the VBA editor by default. To do so, follow the steps in the following section "Managing Library References" to add the Microsoft Office 10.0 Object Library.

19

Toolbars and menu bars are added to the user interface using the global `Application` object's `CommandBars` collection as the starting point. You can also use the `CommandBars` collection to modify and add controls to the existing menus and toolbars. The objects representing individual command bars and controls have a property named `BuiltIn` which indicates whether or not the particular item is part of Access or has been added by VBA code.

Creating a New Toolbar

The easiest thing to do with command bars is to add a new toolbar. You can do it with one line of code:

```
Application.CommandBars.Add "My Toolbar", msoBarTop, False, False
```

The parameters passed to the `Add()` method will add a new toolbar named "My Toolbar," set it to dock on the top of the Access window, not replace the main menu with the new toolbar, and make it go away when the user closes the application.

 Note | If there is already a toolbar named "My Toolbar" when you execute the previous line of code, a runtime error will occur. In a few paragraphs you'll see how to prevent such runtime errors.

However, when you run this line of code the toolbar will not be visible. By default, new command bars have their `Visible` property set to `False`. If you right-click over the toolbar area, you'll see it in the list of available toolbars. To show the toolbar immediately, we'll need to make a few changes to our code:

```
Dim oCmdBar As Office.CommandBar
Set oCmdBar = Application.CommandBars.Add("My Toolbar", msoBarTop, False, False)
oCmdBar.Visible = True
```

After this code is executed you'll see an empty toolbar docked at the top of the application window. You'll be able to manipulate this toolbar using the Customize dialog box (right-click over the toolbar and select Customize). From this dialog box you can manually add items to the toolbar by dragging them from the Commands tab to the new toolbar.

As you'll see in an upcoming section, "Manipulating Command Bar Items," you can programmatically add controls to the new toolbar using the `CommandBar` `Controls` collection property. You can also use the `Controls` collection to manipulate any controls which the user might add to the toolbar using the Customize dialog box.

Note

If you want to prevent the user from using the Customize dialog box to add controls to the toolbar, set the `Protection` property of the `CommandBar` to `msoBarNoCustomize`:

```
oCmdBar.Protection = msoBarNoCustomize
```

Let's examine the parameters of the `Add()` method. The first parameter serves as both the name and the caption for the new command bar. You'll be able to reference the command bar in the `CommandBars` collection using this name, and the name will appear as the command bar's caption in the user interface.

The second parameter determines where the toolbar will initially be placed. The choices are

`msoBarLeft`	Docked on the left
`msoBarRight`	Docked on the right
`msoBarTop`	Docked at the top
`msoBarBottom`	Docked at the bottom
`msoBarFloating`	Will be a floating toolbar
`msoBarPopup`	Will be a shortcut menu
`msoBarMenuBar`	Macintosh only menu

The third parameter is a Boolean indicating whether the new toolbar should replace the main application menu. If `True`, the main menu will disappear until the new toolbar is deleted. Even if the user unchecks the toolbar from the toolbar right-click menu, the main menu will still not reappear.

The final parameter is a Boolean that indicates whether the new toolbar should remain with the database after it is closed. The parameter name is `Temporary`, so a `True` value indicates that the toolbar will not remain, whereas a `False` value indicates that when the database is closed and reopened, the toolbar will remain.

One thing to be aware of when you're writing and debugging your code is that you cannot add a command bar with the same name as an existing command bar. This includes command bars which you add at runtime. If you were to execute the previous code that calls the `CommandBars.Add()` method twice, you'll produce a runtime error 5. To avoid this, you can add the following code immediately preceding the call to `CommandBars.Add()`:

19

```
On Error GoTo NoToolbar
If oAppCmdBars("My Toolbar") Is Nothing = False Then
    oAppCmdBars("My Toolbar").Delete
End If
NoToolbar:
On Error Resume Next
```

This is odd-looking code, so let's dissect it. The first line instructs VBA that if an error occurs, execution should proceed to the label NoToolbar. This is necessary because the next line of code will produce an error if the command bar name specified does not exist. The second line checks to see if the command bar exists. The Is Nothing expression is used to test whether an object instance has been initialized to a running instance. It returns False if it has been initialized.

In this case, a False means that the command bar we want to create already exists. Depending on what we're trying to accomplish, we could just exit at this point. But if you're experimenting with creating command bars, as we are at this point, you probably want to re-create the command bar. So the code inside the If block calls the Delete() method on the command bar.

After the If block you see the continuation label (NoToolbar:) and then the error handler is reset to turn off error handling.

Referring to Command Bar Objects

There are three ways that you can refer to objects in Command Bar object model. First, you can refer to them longhand and with the control name (caption):

```
MsgBox Application.CommandBars("My Toolbar").Controls.Count
```

Secondly, you can refer to them longhand by their ordinal value in their collections (the ordinals are 1-based):

```
MsgBox Application.CommandBars(1).Controls.Count
```

Finally, you can create temporary variables to hold references to the various objects (this is the recommended method):

```
Dim oMyToolBar as Office.CommandBar
Set oMyToolBar = Application.CommandBars("My Toolbar")
MsgBox oMyToolBar.Controls.Count
```

The final method is preferred because it produces more compact code and reduces the chances for errors in your code One of the most common errors is entering the wrong name for a particular member of the collection. When you do this you'll produce a run-time error 5 (invalid procedure call) and completely mystify yourself or your users.

Manipulating Command Bar Items

After you've created a new command bar, you should add some controls to it. Of course, you could just leave an empty command bar and leave it up to the user to give it some controls, but that would be borderline pointless. This section will introduce a few of the command bar controls and introduce you to how to work with them. Be sure to check out the Access Help file for more details on these and the other controls.

The `CommandBar` object has a collection property named `Controls` that contains all of the `CommandBar` objects associated with the command bar. The `Controls` property is of type `CommandBarControls` and has a method named `Add()` which, not surprisingly, is used to add new controls to the collection.

First let's look at a simple button control. To add a simple button control to a command bar, use

```
Dim oButtonControl as Office.CommandBarButton
Set oButtonControl = oCmdBar.Controls.Add(msoControlButton)
```

This will add a blank button that does absolutely nothing. Not very useful, so let's manipulate some of the `CommandBarButton` properties and give the new button some worth.

First, set the `Caption` property to a meaningful value:

```
oButtonControl.Caption = "Click Here"
```

The `Caption` property will serve as the tooltip text (which you can override by setting the `TooltipText` property) as well as the button's caption.

By default, a new button control is represented only with a picture, not a textual caption. You can control the button's appearance as it relates to its picture and caption text using the `Style` property. To create a text-only button, set the `Style` to `msoButtonCaption`. The other possible values for the `Style` property create different combinations of picture and caption text.

Speaking of pictures, you set the button's picture using either its `Picture` property or its `FaceId` property. To use the `Picture` property you'll need to load a bitmap into memory (using the global `LoadPicture()` method) and then assign it to the property. The `FaceId` property is a numeric index into a list of predefined bitmaps. You merely set the property value to the correct number for the picture you want, and the button icon changes to that picture.

Unfortunately the Access Help file does not have a list of the index values and the pictures they represent. In the sample database for today's lesson I've included some code

19

which creates a toolbar displaying a range of `FaceId` values. Figure 19.2 shows the toolbar created with `FaceId` values from 1 to 400.

FIGURE 19.2

The available toolbar "faces" with `FaceId` *values from 1 to 400.*

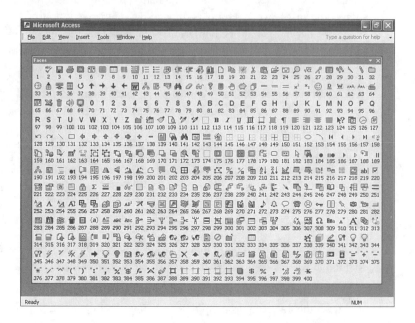

Now that the button has been created, how do you make it actually do something when it's clicked? There is a property named `OnAction` that specifies what happens when the button is clicked. You can set this property to the name of a macro or a `Public` subroutine within your module. When the procedure is executed, the value of the global variable `Application.CommandBars.ActionControl` will be set to the command bar control which activated the procedure. This allows you to use one procedure for multiple buttons and then using this variable you can determine which button caused the procedure to execute. The `CommandBarControl` object provides a `Tag` property which has no usage other than to be a placeholder for random data. You can assign each button a unique, hard-coded value for its `Tag` property and then examine the value of `Application.CommandBars.ActionControl.Tag` to determine which button was clicked.

That was a lot for a simple button control. Fortunately, all of that applies to not just buttons but also to popup menus and menu items. To create a popup menu control on the toolbar, use

```
Dim cbPopup As Office.CommandBarPopup
Set cbPopup = cb.Controls.Add(msoControlPopup)
cbPopup.Caption = "Menu"
```

The `CommandBarPopup` object, like the `CommandBar` object, has a `Controls` property. You add menu items to the popup menu in exactly the same way you add them to a command bar. Listing 19.1 is an example of adding both a popup menu and a command bar.

LISTING 19.1   Adding `CommandBar` Objects

```
Dim cbControl As Office.CommandBarButton
Set cbControl = cbPopup.Controls.Add(msoControlButton)
With cbControl
    .Caption = "My Spell Check"
    .Style = msoButtonIconAndCaption
    .FaceId = 2
    .OnAction = "MenuItemClicked"
    .Tag = "spellcheck"
End With

'un-initialize the object variable
' in preparation for creating a new control
Set cbControl = Nothing

Set cbControl = cbPopup.Controls.Add(msoControlButton)
With cbControl
    .Caption = "My File Save"
    .Style = msoButtonIconAndCaption
    .FaceId = 3
    .OnAction = "MenuItemClicked"
    .Tag = "save"
End With
```

This adds two items to the menu. Both activate a procedure named `MenuItemClicked` which will have to exist before the menu item is clicked. If it does not exist when the menu item is clicked, Access will display an error message. Notice also the use of the `Tag` property. This code produces a menu which, when dropped down from the toolbar, looks like Figure 19.3.

Listing 19.2 is an example of the code for `MenuItemClicked`.

19

LISTING 19.2   `MenuItemClicked`

```
Public Sub MenuItemClicked()
    Dim thisControl As Office.CommandBarControl
    Set thisControl = Application.CommandBars.ActionControl
    If thisControl Is Nothing Then Exit Sub

    MsgBox "You clicked '" & thisControl.Caption & "'"
```

LISTING 19.2   continued

```
Select Case (thisControl.Tag)
Case "spellcheck"
    MsgBox "About to run the spell cheker..."
Case "save"
    MsgBox "Unable to save the file..."
End Select

End Sub
```

FIGURE 19.3

The popup menu in action.

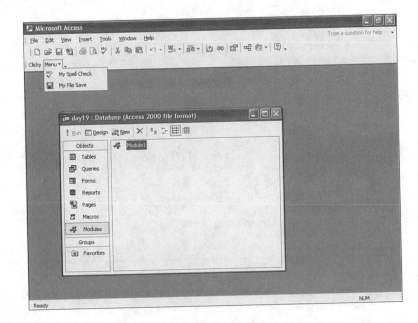

Note

The code snippets in this section are available in the procedure AddMyToolbar contained in the module Module1 in the Day 19 database for today's lesson.

Developer Considerations

This section serves as a catch-all section for topics which did not really fit in any of the previous lessons. Consider it a reference section, if you will. We'll discuss how to develop in Access using multiple developers, manage VBA object type library references, create custom properties, hide the database window, and, finally, how to distribute a finished application.

Multi-Developer Considerations

There are many issues to consider when developing in Access and utilizing multiple developers. The following lists a few:

- Are all developers using the same version of Microsoft Access? Access 2002 can work with files in either Access 2002 or Access 2000 format. Either format can be opened by either version of Access. But if you open an Access 2002 format database in Access 2000, there could be a loss of functionality if you've used any of the features that are new to Access 2002. See
  `http://msdn.microsoft.com/library/default.asp?url=/library/` `en-us/dnacc2k2/html/Odc_acformat.asp?frame=true` for more details.

- Make sure that all developers document their VBA code.

- Use agreed-on naming conventions for your tables, forms, form controls, macros, modules, procedures, and variables.

- Put procedures in place to avoid overwriting one another's work.

- Obtain a copy of the Office XP Developer Edition and install the VBA Source Code Control tools. This will allow you to use Visual SourceSafe to add source control to your project.

Managing Library References

In order to use the Object Browser and have Intellisense work in the Visual Basic Editor, you need to have a library reference established for the objects you're using. By default, there are not many libraries referenced when you run the VB Editor from Access 2002. The next Task describes how to manage the references.

Task: Managing Library References in the VB Editor

1. Open the Visual Basic Editor, either by double-clicking an existing module in the Database window or using the Insert, Module menu item.

2. Use the Tools, References menu item on the VB Editor to open the References dialog box, shown in Figure 19.4. All of the libraries which are already referenced are at the top of the Available References list and their descriptions have the checkbox checked.

3. To add a new library, scroll the list of Available References and check the box next to the library to be added. If the library does not exist in the list, but you know where the library file resides, use the Browse button to locate the library.

4. To remove an unused reference, uncheck the box next to the library description in the Available References list.

FIGURE 19.4

The References dialog box of the Visual Basic Editor.

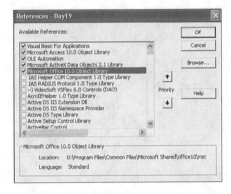

5. Use the Priority buttons to move the referenced libraries up or down in priority order. If two libraries have objects with the same name (and you're not explicit as to which library to use when you define a variable of that object type), Visual Basic will use the object from the library whose name appears higher in the Available References list.

Hiding the Database Window

When you create a stand-alone application, you might not want the Database window to appear. To hide the Database window, you can execute the following two lines of VBA code:

```
DoCmd.SelectObject acTable, , True
RunCommand acCmdWindowHide
```

If you're not creating a stand-alone application out of your database, you can also hide the database window whenever the database is opened using the Startup dialog box. From the main Access menu use the Tools, Startup menu item. On the Startup dialog box uncheck the Display Database Window option.

Distributing Finished Applications

There are two ways to distribute your Access applications. Which you use depends on your target audience. The first way is to simply create an MDE file; the second is to create a standalone Setup.exe executable that will install your database and the Access runtime environment. Using the second method requires purchase and installation of the Office XP Developer's Edition; creating an MDE file does not.

When you create an MDE file, you're actually saving your database's structure in a read-only file that cannot be edited. Additionally, any VBA code in modules is compiled and is no longer viewable in the MDE file. This makes distributing MDE files an excellent way to distribute your application.

To save your database as an MDE file, use the Tools, Database Utilities, Make MDE File menu item. Then specify a name and location for the MDE file and click OK. That's all there is to it. Your current database will remain open in its current state. You'll need to explicitly open the MDE file to see the results.

To create a setup executable, install the Office XP Developer's Edition, save your database as an MDE file, and run the Packaging Wizard (you'll find it under Microsoft Office XP Developer on the Windows Start menu). This wizard will walk you through the process of creating a setup disk which you can distribute.

Suggested Resources for Access and VBA Information

Here are some resources you can consult if and when you need some help with Access programming or VBA:

- `http://msdn.microsoft.com`: The Microsoft Developer Network Web site, where you'll find information not just on VBA but on all of Microsoft's programming and programmable technologies.

- `http://msdn.microsoft.com/vba`: The VBA Home Page.

- `http://www.microsoft.com/office/developer`: Information and support for the Office XP Developer Edition.

- `http://groups.google.com`: Search current and past Usenet newsgroup articles for information. Fast, easy-to-use search engine that lets you benefit from the experience of other Access developers.

- Microsoft KnowledgeBase article Q226118 (`http://support.microsoft.com/support/kb/articles/Q226/1/18.ASP`): List of further resources for programming VBA with Microsoft Office.

19

Summary

Today's lesson began with an introduction of the ActiveX Data Objects. These are a streamlined set of objects which you use to work with data external to the current database. The first section of the lesson provided a reference to ADO's objects and their properties and methods. The section concluded with some examples of how you work with these objects.

The middle part of the lesson provided details on another useful set of objects available in Access 2002, the CommandBar objects. These are used to add toolbars, menu bars, and shortcut menus to the user interface. Although they are simple to use, they are a powerful tool for improving the usability of your database applications.

The lessons concluded with a catch-all section covering a range of other programming topics as well as a reference to other useful VBA resources.

Q&A

Q. If I want to use ADO in another application to manipulate data in an Access database, how do I set up the Connection object?

A. The following code will open a connection to an Access database:

```
Set cn = New ADODB.Connection
cn.Provider = "Microsoft.Jet.OLEDB.4.0"
cn.Open "Data Source=<path & filename of database>"
```

If the database you're connecting to has had user-level security applied (see Day 20, "Maintaining and Securing Access Databases" for details on how to do so), you will need to specify a username and password when you call the Open() method.

Q. How do I free the memory and resources that an ADO object is using when I'm finished with the object?

A. Visual BASIC will automatically release the memory and resources when the variable "goes out of scope" and is no longer used. But you can manually release the connection from memory when you're finished using the variable, by setting it to nothing, literally:

```
Set oConnection = Nothing
```

Workshop

The Workshop helps you solidify the skills you learned in this lesson. Answers to the quiz appear in Appendix A, "Answers to Quizzes."

Quiz

1. When working with ADO, do you have to connect to the data source before you create an instance of a `Recordset` object?

2. When scrolling through a `Recordset` object with the `MoveNext()` method, how will you know when you've reached the end?

3. When you clone a recordset, do bookmarks from the original recordset point to the corresponding record in the clone?

4. When you create a new `CommandBar` object, is it visible by default?

5. Can you add a `CommandBar` object with the same name as an existing `CommandBar` object?

6. What properties of a `CommandBarControl` do you use to set the picture for the control?

7. Are new `CommandBars` automatically saved with the database?

Exercise

For today's exercise, I invite you to peruse the `Day 19` database for today's lesson. There are routines in `Module1` that set up various toolbars and menus.

19

DAY 20

Maintaining and Securing Access Databases

Today's lesson covers some pretty mundane topics. But regardless of how mundane these topics turn out to be, they're some of the most important for keeping your database running.

When your database application is in its infancy, these topics won't appear to apply. But as your project ages and becomes more successful (as they all do, right?) you're going to need to be familiar with how to maintain and secure your database. You need to maintain it against "normal wear and tear" and you need to secure it against malicious intent.

Today You Will Learn

In this lesson you will learn the tasks necessary to maintain your database and keep it running smoothly. Specifically you will learn

- Why you should know what maintenance tasks you can perform
- How to repair a database

- How to compact a database
- How to convert the database to a different format
- What security options are available
- How to secure a database

The Importance of Database Maintenance

It is important to maintain your database because failure to do so can lead to catastrophic loss of information. And in most cases loss of information usually means losing both time and money. These data losses can result from a hardware failure, such as a disk drive crash, a software failure, such as a virus that infects the machine, or as the result of corruption caused by some other means.

There are only two "routine maintenance" activities you need to perform on your database. The first, and most important, is making backups of the database. The second is compacting the database, which is covered in the upcoming section "Compacting a Bloated Database."

For Access 2002 file-based databases (as opposed to Microsoft Data Engine, SQL Server databases), there is no built-in tool to create backups. Instead, you should copy the MDB file (or MDE file, if that's what your users are working with) to a secured backup location. You should do this on a regular basis and should make at least two backups each time. Store one on-site and store the other backup copy off-site.

Repairing a Corrupted Database

Databases can become corrupted in a number of ways. The most common is when the computer loses power while the database is open. More than likely Access will detect that the database is corrupt when you open it. Sometimes, however, it might be that only a certain table has been corrupted. In this case, you probably won't notice the corruption until you attempt to use the affected table.

If Access detects the corruption when you open the database, you will be given the option of repairing the database. Otherwise, you'll have to launch the repair tool manually.

To repair a database, open the database and use the Tools, Database Utilities, Compact and Repair Database menu item. You have to open the database in exclusive mode, so if the database is shared with other users, make sure that no one else has the database opened.

To repair a database that is not the current database, close the current database. Then use the Tools, Database Utilities, Compact and Repair Database menu item. When the Database to Compact From dialog box opens, either select the database to be repaired and click the Compact button or double-click the database to be repaired. The Compact Database Into dialog box appears; enter the name of the new, repaired database. You can use the same name as the existing database, in which case Access will overwrite the existing database.

Compacting a Bloated Database

Through the normal course of using a database, you'll find that its file size increases even though you might be deleting more data than you're adding. This occurs because Access does not attempt to reclaim disk space even though you delete records or shorten the amount of data in records. If this situation gets out of hand, database performance will start to suffer and you might run into problems with disk space.

You follow the same steps to compact a database as you do to repair it. If you want to compact the current database, use the Tools, Database Utilities, Compact and Repair Database menu item. If you do not have a database open when you use this menu item, Access will prompt you to enter source and destination databases (which can be the same file).

You can also set your database to repair and compact whenever you close it. To do so, use the Tools, Options menu item. When the Options dialog box appears, switch to the General tab. To automatically repair and compact the database when it is closed, check the box labeled Compact on Close. Note that this option applies to the current database only, not to Access in general. You need to set this option for each database that you want to compact automatically.

> **Note**
>
> In addition to using the menu item to repair and compact a database, there is also a method on the Access Application object named CompactRepair. You cannot use this method for the current database, however. See the Access Help file for details on using this method.

20

Converting the Database to a Different Format

If you're the only person who will ever use the databases you're creating, this section won't serve much of a purpose. However, if it's possible that others will use the database, you'll at some point run in to a user who, for whatever reason, cannot install

Access 2002. Or you might find that your user base or dataset has grown so large that Access can no longer efficiently hold your data. In these cases, the material in this section will come handy.

This section discusses two topics: converting a database to earlier versions of Access and "upsizing" an Access database to a SQL Server database.

Using Different Versions of Access

If you work in a mixed environment of different departments or if you work with the general public, you need to be prepared for the fact that not everyone will be using the latest version of Access. Fortunately, Access 2002 makes this proposition easy to stomach.

First off, you can use Access 2000 databases directly in Access 2002. Also, by default Access 2002 saves the database in a format which is readable in Access 2000. Of course, there are some new features in Access 2002 that won't be supported in Access 2000, so you should use these new features with care.

Sometimes, however, you might want only users who have Access 2002 to open your database. In this case, you should explicitly convert the database to Access 2002. To do so, use the Tools, Database Utilities, Convert Database, To Access 2002 File Format menu item. This menu item will only appear if the database is not in Access 2002 format. A Convert Database Into file save dialog box will appear. Enter the new destination filename and location.

Likewise, if you need to convert your Access 2002 format database such that users of Access 2000 can open it, use the Tools, Database Utilities, Convert Database, To Access 2000 File Format menu item. This menu item will only be available if the database file is not in Access 2000 format. The database file will now be usable in both Access 2000 and Access 2002.

If you attempt to open an Access 97–created database in Access 2002, you will be instructed to convert it to the latest format. Conversely, there is a menu item for converting Access 2000 or 2002 version databases to Access 97 format (again with reduced functionality). Do so with the Tools, Database Utilities, Convert Database, To Access 97 File Format menu item.

Note

Microsoft has a wonderful Web page detailing the decision as to which file format you should use. You can find this page at
`http://office.microsoft.com/assistance/2002/articles/`
`acDefaultFileFormatAccess.aspx`.

Using the Upsizing Wizard

At some point in the life of a database you might need to consider whether to upsize the database to Microsoft SQL Server. Upsizing the database consists of transferring some or all of the objects in the database to either a new or existing SQL Server (version 6.5 or later) database or to a new Microsoft Access project (ADP) file. Fortunately, Access 2002 provides the Upsizing Wizard to help you perform this task.

Why would you want to upsize? SQL Server provides the following advantages for your databases:

- Higher performance and scalability (more data, more users, more transactions occurring simultaneously)
- Increased availability because SQL Server provides online backups, meaning users don't have to exit the database in order to perform a backup
- Improved security
- Improved transaction and inherent client/server functionality

There are several things to keep in mind before running the Upsizing Wizard. First, you must have at least one table in your database or the wizard will not even start. Second, you must not have any objects open in any manner. If you do, the wizard will display a message informing you of this fact and then will exit. Third, you need to have the appropriate permissions on both the SQL Server you'll be upsizing to and the Access database. On the SQL Server, if you upsize to an existing database you will need CREATE TABLE and CREATE DEFAULT permissions in that database. If you are upsizing to a new database, you'll need CREATE DATABASE on the server and SELECT permission on the Master database for that server. On the Access side, you must have READ and DESIGN permission on all of the objects in the database (more on this in the upcoming "Security Options in Access" section).

After these items are taken care of, make a backup copy of both your Access database file and the SQL Server (or at least make sure a suitable backup exists for the SQL Server). Then make sure that there is enough disk space on the SQL Server to handle your database. Now you're ready to move on to the task at hand: running the Upsizing Wizard.

20

Task: Running the Upsizing Wizard

1. Open the database you want to upsize. If it's already opened, close all objects and return to the Database window. The Upsizing Wizard is only available if you have an open database.
2. Use the Tools, Database Utilities, Upsizing Wizard menu item. If the wizard is able to run, its first dialog box appears as shown in Figure 20.1.

FIGURE 20.1

*The initial dialog box
of the Upsizing Wizard.*

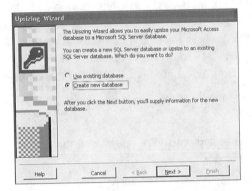

3. On this dialog box, select whether you are upsizing to a new or an existing database on the SQL Server. If you select Create new database, the dialog box that follows will let you specify information for the new database. If you select Use existing database, clicking Next will prompt you to log in to the database. For this task, select Create new database. Click the Next button after you've made your selection.

4. The Upsizing Wizard's second dialog box, shown in Figure 20.2, is used to identify which SQL Server will host the upsized database. Enter or select the server name in the dropdown list. The default entry is (local) which means to use the current machine as the SQL Server.

FIGURE 20.2

*The dialog box of the
Upsizing Wizard where
you enter information
about the SQL Server
database you're
creating.*

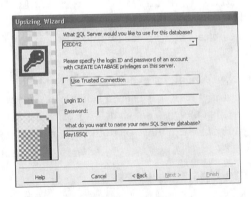

5. If the SQL Server uses integrated security (meaning that your Windows username and password also allow you to access the SQL Server), check the box labeled Use Trusted Connection. Otherwise, enter the username and password for a user with proper permissions on the SQL Server.

▼ 6. Enter a name for the new database. Click the Next button to continue. If the database name you enter already exists on the server, the wizard will inform you of this, suggest a new, unique name, and return you to the current dialog box. If the newly chosen name is acceptable, click the Next button again. If it's not, enter a new name and try the Next button again to see if this new name passes muster.

7. On the third dialog box, you specify which tables should be upsized to the new SQL Server database. Double-click the table names in the Available Tables list to move them to the Export to SQL Server list. When you're finished, click the Next button to continue.

8. The dialog box that appears, shown in Figure 20.3, is where you can specify what attributes of the tables you want to include in the SQL Server version of the tables. If you only want to create the tables on the SQL Server but not copy any data to the server (as might be the case if you've been using Access to prototype your database), check the box labeled "Only create the structure; don't upsize any data." Click the Next button when you're satisfied with the settings on this dialog box.

FIGURE 20.3

The dialog box of the Upsizing Wizard where you specify what table attributes you want to upsize to the new SQL Server database.

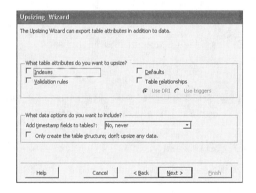

9. On the dialog box that appears next you specify whether you want to create a new Access client/server application (ADP file) for the SQL Server database, link the new SQL Server tables to the existing database, or make no changes. If you select either option other than "No application changes," the "Save password and user ID" checkbox will be enabled. Check this to save the credentials with the database or data project file. Click the Next button when you're finished here.

10. This is the final dialog box for the wizard. If on the previous dialog box you specified to create a new client/server application, you can specify whether you want to open the new ADP file or leave the existing database open. Click the Finish button ▲ and the wizard will start its work.

20

When the wizard is finished upsizing the database, it will display an Upsizing Wizard report window that summarizes what was accomplished. Close this window when you're satisfied with having read through it.

If you specified that a new client/server project should be created and opened, that file will open in place of the database you were working with. If you specified to link the new SQL Server tables to the existing database, the tables you upsized will be renamed to `tablename_local` and in the Tables list you'll see the original table names now have a world icon next to them. This indicates that this is a linked table. Double-click the table name to open it in Datasheet view.

Security Options in Access

In the vast majority of cases, you won't need to provide security for your Access databases. In fact, if you're extremely concerned about security you should be looking at using Microsoft SQL Server as your database platform. SQL Server provides much tighter security as well as the option of integrating your database's security with your network security.

That said, Access 2002 does provide several options for securing your databases. The first (and least secure) is encrypting the database, which will prevent the database from being read outside of Access 2002. Next comes setting a database password. This will prevent anyone from opening the database without entering the correct password. Finally, the most secure method is implementing user-level security.

Encrypting a Database

Encrypting a database is the easiest way to protect your database from certain prying eyes. When a database is encrypted, it cannot be read by utility programs or word processors. However, if you encrypt a database that has not been secured using one of the other methods, you really haven't gained anything. Anyone with Access installed can still open the database and view, edit, or otherwise mess with it.

When you encrypt a database, it must be opened in Exclusive mode. Also, if the database has been secured using user-level security, you must be the owner of the database or a member of the Admins group. Because the database must be opened in Exclusive mode, you must also have Open/Run and Open Exclusive permissions (permissions and groups are discussed in the section "Working With Users, Groups, and Permissions" that follows).

Encrypting a database is simple. First, open the database in Exclusive mode. If the database is already opened but you're not sure it's opened Exclusive, close the database using the File, Close menu item and then use File, Open to display the Open dialog box. Select the file you want to open and then click the dropdown arrow on the Open button. Select `Open Exclusive`. Make sure you have the correct file selected before you manipulate the button because selecting an item in the dropdown will click the button.

Once the database is opened Exclusive, use the Tools, Security, Encrypt/Decrypt Database menu item. An Encrypt As dialog box will appear. Choose the location and a filename for the encrypted copy of the database. Once it's encrypted, you won't be able to tell that it has been encrypted.

To decrypt an encrypted database, follow the exact same steps. There's really not much reason to decrypt a database, but the capability is there should you need to.

Setting a Database Password

The second level of security is provided by setting a database password. Once a password is set, the database cannot be opened without first entering the password. Also, when the password is set the database will be encrypted as in the previous section.

However, setting a password only prevents unauthorized users from opening the database. Once the database is opened, any user can perform any task on either the data or the design of the database. In most cases, this will be acceptable.

To set a database password, close the database (if it's open) and make a backup copy that you store someplace safe (once you've set a database password, it cannot be recovered so if you forget the password you will never be able to open the database again). Open the database in Exclusive mode and then use the Tools, Security, Set Database Password menu item. In the Set Database Password dialog box, enter the password in the Password edit box, and then enter it again in the Confirm edit box. Click OK and the password is now set.

After you have set a database password, you can unset it. Open the database in Exclusive mode and use the Tools, Security, Unset Database Password menu item. The Unset Database Password dialog box appears. You have to enter the current password to unset the password. After you've entered the password, click OK and the database password will be removed.

20

Working With Users, Groups, and Permissions

By far the most secure and functional way to secure a database is to use workgroup security. Workgroup security combines users, groups, and object-level permissions to allow you to restrict access to the objects in a database. When workgroup security is enabled for a database, anyone attempting to open the database must enter a username and password. The username is mapped to a set of permissions that determine what the user is able to do once the database has been opened.

In addition to creating users in a database, workgroup security also supports groups. A group contains a list of users. Each group can have its own set of permissions on the objects in the database. Any user that is a member of the group inherits the permissions from that group in an additive manner. This means that if a user by itself only has read access to a table but the user is a member of a group that has full control on the table, the user will have full control and not read-only permission on that table.

The information about users, groups, and user passwords are stored in an encrypted file known as the workgroup information file. The information about object-level permissions is stored within the database containing the objects. When you're using the Microsoft Access application or the Access runtime to open and work with an Access database, there can only be a single workgroup information file active. You set the active workgroup information file by using the Workgroup Administrator.

By default, the workgroup information file system.mdw is the active file. You can add users and groups to this file if you want, but it's usually better to create a new workgroup information file and then add users and groups to the new file. To create a new workgroup, follow the steps in the next task.

Task: Creating a New Workgroup Information File

1. Start Access 2002. You do not have to have an open database in order to create a new workgroup information file.

2. Use the Tools, Security, Workgroup Administrator menu item. The Workgroup Administrator dialog box, shown in Figure 20.4, appears.

FIGURE 20.4

The Workgroup Administrator dialog box.

3. Click the Create button. The Workgroup Owner Information dialog box appears. Enter a name, organization, and workgroup ID value. Make sure that the workgroup ID is a unique value as this value is used to match a database with the workgroup information file containing the users and groups for the database. Click OK.

▼ 4. The next dialog box is where you specify the name and location for the new file. Click OK when you've entered this information.

5. A confirmation dialog box appears. If you need to make any changes, click the Change button and you'll be returned to the initial dialog box. Otherwise, click OK.

6. You will receive a confirmation message telling you that the file was successfully created and will be returned to the Workgroup Administrator dialog box after you click OK on the confirmation message. The file has been created and is now the active workgroup information file. Click OK to close the Workgroup Administrator
▲ dialog box.

Once you have created the workgroup information file, you can begin adding users and, if needed, groups. By default there will be two groups: Admins and Users. You use the Tools, Security, User and Group Accounts menu item to launch the User and Group Accounts dialog box where you create new users and groups as well as specify to which groups a user belongs. You can also clear a user's password and change the password of the currently logged-in user. This information is stored in the workgroup information file.

Now that you have an active workgroup administration file, you can open an unsecured database and add the necessary security information. After the database has been opened, use the Tools, Security, User and Group Permissions menu item. This will launch the User and Group Permissions dialog box where you specify the permissions that the various users and groups have for existing items. You can also specify what permissions users and groups will have on new items created in the database.

You can set permissions for the database as a whole and for tables, queries, forms, reports, and macros. Additionally, the database and each object within it have a user that is specified as the owner. You can change the owner using the Change Owner tab of the dialog box.

Using the Workgroup Security Wizard

The previous section describes the manual way to set up workgroup security. Doing so involves several steps you must follow correctly. Fortunately, Access 2002 provides the User-Level Security Wizard. This wizard walks you through the task of creating a workgroup information file, adding users and groups to it, and specifying security for the existing objects in the current database.

To launch the wizard, open the database to be secured (if the database is open in Exclusive mode, the wizard will prompt you to allow the wizard to close and reopen it in Shared mode) and use the Tools, Security, User-Level Security Wizard menu item. If you

20

are working in an unsecured database, the first dialog box will have only one option: Create a new workgroup information file. Otherwise, you can choose to create a new file or to modify the existing workgroup information file.

If you're creating a new file, clicking the Next button will take you to a dialog box where you enter information necessary to create the workgroup information file (see the previous section). One big difference is that the wizard creates a unique workgroup ID for you. Click the Next button to continue.

The dialog box that displays next (see Figure 20.5) is where you specify which objects you want to secure. You'll find the items for <New Table>, and so on, on the All Objects tab. By default, all objects will be secured. If you don't want to secure certain objects, uncheck them on this dialog box. Click the Next button to continue.

FIGURE 20.5

The Security Wizard dialog box where you specify which objects will be secured using the wizard.

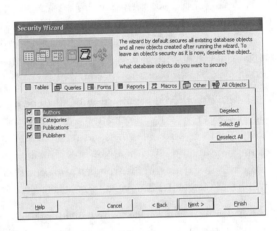

The next dialog box suggests a list of security groups which can be added to your workgroup information file. Each group serves a different function and will be given appropriate permissions on the objects you selected on the previous dialog box. Check the box next to the groups you wish to include. Click the Next button to continue.

On the dialog box that appears you specify whether or not to give any permissions to the built-in Users group. All users are included in the Users group and so any permissions you give to this group will be inherited by all users. If you give the Users group full control over all objects, then you essentially have unsecured the database. If you want to give a base set of permissions to all users, then select the Yes radio button and specify which permissions to assign to the Users group. Click the Next button to continue.

The next dialog box helps you to create new users for your workgroup information file. You can specify the username, password, and personal ID (PID) for each new user. Notice that, once again, the wizard provides you with a unique PID which you can use. When you're finished creating users, click the Next button to continue.

On the dialog box that appears you can specify to which groups the users belong. You can do this by looking at either the list of groups that a user belongs to or the list of users belonging to a specific group. Toggle between these lists using the radio buttons at the top of the dialog box. When you're finished working on this dialog box, click the Next button to continue.

The final dialog box is where you specify where to place a backup copy of the current database before it is secured. Click the Finish button to let the wizard begin its operations.

A report will display when the wizard has finished. When you close the report window you will be prompted to save the report file. You should definitely save the file in case you need to re-create the workgroup information file at a later date.

After running the wizard, you should close down Access and then reopen the database you secured. You will be prompted for a username and password to log in to the database. You can now use the User and Group Permissions dialog box to tweak the permissions on individual objects, if necessary, for the various users and groups.

Summary

Today you learned about the various database maintenance and security tasks you can accomplish with Access 2002. These include repairing a corrupted database, compacting a bloated database, converting a database to a different version of Access, and using the Upsizing Wizard to move the database to SQL Server.

You also learned about the three ways to secure a database: encrypting, setting a database password, and using workgroup security.

20

Q&A

Q. If I lose the workgroup information file associated with a secured database, can I re-create it?

A. Yes. If you have the information used when you created the file, especially the workgroup ID and personal ID values, you can re-create the workgroup information file. Simply create a new file and use the old values.

Q. Can I print a list of the users and groups in a workgroup information file?

A. Yes. Open a database that is associated with the workgroup information file. Then use the Tools, Security, User and Group Accounts menu item. On the Users tab of the User and Group Accounts dialog box, click the Print Users and Groups button.

Workshop

The Workshop helps you solidify the skills you learned in this lesson. Answers to the quiz appear in Appendix A, "Answers to Quizzes."

Quiz

1. Does Access provide a tool for making a backup of a database?

2. What are the benefits of compacting the database on a regular basis?

3. What tool does Access provide for moving a database to a Microsoft SQL Server database?

4. What two groups are included in every new workgroup information file?

Exercise

For today's exercise, create a new database and add some tables to it. Then use the User-Level Security Wizard to several users to the group. After you reopen the database, use the User and Group Permissions dialog box to remove permissions for various objects for a particular user. Make sure that user is not in any groups. Then close and reopen Access, logging in as that user. Attempt to work with the objects whose permissions you modified. Repeat this process to learn what the various permissions allow.

DAY 21

Access on the Web

As Microsoft continues its march to webify every application and computer, it's not leaving Access databases behind the times. Access 2002 continues to expand on the number of methods available to publish your data using a Web browser. Today's lesson shows you the features allowing you to publish data via XML, explains how to publish static and dynamic HTML files or Active Server Pages from your tables, and introduces you to Data Access Pages.

Today You Will Learn

In Day 3, "Automatic Access," you were introduced to HTML and the Page Wizard. In today's lesson you learn

- How to publish a static HTML page from a table or query
- How to publish a dynamic Web page to a Microsoft IIS Web server
- How to export a table or query to an XML file
- How to format the XML output using XSL
- How to create and edit a Data Access Page

Publishing Static Web Pages

Access 2002 provides a very handy mechanism to publish your data to a Web server. The Web server can be open to the entire Internet or can be a company intranet. Using the tools Access provides, you can export tables, queries, forms, and reports. When you perform the export, you can allow Access to format the HTML or you can provide a template file to guide Access as to where to place labels and data.

When you publish a static Web page from Access, the contents of the page do not change after it is published. If the data that created the Web page changes, the Web page will stay the same. You also can publish dynamic Web pages as you'll see in the sections "Publishing Dynamic Web Pages" and "Creating a Data Access Page."

Creating the HTML Template File

Access 2002 can create Web pages from datasheets (either tables or query results), forms, and reports without any input from you. However, you also can provide an HTML template file to be used by Access when creating these Web pages. The template file allows you to enforce your own standards for the Web pages to be created. You can add graphics such as company logos and backgrounds, as well as specify text colors, background colors, and any other style sheet elements.

 Note

An HTML browser can read display format information from a style sheet. The style sheet can provide direction as to which font family to use for certain elements, what font size to use, what margins to provide around elements, and so on.

You can use a specialized Web page editor, such as Microsoft FrontPage 2002 or even a standard text editor, to create the HTML template file. Store it in a common directory so that you'll be able to easily locate it when you perform an export.

In addition to standard HTML elements, your template files should also include special tokens. *Tokens* are keywords that will be replaced with the information that they represent. Place these tokens at the appropriate places in your HTML template file and Access will replace them when you perform an export with this template specified. Table 21.1 shows you the various tokens and what they'll be replaced with on export.

TABLE 21.1   HTML Template File Tokens

Token	Replacement
`<!--AccessTemplate_Title-->`	The object name is placed in the Web page title
`<!--AccessTemplate_Body-->`	The exported data
`<!--AccessTemplate_FirstPage-->`	A link to the first page of a multiple page export
`<!--AccessTemplate_PreviousPage-->`	A link to the previous page of a multiple page export
`<!--AccessTemplate_NextPage-->`	A link to the next page of a multiple page export
`<!--AccessTemplate_LastPage-->`	A link to the last page of a multiple page export
`<!--AccessTemplate_PageNumber-->`	The current page number of a multiple page export

Performing the Export

Regardless of the object you're exporting, you follow the same steps to export its data to a static HTML file. These steps are outlined in the following task.

Task: Exporting a Static HTML Page

1. In the Database window, select the object which you want to export. If you don't have a database you're working with, use the `Northwind` sample database and select any of the tables or queries it contains.

2. Use the File, Export menu or right-click the object and select Export from the shortcut menu.

3. The Export To dialog box appears. Use the Save as type dropdown list at the bottom of the dialog box to select HTML Documents.

4. Select the folder that will be the destination of the HTML page file and enter a name for the file.

5. Check the box labeled Save formatted. To open the HTML file after it is created, check the Autostart checkbox (this checkbox is only enabled if you checked the Save formatted checkbox).

Note

For form and report objects, the Save formatted checkbox will not be enabled and will always be checked. This is because forms and reports must be exported with their design-time layout because you cannot automatically convert a form or report to a datasheet (tabular) view as you can with a query or a table.

21

6. Click the Export button. If Save formatted was checked, the HTML Output
   Options dialog box, shown in Figure 21.1, appears. Otherwise, the HTML file is
   created and you'll be returned to the Database window.

FIGURE 21.1

*The HTML Output
Options dialog box is
where you can specify
a template file or a
character encoding
option to use when
creating the HTML
file.*

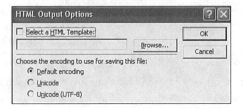

7. To select the template file, check the box labeled Select an HTML Template and
   then either enter the file path and name in the edit box, or use the Browse button to
   locate it.

▲   8. Click the OK button to create the output HTML file.

Note   If the object you selected to export requires any user input before being displayed (such as a parameterized query), you will be prompted to enter the
required information when the export is performed.

Publishing Dynamic Web Pages

If you want to create pages that change each time they're requested (as opposed to the
static pages created in the previous section), Access 2002 provides two options. Which
one you choose depends on the capabilities of both your Web server and the browser
application that will be used to view the page.

If you can guarantee that your clients will be using Internet Explorer 5.0 or later (and
typically you can only guarantee this in an intranet situation) and that they can open the
database from their machines using ODBC or OLE DB (typically this is once again the
case only in an intranet situation), you can use Data Access Pages (discussed in the
upcoming section "Creating a Data Access Page").

If you have no control over the user's browser, or if your database must reside behind a
firewall or cannot be opened by outside users directly, and your Web server is
Microsoft's Internet Information Server (IIS), then you can create pages that will be
dynamic and browser-neutral using the information in this section.

Access can export your database objects into Microsoft Active Server Pages (ASP) format, which are processed by IIS when requested. The IIS server will open a connection to the database, retrieve the data from the object that was exported, and return the appropriate HTML to the Web browser.

Creating an ODBC Data Source

The ASP files created when you export to Active Server Pages format utilize ODBC to retrieve data from the database. ODBC uses what's called a data source to define how to connect to the database. Before anyone can browse through the ASP files you'll create, you need to define an ODBC data source for the database being used.

To create an ODBC data source for a Microsoft Access database, follow the steps in the following task.

Task: Creating an ODBC Data Source

1. Launch the Windows Control Panel. If you're using Windows XP or Windows 2000, double-click the Administrative Tools folder. Double-click the Data Sources (ODBC) icon (on some operating systems, this might be listed as "32-bit ODBC").

2. The ODBC Data Source Administrator appears. Click the System DSN tab. You need a System data source so that the users browsing your pages can reference the data source properly.

3. Click the Add button. The Create New Data Source dialog box appears. Select Microsoft Access Driver (*.mdb) in the list of available data sources. Click the Finish button.

4. The ODBC Microsoft Access Setup dialog box appears. This dialog box contains a lot of buttons and edit boxes. The only ones that need to be filled in are the data source name (remember what you enter here, you'll need it in the section that follows) and the database name and path. Enter a name for the data source, then click the Select button found in the Database area. On the Select Database dialog box, browse to the database you're using for the ASP file and click OK when you've located it.

5. If your database has been secured, select the Database radio button in the System Database area and then use the System Database button to select the workgroup information file for your database (see Day 20, "Maintaining and Securing Access Databases," for information on securing databases and workgroup information files).

6. For help on any of the other options, use the What's This? Help button. When you're finished on the dialog box, click the OK button to return to the ODBC Data Source Administrator.

Exporting to Active Server Pages

To create ASP files to access objects in a database, follow the steps in the following task.

Task: Exporting an Object to Active Server Pages Format

1. Open the database containing the object or objects to be exported. On the Database window, select an object to export.

2. Use the File, Export menu item. The Export To dialog box appears.

3. In the Save As type dropdown list select Microsoft Active Server Pages.

4. Browse to the location where you want to save the page. Note that this location needs to be accessible via a Web server in order for the file to be browsed. Click the Export button to continue.

5. The Microsoft Active Server Pages Output Options dialog box appears. Here you can select a template file to use. The template file follows the same format as discussed in the previous section.

6. Enter the name of the ODBC data source you create in the previous section. If the data source points to a secured database, enter the username and password for the user account that will be used to access the database.

> **Note**
>
> The file that gets created will contain server-side script code. The username and password you enter here will only appear in that code, not in any HTML code that is returned to the user. As long as you're certain that your Web server's directories are properly secured against unauthorized access, you can feel safe about entering the username and password in step 6.

7. Enter the URL for the directory on the Web server where the file will be accessed. If you want to override the default session timeout for this page, enter a new value in the Session timeout edit box.

8. Click OK when you're finished. The ASP file will be created and placed into the file you specified in step 4.

After you create the ASP file and verify that it's in the correct location on the Web server, you can browse to the page in any browser. You should see the data from the object you exported returned in a tabular format.

Exporting Data in XML Format

Another advance made in Access 2002 is the ability to save data from the database into XML files. XML (Extensible Markup Language) is quickly becoming the standard method of transferring data among disparate data sources and across the Internet. With Access 2002, you can save the data into an XML file, the data definition into an XML Schema (XSD) file, and the layout of the data into an Extensible Stylesheet Layout (XSL) file.

The XSD file, the XML schema definition, describes the structure of the data you're exporting. It defines the rules applied to the data within the XML document. This includes the field names and their data types and what attributes apply to each field. Using the XSD file, you can easily transfer the data in the XML file to another system, which supports XML and XSD file import because the XSD file will instruct the other system as to the format of the data in the XML file and allow for automatic importing of that data.

When you choose to export the schema definition, you can choose to either embed it within the XML file itself or to create a separate XSD file. Using an external file allows you to export the schema definition once and then use it repeatedly even though you might export XML data only in the future.

The XSL file is used to transform the data into some display format. By default, when you choose to export the XSL file, Access 2002 creates an XSL file that produces HTML display elements to display the data in the XML file. The HTML display elements are the HTML tags that dictate how the data will appear, such as the <TABLE> and <TR> tags. The XSL file describes how and where fields in the XML file should be displayed. You do not have to export an XSL file when you export to XML. If you're exporting your data to transfer it to another system or application, you won't need the XSL file. Also, Internet Explorer 5.0 (IE) and later can display an XML file natively. But using the XSL file allows you to more easily define how the data should appear when viewed in IE.

Note   If you are exporting a report or a form, Access will automatically create an XSL file to handle the presentation. You will not be able to deselect this option on the Export XML dialog box.

The following task describes how to export data to XML. It uses queries from the Northwind sample database that ships with Access 2002.

21

Task: Exporting a Query to XML

1. Open Access and open the `Northwind` database. Click the Objects bar and then click Queries in the list of objects.

2. Click Quarterly Orders. Use the File, Export menu item. The Export To dialog box appears. In the Save As type dropdown list, select XML Documents (*.xml). You can leave the suggested filename or choose another. You can do the same for the file's folder. Click the Export button.

3. The Export XML dialog box, shown in Figure 21.2, appears. By default, the Data and Schema checkboxes are checked. You also can check the Presentation box to export XSL and HTML files that will display the exported XML data. To accept the default settings used to export the checked items, you can click the OK button and the files will be exported to the folder selected in step 2. If you click the Advanced button, you'll be able to modify these default settings. For this task, check all three options (Data, Schema, and Presentation) and click the Advanced button.

FIGURE 21.2

The Export XML dialog box is where you select which XML component files to export.

4. The Export XML dialog box is modified to include all of the options available when exporting XML (see Figure 21.3).

FIGURE 21.3

The advanced version of the Export XML dialog box.

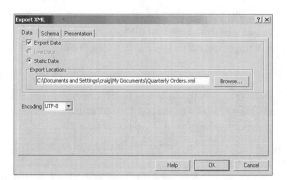

5. Use the three tabs to set options for the three file types. On the Data tab, you can set the location for the XML file and the character encoding format to use. On the

Schema tab, you can specify whether to include primary key and index information from the data and whether to embed the scheme information into the XML file. On the Presentation tab, you specify whether the presentation will be generated on the client or on the server (using Active Server Pages), whether to and where to store any report images if you are exporting a report, and where to store the XSL file.

6. When you've finished setting the options, click the OK button to perform the export. Keep in mind the location you've specified for the exported files.

7. After the export completes, open Windows Explorer and find the folder to which the data was exported. Double-click the .XML file that was created. Your screen should appear similar to Figure 21.4.

FIGURE 21.4

The XML file resulting from exporting the Quarterly Orders query to XML.

8. Return to Windows Explorer and double-click the .HTM file that was created to open it in Internet Explorer. Internet Explorer should display the file similar to Figure 21.5. This is obviously a more human-friendly method of viewing the data.

21

FIGURE 21.5

The HTML page resulting from exporting the Quarterly Orders *query to XML.*

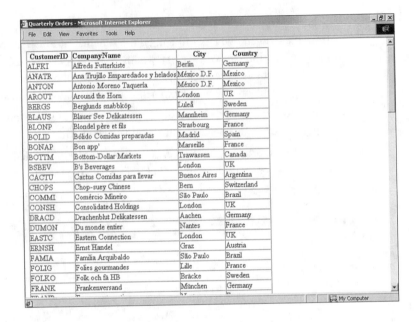

Using Data Access Pages

Now that you've seen how to create standard HTML, as well as how to export XML and XSL, let's take a look at Data Access Pages. Data Access Pages are very similar to form objects in Access, but are designed to be viewed using Microsoft's Internet Explorer Web browser.

Like the previous methods described in today's lesson, when you create a Data Access Page, you're actually creating a Web page. The page is stored somewhere in your filesystem, as opposed to within the Access database file. Still, there is a link that appears in the Pages list of the Database window, and opening an entry in that list will open the Data Access Page in the native viewer for Data Access Pages.

Access provides a designer you can use to edit the Data Access Page in conjunction with that database's other objects (including a Field List task pane). However, you can also edit the page in an external editor, such as Microsoft FrontPage or Visual InterDev. If you do, you won't have access to the other objects in the database, though.

Note

If you're using the Access 2000 file format for your database, you won't be able to edit the page using Access 2000. You will, however, be able to open the page in Page view.

There are four ways to create a Data Access Page:

- Saving an existing table, query, form, or report as a Data Access Page (using the File, Save As menu item).
- Using the Data Access Page Wizard
- Using the AutoPage feature
- Using Design View to manually create a new Data Access Page

In the remainder of today's lesson, you'll build a Data Access Page using the wizard. The page will display information from the Customers table of the Northwind sample database included with Access 2002. After the page is created, you'll modify that page with the Design view, extending it to display information about orders placed by each customer.

Creating a Data Access Page

Like most tasks in Access, there's a wizard provided for creating new Data Access Pages. This wizard will guide you through the creation of a Data Access Page, even allowing you to do a master-detail page, such as displaying all of the orders for a particular customer.

In this section, you create a simple page based on the Customers table. In the section that follows, you will add to this page using the Data Access Page Design view window.

Task: Using the Data Access Page Wizard to Create a Data Access Page

1. Open the database to which you're adding the Data Access Page. For this task, open the Northwind sample database using the Help, Sample Databases, Northwind Sample Database menu item.

2. On the Database window, click the Pages button. Your screen should appear similar to Figure 21.6.

3. Click the New button. The New Data Access Page dialog box appears. Select Page Wizard in the list box at the top of the dialog box and Customers in the dropdown list at the bottom of the dialog box. Click the OK button to continue.

4. If your database file format is Access 2000, you will get a dialog box warning you that you will not be able to edit the page using Access 2000. Click OK to continue.

5. The first screen of the wizard appears, as shown in Figure 21.7. The dropdown list contains all of the tables and queries defined in the database. The table selected in step 3 (Customers) is selected for you. The Available Fields list displays all of the fields in the selected table or returned by the selected query. Select the fields you

21

▼ want to appear in the page by double-clicking them. To add all fields, click the button with the two "greater than" symbols. You can add fields from multiple tables by selecting another table in the Tables/Queries list. For this task, select all of the fields except `CustomerID`. The easy way to accomplish this is to click the button with the two "greater than" symbols and then double-click the `CustomerID` field to remove it from the Selected Fields list. Click the Next button to continue.

FIGURE 21.6

The Pages list of the Northwind *sample database.*

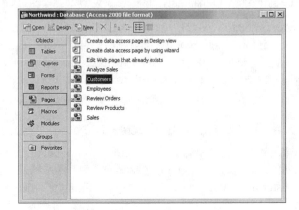

FIGURE 21.7

The initial dialog box of the Page Wizard is where you select the table and fields that the Data Access Page will be based on.

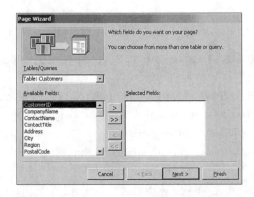

6. The dialog box that comes next is where you set grouping options for the page (see Figure 21.8). For the Customers page, you'll group by the Region field. To do so, double-click the Region entry in the list box at the left side of the screen. If you wanted to have multiple levels of grouping, double-click the field or fields to group by. To move the grouping fields up or down in priority, use the preview area at the right-hand side of the dialog box to click the field to be moved. The field's name will change to bold face. Use the Priority buttons in the middle of the dialog box to move the field up or down.

▼

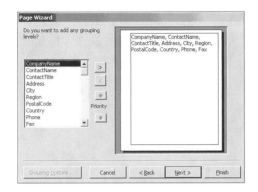

FIGURE 21.8

The grouping options dialog box of the Page Wizard is used to specify how to group the data returned in the Data Access Page.

7. If you want to change the interval for the grouping, click the Grouping Options button. The interval determines when the data will warrant a break between groups. For character fields, you can select Normal or a certain number of characters to match. For the task at hand, leave the setting at Normal and click OK to dismiss the Grouping Intervals dialog box. Click the Next button to continue.

8. The dialog box that appears is where you set the sort order for the records. The sort order applies to records within the lowest level of grouping. For this task, select CompanyName in the dropdown list labeled 1. Leave Ascending as the selected sort order. If you wanted to change to descending sort order, you would click the button to toggle the sort order. Click the Next button to continue.

9. This is the final dialog box. Enter a name for the new Data Access Page and tell Access what you want to do next (either open the page or modify the design). If you have selected to modify the design, you can also specify that you want to apply a theme to the page. Click the Finish button.

10. If you checked the apply theme checkbox on the dialog box, a Theme dialog box will appear after you click Finish. You can use this dialog box to select a theme for your new page.

The Page view of the page that is created with this task is shown in Figure 21.9. If you're on the final dialog box of the wizard you selected to modify the design, you'll be taken to the Design view first. Use the View, Page View menu item to open the Page view.

21

FIGURE 21.9

The Customers Data Access Page created with the Page Wizard.

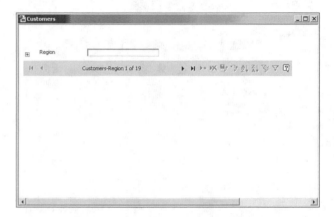

Because of the grouping used and the data in the Region field, the page appears empty. To see an actual record, click the plus sign next to the word Region. By default, the group section is not expanded. We'll correct that in the next section.

After you expand the group section, you'll see two sets of record navigation buttons: one for the Region grouping (at the bottom of the page) and the other for the Customers records within the current region group. Notice that the grouping navigation does not have the record editing, the sorting, or the filtering buttons enabled. All of these actions must take place on or within records in the current group.

Note

At this point, the Data Access Page still has not been saved. When you close the window, Access will prompt you to save it. Name the Data Access Page **Customers**.

One of the wonderful features of a Data Access Page is that it also can be viewed in Internet Explorer. This means that you can take the Web page that's associated with the Data Access Page and install it (along with the database) on a Web server accessible on your intranet. Doing so allows anyone to use the page you build to browse and modify the data presented by the page. Figure 21.10 shows the page displayed in Internet Explorer.

Note

Because Data Access Pages use a direct connection to the database instead of connecting through a Web server, the client machine must be able to connect to the database using the Windows filesystem. In other words, you can't "hide" your database behind your Web server as you can when you create Active Server Pages using the Export menu item.

FIGURE 21.10

*The Customers Data
Access Page viewed in
Internet Explorer.*

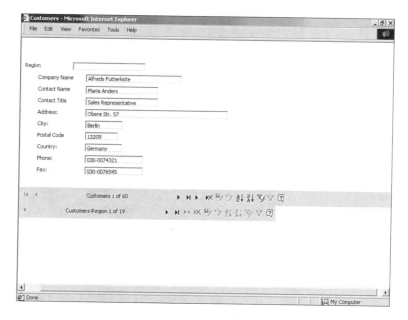

Editing a Data Access Page

Now that you've created a Data Access Page, let's take a look at the Design view for
Data Access Pages. As you can see from Figure 21.11, the designer for Data Access
Pages is very similar to the one for forms and reports. There's a Toolbox, a Field List,
and a Properties window. You work with these just like you work with their form and
report designer counterparts.

FIGURE 21.11

*The Customers Data
Access Page in Design
view.*

21

In the task that follows, you'll correct the fact that the customer record group doesn't expand automatically and you'll add an orders grid. The orders grid will show all the orders placed by the current customer.

Task: Edit a Data Access Page

1. Return to the Database window. On the Objects bar, click the Pages button. Select the Customers Data Access Page and then click the Design button.

2. The Design view appears (see Figure 21.11). To change the behavior of the group expansion, click the dropdown arrow next to the Header: Customers-Region label. Select Group Level Properties from the menu that appears.

3. On the Properties window that displays, change the ExpandedByDefault property to True. Close the Properties window.

4. To add the orders information to the page, you first need to make room for a grid. Click anywhere in the blank area in the Header: Customers region. The resize handles appear along the boundaries of the region (little squares at the sides and corners). Click the bottom handle and drag it downward to make the region taller (leave lots of white space between the Fax field and the header labeled Navigation: Customers).

5. In the Field List pane, the Customers table should already be expanded. Expand the item labeled Related Tables and you should see Orders in the tree.

6. Click the Orders entry. Drag this into the empty area you just created, dropping it at the right side of the white space. When you're in the right area, a border will appear around the Header: Customers region.

7. If the Controls Wizard is enabled when you drop the Orders table onto the page, a Layout Wizard dialog box appears. Because we want to display the orders in a grid-like fashion, select PivotTable (do not use Tabular format as this will produce really ugly results in this case). If the Controls Wizard is not enabled, the orders table will be added with the PivotTable by default.

8. Your page should now appear similar to Figure 21.12. To delete a field from the orders PivotTable, click the column header and then press the Delete key. To practice, delete the EmployeeID field (you'll have to scroll the PivotTable with the horizontal scrollbar to find the column for this field). Save the updated page and switch to Page view. Your page should appear similar to Figure 21.13.

▼

FIGURE 21.12

The modified Customers Data Access Page in Design view.

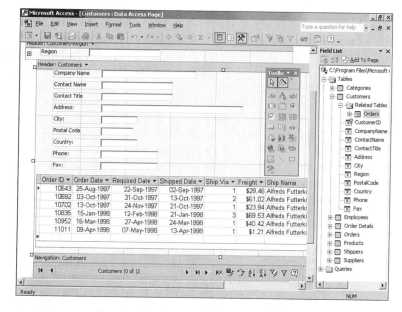

FIGURE 21.13

The modified Customers Data Access Page in Page view.

21

Summary

In this final lesson, you've seen how you can share your information using the Internet. You can choose to share the information in a static way by exporting either HTML or XML files. You can share your data dynamically using Active Server Pages or Data Access Pages. In other words, choose the method you wish to support and Access 2002 provides you the means with which to share the data on the Web.

Q&A

Q. Is Microsoft IIS the only Web server which supports Active Server Pages?

A. No. You can obtain ASP plug-ins for many of the popular Web servers available today. You also need to make sure that there is support for ODBC data connections on the platform in use.

Q. If I create an ASP file attached to my database, is it possible for someone to gain unwanted access to the data?

A. No. Because ASP files use ODBC to open and query your database, they do not need to be accessible through the Web server's Internet connection. This means that you can (and should) store the database file in a directory that is not referenced by the Web server's configuration and is therefore not made accessible via the Web server.

Q. Can the HTML, XSL, and XML files created when I export XML be stored onto a Web server for browsing over the Internet?

A. Yes. Just give out the URL for the HTML page created. You can then export only the XML data on a regular basis and reuse the original XSL and HTML files. Simply replace the existing XML file with the updated copy.

Workshop

The Workshop helps you solidify the skills you learned in this lesson. Answers to the quiz appear in Appendix A, "Answers to Quizzes."

Quiz

1. If you want dynamic data in your Web page, what are the two methods you can use to create the page?

2. How can you standardize your Web pages when you export them?

3. When exporting to XML format, which file contains the actual data? Which file contains display information?

4. Can you use your Data Access Pages on a Web server?

Exercise

For today's exercise, try replicating the Review Products Data Access Page. You can do so using the wizard and then modifying the page in Design view. Open the Review Products page in Design view also, if you need help.

21

WEEK 3

In Review

This week you worked on the advanced topics of Access programming. You are ready to create a full-featured database that you can maintain and secure and you should feel comfortable about the integrity of your data. You have learned to tap into the resources of VBA to automate tasks in Access 2002. In addition, you have learned how to use Access to present information on the Web. With the skills you have learned in the last three weeks, you are more than ready to tackle any programming project using the power of Access 2002.

15

16

17

18

19

20

21

APPENDIX A

Answers to Quizzes

Day 1

1. What's it called when a primary key field is the linked field in another table?

   Answer: Foreign Key.

2. Would you classify the following statement as data or information? "In the last election, Republicans outvoted Democrats 5 to 3."

   Answer: Information.

3. Would you agree with the statement "Because Access is a relational database, there is no need to backup its files"?

   Answer: No, backup instead.

4. Can Access dynamically shrink the database to reflect deleted data?

   Answer: No, it will not automatically. However, by turning on the Compact on Close feature, it will. This option is under Tools, Options and on the General tab of the Options dialog.

Day 2

1. What Access object is optimized for display of data on a screen? A printer?

   Answer: A form. A report.

2. Will double-clicking a form in Database View open it in design view?

   Answer: No, it will open it in Form View.

3. Can you run a macro from the macro design view?

   Answer: Yes, by clicking the Run button.

4. What language does a module use?

   Answer: VBA or Visual BASIC for Applications.

5. Where does Access store data?

   Answer: In tables.

6. Are the columns in a table the fields or the records?

   Answer: Fields.

7. Is the type of data in a record always uniform (of the same data type)?

   Answer: No. Data in fields is one data type. Records can contain heterogeneous data types.

Day 3

1. How can you get more templates for your database wizard?

   Answer: Run Office XP setup again to load additional templates. Microsoft can also have additional templates on its web site. Click the Templates on Microsoft.com hyperlink on the New File Task Pane.

2. Which button on the toolbar toggles view and design view?

   Answer: The far left one on the standard toolbar.

3. What is a reason to run the full report wizard instead of the AutoReport?

   Answer: The full wizard offers many more options for the design of the report.

4. Is the type of data you intend on using in a field important to specify when designing a table?

   Answer: Yes, it is vital.

5. If you add a criterion to a query, do you end up with a subset or superset of the queried object?

   Answer: Subset.

Day 4

1. Can a primary key field have two records with identical values for the primary key field?

   Answer: No. A primary key field must contain unique values for each record.

2. Can the value of a primary key appear elsewhere (another field) in a record?

   Answer: Yes.

3. How often should identical data appear in a properly designed database?

   Answer: Never, but this rule is often violated with no serious consequences.

4. If you create two tables you intend to have a one-to-many relationship, how do you create that relationship?

   Answer: Use the Relationship window. Drag a line between the two fields you wish to join in a relationship and then assign the correct values (if necessary) to each side of the join using the pop-up dialog box.

5. Will the letter Z appear first or last after applying a Sort (Descending) on a field containing all the letters of the alphabet?

   Answer: First.

Day 5

1. What allows the dragging of a control separate from its label?

   Answer: In the upper left corner of the control there is a large black square that can be dragged.

2. How do you remove a control from a form?

   Answer: Highlight it then press the delete key on your keyboard or choose Edit, Cut from the menu.

3. How can you alter a control's size on a form?

   Answer: Highlight it and position your mouse over one of the small black squares, click and then drag.

4. Will a form header appear for all records on a form?

   Answer: Yes. A header is persistent data present for all records.

5. Can two option buttons in an option frame both be set to Yes?

   Answer: No. An option frame requires unique values for its controls.

6. How does filtering by form differ in a datasheet and a form?

   Answer: It doesn't differ.

Day 6

1. How can you filter for data by example in a datasheet?

   Answer: Click the Filter by Form button on the toolbar when in datasheet view.

2. What does the criterion >100 return?

   Answer: Records with values greater than 100 but not equal to 100 in that field.

3. What do the criteria "Cassel" AND "Orchant" yield in the Surname field of qryVoters?

   Answer: Nothing. Records where the name is both Cassel and Orchant (impossible). It will not return records where the name is either Cassel or Orchant. For that you need to write the criterion "Cassel or Orchant".

4. You've set two sorts in the design view of a query. Which field is the primary sort?

   Answer: The one furthest left in the query design grid.

5. What does the SQL keyword ON mean?

   Answer: The ON keyword is used in conjuction with a JOIN keyword. The ON specifies the link between the two tables specified in the JOIN keyword.

6. Can you select by one table's fields, but show another table's fields in a query?

   Answer: Yes, by unchecking the Show checkbox for the fields that you don't want to display.

Day 7

1. How can you customize which fields the AutoReport wizard includes in a report?

   Answer: You can base the report on a query instead of directly on the table. Or, you can let the wizard run, then choose Reports, design view and customize the report.

2. Is there any difference binding a report to a query versus a table?

   Answer: No.

3. What does the Keep Together property of a group do?

   Answer: Access tries to keep the section or group on the same page (along with headers and footers).

4. What does the [Pages] return in the report header?

   Answer: The number of pages in the report.

5. What does the white space in between the double quotes in the following expression do?

    ```
    =[Name]&" "&[LastName]
    ```

    Answer: Creates a space between the two fields.

Day 8

1. What constitutes properties for a macro action?

    Answer: Action Arguments. They tell the macro when to fire.

2. Do entries in the macro Name column appear in the database view?

    Answer: No.

3. Do you need to precede a condition with an equal sign?

    Answer: No. You can also use other Boolean expressions such as "greater than."

4. What does the following condition mean?

    ```
    [City]<>"New York"
    ```

    Answer: The field City does not equal the value, New York.

5. Is the following expression valid?

    ```
    Between #4/5/98# and #4/5/99#
    ```

    Answer: Yes.

Day 9

1. Can you display a hyperlink using a label or a different display text?

    Answer: Yes.

2. Does the expression In("Madrid","London") as a validation rule allow the entry of the city Belfast?

    Answer: No.

3. Does the expression In("Europe") as a validation rule allow the entry of the city Belfast?

    Answer: No. Access doesn't know that Belfast is part of Europe.

4. Do you need to use the built-in message boxes for Validation violations?

    Answer: No. You can create your own message boxes using VBA.

5. What does the expression Not "Denver" do as a validation rule?

    Answer: Prevents the use of Denver as an entry.

Day 10

1. Can you alter one property to change background color for both the form footer and detail area?

   Answer: No, you must change them individually.

2. Can you include a sunken rectangle object within a raised rectangle object?

   Answer: Yes.

3. Can you make some form design changes in form view?

   Answer: Yes, but you must set the form's `Allow Design Changes` to **All** on the Other tab on the Properties list.

4. If you don't have as many colors to choose from for form color as you wish, what can you do to increase your selection?

   Answer: This setting is dependent on the number of colors available to you in Windows.

5. Can you change the identical property for several objects at the same time?

   Answer: Yes. Select the different objects by shift-clicking on each object, then change the property.

Day 11

1. How does Access store date and time information?

   Answer: Using sequential numbers that are formatted into either a date or time format for display.

2. Must you use only built-in functions for use in queries?

   Answer: No, you can use your own functions by programming them using VBA.

3. What is the most commonly used built-in Access function for calculating date or time intervals?

   Answer: `DateDiff()`.

Day 12

1. If you need to organize your information in your report vertically down the page, what technique do you use?

   Answer: Sorting and Grouping.

A

2. Name one method that allows you to show a subset of information in your report.

   Answer: Filtering by changing the underlying query.

3. In Sorting and Grouping, what does the `Keep Together` property do?

   Answer: It tells Access to try to keep the header, detail and footer on one page.

4. When specifying dates in Access, why do you need to specify the "#" symbol around each date?

   Answer: Access might try to divide the numbers that make up the date, because the date separator is also the division operator.

5. There are three parts to a Crosstab query: the Column Heading, the Value, and the _____?

   Answer: Row Heading.

Day 13

1. Do you need to add a table to the QBE before constructing an SQL query?

   Answer: No.

2. Can you query queries using SQL or are you restricted to tables? Hint: Open the query `qryCountTheCounter` from the sample data and switch to SQL view.

   Answer: Yes. You can query on a query

3. What does the `WHERE` statement do?

   Answer: Filters records.

4. Does Access SQL require keywords to appear in all caps?

   Answer: No, but it is a good practice to follow.

5. Can you use Boolean operators such as >, <, and = in SQL?

   Answer: Yes.

Day 14

1. Instead of using the table Datasheet View, what's a more efficient way to modify the field values of a known group of records?

   Answer: Use an `Update` query.

2. When you execute a `Delete` query, can the deletions be undone?

   Answer: No, the records are permanently deleted. To make sure your query will delete the proper records, copy the WHERE clause of the delete query to a select query.

3. Can you create a table by writing a query?

   Answer: Yes, write a `Create Table` data-definition query.

4. How does Access determine what's a parameter in a query's `WHERE` clause?

   Answer: If the right-hand side of an equals statement is enclosed in square brackets and is not a field name, it's a query parameter.

5. How do you reference a form field from within a query?

   Answer: Use the syntax `[Forms]![form name].[field name]`.

Day 15

1. What are the three types of code modules?

   Answer: Form code modules, standard modules, and class modules.

2. Objects have the following:

   a. Properties

   b. Methods

   c. Events

   d. All of the Above

   Answer: (d) All of the Above.

3. Was Bill Gates the inventor of BASIC?

   Answer: No, the language was invented by John Kemeny and Professor Thomas Kurtz.

4. Can you use a macro to execute a Visual Basic procedure?

   Answer: Yes, use the `RunCode` macro action and specify the procedure to be executed.

Day 16

1. How do you ensure that every variable that you use in your procedures is declared?

   Answer: Use `Option Explicit` at the top of the module.

2. What data type would you use for a variable that you know will only store a whole number between –32,768 and 32,767?

   Answer: Integer.

3. What type of module is inherently attached to a form or report?

   Answer: Class module.

A

4. Where do you declare a local variable?

Answer: In the procedure in which it is used.

5. Which data type can store a `Null`?

Answer: Variant.

6. Which type of procedure can return a value: A sub or function?

Answer: Function.

Day 17

1. What function would you use to convert a string variable to a currency variable?

Answer: Cstr.

2. If you were to follow the naming conventions that this book follows, what prefix do you use to notate a variable that is a string data type?

Answer: str.

3. What does the name of the function `IIf()` stand for?

Answer: Immediate If.

4. There are four types of operators. They are arithmetic, concatenation, comparison, and _____?

Answer: logical.

5. What VBA keyword do you use to resize a dynamic array?

Answer: Redim.

6. The low and high index numbers in an array are called _____?

Answer: bounds.

7. If you think your code is stuck in an endless loop, how do you stop it?

Answer: Press Ctrl + Break (Break key is also the Pause Key).

Day 18

1. An object is defined by what?

Answer: By its class.

2. The `Property Let` is used when retrieving the value of the property. True or False.

Answer: False.

3. Can you define more than one event in a class?

Answer: Yes.

4. What keyword allows you to instantiate a variable without using the Set statement?

   Answer: `New` Keyword.

5. What keyword allows an object to "listen" to another object's events?

   Answer: `WithEvents`.

6. Is VBA programming object-oriented or object-based programming?

   Answer: Object-based.

7. What method of the collection object would you use to get rid of an item in the collection?

   Answer: `Remove` property.

8. What keyword do you use to gain access to Windows API functions?

   Answer: `Declare`.

Day 19

1. When working with ADO, do you have to connect to the data source before you create an instance of a `Recordset` object?

   Answer: You can create the `Recordset` prior to connecting to the data source.

2. When scrolling through a `Recordset` object with the `MoveNext()` method, how will you know when you've reached the end?

   Answer: When the `EOF` property returns `True`, you have reached the end of the recordset.

3. When you clone a recordset, do bookmarks from the original recordset point to the corresponding record in the clone?

   Answer: Yes.

4. When you create a new `CommandBar` object, is it visible by default?

   Answer: No. You have to explicitly set the `Visible` property to `True`.

5. Can you add a `CommandBar` object with the same name as an existing `CommandBar` object?

   Answer: No. Doing so will generate a run-time error 5. If there's a chance you might be recreating an existing `CommandBar`, attempt to delete the `CommandBar` first.

6. What properties of a `CommandBarControl` do you use to set the picture for the control?

   Answer: Either the `Picture` or the `FaceId` property.

A

7. Are new `CommandBars` automatically saved with the database?

Answer: No. You have to set the `Temporary` parameter of the `Add()` method to `False` in order to preserve the new command bar after the application is closed.

Day 20

1. Does Access provide a tool for making a backup of a database?

Answer: No. You must manually back up the database by copying the MDB file to a backup location.

2. What are the benefits of compacting the database on a regular basis?

Answer: Performance and disk space.

3. What tool does Access provide for moving a database to a Microsoft SQL Server database?

Answer: The Upsizing Wizard.

4. What two groups are included in every new workgroup information file?

Answer: Admins and Users.

Day 21

1. If you want dynamic data in your Web page, what are the two methods you can use to create the page?

Answer: Export to Active Server Page or use a Data Access Page.

2. How can you standardize your Web pages when you export them?

Answer: Through the use of a template file.

3. When exporting to XML format, which file contains the actual data? Which contains display information?

Answer: The XML file contains the data, the XSL file contains the display information.

4. Can you use your Data Access Pages on a Web server?

Answer: Yes, but only if the users of the pages can open the database referenced by the pages using the Windows file system.

INDEX

Symbols and Numbers

* (asterisk), 341
[] (brackets), 123, 345
() (parentheses), 413
(pound), 50, 427
_ (underscore), 420
3D effects, adding to
  forms, 280-281

A

Access
  case-sensitivity, 340
  hardware requirements,
   28-29
  launching, 35
  origins of, 27
  SQL Server development
   and, 28
  versions of, 27
accessing
  data source with
   Connection object,
   485-487
  help systems, 63
  VB Editor, 465
**action arguments and
  macros, 219**
action queries
  adding to toolbars, 352
  Append, 356-358
  Delete, 358-359
  Make Table, 360
  overview of, 352
  Update
   creating, 353-355
   overview of, 352-353

**actions and macros, 219,
  224-225**
**Active Server Pages (ASP),
  exporting to, 528**
**ActiveX Data Objects
  (ADO)**
  avoiding conflicts with
   Data Access Objects
   (DAO), 484-485
  Connection object,
   485-487
  connections, creating,
   491-492
  Field object, 490-491
  Fields collection,
   489-490
  model, using, 485
  overview of, 459, 484
  Recordset object,
   487-489

Q

R

X – Y – Z